The Government and
Politics of France

By the same author

THE FRENCH POLITICAL SCENE
FRANCE BETWEEN THE REPUBLICS
FRENCH POLITICS: THE FIRST YEARS OF THE FOURTH
REPUBLIC
FRANCE: THE FOURTH REPUBLIC
ALGERIA AND FRANCE
INTRODUCTION TO POLITICS
THE FIFTH FRENCH REPUBLIC
FRANCE (Oxford Modern World Series)
THE UNEASY ENTENTE
DEMOCRACY

DOROTHY PICKLES

The Government and Politics of France

VOLUME I

Institutions and Parties

METHUEN & CO LTD
LONDON

First published 1972 by
Methuen & Co Ltd
11 New Fetter Lane, London EC4
© *1972 Dorothy Pickles*
Printed in Great Britain by
Butler & Tanner Ltd, Frome and London

SBN 416 30000 6 hardback
SBN 416 29990 3 paperback

distributed in the USA by
HARPER & ROW PUBLISHERS, INC.
BARNES & NOBLE IMPORT DIVISION

Contents

v

Contents

Preface

When I originally wrote *The Fifth French Republic*, it seemed improbable that the Constitution of the Fifth Republic would outlive its predecessor. When I revised it extensively in 1965, it still seemed far from certain that it could survive the resignation or death of its first President. Now that it has done both these things, it is clearly time for a fresh look at French government and politics. This is, therefore, an entirely new study of a continuing political system. For the régime has now a respectably long past, even if its future is not clearly predictable. And it has a political as well as a constitutional record.

In this first volume, an attempt has been made to analyse the evolution and functioning of the main institutions – the Constitution itself, the electoral system, the relations between Parliament and Government and the constitutional and political rôle of the President – and also to look at the evolution of the main political parties, their relations with each other, their attitudes towards institutions, and to the new phenomenon in French politics represented by the existence of a single dominant party in power without interruption for over a decade. The second volume will be concerned with the politics of the Fifth Republic – the aims, achievements and failures of Gaullist Governments – political, economic, social and in the field of foreign policy – and the alternative policies of opposition parties.

Since many readers interested in French politics do not necessarily require the information regarding sources, or the additional detail that will interest some students, the paraphernalia of footnotes has been omitted and the relevant sources or additional material banished to a comprehensive section of Notes at the end of the book.

It is always a dangerous adventure to publish a study of current French politics, and in many ways it is today even more hazardous than usual. I can only hope that the present book will contain no more than a permissible minimum of errors of fact or of judgement and that some of the organizations mentioned will at least be still in existence on the day of publication.

Dorothy Pickles
February 1972

Abbreviations

ACADI	Association des Cadres dirigeants de l'Industrie
AES	Alliance des Etudiants pour le Socialisme
AJS	Alliance des Jeunes pour le Socialisme
APAR	Amicale parlementaire agricole et rurale
APPCA	Assemblée permanente des Présidents de Chambre d'Agriculture
CD	Centre démocrate
CDP	Centre Démocratie et Progrès
CDR	Comités de Défense de la République
CEIR	Centre d'Etudes et d'Initiatives révolutionnaires
CERES	Centre d'Etudes, de Recherches et d'Education socialistes
CETA	Centre d'Etudes techniques agricoles
CFDT	Confédération française démocratique du Travail
CFPC	Centre français du Patronat chrétien
CFT	Confédération française du Travail
CFTC	Confédération française des Travailleurs Chrétiens
CGA	Confédération générale de l'Agriculture
CGC	Confédération générale des Cadres
CGPF	Confédération générale de la Production française
CGPME	Confédération générale des petites et moyennes Entreprises
CGT	Confédération générale du Travail
CGT-FO	Confédération générale du Travail – Force ouvrière
CGTU	Confédération générale du Travail unitaire
CID	Comité d'Information et de Défense
CIR	Convention des Institutions républicaines
CJDE	Centre des jeunes Dirigeants d'Entreprises
CJP	Centre des jeunes Patrons

CNI[P]	Centre national des Indépendants [et Paysans]
CNJA	Centre national des jeunes Agriculteurs
CNPF	Conseil national du Patronat français
CRR	Centre de la Réforme républicaine
EDC	European Defence Community
EEC	European Economic Community
FEN	(i) Fédération de l'Education nationale
FEN	(ii) Fédération des Etudiants nationalistes
FER	Fédération des Etudiants révolutionnaires
FGDS	Fédération de la Gauche démocrate et socialiste
FNEF	Fédération nationale des Etudiants de France
FNSEA	Fédération nationale des Syndicats d'Exploitants agricoles
GUD	Groupe Union-Droit
JAC	Jeunesses agricoles catholiques
JCR	Jeunesse communiste révolutionnaire
JRI	Jeunes Républicains indépendants
MJR	Mouvement jeune Révolution
MRP	Mouvement républicain populaire
OAS	Organisation de l'Armée secrète
ORTF	Office de Radiodiffusion–Télévision française
OURS	Office universitaire de Recherche socialiste
PDM	Progrès et Démocratie moderne
PRL	Parti républicain de la Liberté
PSA	Parti socialiste autonome
PSU	Parti socialiste unifié
RGR	Rassemblement des Gauches républicaines
RPF	Rassemblement du Peuple français
SFIO	Section française de l'Internationale ouvrière
SGEN	Syndicat général de l'Education nationale
SNC	Syndicat national des Collèges
SNES	Syndicat national de l'Enseignement du second Degré
SNE-sup	Syndicat national de l'Enseignement supérieur
SNI	Syndicat national des Instituteurs
UCRG	Union des Clubs pour le Renouveau de la Gauche
UDCA	Union de Défense des Commerçants et Artisans
UDR	Union des Démocrates pour la République

UDSR	Union démocratique et socialiste de la Résistance
UDT	Union démocratique du Travail
UDVᵉ R	Union des Démocrates pour la Vᵉ République
UGCS	Union des Groupes et Clubs socialistes
UJCML	Union des Jeunesses communistes marxistes-léninistes
UJP	Union des Jeunes pour le Progrès
UNATI	Union nationale des Travailleurs indépendants
UNEF	Union nationale des Etudiants de France
UNEF–Renouveau	Union nationale des Etudiants de France–Renouveau
UNR	Union pour la nouvelle République

PART I
Institutions

CHAPTER I

The Constitution

THE RELEVANCE OF THE CONSTITUTION*

Ten years after the acceptance of the Constitution of the Fifth Republic by 79·25% of French voters, one of the best-known French political commentators noted that

> ... after seventeen Constitutions in a little over a century and a half, all of them intended to last for ever and phrased accordingly, Constitutions rarely applied, regularly amended, and whose utility was sometimes exhausted before having been really tested, it is only too easy to justify scepticism and indifference about Constitutions. Eleven years ago, it took General de Gaulle's skill to convince people that the 'evils of the system' were responsible for all their problems. Today, Frenchmen think more about changing their cars than their Constitutions.[1]

It by no means follows that the public's boredom or resignation regarding constitutional issues will necessarily ensure a long life for the Constitution of the Fifth Republic. French political crises have a habit of turning unexpectedly into constitutional crises. All the same, twelve years after the constitutional referendum of 28 September 1958, there was certainly far less talk about the Constitution, as well as far less opposition to it, than there had been during the first five or six years of its existence. The months following General de Gaulle's resignation, after his defeat in the referendum of 27 April 1969, at least answered one major constitutional question: Would the régime be able to survive his retirement? His death in 1970 answered, if only provisionally, another: Would it be able to survive his

* For the text of the Constitution, see Appendix II.

death? It could not yet answer the question as to whether the Gaullist party would in the long run be able to retain its cohesion without his presence.

It was said of the Fourth Republic that it decayed less through the inadequacy of its procedures than through the inadequacy of its politicians. The Fifth Republic certainly survived for the first eleven years thanks more to the ability of its first President to use (and abuse) the provisions of its Constitution than to the provisions themselves. But though French political and constitutional history provides ample evidence of the fact that Constitutions work well or badly according to the way politicians use them, this has never prevented French politicians from attaching enormous importance to the provisions of the written text, even to the extent of wasting a precious year in the difficult post-war conditions of 1945–6 arguing about constitutional and electoral matters. The result was a Constitution acceptable to only a third of the electors (a third did not trouble to vote) and, within a few years, fresh argument about its revision, an argument that continued intermittently until, in 1958, the Constitution itself was swept away.

It is understandable that a country such as France, which has had a troubled political and constitutional history, and in which political and constitutional disagreements still persist, should attach importance to the written text of a Constitution as a hoped-for expression of political consensus, or, at worst, a weapon on the side of the victors that could help to consolidate their victory. What is often less easy for non-Frenchmen to understand is the extent to which, particularly on the Left, certain constitutional principles have acquired a symbolic significance and have become a part of party mythology. 'The Republic one and indivisible', 'the sovereignty of the people', 'a secular, democratic and social Republic', along with other phrases, have become part of a *mystique*, and so constitutional rigidities have been added to political rigidities. There is attachment not merely to the terms of the current written Constitution, but also to their conformity with the principles or the terminology of past Constitutions.

General de Gaulle certainly attached importance to the terms of the 1958 Constitution and recommended it as a cure for France's political ills. But he was never under the illusion that the medicine would prove effective unless administered by him. His own interpretation (or mythology) was an essential ingredient. The Gaullist party, however, has, during these years in power, become increasingly aware of the need for a process of continuous adaptation of some constitutional and political rules in the interest of more effective Parliamentary government.

The same cannot be said of the opposition parties, whose inability to transform themselves into either an effective opposition or a credible alternative Government contributed a great deal to Gaullist stability. Up to 1962, they were, in practice, helpless, owing to General de Gaulle's indispensability while the Algerian war lasted. But they wasted those years by indulging to their heart's content in the traditional left-wing passion for constitution-making, and the following years in party wrangling and electoral tactics. There is no reason to believe that the French interest in – indeed passion for – constitution-making is dead. The fundamental divisions of opinion and political antagonisms are still there. And (as the 1968 troubles made clear) political quarrels can still only too easily escalate into constitutional crises, while the rigidity of constitutional and political attitudes still makes it easier to challenge a Constitution than to replace it. Any study of French institutions must, therefore, begin with some consideration of the written constitutional text, since that is the framework in which French parties have seen them in the past, in which they see them today and will probably see them in the future.

TRADITIONAL REPUBLICAN CHARACTERISTICS OF THE CONSTITUTION

If the Gaullist party and the régime do survive, one of the principal reasons may well be that, once the hullabaloo over the most criticized innovations of the 1958 Constitution had died down and Deputies had got used to its existence, it could be recognized as resembling its Republican predecessors, if not like a brother, at least like a cousin. The first reactions to it from almost every significant French political party, and every political scientist outside the Gaullist ranks, had been to regard it as an instrument created for General de Gaulle, if not actually created by him. It was criticized as being 'quasi-monarchical',[2] unworkable and badly drafted,[3] and essentially ephemeral.[4] Over the years, it revealed itself as being in many respects in the French Republican tradition, and so at least one reason for wanting to replace it virtually disappeared.

In the first place, notwithstanding the overwhelming majority by which the electorate had approved it, it failed, as its predecessors had done, to represent a political consensus, and so, for some years, one of the few things on which opposition parties were agreed was their objection to some of its provisions. They were by no means agreed on how to replace these provisions. In 1791, the first Constitution (Monarchical) had sought to eliminate once for all the evils of the *ancien régime*. So certain of their success had its authors been, that the Constitution had prohibited all amendment during the first two Parliaments and then made revision dependent on agreement by three consecutive Parliaments. Since each Parliament was to sit for two years, these provisions would have effectively deferred any revision for ten years.[5] In practice, it was short-lived, as were all its Republican successors, except that of 1875. Each Constitution in turn, whether Republican, Monarchist or Imperial, sought to consolidate a political victory. Unlike American and British Constitutions, both of which have contributed in differing ways to the strengthening of national unity, French Constitutions have almost always helped to increase political disunity, because they have so often been at the centre of political battles both before and after their acceptance.

For some years at least, the Constitution of 1958 was no exception to this rule. It tried to correct past errors, by giving to President and Government constitutional powers intended to prevent the development of a powerful and undisciplined legislature. The Constitution of the Fourth Republic had provided for a weak President, because its supporters could not forget Louis Napoleon and were afraid of the ambitions of General de Gaulle. They had also provided for a weak Senate, because they did not want to see Governments of the Fourth Republic hampered as those of the Third Republic had been by the Senate's ability to delay legislation indefinitely. The result had been a National Assembly able to overturn Governments at a whim (or alternatively to make their lives untenable), but unable to discipline itself sufficiently to provide coherent alternative Governments. But even those politicians and statesmen of the Fourth Republic who were not themselves opposed to the creation of a stronger executive regarded the authors of the 1958 Constitution as having weighted the scales too heavily on the side of the executive. For instance, neither François Mitterrand nor Pierre Mendès France wanted to see a repetition of the errors of the Fourth Republic, but neither could accept the new Constitution, because it gave, in their view, too much power to the President, and because they believed General de Gaulle to be imposing it on the French people as part of the price to be paid for his agreement to return to power and to deal with the Algerian problem. The 1958 Constitution alienated from the outset, therefore, substantial elements of public opinion whose support, or at least neutrality, its authors might otherwise have been able to count on. The thirteenth written Constitution in 180 years, and the fifth Republican Constitution, thus got off to a relatively unpromising start,[6] as indeed both its immediate predecessors had done.

The second way in which the 1958 Constitution resembled its predecessors was in its reaffirmation of the recognition of certain human rights. The 1789 Declaration of the Rights of Man and the Citizen had been incorporated in the 1791 Monarchical Constitution, and also in the 1848 Republican Constitution. That of 1946 had re-affirmed recognition of the rights contained in the 1789 Declaration and added a number of new social and economic rights. Of the five Republican Constitutions, only that of 1875 had omitted all reference to rights or duties.[7] And there were constitutional lawyers who maintained that the rights included in the 1789 Declaration still preserved constitutional and legal validity under the Third

Republic, notwithstanding their omission from the constitutional text.

> We firmly believe [wrote Léon Duguit] that a law contrary to the provisions of the Declaration of Rights of 1789 would be an unconstitutional law.[8]

This view was challengeable on the ground that the Third Republic provided no machinery for the enforcement of constitutional rights if the legislature chose to ignore them. The principle of the sovereignty of Parliament was, in practice, supreme, and any obligations imposed by the Declaration of the Rights of Man remained, in the view of more conservative constitutional lawyers as well as of politicians, only moral rights, unless backed up by the tacit or explicit approval of the legislature.[9] The position was not quite the same under the Fourth and Fifth Republics, but it presented its own problems. The recognition of rights was included in both the Constitutions, but only in a Preamble. 'The Preamble', wrote Marcel Prélot, 'has from the point of view of the legislator only moral authority.'[10] A prominent conservative politician of both the Third and Fourth Republics, Jacques Bardoux, even stated in the National Assembly in 1946 that 'a Declaration divided into articles has the authority of a juridical code. A preamble divided into paragraphs has no more authority than an academic preface.'[11]

It is certainly true that the application of such principles requires laws and that no law can be challenged in any French court, even if its aims are in contradiction with the principles of the Constitution. In this sense, guarantees of rights, whether in the body of the Constitution or in a Preamble are, in the words of an eminent member of the *Conseil d'Etat*,* only 'a guide (*un indicateur*) to both legislator and judge',[12] and as such have no more than moral authority. But in the absence of legislation, both ordinary and administrative courts have based their decisions on these principles. For instance, in 1950, a civil court based its decision explicitly on the Preamble in a case involving infringement of property rights. Recalling the terms

* On the *Conseil d'Etat*, see Appendix 1.

of the solemn reaffirmation of the rights and liberties of man and the citizen in the Declaration of Rights of 1789, and the fundamental principles recognized in the laws of the Republic, it concluded that

> ... it can be deduced from this solemn reaffirmation that, constitutionally, the right of property remains inviolable and can be denied only by the will of the nation expressed in a law, and to the extent laid down by law.[13]

Among the rights included in the Preamble of both Constitutions is the right to strike 'within the framework of the laws regulating it'. Throughout the Fourth Republic and the first five years of the Fifth, no such legal framework was created. Yet the general right to strike was recognized, in so far as its exercise was not prohibited by provisions of laws dealing with the right to strike of specific categories of the population.[14]

There also developed under the Fourth Republic an accepted case law, especially in the administrative courts, which broadened the concept of legality to include what were called 'general principles of law', defined as 'non-written legal rules, having the authority of law, and, in consequence, binding on administrators and decree-making bodies', and stated to be 'derived more or less directly from the principles of liberty and equality which have, since 1789, constituted the basis of the French political system, and are today recognized by the Constitution'.[15] In 1962, the *Conseil d'Etat* annulled a presidential decree setting up a military court to try officers accused of offences in relation to the Algerian war, on the ground that the court was illegally constituted, owing to its failure to make provision for appeal. As the decision put it, 'the procedure, and the exclusion of all right to appeal' constituted in the circumstances an unjustified infringement of 'the general principles of the penal law'.[16] In relation to the safeguarding of rights by the courts, therefore, and especially in relation to their attitudes to the provisions contained in the Preamble, the Fifth Republic continued the practice of the Fourth.

Another constitutional principle of the 1958 Constitution that reaffirmed those of earlier Republican Constitutions was the declaration of the indivisible unity of the Republic (article 2). The 1791 Constitution used the phrase '*Le Royaume un et indivisible*'. The wording in the 1958 Constitution – 'France is an indivisible, secular, democratic and social Republic' – is identical with the wording in the Constitution of the Fourth Republic. The requirement of the 1958 Constitution (article 27) that the Deputy cannot be subjected to any 'imperative mandate' – 'Any specific instruction to a member of Parliament is null and void' – was not included in the Constitution of the Fourth Republic, which reflected the views of the three large, disciplined parties of the Left. But it was by no means new. It was included in the Constitution of 1791, those of 1795 and 1848, and (though the short 1875 Constitution does not include it) in the Organic Law of 30 November of the same year.[17]

What is no less striking than these specific instances of the continuity of Republican traditions is the general resemblance between the systems of the Fourth and Fifth Republics, as outlined in the constitutional text. The general framework of Parliamentary government is basically similar – the judiciary is independent; the Government is collectively responsible to Parliament (articles 49 and 50) and, subject to this responsibility directs and decides national policy (articles 20 and 21). Indeed, these were two of the five principles of constitutional reform accepted by General de Gaulle in the law of 3 June 1958, the other three being the retention of universal suffrage, the separation of legislature and executive, and the undertaking to provide a new constitutional status for the overseas territories. The office of President remains distinct from that of Prime Minister, and the former remains politically irresponsible, except on a charge of high treason.

Even in its omissions, the 1958 Constitution resembles its predecessors. Like the Constitutions of 1875 and 1946, it takes for granted the continuance of existing Parliamentary procedures (except, of course, for the specific modifications discussed later). It assumes the continuance of the existing administrative structures, of existing local government organs and methods, of the existing educational system. It assumes, as its predecessors had done, the continuance of the existing system of administrative law, interpreted by the *Section du contentieux* of the *Conseil d'Etat*, together with the administrative functions performed by that body. Like its predecessors, too, it omits electoral rules from the Constitution. Tocqueville noted in his *Ancien régime et la Révolution* that the administration had remained virtually unchanged throughout all the constitutional changes that had taken place since the Revolution. The Fifth Republic clearly intended to respect that tradition.

CONSTITUTIONAL INNOVATIONS OF THE FIFTH REPUBLIC

The 1958 Constitution, nevertheless, made a number of innovations, some highly important, others less so. These are discussed in some detail in following chapters, in the context of the actual working of political institutions. But it is worth mentioning here the most striking of the changes, in particular those that were most controversial and that have been responsible for the description of the Fifth Republic as being *hors série*, or *sui generis*.[18] One change that was not a subject of political controversy seemed perhaps at first sight odd. In article 4, a Constitution recommended to the nation by General de Gaulle, whose disrespect for political parties was notorious, recognizes (as no Republican Constitution had done before) the rights of political parties to exist and to function, and their obligation 'to respect the principles of national sovereignty and of democracy'. In fact, the article was suggested by the Constitutional Consultative Committee, most of whose members were Deputies or Senators.[19] But the Government nevertheless accepted it, and the provisions have remained unquestioned. It was at first generally assumed that the wording of the article (the use of 'parties' in the plural and the reference to democracy) might be intended to facilitate the banning of the Communist party if necessary. In reality, no such step was apparently ever contemplated.[20]

The three most controversial innovations concern the rôle of the President, modifications of the traditional relations between Government and Parliament, and the institution of 'incompatibility' between the functions of a Minister and a member of the legislature. Under the Third Republic, the President was described by an eminent constitutional lawyer as 'a mute and powerless onlooker',[21] and had at one moment risked being, under the Fourth Republic, no more than 'a clerk and a postman'.[22] Under the Fifth Republic, he is accorded specific powers to be exercised without a counter-signature and can, under article 16, assume sole control of the Government in a declared state of emergency. And he alone is the effective judge both of the circumstances justifying his declaration of a state of emergency and of the measures that he proposes to take to deal with it. The article is known to be one to which General de Gaulle, who was haunted by the impotence of 'the State' under the two previous régimes, attached particular importance.[23]

This reserve power, together with the President's right to dissolve the National Assembly, to accept or refuse a request, either by the Government or by the Deputies, to have a Bill submitted to a referendum instead of to Parliament, and with his election, from 1965 onwards, by the whole electorate, provided a novel combination of quasi-presidential and traditional Parliamentary government. Indeed, Maurice Duverger maintains that the combination has existed in only three other democratic régimes.[24] The two principles are not necessarily incompatible, however, and Maurice Duverger was himself one of the most eloquent proponents of a system that would combine the election of the President of the Republic by universal suffrage with the responsibility of the Government to the National Assembly.[25] As it exists in France under the Fifth Republic, it is, he says, characterized by the President's possession of powers that he can exercise without the need for a counter-signature. The problem created by this presidential power alongside the retention of Governmental responsibility is, he recognizes, that of reconciling the two, 'which is not easy'. And as an illustration of the difficulty, he goes on to ask exactly what the powers of the President are in his capacity of President of the *Conseil des Ministres*.

His role is certainly not purely formal, as is that of a Parliamentary Head of State, whose presidency of the *Conseil des Ministres* remains symbolic and whose influence on its decisions is purely moral. On the other hand, he cannot himself take decisions, as does the president of the United States, whose Ministers must bow to his will. Our system lies somewhere between the two. In most cases, it is necessary for there to be agreement between President and Ministers.[26]

But what if there is not? This problem of the 'bicephalous executive', or 'executive dyarchy', remained unresolved throughout the presidency of General de Gaulle. M. Pompidou gave his own description of the system in 1970, but without providing any more guidance on the consequences of disagreement between President and Prime Minister.

I think [he said] that our Constitution is half-way between a properly presidential régime and a properly Parliamentary régime. The balance between the two – which is moreover difficult – has the advantage of making our political system capable of firmness, stability and at the same time of flexibility. As Prime Minister, I have heard General de Gaulle maintain that there was no dyarchy. But on the whole, I think the system is not a bad one.[27]

All of which leaves the political scientist to conclude that, ultimately, the issue of where executive power lies may have to be decided by a trial of strength. There is certainly nothing in the text of the Constitution to prevent a President less politically dominating than General de Gaulle or less politically active than President Pompidou from adopting habits more consonant with earlier French Republican traditions. The Constitution of 1958 is flexible enough to be adapted to either a weak or a strong President, provided only that the issue of the division of functions between President and Prime Minister does not become a matter of acute political controversy. But as it stands, and as it was applied during the first twelve years of the régime, nothing in the Constitution could necessarily prevent a clash from developing between a President determined to rule and a

Prime Minister determined to use his own powers under articles 20 and 21 to do the same.

The second controversial change is the increased power accorded by the Constitution to the Government to prevent Parliamentary harassment or obstruction, snap defeats,[28] and frequent challenges to its safety, whether by votes of confidence or by votes that can be used to diminish confidence, even without endangering the life of the Government. Measures to strengthen Governments *vis-à-vis* the National Assembly were on the whole welcomed by ex-Ministers of the Fourth Republic who had been trying to achieve a similar result during the last days of the régime.[29] But the 1958 Constitution went very much farther than anything suggested earlier, and the transference of a number of subjects hitherto belonging to the lawmaking field to that of Governmental decree-making was too much for many politicians to stomach.

The traditional right of Parliament to legislative supremacy had, indeed, been laid down as far back as the Constitution of 1791:

There is in France no authority above the law. The king rules by the law and can demand obedience only in the name of the law.[30]

From 1958 onwards, certain matters were laid down as belonging to 'the field of law' (*le domaine de la loi*). All others not specifically enumerated belong to the field of the Government, which is entitled to introduce by decree measures that have hitherto been regarded as requiring laws.

The third innovation was the institution of 'incompatibility' between the functions of Minister and of Deputy or Senator. Though such 'incompatibility' had existed under neither the Third nor Fourth Republics, it was not a new idea[31] and opinion was not in general unsympathetic to it. The Socialist party, for instance, approved of the innovation (though not by a very large majority). There has never been in France any requirement that Ministers should be members of Parliament, and non-Parliamentary Ministers have been included in Republican Governments from time to time. Since a Minister is entitled to attend debates and to speak in either assembly (though not of course to vote, except in an assembly of which he is a member), these exceptions do not create the difficulties that would arise in Great Britain if Ministers were not members of Parliament.[32] The separation of executive and legislature reflects, of course, Gaullist dislike of party pressures on Ministers and the dislike of many non-Gaullist as well as Gaullist politicians for a system in which Governments could be easily defeated by ambitious politicians anxious for office.

Three other constitutional innovations, less politically controversial, should be mentioned. They were: the creation of a Constitutional Council, the institution of the 'Community', and the transformation of the Fourth Republic's Economic Council into an Economic and Social Council. The Constitutional Council has three distinct and carefully defined functions.[33] The first is to *decide* certain issues. If the President of the assembly in which a Bill is under discussion accepts as belonging to the law-making field a matter that the Government considers to belong to that of decree-making, then the latter can refer the matter to the Constitutional Council, whose decision is final and binding. Or, if the President of the assembly concerned has doubts, he can refer the Bill on his own initiative. Similarly, a Government's intention to amend a post-1958 law by decree must be referred to the Constitutional Council, which decides whether this procedure is in accordance with the constitutional definition of the respective fields of law and decree-making.

The second function of the Constitutional Council is to *give an opinion* in certain circumstances. It *must* be consulted on the President's intention to invoke article 16, which gives him emergency powers, and on the conformity of organic laws and of the Standing Orders of both assemblies with the Constitution. In the first case, it expresses a formal opinion, giving reasons, but the President can ignore this if he wishes. In the second, if it reports that either an organic law or any part of the Standing Orders is not in conformity with the Constitution, it is left to the Government or to Parliament to take the appropriate steps to regularize the situation. The amended text must be re-submitted to the Council. The Council *may* be consulted by President, by Prime Minister, or by the Presidents of either assembly, on the conformity with the Constitution of a law about to be promulgated, or of an international agreement. A provision declared by the Council to be unconstitutional cannot be promulgated or applied.

The Constitutional Council's third function is to *supervise the conduct of elections* (including the presidential election and referenda) and to proclaim the results. It also decides on the validity or otherwise of contested elections, on which its decisions are final. This last task had traditionally belonged to Parliament, each assembly deciding on the validity of the election of its own members. This sometimes produced decisions that were politically biased.[34]

An organic law of 29 December 1961 gave the Constitutional Council new functions related to Parliamentary elections. In cases where there may be doubts regarding the constitutionality of the retention of certain business or professional occupations by candidates who have been elected as Deputies or Senators, the matter is deferred to the Constitutional Council by the *bureau* of the assembly concerned, the Minister of Justice or the member himself. The Council's decision is final. A similar procedure is followed if a Deputy or Senator decides during his period of office to take up business or professional occupations that may be challenged as being constitutionally 'incompatible' with membership of Parliament. An organic law voted on 20 December 1971, and promulgated on 24 January 1972, added to the number of such 'incompatibilities', as a result of several highly publicized cases of alleged fraud (then *sub judice*) that had involved Deputies.[35]

These functions do not amount to anything like a power of judicial review. The Constitutional Council has no general responsibility for ensuring respect for the Constitution. It can express its opinion only if consulted in the circumstances described, and it has no powers to enforce its decisions. In matters where consultation of the Council is optional, it has no official means of making its views known if no authorized person consults it. No ordinary citizen, for instance, can appeal to it, except on electoral matters. Nor is it really a judicial body. There is no condition that its members must be lawyers and many of them have not been. It is composed of a minimum of nine members, three of whom are appointed by the President, three by the President of the Senate and three by the President of the National Assembly. Former Presidents of the Republic are, in addition, life-members *ex officio*. Councillors sit for nine years, a third being replaced every three years, and are not eligible for a second term. The President of the Council is appointed from among the members by the President of the Republic. It is evident that there is nothing to prevent nomination on political grounds, and the political views of some members have clearly played some part in their nomination. Members may even have leave of absence to contest an election and may return to the Council if defeated.

The creation of the 'Community', to replace the French Union (which had, in 1946, replaced the pre-war French Empire) was provided for by articles 77–87. For the first time in French history, the assimilative principle that had dominated French thinking since the Revolution was replaced by a more complex system offering a choice between three types of relationship between the mother country and overseas possessions. And for the first time, a French Constitution, referring to the organization of overseas dependencies, used the word 'independence'.

The first of the three types of relationship, integration within the Republic, was the status chosen in 1946 by the four overseas *départements* (Martinique, Guadeloupe, Réunion and Guiana). They retained this status under the Fifth Republic. Some provision was made, however, for modification by measures intended to take account of local conditions. The second, the status of Overseas Territories of the Republic, had been, under the Fourth Republic, that of the eighteen overseas dependencies. But the Constitution of the Fifth Republic offered them a choice, either to retain that status, or, either separately or in groups, to choose a new status, that of 'member-State of the Community'. 'The Community' was not clearly defined. The Constitution merely stated that it was 'based on equality and the solidarity of its member peoples' and that its institutions were founded on 'the common ideal of liberty, equality and fraternity' and were intended to 'permit of democratic evolution'. It granted to member-States the right to 'self-administration and the free and democratic management of their affairs' (article 77).

The choice was to be made in two stages. First, a vote of 'Yes' in the constitutional referendum signified the desire for continued association with France. The single Territory that voted 'No' (Guinea) immediately became independent. Second, within a period of four months, five Territories (St Pierre-et-Miquelon, the Comoro Archipelago, French Somaliland, Polynesia and New Caledonia) chose to retain their status under the Fourth Republic. They therefore remained within the Republic, but with some degree of autonomy, and continued to elect Deputies and Senators to the French Parliament.[36] The remaining twelve Territories opted for the new status. They thus ceased to be a part of the Republic and assumed control of their own affairs in a field of competence that *excluded* foreign policy, defence, currency, common economic and financial policies – all of which remained matters for the Community – which, of course, included France. It also excluded justice, higher education, transport and telecommunications, unless special agreements were made transferring competence in these fields to specific States.

The exact meaning to be given to the constitutional provision that the member-States were to 'enjoy autonomy' and to 'administer themselves and manage their own affairs freely and democratically' (article 77) is immaterial, for almost before the ink was dry on their respective Constitutions and the administrative organs of the Community had been set up, all twelve decided to avail themselves of the possibilities provided by articles 85 and 86 to become completely independent. Senegal and Soudan decided to become independent in September 1959. The following year, all the rest followed suit. The procedure for accession to independence was simplified by a revision of articles 85 and 86, making it possible for all articles concerned with the Community to be revised by a simple agreement between all the States (including France) and for any State that so desired to remain a member of the Community even after independence. By June 1961, all had become members of the United Nations.

Although six States (Senegal, Madagascar and the four States of the former Equatorial African Federation) decided to remain within the Community, this had by then to all intents and purposes disappeared. Its organs no longer functioned, although the relevant constitutional provisions remained unrevised. Its executive never met after March 1960, and its Senate, which met only twice in 1959, was regarded as having been dissolved. From then on the relations between France and these twelve former possessions, though friendly, and certainly closer than relations between France and other foreign countries, thanks largely to the amount of French technical and financial (and sometimes military) aid, have belonged to the field of foreign affairs.[37]

The provisions (in articles 69–71) for a third assembly, the Economic and Social Council, were, strictly speaking, not an innovation, for this body is a direct descendant of the Fourth Republic's Economic Council, whose functions had been to consider general questions concerning the economy and especially those arising from the application of National Plans. The effectiveness of the Fourth Republic's Economic Council had been reduced, in the first place, by the Government's failure to pay attention to its recommendations.[38] The functional basis of its composition – it consisted mainly of representatives of employers' and workers' organizations and of interest groups – made it unfitted for a general legislative rôle, even if only advisory, since, on issues requiring specialized knowledge, the main spokesmen were likely to be those with their own special interests to defend. Though still similarly composed,[39] the Economic and Social Council of the Fifth Republic has had a much more restricted field of activity. Its advice is virtually limited to matters on which it is consulted by the Government. Its sessions are no longer public. And much of its work is done in technical sections including co-opted outside specialists. It is, therefore, less subject to politicization and is consequently even less interesting to the general public. There has been little evidence that Governments of the Fifth Republic have paid more attention to its opinions than those of the Fourth Republic paid to those of its predecessor.

REVISIONS OF THE CONSTITUTIONAL TEXT

Throughout the first twelve years of the Fifth Republic, there were only three textual constitutional revisions, and two of these were carried out by procedures other than those laid down in the Constitution (article 89) as governing revision. The first, on 4 June 1960, modified articles 85 and 86 in an unusual way. The use of the procedure employed was the subject of some criticism, though there were sound political reasons in this case for refusal to use article 89, whether or not this constituted a technical irregularity.[40] The second, and only important revision, in October 1962, was that of articles 6 and 7, laying down the rules for the election of the President of the Republic. Though opinion on the desirability of the revision itself was divided, there was virtual unanimity outside the Gaullist party that the procedure chosen by the President (that of a referendum) was unconstitutional. The controversy proved to be short-lived, however, partly because opinion in all parties became rapidly reconciled to the new method of election by universal suffrage, and because the public's acceptance of the proposal was regarded as having legitimized the unconstitutionality of the method. In other words, article 3, which states that 'National sovereignty belongs to the people, who exercise it through their representatives and by way of referendum' clearly carried more weight than considerations of technical constitutional requirements. The third revision, on 30 December 1963, merely provided for slight changes in the dates for the opening and closing of Parliamentary sessions.[41]

THE EVOLUTION OF CONSTITUTIONAL OPINION

Far more important than these formal revisions was the evolution of constitutional and political practice between 1958 and 1971. This forms the subject of the following chapters. But the evolution of opinion in the opposition parties on the Constitution itself is not without importance, since it indicates the extent to which most people came to accept some part of the innovations that they at first strongly opposed. There had been already considerable dissatisfaction with the Constitution during the previous régime and, during its later years, there had already grown up, mainly on the Left, a relatively small but influential body of opinion in favour, if not of a presidential régime, at least of one that included certain presidential features. The arguments put forward in favour of what was called by Maurice Duverger '*le parlementarisme rationalisé*' were that, while a Parliamentary system was traditional in France and valued as such, in the absence of anything like a political consensus, it was bound to work badly. The only solution seemed to be to find some way of deliberately creating a majority, and the Duverger recipe was to have the head of State elected by the whole nation, to hold office for the same term as the Deputies elected to the National Assembly. If the electorate behaved rationally, this system should, in his view, help to ensure that both President and National Assembly represented the same majority in the country. For the essential bi-polarization involved in the election of a President would, he thought, encourage the tendency towards a two-party system. Since a Government defeat would automatically entail a presidential resignation, such a general agreement would be safeguarded by the obligation of both President and Assembly to face the electors at the same time.[42]

A 'neo-Parliamentary' system of this kind, conserving the duality of the executive, the right of the legislature to dismiss the executive, and the right to dissolution, was criticized both by supporters of a real presidential system, such as Professor Georges Vedel, and by other quasi-presidentialists. One politician described it as likely to produce the worst of both worlds. 'If', he said, 'Republican votes were to be divided between Maurice Thorez and Pierre Poujade, what a magnificent choice that would be between the plague and cholera.'[43] For authentic 'Presidentialists', what was required was, in addition to the election of the President by universal suffrage, a separation of powers such as exists in the United States, where neither votes of confidence nor dissolution can cut short the period of office of either legislature or executive.[44]

During the Fifth Republic, though none of the orthodox parties went as far as this in advocating a presidential form of government, there was evidence of some degree of 'quasi-Presidentialism' in the discussions, particularly in the Socialist party, of systems somewhere in between the classic forms of Parliamentary government and those advocated by the supporters of more openly presidential systems. For instance, neither Gaston Defferre nor Guy Mollet wanted to see a President-cum-Prime Minister, but nor did they want to return to a President who would be the powerless figure-head of the Third and Fourth Republics. The Socialist party, therefore, supported (if with some reservations) the position of the President as outlined by Gaston Defferre between 1964 and 1965, when he was hoping to be the presidential candidate of a united Left. The President was, in his view, to represent not a policy, but what were described as '*les grandes options*' – that is, a general political outlook, not going beyond the main head-lines of a policy. He was to be in general sympathy with a policy carried out in the traditional way by the Prime Minister and the responsible Government of a Parliamentary system.[45]

This general objective (it was never really worked out as a system) was, of course, open to exactly the same objections as was the dual executive proposed by Maurice Duverger. How could presidential and general elections be guaranteed to produce similar political majorities? The criteria governing the electors' choice of a man and of a party could vary considerably, as any study of the divergencies between the results of presidential and general elections during the presidency of General de Gaulle reveals. If President and legislative majority differ, then either the Assembly must give way, which means that, effectively, there would be presidential rule, or the President must give way, in which case the *grandes options* would have served no useful purpose. The growth of a system of mutual accommodation such as exists in the United States would be at best a very long-term prospect. It is hard to see, in any case, what useful purpose could be served by the *grandes options* unless they represent merely an attempt to create the impression that the President is no longer a figure-head, without giving him any real political powers. If this was all it meant, then, at least, it was an indication of a changing attitude to the rôle of the President, whose powerlessness had been desired by most of the Left in 1946, though this attitude was as yet not clearly defined in institutional terms.[46]

There were also in the first years of the Fifth Republic various other proposals, ranging from those of Paul Reynaud on the Right to those of the MRP and Socialists on the Left, intended to produce by constitutional rules the kind of stability regarded as being due in the Anglo-Saxon countries to the existence of a two-party system. One which had considerable support was what was described as *le contrat de majorité*, or *le contrat de législature*. Like the Duverger proposal, this would involve a dissolution whenever a Government was defeated, which as M. Guy Mollet put it, would mean in practice not a *gouvernement de législature*, that is, a Government lasting throughout a Parliamentary term, but a Parliamentary term coming to an end with every Government defeat. Other variants of this proposal included the adoption of the German device of making a Government resignation enforceable without a dissolution only if there was an alternative Government able and willing to replace it. This had a good deal of support in the ranks of the MRP.[47] Some Socialists preferred the Swiss system of a *contrat de majorité* without the possibility of dissolution, that is, a Government holding office for a fixed period. Pierre Mendès France believed that a Government ought to hold office for the full life of a Parliament, and that this should coincide with the term of the current National Plan. He also thought (contradictorily) that the President should have the right of dissolution in case of conflict between Government and Assembly.[48]

The objection to all these devices is essentially the same. They depend, for their successful working, on some effective fiduciary basis – a two-party system or a general willingness to abide by political rules or a general consensus on the Constitution, together with a general willingness to apply its provisions. Such a basis has never existed in France for any considerable period, even during the Third Republic. It did not exist during the early years of the Fifth Republic, though one of the avowed aims of Michel Debré, one of the chief architects of the Constitution, was to create conditions in which such a basis could be created. There is no convincing evidence that any such basis is likely to develop in the foreseeable future. If it does not, then the dormant interest in constitutional revision or constitutional change is likely at some point to become active again, and the Fifth Republic could become, like its predecessors, a régime whose Constitution never succeeded in becoming the accepted framework for the political life of the nation.

CHAPTER II

The Electoral System

THE HABIT OF ELECTORAL CHANGE

Electoral rules were included in Republican Constitutions up to 1848, but neither the Third nor the Fourth Republics treated elections as a constitutional matter.[1] The main reason for this was, by then, the reluctance to 'constitutionalize' a particular system, since experience had shown that the French were even more ready to change their electoral systems than their Constitutions. Under Monarchic as well as Republican systems, amendment and changes of electoral systems were frequent. During the Third Republic the system was changed four times (in 1885, 1889, 1919 and 1927). After the second world war, it was changed in 1945 and again in 1951. In addition to these changes there were a number of amendments that did not radically change the system (in 1924 and 1946, for instance), and some intended radical changes that were never actually made, owing either to the fall of the régime (1940), the inability of the Deputies to agree on a proposal (1951 and 1955), or to disagreements between the two assemblies (1957). In 1951, eight systems were debated and in 1955 eleven, without agreement being reached in the National Assembly.[2]

Deputies have traditionally regarded the choice of the electoral system as a matter for Parliament, and the Constitution of the Fifth Republic recognizes that it is a matter to be decided by law. But the choice of the particular system to be used for the first election of the Fifth Republic was entrusted, under article 92 of the 1958 Constitution, to the Government headed by General de Gaulle.[3] The system chosen, that of the single-member constituency with two ballots, was the one that had been used for 13 of the 16 elections of the Third Republic, and for 17 of the 21 elections held from 1876 to 1956. It had not, however, been used since 1936. It was the only system used since 1875 that had lasted for more than ten years,[4] and it remained in force from 1958 to 1972 without any proposals for change being put forward (though there were one or two changes of detail). It would be rash all the same to conclude that electoral controversy is a thing of the past, and that French politicians have lost their passion for drawing up complex and varied electoral systems. The Communist party has remained steadfastly in favour of proportional representation. The Christian Democrats – the *Mouvement républicain populaire* (MRP) up to 1967 – also supported proportional representation and would do so again if they were to regain their former strength. The Socialist party has always been divided, being for practical reasons in favour of the greater flexibility of the single-member system with two ballots, but favouring the proportional system in theory as being a more logical and statistically accurate method of representation. Conservative parties have always opposed proportional representation. For the time being, however, the issue remains dormant.

GENERAL CHARACTERISTICS OF THE FRENCH SYSTEM

There are a certain number of general similarities between the electoral system of the Fifth Republic and those of its two predecessors, whether or not the system has been that of the single-member constituency with two ballots, or some form of proportional or quasi-proportional representation. Elections to the National Assembly (the Chamber of Deputies under the Third Republic) have always been by direct, 'universal' suffrage, and to the second Chamber, the Senate, by indirect suffrage exercised through an electoral college, composed of Deputies for *départements*, Mayors of *communes*, and representatives of Councils of the *départements*. Though the term 'universal suffrage' occurs regularly in the text of Constitutions from 1848 onwards,[5] it has not always had the same meaning in practice. It means that the suffrage is regarded in principle as a general right, not restricted to an élite based on heredity, wealth or social distinction. But the exercise of the right has been limited by the conditions prevalent at the time in most Western democracies. Since 1875, these have related mainly to age, sex, nationality and sanity. From 1944, women have voted on the same terms as men.[6]

Election to the popularly elected Assembly has always been for a fixed maximum term (four years under the Third Republic, five under the Fourth and Fifth), though not for a rigidly fixed term as in the United States. Provisions for dissolution have been included in all three Constitutions, though, in the first two, only in certain defined circumstances. The Senate has always sat for a longer term than the National Assembly (nine years under the Third and Fifth Republics, six under the Fourth), a proportion of its members being renewed every three years, whereas all Deputies have been elected at the same time.

All three régimes have provided for the representation of their overseas possessions in both assemblies, though the scope of the representation has varied widely. Under the Third Republic, only French citizens in the Overseas Territories voted, and since citizenship was granted only to a small élite of non-Europeans, this meant that a mere handful of native colonial representatives sat in either assembly. In any case, the total number of representatives was small, and representation was limited to Algeria, the 'old colonies' of Guadeloupe, Martinique, Réunion and Guiana, all of whose inhabitants possessed French citizenship, together with parts of Senegal and the Indian enclaves.[7] In the first years of the Fourth Republic, the suffrage was extended to all Overseas Territories. In Madagascar, Algeria and the African Territories, there were for some years two separate electoral rolls, which meant that there was over-representation of European residents and the small number of 'assimilated' native electors who had been granted French citizenship and so voted on the European roll. By 1957, when universal suffrage and a single electoral roll had become the rule, 84 Deputies out of 626, and 64 out of 320 Senators sat for overseas possessions (including Algeria and the four 'old colonies'). By 1962 as a result of decolonization, overseas representatives had been reduced to six Deputies and seven Senators representing the remaining six small Overseas Territories, only one of which was in Africa. Though from 1960 to 1962, 71 Deputies and 34 Senators had continued in theory to represent Algeria and the Saharan *départements*, in practice many had ceased to sit before the achievement of Algerian independence in July, 1962.

In Republican France, candidates for election are not required, as they are in the United States, to be resident in their constituencies. Like the MP in Great Britain, the Deputy is regarded as the representative of the nation as well as of the constituency. The Constitution of 1793 (article 29) expressly stated this rule and, in 1871, after the cession of Alsace-Lorraine to Germany, it was expressly decided that the representatives for the region should remain in Parliament, because they had been elected as part of the representation of the whole nation. A more recent example of this attitude is provided by the correspondence in 1970 between the newly elected Deputy for one of the Nancy constituencies, M. Jean-Jacques Servan-Schreiber, and the President of the National Assembly, M. Achille Péretti. In a letter to the latter, M. Servan-Schreiber had referred to himself as '*député de Lorraine*'. The President of the Assembly objected to this phrase. '. . . even as the member for the first constituency of Meurthe-et-Moselle', he wrote, 'you are much more than "Deputy for Lorraine"; you are a Deputy for the entire nation'.[8] This is less than the whole truth about the Deputy. Many Deputies (and Senators too) live in their constituencies, and a relatively large proportion of them are either Mayors of a *commune* within the constituency or members of the Council for the *département* that includes the constituency. They combine the functions of national representative, not only with those of local government, but also with those of spokesman for local interests.

As in Western democracies generally, the vote in France is not obligatory, though a relatively high proportion of the electorate does normally vote.[9] Perhaps the fact that elections are always on Sunday has something to do with that.[10] Since 1913, the vote has been secret. But in spite of the existence of polling booths and envelopes for ballot papers, it is not always possible to avoid information on how some people have voted from leaking out in small rural areas, owing to the fact that votes are counted and the local result announced in each polling station, and then totalized in the centre for the constituency, instead of being counted there as is the custom in Great Britain.

THE CANDIDATE'S 'SUBSTITUTE'

An important innovation of the Fifth Republic, and one that has given rise to much controversy, is the 'incompatibility' rule. The effects of this on the behaviour of Ministers and Deputies are discussed later. The electoral consequence of the provision of article 23 of the Constitution, that membership of the Government is incompatible with membership of either legislative assembly, has been the appearance on the electoral scene of the substitute (*'remplaçant'* or *'suppléant'*), who must be chosen by the candidate, and whose name must figure on the ballot paper along with his own. In case of the candidate's election and his subsequent death or appointment to Government office (and also in two other specified cases[11]), the substitute replaces him for the remainder of the term for which he would otherwise have represented the constituency.[12] In the case of any other disqualifications, a by-election is held.

The substitute must consent to nomination, and once given, his consent cannot be withdrawn. Nor can he withdraw after the first ballot. On the other hand, once nominated, he cannot be got rid of by the candidate.[13] And if the candidate dies between the two ballots, he is replaced by the substitute, if he would have been qualified to stand at the second ballot. Nor can a substitute take a political line opposed to that of the candidate, though substitutes are often chosen precisely because they may be acceptable to the electors for reasons other than those that the candidate hopes will make him acceptable. For instance, a free-thinker or a Protestant candidate might well choose a Catholic substitute, or an urban candidate choose a farmer, and so on.

The substitute who is called on to replace a member of Parliament has the right and duties of a member, and so must also be qualified to be a candidate. He has, however, one disability. At the following election, he is not allowed to stand in the same constituency *against* the member whom he has replaced. This restriction was intended to give a Minister who loses office a better chance of success if he wishes to return to his old seat. In practice, Ministers who have been Deputies, and who realize that they might want to become Deputies again, have continued to regard themselves, and have also been regarded by their parties, as having a 'special relationship' with their former constituencies. As Ministers, they are an electoral asset to their party, and as potential Deputies they are obliged in their own interests to nurse what might at any time become their constituencies again. It became the general practice, therefore, during General de Gaulle's presidency, for substitutes to agree to resign in order to permit former Ministers whom they were replacing to fight by-elections. On 19 October 1970, six former Ministers all fought by-elections. In five cases, their substitutes had resigned in order to allow them to do this.[14]

THE RULES GOVERNING ELECTION TO THE NATIONAL ASSEMBLY

The National Assembly includes 487 Deputies, of whom 470 represent metropolitan France's 95 *départements*.[15] Ten represent the four overseas *départements* of Guadeloupe, Martinique, Réunion and Guiana, the first three having three Deputies each and the fourth one. Since 1946, these have constituted *départements* of the French Republic. Of the six small Overseas Territories, also forming part of the Republic but not having the status of *départements*, five have one Deputy each, and the sixth (the Comoro Archipelago) is a double-member constituency.[16]

Under the single-member system, the constituency boundary was originally the *arrondissement*, but the increase in industrialization and the consequent shifts of population produced great variations in the populations of constituencies. From 1927 onwards, therefore, *cantons* and *communes* were grouped in order to give constituencies of roughly equal size. In spite of a comprehensive redistribution in 1958, when the system was reintroduced after 22 years, there are considerable variations in the size of constituencies.[17] But the great majority have had an electorate of between 45,000 and 75,000.

To be elected at the first ballot, candidates must obtain an absolute majority (one half of the votes cast, plus one), and a number of votes equal to a quarter of the electors on the register. If no candidate in a constituency achieves this result, as happens in the majority of constituencies,[18] then there is a *'ballottage'*, which means that a second ballot is held the following Sunday, at which the candidate who heads the poll wins the seat. Under the Third Republic, new candidates could present themselves between the two ballots. This is now forbidden and, of the candidates at the first ballot, only those who have obtained at least 10% of the votes at the first are qualified to stand at the second.[19]

Where no electoral alliance has been made before the election, the two days immediately following the first ballot are used by candidates who are either eliminated at the second ballot by the 10% rule, or who are prepared to eliminate themselves as they do not expect to win, as a time when they can seek to negotiate an agreement enabling them to withdraw and advise their supporters to vote for one or other of the more favoured candidates. If no agreement is reached, the candidate can withdraw, either without giving his supporters any advice, or advising them as he pleases. Or he can decide to stand, even though he has no hope of winning. In any case, the electors are perfectly free to follow or ignore any advice. In the 1962 elections, there was a loose agreement on a constituency basis between four opposition parties on the Left or Centre-Left. In 1967, there was a formal agreement on a national basis between the Federation of the democratic Left (including three parties), the small, independent Socialist party, the PSU (*Parti socialiste unifié*), and the Communists, providing that their candidates would stand down at the second ballot in favour of the 'best-placed' candidate, by which was generally understood the candidate of whichever of the signatory parties was most likely to defeat the Gaullists. In some cases this meant voting for the candidate belonging to a party not having signed the agreement, provided he was generally acceptable to the Left.

All candidates must be French, over 23 years of age, and in possession of their civil and political rights. After the second world war, a number of persons convicted of collaboration with the enemy were expressly deprived for a specified period of the right to vote. This entailed deprivation of their right to be candidates, since candidates are required to possess the qualifications of a voter, though it is not essential for their names to be actually included in the register. In the early years of the Third Republic, multiple candidatures were permitted. For instance, in 1871, Thiers was elected in 26 constituencies. The potentialities of multiple candidature as a test of personal popularity were exploited in the 1880s by General Boulanger, with the result that a law of 17 July 1889 made it illegal. It is possible, however, for an elected Deputy to stand as a candidate in a by-election in another constituency, as was demonstrated in 1970, when M. Jean-Jacques Servan-Schreiber, having been elected a Deputy for Nancy the previous June, was a candidate in a by-election in Bordeaux the following September. The candidature aroused much controversy, though, as was pointed out, nothing either in the Constitution or the electoral laws forbids an elected Deputy to fight an election in another constituency. He would, however, be obliged to resign from one of the constituencies, if elected, since he could not actually represent two constituencies.[20]

Candidates must make a deposit of 1000 francs,[21] but this is reimbursed to all who obtain 5% of the votes cast. They must make a declaration of candidature at least 21 days before the first ballot, giving their names, date of birth, profession and the name of their substitute. During the election campaign, the State provides facilities for a limited amount of publicity, including the provision of official hoardings for each candidate. All other bill-posting is prohibited, a regulation widely flouted in practice. The cost of printing and postage of election addresses and cards is reimbursed by the State in the case of candidates who obtain not less than 5% of the votes cast. Time on the radio and television services is strictly allocated, the aim being to provide equality as between Government and opposition candidates.[22]

Although these rules ensure a minimum of theoretical equality, their efficacy is diminished by several electoral habits. The first is that, although no electoral propaganda in the form of advertisements may be published in the press during the electoral campaign, nothing prevents a candidate from financing and distributing his own newspaper during this period, for there is no ceiling on election expenses as there is in Great Britain. He can also send so-called private letters to electors in sealed envelopes. The allocation of radio and television time devoted to party election broadcasts during the campaign applies only to the French radio system, but parties are free to buy time on foreign radio stations that have a considerable public in France.

Electors must be French, over 21 years of age and in possession of their civil and political rights. Their names must be on the electoral register, which is revised annually in every *commune*. Though voting is not obligatory, a relatively high proportion of the electorate do vote. The lowest proportion since the war was in 1962, when only 69% voted; the highest proportion was in 1956, when over 82% did.[23] It is possible to vote by proxy or to have a postal vote in certain circumstances. The postal vote was used only exceptionally under the Third Republic (in 1919 and 1924), in the first case to allow inhabitants of the devastated areas to vote and in the second to allow those serving in Germany to do so. In the post-war years of the 1940s, refugees also constituted a problem, as did the returning prisoners of war and the absence from France of those serving in the army. The Fourth Republic, therefore, extended the right to a postal vote and added the possibility of proxy voting, but intended these methods to be used only by those whose occupation involved their unavoidable absence from the *commune* in which they had to vote on the day of the election. The right to a postal vote existed only for a general election. In

1958, the right was greatly extended, for the constitutional referendum as well as for the election, and doubts were already being expressed by 1959 regarding the loopholes in the regulations permitting either pressure on the elector voting by correspondence, or fraud by the authorities. For instance, the Ordinance of 20 August 1958 extended the right to a postal vote to the sick and to invalids unable to get to the polls; an Ordinance of 5 September granted the right to commercial travellers, and officials; another of 20 October added to the list journalists, travelling tradesmen and seasonal workers; and yet another added students, artists and other categories, and extended the right to the postal vote to municipal and cantonal elections.[24]

Though the fears that these measures would lead to abuse of the system proved well-founded, relatively few French electors in fact make use of the postal vote. Only 0·94%, for instance, did so in the 1958 referendum, and 0·95% in the elections the following November. But in 1958, in Corsica, which has a long history of corrupt elections, 4·02% of the votes counted (or declared to have been counted) were (or were declared to be) postal votes, and during subsequent elections there were several appeals for invalidation of Corsican elections on the grounds of a massive use of fraudulent postal votes. In a letter to *Le Monde*, after the 1967 election, the *Rapporteur-général* of the Finance Commission of the *Conseil général* in Corsica wrote that, in each of the three Corsican constituencies,

> a thousand votes have been 'posted' by people other than electors, and 70% at least of the postal votes, that is 3500 out of about 5000, in each constituency, are in one way or another illegal.[25]

In its decision invalidating the election in the Corsican constituency of Bastia, the Constitutional Council reported somewhat more soberly that 'a number of the postal votes did not come from electors who had requested them'.[26] The situation in Corsica was no doubt unique, but the problem of the misuse of postal votes was a real one.

THE RULES GOVERNING ELECTION TO THE SENATE

The system of election to the Senate is more complicated. In accordance with French electoral traditions, it is an indirect system, Senators being chosen by an electoral college made up of directly elected representatives. The constituency is the *département*. In each of France's 95 metropolitan *départements*, and in the four overseas *départements*, the electoral college includes the Deputies and the Councillors for the *département*, together with Municipal Councillors or their delegates. In *communes* with populations of over 9000, and in all *communes* in the Paris region (which consists of the *département* of Paris and six suburban *départements*), all Municipal Councillors are electors and *communes* with over 30,000 have the right to an additional delegate for every thousand inhabitants. In *communes* with under 9000 inhabitants – that is, over 37,000 out of a total of nearly 38,000 *communes* – the electors are chosen from among Municipal Councillors, each *commune* having from one to fifteen, according to the size of the Council. In each of the six Overseas Territories, the electoral college consists of the Deputy, the Territorial or General Councillors and Municipal Councillors, together with the elected Presidents of other municipal and rural communities. In all, some 102,000 electors, of whom between 75,000 and 80,000 represent metropolitan France,[27] elect 264 Senators for metropolitan France, seven for the four *départements* and six for the Overseas Territories. In addition, six Senators represent French citizens resident abroad, making 283 in all.[28]

Three systems of election are used. The twelve most populous *départements* of metropolitan France elect 69 Senators by proportional representation, Paris has 12 Senators and the six new suburban *départements* formed in 1967 have 27, while the remaining five heavily populated urban *départements* of Bouches-du-Rhône, Nord, Pas-de-Calais, Rhône and Seine Maritime have 30.[29] The remaining 83 metropolitan *départements*, the overseas *départements* and Overseas Territories elect 208 Senators (of whom 195 represent metropolitan *départements*) by the majority system with two ballots, an absolute

majority of the votes cast being required for election at the first
ballot, and a number of votes equal to at least a quarter of the
electors on the register. At the second ballot (which takes
place the same day) a relative majority only is required. The
third system applies only to the six Senators who represent
French residents abroad. These are chosen in the first instance
by the High Council for French residents abroad, which is
made up of *ex-officio* and elected members, together with
members nominated by the Ministry of Foreign Affairs. Names
are submitted to the High Council by its regional sections[30]
and the Council's choice must be ratified by the other Senators.
If 30 Senators oppose any nomination, then there is a secret
ballot to decide all six. A relative majority only is required for
election.

Senators must be aged at least 35 (the Third Republic had
a qualifying age of 40). They are elected for nine years, as under
the Third Republic, and one-third are renewed every three
years.[31] Like candidates for election to the National Assembly,
senatorial candidates must be replaced by a substitute in case
of death or of one of the incompatibilities. Senators elected by
the majority system have, therefore, to present themselves to
the electorate along with a substitute, as do candidates for
election to the National Assembly. Senators elected by proportional representation are replaced when their seats become
vacant, for whatever reason, by the candidate heading the list
of non-elected candidates.

ADVANTAGES AND DISADVANTAGES OF
THE ELECTORAL SYSTEM

Two advantages of the Senatorial electoral system, in the
context of French politics, are that it provides a legislative
Assembly that has continuity, and one that, though democratically elected, can no longer claim to be a serious rival of the
National Assembly. The system is criticized, however, for
providing a reflection of public opinion that is both out of date
and biased. It risks being out of date, because Senators are
elected by a body of local representatives who may themselves

have been elected up to six years earlier, and because they hold office for nine years, at the end of which they may well be seriously out of touch with opinion. It is biased, because it heavily over-represents rural opinion, and, in particular, that of small villages. This was, of course, one of the purposes of the system under which Senators were elected during the Third Republic, when the Senate could, and sometimes did, act as a conservative check on the Chamber of Deputies. But in a context of growing industrialization, over half of the Senatorial electoral college of the Fifth Republic still represents *communes* of under 1500, which account for only just over a quarter of the population, while just over a fifth of the senatorial electoral college represents the population of *communes* with over 10,000 inhabitants, that now make up over half the population.[32] A comparison of the senatorial representation of the five largest provincial *départements* with that of the five smallest *départements* is peculiarly illuminating on this point. The former, which includes agglomerations with an electorate totalling over four millions, elect 30 Senators. The latter, with an electorate of under 400,000, elect five Senators. In other words, the small rural *départements* have one Senator for every 74,000 electors, while the large urban *départements* have one for every 135,000 electors. The attribution of at least one Senator to every *département*, however small, and of one senatorial elector to every *commune*, however small, greatly increases the overweighting of rural opinion in the Senate.

It can be argued that this disproportion is unimportant, since it concerns a subordinate assembly. But there is also some overweighting of rural opinion in the National Assembly (though much less) and the close relationship between Parliamentary representatives and the local constituency must, therefore, increase the political pressure that rural interests can exert on Parliament.

In approving a system of presidential election very similar to that for the Senate, M. Debré had argued in 1958 that France was, after all, a country of small villages.[33] The Gaullist party soon realized, however, that one consequence of this fact was that the strength of Gaullism in the National Assembly was much greater than in the Senate. In 1968, this was still true. The Senatorial elections of that year showed that of the 94 seats concerned, 24 returned non-Communist left-wing Senators; 22 returned representatives of Centre or Radical parties; 22 returned Conservatives; 15 returned Communists, and only 14 elected Gaullists. Of these 14, eight were elected for the Paris region, where Gaullism was particularly strong. In other words, France's small villages had remained bastions of pre-Gaullist political attitudes. The recognition of this fact no doubt helped to explain why the Gaullists wanted to change the constitution of the Senate in 1969.

The system of election to the National Assembly is traditionally defended on two main grounds. The first accepts, implicitly or explicitly, some degree of over-representation of rural opinion in the interests of obtaining constituencies small enough to make real personal contacts possible between electors and elected. The former, it is argued, are able to vote for a candidate who is an individual, and not simply a party nominee, which is inevitably the position with a proportional system based on large constituencies of 500,000 or so, rather than on small constituencies of 50,000. Critics have pointed out that, in France, these contacts have helped to encourage 'parish-pump' politics and have been productive of strong sectional and local pressures on the Deputy, particularly if he combines, as so many Deputies do, the functions of Deputy with those of Mayor.

The second, and more important, defence of it is one favoured more by university professors than by practical politicians. It maintains that the device of the second ballot encourages, or should encourage, the bi-polarization of opinion, thus permitting a multi-party system to retain its freedom of choice without incurring the penalty of either politically incoherent or minority Governments.[34] The first ballot registers choice, the second eliminates, or can eliminate to some extent, those candidates who cannot hope to be elected. If they agree to withdraw and to advise their supporters to vote for one or other of the more favourably placed candidates, then at its best, the system can provide a coherent choice between a prospective

Government and a prospective opposition. It can provide the kind of crystallization of opinion that a two-party system in some other countries achieves voluntarily. At any rate, it offers the elector the possibility of deciding, on the basis of the evidence provided by the first ballot, whether to vote in the hope of victory, or merely to express his convictions.

Critics have not failed to point out that, in actual fact, the system provides, not coherent Parliamentary majorities, but only electoral majorities based on alliances concluded for purely tactical electoral reasons. If, as has often happened, no party agreements are possible on a national level, and parties make *ad hoc* agreements on a constituency level, then the candidate elected at the second ballot certainly receives more votes than any other candidate, but exactly what the vote is for has to be decided later within the National Assembly. In such circumstances, Deputies are subject to multiple and contradictory pressures. If M. Durand (a Socialist) has been elected in constituency X with the aid of Communist votes, while M. Dupont (another Socialist) in constituency Y owes his election to Centre votes, then the attitudes of each within his party (or within the Government) will naturally reflect the consciousness that he may need the same support to be re-elected. He is also subject to the normal pressures from constituency interests. The danger is, therefore, that, at its worst, the system makes the formation of coherent Governments more difficult and increases the ability of Deputies to use their power to threaten Governments. This was the disease from which both the Third and the Fourth Republics suffered (though the latter could not blame the same electoral system). Either the Assembly dictated to Governments, producing what was called *gouvernement d'assemblée*, or it was too divided to do this coherently and exercised contradictory pressures conducive to Governmental deadlock – the state known under the Fourth Republic as *immobilisme* – in which parties could combine only to destroy and so had to compromise by enduring Governments only so long as they did virtually nothing.

It has also been argued in defence of the second-ballot system that it encourages political moderation, since parties must combine to win elections and the extremist parties cannot do this. This was the thesis on which the elections of 1951 were fought. Although the system was quasi-proportional, it provided for electoral alliances intended to produce the same effect as a second ballot, and expressly intended to reduce the strength of the two parties least able to combine with others, yet totally unable to combine with each other – the Gaullists and the Communists. It achieved this result in the case of the Communist party, but not in the case of the Gaullists, who, though mainly isolated, emerged as the largest party for political reasons strong enough to defeat the electoral calculations.

During the first ten years of the Gaullist régime, Gaullists and Communists were no longer in this state of political isolation. Indeed, the hankering of the Socialists for an electoral understanding with the Communists drove them to conclude electoral alliances which were not based on any real agreement on policy issues, but which alienated other possible allies. The fact that too many members of the Federation of the Left had been elected in 1967 only thanks to Communist votes made it electorally impossible for the Socialists (the dominant member of the Federation) to withdraw from the alliance with the Communists in the 1968 election, though by then the Federation was moribund. The Socialist alliance with the Communist party frightened away from the Left a number of voters belonging to the Centre, thus increasing the dependence of many Socialists on Communist votes for their re-election in a subsequent election.

The system has also been criticized mainly on two grounds. The first is that the negotiations between the two ballots involve a great deal of political bargaining between parties that is carried out in secret. This cannot be treated as a serious objection, since bargaining and negotiations within parties, as well as within electoral and governmental coalitions, are regular and inevitable procedures of democratic politics. They are, indeed, desirable procedures for, if the number of parties and the number of issues on which there are divisions of opinion are to be kept within reasonable bounds, the only democratic method of doing so is by means of discussion and negotiation.

The second criticism is a technical one. It is that the single-member system, whether with one or with two ballots, inevitably produces some disproportion between the numbers of votes and the numbers of seats. It is undeniable that this often happens, but the difficulty is to identify the political and electoral contributions to any particular electoral result. For instance, to quote only the examples provided by the four elections held between 1958 and 1968, that of 1958 gave the Gaullists 40% of the seats, though they had only 18% of the votes at the first ballot. The Gaullist victory was obviously due to the political circumstances, but the electoral system certainly also gave the Gaullists a disproportionately high share of Parliamentary seats. In 1962, the Gaullist party won 49% of the seats, with 31·9% of the votes at the first ballot. The Communist vote was in fact only 100,000 higher in 1962 than in 1958, yet the party had nine members elected at the first ballot as against one only in 1958. At the second ballot, with half a million *fewer* votes, 32 Communist Deputies were elected, thanks to the left-wing electoral agreement. In 1967, thanks to the left-wing electoral alliance, including the Federation of non-Communist parties, the independent Socialist party and the Communists, the number of Communist Deputies rose from 41 to 73, and the number of 'Federation' Deputies from 91 to 116, although the combined left-wing vote increased only from 41·2% to just over 42%. In 1968, when the alliance worked less well, and when the Left was suffering from the repercussions of the May events, a combined Socialist–Federation vote at the first ballot of 36·5% and of nearly 42% at the second did not prevent the loss of over half their seats and the reduction of their members from 193 to 91. On the other hand, in 1968, the 358 Deputies of the majority were elected by 46·4% of the electors.

In two of these four elections (1958 and 1968), the working of the electoral system was vitally affected by the political situation which, indeed, was the main cause of the Gaullist victory. The extent to which either Gaullists or opposition parties were able to form effective electoral alliances (a matter also dependent on political factors) undoubtedly affected the *scale* of the victory or defeat. In other words, the single-member system with two ballots can exaggerate an existing movement of political opinion, but it is this movement of opinion itself which is primarily responsible for its ability to do so. In 1962, when the relations between the opposition parties did not favour a very effective alliance, and when there was no political crisis to encourage them to combine, the relation between votes and seats was much less disproportionate and the interest of the electors in the contest was much smaller.

It could be argued that a disproportion that merely increases the scale of an electoral victory, thus providing a clear result and a workable majority, is preferable to an accurate reflection that may blur Governmental responsibilities. A clear majority is, indeed, more necessary in France than in countries with a tradition of more stable government. For there is a tendency to attribute the responsibility for political instability either to the electoral system or to the political complexion of Governments, instead of to the attitudes of parties themselves. The facts support neither of these facile conclusions. Between 1945 and 1958, France had a proportional system for three elections and a quasi-proportional system for the remaining two. Between the wars, she had a quasi-proportional system for two elections and the single-member system for the following three. But political instability was similar under all systems.[35] Nor were predominantly left-wing Governments either more or less stable than right-wing ones.[36]

The simple fact is that there has never been any conclusive evidence that any French electoral system could achieve what its supporters have hoped for from it. France's obsession with electoral change is only a symptom of the fundamental political disease of French politics, which is the inability to achieve sufficient political consensus to make either constitutional or political stability possible. Dissatisfaction with the working of the political system too easily becomes dissatisfaction with the whole system of political institutions. Constitutional and electoral change both reflect the perennial French illusion that it is possible to manipulate institutions in such a way as to create the necessary conditions for political stability. A similar illusion that institutions can mould politics has been perceptible in France's foreign policy.[37] But an electoral system is essentially a reflection (with some distortion) of a political situation and of political habits, not a creator of either. In practice, the French themselves have always attached a great deal of importance to this function of reflection – but without being willing to accept its consequences!

The most that can justifiably be claimed for the system of election of the Fifth Republic is that it is both simple to grasp and familiar, and so, perhaps, has a better chance than any other of removing from the arena of political conflict at least one of the many issues that divide French parties. Like all political institutions it works best in favourable political circumstances. If French politicians could produce these, if they could, so to speak, look after the political pence, then elections, like the pounds, could be left to take care of themselves.

CHAPTER III

Parliament

THE PLACE OF PARLIAMENT IN REPUBLICAN POLITICS

Gaullists and non-Gaullists are agreed that the French system, as defined in the 1958 Constitution, is one of Parliamentary government. The importance of Parliament is reaffirmed in article 3: 'National sovereignty belongs to the people, who exercise it through their representatives and by way of referendum.' In spite of the increased powers conferred on the Government, the National Assembly retains the right to compel Governments to resign (article 50). Parliament alone can vote laws (article 34), and authorize the declaration of war (article 35). The status and the rights and duties of individual members of Parliament remain basically the same as they were under the two previous Republics, and most of the rules governing the conduct of Parliamentary business are unchanged too. Nevertheless, an authority with the prestige of André Siegfried was not alone in the belief that the Fifth Republic was 'no longer in the Republican tradition'.[1]

That tradition, expressed first in the Monarchic Constitution of 1791, is characterized by one fundamental principle: the supremacy of law as voted by Parliament. It has implied two beliefs. The first is the conviction that Parliament alone should decide the limits of its own competence.

The power to make the law is part of the exercise of sovereignty, entrusted by the people to its representatives. . . . The power can no more be enclosed within pre-established limits than can sovereignty itself. It is a power that includes freedom of initiative and consequently freedom to deal with any question or any subject without any restriction of the sphere of activity. It means that the right of the legislative body to act is in principle limitless.[2]

The second is the belief of both French legislators and the French public that a special prestige attaches to Parliament as the authorized law-maker. The strength of the belief in Parliament as the only valid expression of the national will helps to explain the tendency of French Republics to favour strong Parliaments and weak Governments.[3] They have shared the opinion expressed by Roederer to the Constituent Assembly in 1791 that 'executive power is essentially an agent'.[4] Though circumstances have often made it imperative to give Governments power to govern for limited periods by decree, such periods have always been regarded up to the Fifth Republic as essentially temporary delegations of sovereign power, granted on certain conditions only, and withdrawable at the will of the legislature. The definition in the 1958 Constitution, therefore, of a circumscribed area of legislative power, even though it left in the hands of Parliament all the vital powers, including those to which Parliament has traditionally attached importance, was among the most contested of its innovations. It is not that Governments are felt to be unsuited to exercise the powers now entrusted to them. Parliaments have, indeed, repeatedly granted them far greater powers at one time and another. What is objected to is that the 1958 Constitution recognizes as a principle, and not merely as a matter of expediency, that the decision as to what is and what is not Parliament's sphere of action is no longer a matter for Parliament to decide for itself.

THE RIGHTS AND DUTIES OF MEMBERS OF PARLIAMENT

That change has not, however, significantly affected the rules governing the rights and duties of Deputies and Senators, or the general rules governing the organization of Parliamentary business. Members of Parliament enjoy, as they have done under previous régimes, the privilege of 'Parliamentary immunity', which means that they are not liable either during or after their membership of Parliament to criminal or civil proceedings in respect of any opinion expressed by them in the exercise of their Parliamentary functions in the Chamber of which they are members. They are, of course, liable for anything actionable said outside Parliament. But, while Parliament is sitting, proceedings may be taken against them for alleged offences only with the authorization of the assembly of which they are members, unless they are caught *flagrante delicto* (in which case they may be arrested, though the assembly can stop proceedings if it so decides),[5] or unless the matter is a minor one (such as a parking offence, for instance) or a civil matter in which no question of arrest is involved and which will not prevent the member from carrying out his Parliamentary duties. When Parliament is not sitting, proceedings are possible, but even then the authorization of the *bureau* of the assembly is required for the member's arrest, except in three cases: when he is caught *flagrante delicto*, when a court has made a final finding of guilt, or when the assembly has agreed during a previous session to suspend his immunity. In general, Parliament has preferred to suspend a member's immunity in order to allow proceedings against him, rather than authorize his arrest.

Members of Parliament also enjoy certain financial rights and privileges, including the right to a certain amount of free or cheap travel, the right to send political correspondence from the Assembly post-free (a term very generously interpreted), and the right to a tax-free residence allowance. Though lower than those of an American Congressman, their salaries were, until recently, higher than those of British MPs. Since 1946, they have been calculated on the basis of the salary scale of the highest category (*hors échelle*) of civil servants,[6] which means that Parliament does not have the embarrassing responsibility of deciding whether or not to award itself salary increases. Members are, however, liable to a number of deductions, including contributions to their Parliamentary groups and to their parties. Communist Deputies, for instance, hand over the whole of their salary to the party, which returns to them a proportion that the party considers suitable.[7]

There has been one interesting innovation in the Parliamentary rules under the Fifth Republic, the aim of which is to cure the chronic absenteeism of members. The member's salary is now divided into two parts, a basic salary and an 'attendance bonus' (*indemnité de fonction*) which amounts to a quarter of it. In order to qualify for the latter, the Deputy is required to take part in a certain percentage of the votes, both in Parliament and in Committee. Failure to do so involves the loss of some or all of the bonus, the precise amount of the fine depending on the degree of absenteeism.[8] Another innovation, also aimed at reducing absenteeism, is the prohibition of proxy voting, except in six specified conditions which must be notified in advance and in writing. They are: (i) illness, accident or family circumstances; (ii) absence on military service; (iii) absence on a temporary Government mission; (iv) attendance abroad at a meeting at which the member is representing the Assembly or the Senate; (v) absence from France on the occasion of a meeting of Parliament in special session; (vi) *force majeure*.[9]

The French Parliament has no system of 'pairing', but proxy voting was generally accepted throughout the Fourth Republic. Either one member of the Parliamentary group cast all the votes of the group (the Communist system) or members left signed voting papers with one or more proxies. The Fifth Republic has not only made proxy voting unconstitutional (article 27) except in the above-mentioned conditions, but has introduced a system of electronic voting (so far in the Assembly only) which can be operated only by the Deputy's individual key.

These rules have been fairly easily circumvented by Deputies. They require attendance only for recorded votes (*votes publics*), which excludes votes by a show of hands or by standing up, and does not require the Deputy to have attended the preceding debate. There have consequently been persistent complaints that speeches are made to empty benches, followed by an influx of members when it comes to the vote. The citizen reading in his paper the next morning that a Bill has been voted by 240–180 is, therefore, unaware that no more than 20–40 Deputies may have been actually following what was going on. And, of course, the requirement does not affect debates that are not followed by a vote (in particular those at question time) which have a dismal record of poor attendance. The rule has also been easy to evade because, by general admission, the 'valid explanations' that justify absence have been very liberally defined. Marcel Prélot, himself a Senator, went so far as to say that the penalties rapidly became theoretical.[10] And the press has provided illuminating accounts of the dexterity rapidly acquired by Deputies in using – or rather misusing – the electronic system to record their colleagues' votes.

> When a vote is announced [wrote Pierre Viansson-Ponté in 1963] a few Deputies rise and pass at great speed along the red benches, lightly pressing buttons on each desk as if they were playing on some immense keyboard. A humorist could say that the Palais Bourbon has become the Salle Pleyel. . . . This curious gymnastic exercise, in which the ushers sometimes join, is no tribal rite, but merely the Deputies present obligingly and agilely casting votes for their absent colleagues.[11]

THE ORGANIZATION OF PARLIAMENTARY BUSINESS

Parliament meets for two sessions during the year. One begins on 2 October and lasts 80 days, and is mainly concerned with the budget. The other begins on 2 April and lasts 90 days. It is mainly concerned with legislation, and is no longer interrupted in order to allow Deputies to attend party conferences, some of which were in May. Special sessions can also be held. They are convened by the President of the Republic on the request of the Prime Minister or of a majority of the Assembly and have a specific agenda. Up to March 1960, this provision (articles 29 and 30) was generally interpreted to mean that the President *must* convene a special session if the constitutional conditions were complied with. The President, however, interpreted it as giving him the right to decide whether to call one. A special session requested by the National Assembly cannot exceed 12 days, and a fresh one cannot be held on the request of the Assembly within the month following the closure of the previous one. In addition Parliament meets for a special session 'as of right' in two circumstances. The first is following a general election, when it meets for a period not exceeding a fortnight (article 12). The second is during a national emergency as defined by article 16, when it can sit for the duration of the emergency.

On the opening of the October session each Chamber elects its *bureau*, that of the National Assembly comprising its President, six Vice-Presidents, twelve Secretaries and three *Questeurs*, that of the Senate comprising its President, four Vice-Presidents, eight Secretaries and three *Questeurs*. The Secretaries, usually young members, supervise official records and check votes. The *Questeurs* are responsible for certain administrative and financial arrangements. The *bureau*'s functions are administrative and political, and include examining reasons for proxy-voting, deciding whether private members' Bills are in order, advising on the constitutionality of amendments, verifying the existence of a quorum, deciding on disciplinary measures, etc. The first meeting of a new Assembly is presided over by the oldest member (*le doyen d'âge*)[12] until the newly elected President of the Assembly takes the Chair. He is elected by secret ballot for the duration of the Parliament, other members of the *bureau* being elected annually.[13]

Like the Speakers of the House of Commons and the House of Representatives, the President of the National Assembly is a spokesman and chairman, but without the degree of unchallenged authority and discretion possessed by the Speaker of the House of Commons, though he has been given more power than his predecessors have had to call members to order, to prolong or curtail debate, or apply the closure. He is not under the same obligation as a British Speaker to refrain from involvement in party politics. He remains an active member of his party and attends and speaks at party conferences. In the past, he occasionally left the Chair and intervened in debate, and even more occasionally voted. Presidents of the Assembly have not so far acted in either of these last two ways under the Fifth Republic.[14] He enjoys considerable prestige, being fourth in the order of precedence and presiding over a meeting of the two Houses at Versailles, when this meets to vote a constitutional revision. He sees that the Standing Orders of the Assembly are complied with, acts as a link between the two Chambers and between the Assembly and the Government, receives communications from members, distributes Bills to the legislative committees, calls meetings of them as well as meetings of the Conference of Presidents (the body responsible for drawing up the weekly agenda) and transmits to the Government the texts of Bills voted.

He has also been given additional functions by the Constitution of the Fifth Republic. He can rule private members' Bills or amendments out of order if he believes that they do not come within the constitutional definition of the law-making sphere, or he may defer the matter to the Constitutional Council for a ruling. If he holds that clauses of either international treaties (article 54) or of laws *before* their promulgation (article 61) are not in conformity with the Constitution, he defers the matter to the Constitutional Council. He *must* be consulted by the President of the Republic before the latter declares a state of emergency under article 16, or before he decides to dissolve the National Assembly. He chooses three members of the Constitutional Council.

M. Chaban Delmas, who was President of the Assembly from 1959 to 1969, took on himself the duty on one occasion of interpreting certain constitutional provisions that were under dispute, and on which the Constitutional Council had found itself incompetent to pronounce. His authority to do this was challenged by a number of Deputies, and even implicitly by the President of the Republic himself, whose opinions regarding the dispute M. Chaban Delmas had endeavoured to explain to Deputies. This was, however, an isolated occasion.

In the French Parliament, both the National Assembly and the Senate are divided into a variable number of 'organized groups'. Though the titles differ somewhat in the two Houses, the parties represented in them are roughly the same. To be recognized as an 'organized group', that is, one with the right to be represented in the two main organs on which the organization of Parliamentary business depends – the Conference of Presidents and the standing legislative committees – a group must have 30 members in the Ássembly (in the Senate the figure is 14). The groups can also have affiliates (*apparentés*).

Affiliates are usually in general sympathy with the group's political views and vote with it, but it is also possible to affiliate purely as a matter of administrative convenience, without any political obligation to vote with the group.[15] All groups are required to make a 'political declaration', but this is generally little more than a collection of pious platitudes.[16] The Conference of Presidents (so called because it includes the President and Vice-Presidents of the Assembly, the Presidents of the legislative committees and of the Parliamentary groups, together with the *Rapporteur-général* of the Finance Committee and a representative of the Government) draws up the weekly timetable. This body has far less authority, however, than it had under the previous régime, since the Government now has the right to priority for Government Bills and private members' Bills accepted by it, and so can effectively control the timetable.

Both assemblies meet normally on four afternoons a week (Tuesday to Friday inclusive), committees sit in the morning (though not every morning), and time on one afternoon a week is reserved for questions (usually Friday in the Assembly and Tuesday in the Senate). There is no quorum either for debate or for voting, unless a group President specifically asks the *bureau* to verify that a quorum exists, in which case it is defined as the presence within the Assembly precincts of an 'absolute' majority of its total membership, excluding vacant seats. Voting may be by a show of hands, by standing up if this gives a clearer result, by a 'public vote', which requires each Deputy to place a voting paper (white (for), blue (against), red (abstention)) in a ballot-box, and finally by a 'public vote at the rostrum', which requires a roll-call, each Deputy mounting the rostrum to record his vote.[17] The last two are now replaced normally in the National Assembly by the electronic system, in which the Deputy records P (*pour*), C (*contre*) or A (*abstention*). Authorized proxies are provided with a duplicate of the Deputy's key.

LEGISLATIVE PROCEDURE

Bills may be introduced in either House, except for Finance Bills which must be introduced in the National Assembly. They go first to the appropriate committee. There are now only six permanent or standing committees, chosen at the beginning of the Parliament and then at the beginning of each April session. These are specialist committees, four of them, consisting of a maximum of 61 members each,[18] dealing respectively with Bills concerning Defence; Foreign Affairs; Finance; Laws, constitutional laws and administrative matters. The remaining two, consisting of a maximum of 121 members each, deal respectively with Bills concerning production and trade (including agriculture, fishing, communications, tourism, public works, town planning, etc.), and with cultural, family and social matters (including education, health, social security, labour, population, etc.). Their political complexion reflects proportionately the strength of the different groups in the Assembly. No member may belong to more than one committee.

Under the previous régime, there had been 19 committees, with a uniform membership of 44. Among the reasons for the change were hopes that it would prove more difficult to pack the larger and less specialized committees with representatives of interest groups, and this has proved to be the case. It was also hoped to reduce the political importance of the committees. When their sphere of competence coincided roughly with that of a single Ministry, the committee chairman tended to acquire the importance of a shadow Minister, particularly in the conditions of debates under the Fourth Republic, when it was the Bill as amended by the committee, and not the Minister's Bill, that was usually debated in the National Assembly. It was also hoped to reduce the number of committees to which a Bill had to be submitted for an opinion, in addition to the main committee responsible for making the report in the Assembly. In practice, however, the habit of submitting Bills to other interested committees has been retained and so, even with the larger committees, there is still a good deal of time-wasting. For instance, the guide-line Bill on urban housing and planning (*projet d'orientation foncière et urbaine*), voted in 1967, interested three commissions which could not co-operate. It was therefore analysed in the Assembly four times, once by the Minister, and then by three *rapporteurs* of committees, all making different proposals.[19]

Debates on a Government Bill[20] begin with a ministerial statement, followed by the commission's report (a reversal of the order under the previous régime). Deputies first debate the general principles, and then vote on each article, finally voting on the text as a whole, as amended during the debate. After this 'first reading', the Bill goes to the Senate (or to the Assembly if it has been read first in the Senate) where the process is repeated. If passed by both Houses it is promulgated within 15 days, unless the President of the Republic asks for a reconsideration of it. This request must be granted. If he does not, and if the Bill is not challenged (under article 61) as unconstitutional by either the President of the Republic, the Prime Minister or the President of either House, then on publication in the *Journal Officiel* it becomes law.

Ministers may not be members of either House but may be present at debates and speak in either. The debate may be 'restricted' (now rare), 'open' or 'organized'. A restricted debate requires the Government's request or assent and the assent of the relevant committee and only proposers of Government amendments, Presidents and *rapporteurs* of committees can speak in debate, except for a final speech of not more than five minutes by one member of each group. In an open debate, intending speakers notify the President of the Assembly in advance and he decides on the order in which to call them. The decision to have an organized debate is taken by the Conference of Presidents or by the Assembly itself. A fixed time is allotted and shared out between the representatives of the different groups in proportion to their strengths in the House. One spokesman for each group is usually allowed a brief statement at the end to explain how his group has decided to vote and why (*l'explication de vote*). Some Bills are adopted without debate, especially private members' Bills. When there is a debate on the latter, then it begins with the committee's report and the Government does not intervene unless it so desires.

The relations between the two Houses are now such that the

Senate occupies a potentially stronger position than it did under the Fourth Republic. Unless the Government intervenes, a Bill on which there is disagreement can (as under the Third Republic) in theory shuttle back and forth indefinitely between the two Houses (the process known as *la navette*). In practice, this does not happen, because the great majority of Bills are now Government Bills, and so the Government is anxious to see them passed. After a Bill has been read twice in each House without agreement being reached (or once, if it is being dealt with under the 'urgent' procedure),[21] the Government can decide on the appointment of a *Commission paritaire*, that is a joint committee of fourteen members, seven (with seven substitutes) chosen by and from each House. If it reaches agreement on the points in dispute (which alone can be considered) the Bill is voted on in both Houses, with such of the amendments as the Government accepts. If the committee does not reach agreement, or if the agreed text is defeated in either House, then either the Bill falls, or is shelved, or a fresh attempt is made to reach agreement; or else the Government intervenes, in which case, after a further reading in both Houses without agreement being reached, the National Assembly is asked to vote either the committee's amended text or the Government's latest version of its own Bill with any acceptable Senate amendments. Unless the Bill is one amending an organic law, the Assembly requires only a majority of those voting to pass it.

All this means, of course, that Bills in which the Government is not interested can be blocked in the Senate. But except for this contingent veto, which has not been of any importance, the Senate remains a subordinate legislative Chamber as it was under the Fourth Republic. Even the provision requiring its consent to Bills relating to the Senate (article 46) could have proved ineffective in practice, for when General de Gaulle proposed to change the composition and functions of the Senate in 1969, he intended to do so by referendum and not by the Parliamentary method under article 46. The last-minute concessions made in December 1971 by the National Assembly to meet the Senate's objections to clauses of the Bill amending the 'incompatibility' rule, were generally regarded as being due to the fact that this was an organic Bill relating to the Senate (as well as to the Assembly). Failure of the two Houses to agree would, therefore, have prevented the Bill from being voted, since, in these circumstances, the Assembly cannot override the Senate.

Under the Fifth Republic, an 'organic law' deals with one of the nineteen subjects that the Constitution specified as requiring an organic law in order to complete its own provisions.[22] These laws may be amended by what are also called organic laws, but only one additional organic law is provided for, and on this nothing has so far been voted. A special procedure is required to vote organic laws, as they are really minor constitutional measures. Organic Bills must be tabled a full fortnight before being debated. The two Houses must agree, or failing agreement, the Assembly can override the Senate only by voting the amendment by an 'absolute' majority of its membership, and not even then if the amendment relates to the Senate. Organic laws are promulgated only when the Constitutional Council has declared them to be in conformity with the Constitution.

The procedure for voting finance Bills also differs from that of ordinary legislation. Most of the changes are intended to prevent Parliament from using delay in voting the budget in order to force the Government to make concessions, as happened under the Fourth Republic.[23] A strict timetable is imposed on both Houses. The Assembly must complete its first reading within forty days of the Government's introduction of the Bill, failing which the Government sends it to the Senate to be read within a fortnight. If the Parliamentary procedure has not been completed within 70 days of the introduction of the Bill in the Assembly, the Government is free to apply its provisions by Ordinance.

If, however, the Government fails to introduce the Bill in time for it to be promulgated before the beginning of the financial year (in January), it may ask Parliament to authorize taxation, and it allocates by decree expenditure on continuing services. Either a request is made to the Assembly ten days before the end of the session to vote under the 'urgency' procedure those parts of the law covering the collection of taxes and the general headings of expenditure, or alternatively the Government may ask, two days before the end of the session, for the vote of a special Bill entitling it to collect taxes in anticipation of authorization by the finance law.[24]

It is not possible to give any assessment of the efficiency of these provisions, because no Government between 1959 and 1971 had to encounter the kind of opposition encountered by Governments in trying to vote their budgets under the previous régime. Governments have presented their budgets on time and had them voted on time. There has, therefore, never been any need to have recourse to the procedure outlined in the above paragraph. It is easy to imagine however that, in an Assembly with a stronger opposition and a less disciplined majority, requests to the Assembly to vote the budget speedily might be treated cavalierly. In any case, the Assembly remains as free to reject the budget as it has always been. The provisions of the 1958 Constitution seek to prevent a situation such as that of 1952, when M. Edgar Faure's Government was unable to persuade the Assembly to vote the taxes to meet the expenditure that it had already voted.

The Constitution of 1958 also prohibits members of Parliament from introducing Bills or proposing amendments that would have the effect of increasing expenditure or decreasing revenue (article 40). Such a provision exists in Great Britain and is not regarded by British citizens as detracting in any way from Parliament's sovereignty or prestige. It existed also under the Fourth Republic, but was consistently evaded, and has continued to be evaded to some extent under the present régime. Not only do French Deputies regard their right of financial initiative as an aspect of Parliamentary sovereignty, but, in their capacity as representatives of local and sectional interests, as well as for electoral reasons, they have always been anxious to protect certain vested interests – for instance, to vote for increases in pensions (particularly of ex-Servicemen), for the rights of home distillers to tax privileges, and of peasants and small tradesmen to tax concessions or opportunities to evade taxes (or both). The easiest way to appear diligent in the defence of constituents is to propose to spend more on them and take less from them in taxes, and Communist Deputies were no less assiduous in doing this under the Fourth Republic than any representative of 'capitalist' parties. Indeed a Socialist Deputy calculated that 27 Communist Bills introduced during the first Parliament, but not debated, would have cost between 2000 and 3000 milliard francs![25] Though article 40 has been interpreted by the *bureau*, the President of the Assembly and the Constitutional Council more strictly than were the Fourth Republic's measures seeking to achieve the same end, Gaullists have by no means been immune from sectional and electoral pressures and it cannot be said that old habits have been eliminated. But the increasing use of 'framework' and 'guide-line' laws and of long-term measures such as programme-laws, the application of the five-year National Plans, and the general need in the interests of modernization and economic efficiency to plan ahead, have made the annual budget much more than formerly, if still less than in Britain, a method of criticizing general policy rather than of obtaining modifications in esti-mates. The time limit for voting the budget has helped the Government so far. Both Deputies and Senators complain bitterly that they have not even time to consider adequately the proposals that they are confronted with, much less to produce counter-proposals. In fact, budgets have rarely been significantly amended.[26]

The Senate has more power in the field of finance than has the British House of Lords for, although the finance Bill must be voted first in the National Assembly, it must also be voted in the Senate, which can be overriden only in the conditions already described. These have not so far proved any serious obstacle to the domination of the National Assembly. In one way, they make it easier than it was under the Fourth Republic, when the Senate (up to 1954) could be overridden only by an 'absolute' majority of the membership of the National Assembly, when it had itself voted the Bill by a similar majority, a condition that political divisions during the Fourth Republic made the National Assembly at times incapable of fulfilling.[27]

THE DEMOTION OF PARLIAMENT

The procedural devices by which Gaullist Governments have been enabled to resist Parliamentary obstruction and pressures during debates and to avoid Government defeats not involving Deputies in an election are discussed in the following chapter, because they concern the working relationship of Governments with Parliament, rather than the functions of Parliament itself. The powers of Parliament have been reduced under the Fifth Republic in three main ways: by restrictions on the law-making sphere; by General de Gaulle's resort to legislation by referendum, thus by-passing Parliament; and by the interpretation of constitutional provisions either (unofficially) by the President or (officially) by the Constitutional Council.

In addition to constituting a break with Parliamentary tradition, the new definition of Parliament's right to make the law has proved very difficult to apply. In addition to constitutional law, the Fifth Republic has now, in effect, three kinds of law where only one existed before. There are organic laws, which, though the term existed during previous régimes, did not previously constitute a special category of law requiring a different procedure from ordinary legislation. Under article 34, ordinary laws now fall into two main categories, those which *determine the rules* concerning a list of enumerated subjects, and those which *determine the fundamental principles* of a further list of enumerated subjects. The first category includes the most important of the matters that Parliament has always claimed the right to deal with – those relating to fundamental liberties of the citizen, civil status and civic rights, liability to taxation, obligations of national defence, penal procedure, amnesty, electoral laws, categories of public corporation, and nationalizations. The second category includes matters on which Parliament retains the right to lay down only the general principles and framework – matters such as local government, education, property and commercial rights, trade-union law, social security and the organization of national defence. Finance laws and programme laws are also included in the list. Detailed application in these fields is now a matter for the Government. Subjects not coming within either of these categories belong also henceforth to the executive field. A law is no longer what it has hitherto been in French Republics.[28] Parliament still votes the law, but the matters on which it is qualified to vote are decided by the Constitution.

Not surprisingly, the task of deciding exactly where to draw the line between general principles and detailed application has given rise to a great deal of controversy. Responsibility for resolving conflicts is entrusted under article 37 to two bodies, according to circumstances. In the case of laws voted before the Constitution of 1958 came into effect, the Council of State is responsible. A Government that wishes to amend such a law by decree, on the ground that the matters covered by it now form part of the executive field, must first consult the Council of State. In the case of laws passed since the coming into force of the 1958 Constitution, that is, of course, including all new laws, the responsible body is the Constitutional Council. In addition, a Bill introduced in either House can be challenged under article 41 by the Government and, if the President of the House concerned agrees, be ruled out of order on the ground that it deals with matters not in the domain of law. If the President of the appropriate House does not agree, the matter is submitted to the Constitutional Council for a ruling, which is final.

In reality, the limiting conditions within which these two organs work are different, and some laws are outside the competence of the Constitutional Council. There is no constitutional provision enabling Parliament to appeal against a Government decree on the ground that the matter requires a law. But a citizen or body considering itself to be affected by the rule can appeal to the administrative courts to annul it on the ground that the Government had no legal or constitutional right to make it.[29] Nor has the Constitutional Council, in its own view, any power to declare unconstitutional a law voted by referendum instead of by Parliament. This was made clear when the President of the Senate submitted the question of the constitutionality of the referendum of October 1962 to the Council. Although no express provision, either in the

Constitution or in the organic law relating to its functions, mentions the methods by which a law is voted, in the opinion of the Council, both the spirit of the Constitution – according to which the Council is 'an organ regulating the activities of the public authorities' – and also the letter of it – in the shape of article 11 dealing with the referendum – justified the conclusion that it was incompetent, for the article made no reference to the possibility of 'any formalities between the adoption of a Bill by the electorate and its promulgation by the President of the Republic'.[30]

The attitudes of the two organs have certainly differed, at least in the opinion of many French politicians and jurists. Marcel Prélot described the Constitutional Council as 'seeking to prevent encroachments by the legislator, whilst the Council of State, through appeals on grounds of *ultra vires*, protects the legislative domain from encroachments by the Government'.[31] This is probably how most people in France see them. But the scales are certainly not weighted evenly between the two.

During the early years of the régime there were a number of decisions by the Constitutional Council on conflicts relating to the respective fields of Government and Parliament, and a number of criticisms suggesting that the Council was interpreting the Constitution in a way that helped to strengthen the hand of the Government as against Parliament. By 1961, however, there was growing up a body of case law to serve as a guide in subsequent conflicts, and much less was heard in the following years about the Council's suspected pro-Governmental bias.[32]

Critics perhaps had more ground for complaint regarding its failure, or its powerlessness, to give a ruling. The example just quoted relating to the referendum was not an isolated instance. When consulted by the President of the Senate in September 1961 on the question of a private members' Bill on farm prices, the Council rightly ruled it out of order on the ground that the matter was one for the Government to decide. But when dissatisfied Deputies tabled a motion of censure on the same subject, the Council, consulted by the President of the Assembly as to the constitutionality of a motion of censure during a special session held under emergency conditions (as defined in article 16), equally rightly held that it had no competence to give a ruling. The President of the Assembly was, therefore, left to rule it out of order, giving his own explanation of the constitutional position, a solution that satisfied nobody outside the Gaullist party.[33]

The Constitutional Council's rôle in the complex and disputed issue of the introduction of brand advertising on the State radio and television services shows up even more clearly the practical difficulties created by the constitutional distinction between 'fundamental principles' as a matter for the legislature, and detailed application as a matter for the Government. The Constitutional Council had decided in 1964 that the 'fundamental principle' governing the radio and television service belonged to the field of law.[34] But in 1968, after months of wrangling on the subject of the Government's intention to authorize by decree a limited amount of brand advertising, there were three main constitutional questions in dispute, regarding the respective powers of Government and Parliament. First, would this change the fundamental nature of the service? If it did, then it must be introduced by law. Second, even if the Government's competence in this matter was to be accepted, was it possible to provide the service with the financial resources accruing from brand advertising without bringing in a law? An amendment to the finance law of 1961 (the *amendement Diligent*) had stated that the French radio service could not accept new financial resources without authorization by law. Would the contemplated additional resources be regarded as '*new*' or merely as '*a variation*' of existing amounts? In the former case, the matter belonged to the field of law, in the latter to the executive field.[35] At this stage an opposition Deputy tried to jump the gun by bringing in an organic Bill to complete article 34 (the long-awaited final organic law). This raised a third problem, for it revived the controversy, in abeyance since the months following the publication and voting of the Constitution, regarding the permitted scope of such a Bill. Article 34 described the purposes of the permitted organic law as being 'to complete and make more precise' (*préciser et compléter*) the existing provisions. This phrase can be interpreted, either broadly, to include an extension of the enumerated functions comprising the field of law-making, or restrictively, merely to define more clearly the existing ones.[36]

For political reasons, the Government was anxious to introduce its proposed measures by decree. In view of the amount of opposition to the plan, the virtual absence of a Gaullist majority in the National Assembly made the passage of a law problematical. The Constitutional Council was, therefore, consulted as to whether the Government's proposed decrees did or did not belong properly to the rule-making field. The Council's decision was that, if they left the 'category' of the institution unaffected, they could be authorized. But whether the category, that is, the fundamental principles of the radio service, would or would not be affected by the decrees was precisely the question at issue!

Maurice Duverger's comment that, if the Government had received an ambiguous answer (*une réponse normande*), the explanation was that it had asked an ambiguous question (*une question normande*),[37] though justified, is really beside the point. For this was not the first occasion on which the Council had been either unable or unwilling to provide guidance on a question concerned with constitutionality. Though the Government dropped the plan, the months of debate, together with the constitutional ambiguity, had certainly demonstrated the difficulties involved in trying to apply the constitutional provisions relating to the fields of law and of rule-making, even with the aid of the Constitutional Council.

President de Gaulle's use of the referendum as a legislative instrument in circumstances in which such use did not appear to be authorized by the Constitution, though it effectively removed from members of Parliament decisions that non-Gaullists regarded as being constitutionally theirs to take, did not in practice cause more than minimal deprivation. Of the five referenda between 1958 and 1971, the first, in 1958, had been authorized by Parliament. The following two were concerned with Algeria and were held in the special circumstances created by the Algerian war. A majority, both in Parliament and in the country, certainly approved of the decisions, even if they disliked the method by which they were taken. Of the remaining two, that of 1962 to alter the presidential electoral system, though unpopular with all non-Gaullists, was resented for constitutional reasons rather than for reasons connected with the merits of the proposal, which had a number of supporters in the opposition parties. That of 1969 on regional reform and the composition and functions of the Senate was undoubtedly generally unpopular, for political as well as constitutional reasons. But as it proved no less unpopular with the electorate than with Parliament, the defeat of the General's proposal left the situation unchanged.

Nevertheless, it would not be true to say that no harm was done by the referenda. The use of them was widely regarded as part of a deliberate attempt by General de Gaulle to diminish the authority and importance of Parliament. And though there was no evidence – at least up to the end of 1971 – that General de Gaulle's successor intended to make similar use of the referendum – and no evidence that he would have had the political prestige to enable him to do so even if he wished – the precedents now exist and could be used as supporting arguments by a President who might, for whatever reason, seek to damage Parliamentary prestige or Parliamentary authority.

The ruling out of order by the Constitutional Council of private members' Bills and amendments as involving an increase of expenditure, and the Council's restriction of the opportunities open to the Assembly to criticize the Government by votes of resolutions or by votes following debates on Oral Questions, certainly did deprive Parliament of some of its traditional methods of expression. But it is doubtful whether, in the political circumstances of the 1960s, these restrictions really did more than lessen opportunities for political gestures without real consequence, and for the kind of obstruction and harassment to which Governments of the Fourth Republic were continually subject. As is pointed out in other chapters, some of the restrictions had been openly desired in 1958 by a number of the political leaders of the Fourth Republic. But there is no doubt that many Deputies and Senators resented both in principle and in practice the right of the Constitutional Council to impose limits on Parliament's control of its own Standing Orders.[38] Resolutions are now in order only if they deal with internal matters concerning the organization of each assembly, if they are decisions to bring someone before the High Court of Justice, or if they are to set up committees of enquiry or supervision.

THE FAILURE OF PARLIAMENT

In spite of the deliberate demotion of Parliament by the constitution-makers, members of Parliament under the Fifth Republic have been to a considerable extent responsible for demoting themselves. They certainly made use of the motion of censure. It was used eighteen times in all, between 1959 and 1971. Of these, eight were votes against a Government request for confidence, in conditions described in the following chapter, and ten were initiated by Deputies under the terms of article 49. Only one motion was carried, but the reasons for the failure of the others were political, not institutional. The quarrels and impotence of the opposition parties, which are discussed in later chapters, were by far the most important causes of the discredit of Parliament, which has been added to its demotion. Even within the existing political framework, though it precluded any prospect of an electoral victory for the opposition parties – and would probably have continued to do so even if they had succeeded in looking remotely like an alternative Government – Deputies and Senators could have made far more effective use of the opportunities for criticism and propaganda that the Parliamentary machine still possesses. In the first place, they could have used Oral Questions (with or without debate) more effectively, even without the vote that they were denied. In the event, they continued under the Fifth Republic, as they had done under the previous régime, to put questions concerned mainly with local or sectional interests, and far too often devoid of any national or political interest.

The result was that 'Question times' totally lacked the drama and pace that characterize question time in the House of

Commons (and members of the House of Commons do not vote on questions either!). In the Senate of the Fourth Republic, M. Michel Debré, who invented the procedure of Oral Questions with debate, was able to use them to some effect, precisely because they provided him with an opportunity to criticize Governments of the day. But instead of the rapid cross-fire (and sometimes fireworks) that are an essential element of the question and answer technique of the British House of Commons, Questions in the National Assembly have been long, dull speeches, prepared in advance and read. Replies have often been delayed for months (sometimes even for years) and Ministers have sometimes not turned up, or have left the reply to a junior Minister. There has been no debate, merely what the French call a deaf men's dialogue, often conducted before virtually empty benches. At times even the questioner himself has either not turned up, or has left the premises at latest as soon as his question has been answered. Deputies have blamed Ministers, but this is one field in which their own conduct could have stimulated Ministers to take more notice of them. Instead, they have bored themselves and so have bored the electorate.[39]

In 1970, a new device was introduced in order to inject some interest and spontaneity into the dreary waste of question time. *Questions d'actualité*,[40] as the name implied, were intended to produce a snappy exchange of views on subjects of both topical and national interest. They began with an audience of 100 and with the Prime Minister present. But the only discernible speed up to the end of 1971 was that with which they degenerated into slightly shorter written and read formal speeches on subjects that rarely had any national or political interest. Both the Prime Minister and the President of the Assembly admitted that the experiment had not been very successful.[41]

Nor was it only at question time that Parliamentary benches were virtually empty. Mention has already been made of absenteeism in relation to the voting habits of Deputies under the Fifth Republic. The persistent continuance of absenteeism has been a constant theme of political commentators. It may

have been possible to explain away some of the absenteeism
at question time by the fact that on Fridays Deputies have left
for their constituencies and on Tuesdays Senators have not yet
returned. But commentators have pointed out that some
Deputies leave their constituencies (or more probably their
town halls) on Wednesday and return to them on Thursday
night. It is difficult to explain away an audience of 35 dwindling
to 12 for a four-and-a-half-hour debate on employment problems, or an audience of 40 for an important foreign-affairs
debate. And the debate on the reform of the regions and the
Senate, subjects to which the press contributed hundreds of
columns of newsprint during the months preceding the 1969
referendum, attracted only between 60 and 80 Deputies. Press
reports continually emphasized poor attendances at budget
debates, and also at meetings of the Finance Committee.[42] After
his election to the presidency of the Assembly in April 1969,
M. Achille Péretti noted that the problem of absenteeism was
'a battle that still had to be won'.[43]

The truth is that both Deputies and Senators have kept old
habits in new situations. The motion of censure, resorted to as
a familiar political gesture, has achieved only publicity, and
often only bad publicity. Direct political pressures, whether in
Assembly committees or in Assembly debates, no longer
achieve the results that they did under the unstable and short-
lived Governments of the previous régime. Senators have gone
on defeating Bills, and having their votes overridden by the
National Assembly. And these techniques have helped to
increase some of the problems that both Houses rightly complain of and about which something perhaps could have been
done. There have been consistent complaints of the inefficiency
of the organization of business in Parliament. Bills are often
delayed in Committee, so that they reach both Deputies and
Senators too late to allow adequate study of them. Debates are
consequently exchanges between well-informed Ministers and
ill-informed members of Parliament. Senators complain that
too few Bills are sent to them at the beginning of the session
and far too many at the end. Indeed, in both Houses, floods of
Bills are normally hastily voted during the last days of the

session. Debates are dull as well as uninformed because
Deputies continue, in spite of the prohibition in the Standing
Orders, to read their speeches, as they used to do.[44]

Their suggestions for improvement of Parliamentary machinery often tend, too, to be less practical than nostalgic. These
have included the staggering of budget debates over two sessions, instead of crowding them into one; more opportunities
for Deputies to speak in debates; more use of the *ad hoc* legislative committees that the Constitution provided for, but that the
Government has usually preferred not to appoint; increased use
of the permanent legislative committees, in order to take some
of the burden of work away from the floor of the House and
allow more time for debate; better use of Oral Questions, and
more say for opposition groups in determining priorities for
questions in the Parliamentary timetable; and more opportunities for private members' Bills.[45]

There are strong reasons why the last-mentioned proposal
should be resisted. Critics have long held that the curtailment
of the floods of private members' Bills, most of which never
emerged from Committee and of which only 6–7% at most
ever reached the statute book, has meant a gain in Parliamentary
efficiency. Most of those that did become law were, in the
words of André Philip, a former Socialist Deputy and Minister,
'more suited to a local council'.[46] The traditional French view
that the British Parliament talks, while the French Parliament
legislates, is a survival from the past. It was out-dated during
the previous régime and has become even more so with the
increasing volume of economic and social legislation, and the
consequent need for legislative co-ordination and planning in
the form of programme-laws, guide-line laws and long-term
planning in general.[47] It is true that opinion polls are reported
to show a consistent and widespread discontent with the rôle
of Parliament. But the explanations of this discontent tend to
reflect the political conservatism of the public, just as the proposals of Deputies and Senators reflect their own conservatism.
That Parliament no longer controls the Government, that
technicians are becoming increasingly important, and that the
familiar Parliamentary battles have been replaced by less public

negotiations between Government and majority party are political facts that cannot be ignored. But it by no means follows that the way to deal with them is simply to return to familiar ways.

France is, of course, not alone in having Parliamentary procedures that are ill adapted to the second half of the twentieth century. All Western democracies are facing similar problems and challenges. The difficulties are intensified in France by both economic and political factors – the problems of economic modernization, and the nature of the French party system. There are also special complications, which may or may not prove lasting, and which are discussed in the following chapters – the uncertainties of what is as yet a relatively untried, if no longer new régime, the fragmentation of the opposition parties, and the adaptations imposed on the majority parties by the disappearance of de Gaulle. One of the biggest problems facing the French Parliament, however, is the fact that its members have not yet found a satisfactory rôle for themselves and few on the opposition side have even tried to find one. Until they do, they are unlikely to be able to persuade the public to take a more favourable view of politics and politicians than they have done for the past quarter of a century.

CHAPTER IV

The Government

As laid down in the 1958 Constitution, the function of the Government is to decide and direct the policy of the nation (article 20). The 1946 Constitution had made no specific reference to Governmental functions, stating merely that the *Président du Conseil* (the word 'Prime Minister' was nowhere used in the text of the Constitution) 'ensures the application of the law' (article 47). The traditional attitude towards Governments was expressed, however, by M. Guy Mollet, who was for a time President of the Constitutional Commission responsible for the draft Constitution of the Fourth Republic. 'The Government', he said, 'consists of the Assembly and the Cabinet.' The phrase, as its context shows,[1] is indicative of the suspicion with which Republican politicians have always regarded Governments. In normal conditions they are seen as, at best, a necessary evil, to be turned out at a whim. 'In three-quarters of a century,' wrote Jacques Fauvet in 1957, 'there have been more Governments than years.'[2] Up to the Fifth Republic, the one political fact about France known to every fourth-form schoolboy was that it was a country of weak and unstable Governments.

This is far from the whole truth. In abnormal conditions, whether in the face of external danger, of internal unrest or merely of actual or potential deadlock in Parliament (which has often been far from abnormal), French Governments have been granted extensive powers to govern in place of Parliament. Indeed, a British correspondent in Paris once remarked that every French Prime Minister's dream was 'to get the

Deputies to take their holidays when other people do, and to stay away even longer'.[3] Governments of the Third Republic governed by 'decree-laws', with the authorization of Parliament, for quite considerable periods between the wars. And the Fourth Republic's members of Parliament lost little time in circumventing the obstacles that they had created for themselves by their prohibition in the 1946 Constitution of any delegation by the National Assembly of its legislative power.[4] Even the most jealous Parliamentarian defenders of the ascendancy of the legislature have accepted without question the inherent right of the Government to exercise certain police and administrative powers which are regarded in France as essential attributes of the executive function, and, as such, exercisable without legislative authorization, either general or specific.

The prevalence of unstable Governments has been responsible for the view held by both General de Gaulle and his successor to the presidency, M. Georges Pompidou, that France was a country that was inherently virtually ungovernable. The existence of a stable, highly centralized and powerful administrative machine has left no French citizen in any doubt as to the accuracy of the popular view that France is not governed, but is administered. A French sociologist recently went so far as to suggest similarities between the French and the Soviet conceptions of administrative authority.[5] The tightly knit administrative network has tentacles that stretch all over France. The Minister of the Interior heads a vast empire of Regional Prefects, Prefects and Sub-Prefects, the last two having each his own empire, in the form of the supervision and control within the *département* of municipal councils, of which there are almost 38,000. The Prefect also acts as both the servant and the controller of the *Conseil général* of the *départements*. Other Ministries also have representatives in the *départements*, responsible to their superiors in Paris, but subject to the Prefect's co-ordinating powers within the *département*. The Ministry of Education exercises direct control over finance, staffing, curricula and examinations of all State schools and, up to 1970, controlled universities in France. The whole pyramid of officialdom has its own legal status. Conflicts between its members and citizens are dealt with by a hierarchy of administrative tribunals, headed by the Council of State, which, as well as being the supreme court of administrative law, exercises supervision and control over the activities of local authorities.

The authority and cohesion of this vast machine has not only enabled it to emerge virtually intact from all the political upheavals of the last century and a half, but has built up an image of State control that has led Frenchmen often to belittle the consequences of political and Governmental instability. But it has also been partially responsible for creating in the administrative field a love–hate relationship no less striking than that which characterizes the relations between Parliaments and Governments. On the one hand, there is a lack of strong and independent local government, a lack that has been partially created by and partially perpetuated by the presence of a strong centralized administration. There is an over-reliance on the State and, because its power and influence are so pervasive, a permanent resentment of it, seen in recurrent attempts to loosen the grip of Paris by the creation of some form of regionalism, the most recent of these attempts being in 1969. The relationship between officials and the public reflects and emphasizes the gulf between 'us' and 'them' – between the citizen and the State. It was no accident that Alain, one of the most influential intellectuals of the most influential left-wing party in the first quarter of the twentieth century, should be mainly remembered for a book entitled, *Le Citoyen contre les Pouvoirs*. Alphonse Daudet's provincial *sous-préfet*, rehearsing his speech in the French countryside, addressed his imaginary audience as '*Messieurs et chers administrés*'. The French citizen has tended to remain essentially an '*administré*' (the word is not translatable in terms of British political relationships), in that, whether politically revolutionary or reactionary, he still tends at one and the same time continually to demand and to rely on action by the State, and to resent equally its activity and its inertia.

It has often been claimed by Frenchmen, and by some foreign

observers as well, that the instability of Governments is more apparent than real. Even during periods of constant Government changes, some Ministers withstand the storms and continue to hold office through successive Government reshuffles or reconstitutions. On the other hand, during the years from 1959 to 1971, which exhibited a degree of Governmental stability hitherto unknown in Republican history, some Ministers came and went with a frequency hardly rivalled during the bad old days of the Third and Fourth Republics.

> Under the Fourth Republic [said a Socialist Deputy in 1961] Prime Ministers changed, but Ministers remained: under the Fifth the Prime Minister remains but the Ministers change.[6]

This was substantially the situation four years later. By the end of General de Gaulle's first septennate, there had been only two Prime Ministers and three Governments, both Prime Ministers being Gaullist, supported by a Gaullist majority in the National Assembly.[7] Yet only three members of the 1958 Government headed by General de Gaulle were still Ministers, and only one, the Foreign Minister, M. Couve de Murville, was still in the same post. During the first ten years of the Fifth Republic, there were 25 Government reshuffles (some of them, admittedly, no more than changes of one or two individuals) and, by 1969, France had had twelve Ministers of Education, eleven Ministers of Information, six Ministers of Justice, Finance and the Interior and five Ministers of Agriculture and Labour. During the second Parliament of the Fourth Republic, however, though there had been eight Prime Ministers (and seven effective Governments) in a period of between four and four and a half years, three Ministers served in six of the Governments, seven in five and thirteen in four. The Minister of Education was always a Radical and so (with one exception) was the Minister of the Interior.[8] Between 1944 and 1954 (except for one month in 1946) there were only two Foreign Ministers, both belonging to the same party, although there were 17 changes of Government during those years.

Such ministerial stability can certainly increase the effectiveness of individual Ministers, particularly of Foreign Ministers, who are by tradition somewhat more independent of Governmental control in areas which are not at the centre of acute conflict. But this cannot compensate for the absence of both cohesion and positive political direction which results from Governmental changes that reflect conflicts or deadlocks on political issues. The changes in ministerial personnel under the Fifth Republic have not been of this kind, though the changes under the Fourth Republic only too often were. From 1959 to 1971, Gaullist Prime Ministers could count on a relatively united and predominantly Gaullist Governmental team, and a similarly united and disciplined majority in the National Assembly.

This has meant two significant changes in the relations between Government and Parliament. First, whatever the complaints of opposition Deputies regarding the high-handedness of the Government, in reality the Government's record as far as consulting Parliament and the country are concerned has compared favourably with that of the previous régime. For some years, Governments of the Fourth Republic did not submit the National Plan to Parliament at all, and the Coal–Steel Pool was presented to it only at so late a stage that it was virtually a *fait accompli*. The plan for a European Defence Community, which was submitted to Parliament, was accepted only after two years of bitter controversy, and was not submitted for ratification for the following two years, because no Prime Minister was confident that he would not be defeated on the issue. When M. Mendès France finally did submit it to Parliament, it *was* defeated. Under the Gaullist régime there have at least been Parliamentary debates of sorts on the National Economic Plans. On controversial matters such as the reform of the presidential electoral system, the introduction of regionalism and the reform of the composition and functions of the Senate, the country was consulted in referenda, following extensive press discussion as well as discussion in Parliament.

The second political difference has been that the dialogue between Government and Parliament has been conducted under rules, some of them incorporated in the Constitution, others in the Standing Orders, that have been deliberately framed to free Governments from obstruction and pressure, in the hope that a habit of stable government could be created. It remains to be seen, of course, whether political habits can be created in this way, in the absence of a party system geared to permanent confrontation between a coherent Government and a coherent opposition. If they cannot, then the Gaullist organization of Parliamentary government may prove to be no more than an interlude.[9] In any case, the changes that it has introduced do not amount to anything like a revolution. There is still a wide area of continuity. The general structure and functions of Government remain much as they were under previous régimes, and, of the procedural changes, some were little more than a 'constitutionalization' of reforms already in operation during the later years of the Fourth Republic, while others would in all probability have been submitted to Parliament if the Fourth Republic had survived. The difference is that, whereas any Government before that headed by General de Gaulle in 1958 would have had at best a hard battle to get procedural reforms accepted, and at worst might well have been defeated, General de Gaulle was expressly granted by Parliament the right to draw up a Constitution that would not be submitted to Parliament but to the nation, and so was able to include a number of them in the Constitution itself.

CONDITIONS OF OFFICE

Ministers are held penally responsible for crimes and misdemeanors committed by them in the course of their duties, and cases brought against them are tried by the High Court of Justice, a special court set up to try Ministers and, if necessary, the President of the Republic, on charges of high treason. In an effort to ensure their independence and incorruptibility, members of the Government are barred from combining office with the exercise of certain occupations. These include employment in the public service (civil servants appointed to ministerial office must be detached from service for their period of office), professional activities – such as that of lawyer, director of a public or semi-public concern either subsidized by or used by the State, or that of national official of a professional organization (for instance, a trade union or employers' association).

These restrictions are not really new, nor are they irksome, since the job of Minister leaves little time for outside activities. There is no bar on Ministers retaining unpaid, elective offices such as those of Mayor or local Councillor, or Chairman of the council for the *département*. As has already been pointed out, Deputies frequently combine the two rôles of local and national politician. The new restriction, however, imposed under article 23 of the 1958 Constitution, though not new in Republican history, has created a great deal of controversy. This article, making membership of the legislature and ministerial office incompatible, places the Minister who is a politician and not a technician in a very difficult situation, though this was not the intention. The rule by which any Deputy or Senator who accepts ministerial office must resign his seat within a month, and be replaced in Parliament by the substitute elected with him in the conditions described in chapter two, was justified by Gaullists – and by some non-Gaullists – on several grounds. It was hoped that it would remove one factor making for governmental instability, namely the incentive for Deputies to overturn Governments in the hope of increasing their own chances of obtaining office. A Deputy now knows that the price of accepting office is that he will have no seat to go back to if he loses the job. For a Minister who leaves office cannot, under the new rule, regain his seat in the Assembly (or the Senate) until the following election. A second justification of the rule was the hope that it would protect Ministers from the political pressures of party and constituency interests. If they did not choose to contest elections, then such pressures were expected to become ineffective.[10]

In the light of all that has been written and said about the ties between French national and local politics, it seems inconceivable that anybody could seriously have believed that the 'incompatibility' rule could, so to speak, insulate the Minister in this way from what General de Gaulle believed to be the evil effects of party politics. Within a few years, even he had realized how many additional votes candidates who were also Mayors and local Councillors were worth, and how many votes a Minister who was both a Gaullist and a Mayor or local Councillor could command if he stood as a Parliamentary candidate. By 1965, Gaullist Ministers were fighting local elections in strength, and in 1967 were instructed by the President to stand as candidates in national elections. The constituencies had never been in any doubt regarding the electoral value of Ministers, while Ministers who hoped to regain their seats (and as has been pointed out, security of ministerial office was by no means guaranteed under the Gaullist régime) had to find some way of keeping those seats warm. They found local and constituency contacts the best way. As one of the many opponents of the rule put it:

> The former Deputy who has become a Minister continues to act as if he were still the Deputy, whilst his substitute, who has become the Deputy, remains in the eyes of all the substitute for such and such a Minister! . . .

This situation, goes on the writer, is inevitable, for, if the Minister leaves the seat to the substitute and looks for another, where he is relatively unknown – and, more important, where his ministerial benefactions have not smoothed his way in advance – then he risks defeat, '. . . and why should he risk defeat, when, for months or years, he has been supplying governmental "manna" to his gratified electors?'[11]

The result, as Maurice Duverger has pointed out, was that the traditional relationships between Ministers and their constituencies were restored, but by the opposite route:

> Formerly, Ministers were first Mayors or local Councillors, then Deputies or Senators, and then Ministers. Under de Gaulle, they were Ministers first, then Deputies, and then Mayors or Councillors for the *département*.[12]

This process was assisted by the breakdown in practice of the provision that the substitute retains the seat until the following general election, and its replacement by the 'gentleman's agreement' that he resigns it to make way for the Minister he is replacing, if the latter leaves office and wishes to regain his seat.

An example of the way in which political realities have defeated constitutional intentions was provided by the by-election in Bordeaux in September 1970. It was caused by the death of the substitute for the Prime Minister, M. Chaban Delmas. The latter, who had been Mayor of Bordeaux since 1947, and was generally regarded as having done a great deal for the town, had no interest in seeing his seat go to somebody else, who, unlike the substitute, might displace him permanently. He, therefore, stood as a candidate, thus killing three political birds with one stone. His prestige won the seat easily for his substitute; it remained potentially his; and the campaign was a successful exercise in Government propaganda. A former Gaullist Minister and Professor of public law, M. J.-M. Jeanneney, a supporter of the 'incompatibility' rule, had two main comments to make. On the general situation created by the working of the rule he noted that, with the development of the habit of choosing Deputies or Senators as Ministers, 'every Minister is virtually a Parliamentary candidate, and every Deputy is a would-be Minister'. He saw the Prime Minister's candidature in Bordeaux as 'either an offer to serve local interests in his capacity as Prime Minister, which is shocking, or else a request to the electors of a single constituency to approve his national policy, which is indefensible'.[13] Nevertheless, in spite of the growing unpopularity among politicians of the incompatibility rule, and despite a half promise by M. Pompidou, when he became President, to do something about it, nothing was done in the following two years.[14] Yet M. Pompidou's own actions and words had provided in themselves an eloquent demonstration of the failure of the incompatibility rule to produce a separation, let alone a divorce, between Ministers and party politics. By 1962, the number of 'politicians' as opposed to 'technicians' in the Government was increasing, but none yet occupied a key rôle. 'Politicization' steadily increased during the premiership of M. Pompidou. By 1966, only three members of his Government could legitimately be described as 'non-political' – and

two of these were loyal Gaullists. The Prime Minister himself became a municipal Councillor in 1965 and a Deputy in
1967, when 26 out of his 28 Ministers fought in the general
election. In a television interview in July 1966, the Prime
Minister defended ministerial candidatures on the ground that,
if the opposition leaders contested elections, then Government
leaders should do so too. And he added: 'Do you imagine that
if I were beaten I should remain Prime Minister? In presenting
himself for election, a Minister is risking his job.'[15] Nevertheless, he re-appointed two of his Ministers who were defeated
in the 1967 election.

THE ORGANIZATION AND FUNCTIONS OF THE GOVERNMENT

As far as the framework of Governmental organization is concerned, singularly little has changed. The Government remains
responsible for the direction and co-ordination of national
policy. It remains a collective organ responsible to Parliament and carrying out its work by means of two organs. The
first, the *Conseil des Ministres*, normally included (up to 1969)
all Ministers, irrespective of their position in the hierarchy,
and it continues to be presided over by the President of the
Republic. The second, the *Conseil de Cabinet*, is presided over
by the Prime Minister. Under the Third Republic, the *Conseil
des Ministres* was really a ratifying body, the decisions being in
reality taken by the *Conseil de Cabinet*. The rôle of the President
of the Republic was, therefore, almost entirely formal. Under
the Fourth Republic, its importance was greatly increased,
while that of the *Conseil de Cabinet* declined. Under the Fifth
Republic, the *Conseil des Ministres*, under the chairmanship of
the President of the Republic, is the sole organ of decision-
making in theory and practice and the *Conseil de Cabinet* has
rarely met.[16] Much more use has been made, however, of
inter-ministerial committees, the most important of which
have also been presided over by the President of the Republic.
These have enabled decisions to be reached by a small number
of Ministries concerned with a limited number of subjects,

and so have made it easier for the President to present the full Council with something like a *fait accompli*.[17] In 1969, it was decided that meetings of the Council of Ministers would in future normally be attended only by those with the rank of 'Minister', except for one Secretary of State, who, in his capacity of Government spokesman, is responsible for announcing the communiqué after the weekly meeting of the Council of Ministers.

French Governments of the Fifth Republic have numbered between 25 and 40 members, the most important in status (although not necessarily in responsibilities) being *Ministres d'Etat*. These are usually senior statesmen, sometimes former Prime Ministers, and have sometimes been without portfolio. They usually number between four and six. 'Ministers', who number from 12 to 20, are responsible for the main departments of State. *Ministres-délégués auprès du Premier Ministre* were a creation of the Fourth Republic. They do not usually exceed one or two, and are often entrusted with some special (and perhaps not permanent) function. But apart from the specific dependence on the Prime Minister's office they do not differ in any significant way from 'Ministers'. Junior Ministers, called 'Secretaries of State', vary greatly in numbers, the smallest number under the Fifth Republic being four, the largest twenty.[18] Their function is similar to that of British Parliamentary Under-Secretaries. In speaking of members of the Government, however, the term 'Minister' is generally used to refer to all of them, irrespective of rank.

Most Ministers have been, since 1966, Deputies or former Deputies. Very few of them have been Senators – only three in M. Debré's 1959 Government and subsequently never more than one. All Ministers have a *cabinet ministériel*, that is, a personal secretariat of a kind unknown in Great Britain. It has been described as 'a flexible bridge linking administrators and politicians'.[19] Appointments to it are entirely in the Minister's hands, and members of the *cabinet* are responsible to him alone, although they are paid out of public funds. Their appointments automatically end with the Minister's departure from office. The personal nature of the appointment has resulted in frequent criticisms that the *cabinet* tends to be largely a body of the Minister's personal and political friends, not excluding his relations. This has certainly ceased to be true, partly owing to the limitation of numbers since 1951, and partly owing to the growing complexity and scope of ministerial functions. About 80% are now regular civil servants, who can be seconded in order to serve Ministers in this capacity. The functions of the *cabinet* are technical, administrative and political. Within it,

> . . . there must be total loyalty to 'the chief': the *cabinet* is there to advise, to make informed judgments, to take account of the political wishes of the Minister, explain these to officials and members of Parliament, and see that they are carried out.[20]

The *cabinet*, then, is a team, in which three rôles are of capital importance; that of the *directeur*, usually a high official with experience of the administrative machine and ability to co-ordinate; that of the *chef de cabinet*, generally in political sympathy with the Minister; and that of the technical advisers, who are the chief link between the politician and the technical and administrative expert. At its worst, the *cabinet* has sometimes been – as described by a former French Ambassador – 'an expression, not only of the Minister's suspicion of the department of which he has become the head, but also a safeguard against its tyrannical power'.[21] At its best it can provide the Minister with a team that can combine the functions of private secretary, public-relations officer, Parliamentary private secretary, technical expert, technical adviser and politically sympathetic 'guide, philosopher and friend'.

The Government, under the leadership of the Prime Minister who is its spokesman and chief executant, is collectively responsible to the National Assembly for its conduct of the affairs of the nation, and the resignation of the Prime Minister, or the defeat of the Government in the National Assembly, involves the resignation of the whole Government. Ministers are individually responsible for their conduct of the affairs of their department, and are chosen and dismissed by the Prime Minister. Prime Ministers of the Fourth Republic regarded themselves, and were generally regarded, as being effective heads of Government, the head of the State acting merely in the 'dignified capacity' that Bagehot described as being the rôle of the British monarch. Both the actions and words of Prime Ministers of the Fifth Republic indicate that they share the powers of head of the Government with the President of the Republic. General de Gaulle sometimes went so far as to say that he was the sole head, implying, when he did not say it in so many words, that the Prime Minister was simply an executant or agent. Some Gaullists have agreed with this view. A former Gaullist Minister, M. Jacques Soustelle, who may not perhaps be regarded as wholly unbiased in his opinions of General de Gaulle, has described Ministers as so many 'clerks tied down to administrative jobs'.[22] The practice, as opposed to the theory, of government under the Fifth Republic has also been described as a system in which 'the Head of the State has the eminent rôle and the Prime Minister the useful rôle'.[23] There is, however, a good deal of evidence that General de Gaulle often intervened directly in the field of activity generally thought of as being that of the Prime Minister.

The extent to which the system has been or still is 'a dyarchy', as is frequently alleged by politicians as well as by political scientists, is an important political question that will be returned to later. But since, in constitutional practice as well as theory, it is the Prime Minister and the Government alone who can be held responsible and dismissed by the legislature from their posts, it is necessary first to discuss how the Government acts and how effectively the legislature can exercise control over it. In the relations between the Government and Parliament, it is still the Prime Minister who is the key figure. In some ways, his status has improved as, indeed, it also did during the Fourth Republic. This is indicated by the attribution to him of a number of new responsibilities, in addition to the traditional ones of general direction of the work of the Government, responsibility for national defence, the armed forces and administration, for the execution of laws, and for appointments to certain civil and military posts not reserved to the President. Although the Constitution specifies that requests to

the President for a referendum, or for private members'
Bills to be declared out of order, are made by 'the Government', it specifies that it is 'the Prime Minister' who requests
a special session, proposes a constitutional amendment, tables
Bills (though his right is not exclusive), 'pledges the Government's responsibility' either on his programme or on a Bill,
or seeks the approval of the Senate.[24] It is the Prime Minister,
too, who has the power to decide whether or not to refer a law
or a treaty to the Constitutional Council, and who must be
consulted by the President before he uses his power to dissolve
the National Assembly or to assume emergency powers under
the terms laid down by article 16.

Obviously, no Prime Minister in his senses would act so
independently of his colleagues as to forfeit their confidence
and so threaten the stability of the Government. The extent to
which a Prime Minister does take these decisions himself is
therefore bound to vary with the personality of the holder of
the office, and with circumstances. But since the Constitution
specifies in some cases that prime ministerial action must be
preceded by discussion in the Council of Ministers, and in
other cases mentions his name alone, the distinction could
imply some area of prime ministerial discretion that represents
an increase in the status of the office.

On the other hand, the Prime Minister is specifically empowered only 'in exceptional circumstances', and by express
delegation (article 21), to deputize for the President at meetings of the Council of Ministers and 'when necessary' at meetings of certain committees. These conditions underline the
fact that, under the previous régime, it was the Prime Minister
and not the President who normally presided over organs in
which the real decisions were taken. And whereas the President
now 'consults' the Prime Minister (but with no obligation to
accept his advice) before exercising emergency powers and the
right of dissolution, which do not now require a ministerial
counter-signature, under previous régimes, all the President's
acts except pardons required a counter-signature.

The functions of Government are carried out by means of
what are called inherent powers (*pouvoirs autonomes*) and rule-

making powers (*pouvoirs réglementaires*). The former, which have always existed in France, are exercised independently of Parliament, and are justified as comprising the essential power that any executive body must have to ensure that the purposes for which it exists can be achieved. These include governmental powers (*pouvoirs de police*) required to maintain order, ensure that public health is not endangered, and so on, and administrative authority to enable the public services to continue to function without interruption, even in unforeseen circumstances. The latter are expressed in the form of decrees to apply laws or to modify their provisions. Owing to the constitutional distinction between law-making and rule-making fields, discussed in the previous chapter, the Government now has much wider powers of rule-making than any previous Republican régime has had in normal conditions.

Decrees can be decided on, either in the Council of Ministers, in which case all Ministers sign them, as also does the President, or without consultation of the Council of Ministers, by the Prime Minister himself. Those in the most important categories must be submitted for the advice of the Council of State, though the Government is not obliged to follow this advice. When Parliament meets in a special session that has been requested (that is, excluding the two special sessions when it meets as of right) the decree convening it is signed by the President of the Republic, but must be counter-signed by the Prime Minister. President de Gaulle regarded himself as being constitutionally free to refuse to sign such a decree.

Some governmental powers are delegated by the Prime Ministers to Ministers, who may then issue their own rules (*arrêtés ministériels*) on matters concerning their departments. Since 'the essence of laws lies in their application', there is inevitably an area within which the rule-making power can make its own influence felt through the processes for which it is responsible. Interpretations of provisions of laws, timing of their application, use of loopholes that a law may have left for the exercise of discretion by the administrative authorities – all these and other factors can expedite or delay application, and sometimes defeat to a certain extent the will of the legislature. The farmers' unrest of 1961 was largely due to delays in applying the 1960 'guide-line' law. A law that specifies application through certain administrative measures cannot be applied until the executive authorities have carried out these instructions.

Such devices are a natural part of the administrative process and have always existed, even under régimes such as the Third and Fourth Republic, which were characterized by a degree of Parliamentary domination of the executive often described as amounting to *gouvernement d'assemblée*. The normal dilatoriness of a vast, bureaucratic machine has, therefore, contributed its share of involuntary obstruction of the working of the machinery of Parliamentary government. To the extent that the area of activity of the Gaullist administration has been wider, the opportunities for bureaucratic inefficiency, slowness or inertia have been greater, and commentators have not failed to point out the shortcomings of Gaullist officialdom.

RELATIONS BETWEEN GOVERNMENT AND PARLIAMENT
(i) RESPONSIBLE GOVERNMENT

Whether it be seen as semi-presidential, Orleanist, 'rationalized', or 'personalized', the system provided for by the 1958 Constitution and applied by Gaullist Governments is a type of Parliamentary government. The essential condition of Parliamentary government is the ability of democratically elected representatives to criticize, supervise and, if necessary, defeat the Government. The 1958 Constitution defines the conditions in which Governments can be defeated. It does so limitatively, which must, therefore, raise the question as to whether the right, though admitted, is adequate.

Governments can be defeated in three ways, and in three ways only. First, the National Assembly can defeat the Government, either on a declaration of its programme, or on a declaration of general policy. After deliberation in the Council of Ministers, the Prime Minister 'pledges the responsibility' of his Government, and if he fails to obtain a simple majority (i.e. a majority of those voting), the Government must resign. The

conditions laid down in article 49 (1) are somewhat ambigu-
ously formulated, in that they do not specify any time limit
within which a Prime Minister who assumes office shall present
his programme, while the decision whether or not to make a
declaration of general policy belongs to him, and so there is
nothing to prevent him from deciding not to make one at all.
There is also scope for different interpretations of the word
general in 'a declaration of general policy'.

At first, the practice of the Fifth Republic was for the Prime
Minister to present his programme shortly after assuming
office, as Prime Ministers of previous régimes had done, though
with some variations of procedure.[25] The first Prime Minister
presented his programme in January 1959 and made a declaration of general policy in October of the same year, which was
followed by a vote of confidence. M. Pompidou also presented
his programme, on his appointment in 1962, and made a
declaration of general policy in December, after his reappoint-
ment following the 1962 election. Subsequently, he made only
one declaration of general policy (in April 1966), but this was
not followed by a vote. M. Couve de Murville (in 1968) and
M. Chaban Delmas (in 1969) each made a general declaration
on their assumption of office, but neither was followed by a
vote. It is too soon to say whether the Government's intention
is to let the procedure fall into disuse, or whether temporary
circumstances have been the deciding factor. It must be remembered that, if the Prime Minister is free to make up his
own mind on this, the National Assembly is equally free to
introduce a motion of censure, though this procedure makes it
much more difficult to defeat a Government.[26]

The interpretation placed by the Government on the phrase
'a declaration of "general" policy' was cleared up very rapidly
and has not been seriously challenged since. There had been
objections to the refusal of a vote after the Foreign Minister's
declaration of foreign policy in April 1959, and in October,
when the Prime Minister made a statement on Algeria, he
included a section on other questions in order to make clear
that the Government accepted a vote only on a declaration
concerned with the affairs of more than one department.

Ministerial declarations (most frequently made on foreign policy) are never concluded by a vote.[27]

The second method of defeating a Government (article 49, 2) is by an ordinary vote of censure such as was used under the Third and Fourth Republics. There are, however, new conditions under the Fifth. Such a motion must obtain the signatures of a tenth of the members of the Assembly – that is, from 1962 onwards, of 49 Deputies, if there are no vacant seats.[28] The Constitution requires a delay of 48 hours between the tabling of the motion and the opening of the debate, and this must take place at latest on the third day following the expiry of the 48 hours.[29] Only those in favour of the motion vote, and an 'absolute' majority of the membership of the Assembly is required to defeat the Government, which must then resign. Deputies who do not vote thus in effect count as supporters of the Government's case. If the motion is unsuccessful, the signatories cannot sign another during the rest of the session.

The third method (article 49, 3) is a response to the Government's announcement that it is 'pledging its responsibility' on the passage of a Bill, or part of a Bill. If there is no challenge, then the Bill is regarded as having been passed and the Government as having received that confidence without a vote. A challenge is expressed by the tabling of a vote of censure, again by a minimum of one-tenth of the members. In this case, the debate in progress is suspended for 24 hours from the announcement that this is to be done. In the case of censure motions challenging the Government's request for confidence on a Bill, there is no limit to the number that Deputies may sign during the session. Motions of censure are not subject to amendment.

The conditions and limitations associated with the procedures outlined above do indubitably impose restrictions that French Deputies have hitherto not been accustomed to. It is not denied that, in political circumstances other than those that have existed since the 1958 Constitution came into force, they might prove vexatious. But up to 1971, they were clearly not in practice restrictive, except in so far as they achieved one of the Government's objectives, which was to prevent time-wasting by frequent obstructive and demagogic censure motions. For one thing, throughout that period (except for 1967–8), the Government majority was such that censure motions could not hope to succeed. The one exception, in 1962, is explained both by the fact that it took place just after the end of the Algerian war and was thus in the nature of a test of Gaullist strength, and by the fact that it was on a constitutional issue (the use of the referendum to amend articles 6 and 7) on which many people not opposed to Gaullism were in disagreement with the President. It is precisely in such exceptional circumstances that a motion of censure might be considered desirable. But a little elementary arithmetic shows that throughout the first twelve years of the régime, Deputies made far less use of the method than the restrictive rules allowed. During that period, the left-wing opposition parties, which provided almost all the votes on censure motions, and were responsible for tabling almost all of them, numbered between just under 100 from 1959 to 1962 and something over 150 from then onwards. On the least generous assumptions, they could have tabled, during the seven complete sessions of the first Parliament and the eight complete sessions of the second, a *minimum* of 31 motions of censure under the rules laid down in article 49 (2), together with as many motions under the rules of article 49 (3) as there were Government requests for confidence. Of those in the category subject to limitation, they actually tabled four in the first and two in the second Parliament. Of those in the unlimited category, they tabled five in the first and none in the second. And during the third Parliament, when there was only a very slender Government majority, they tabled three in the first category, in which the rules would have allowed them a minimum of nine.[30] There are a number of possible explanations of these facts, not related to the Constitution, one of which is that the motion of censure has been not merely ineffective as a political weapon, but also at times productive of additional dissensions within the opposition parties. What is less comprehensible is the failure of Deputies to make better use of questions and debates in which they could criticize the Government even if they could not vote.

Where Deputies have found constitutional and procedural restrictions far more irksome has been in the normal day-to-day business of legislation and of criticism of Government policy and behaviour. The main restrictions in this category have been Government control of the timetable, the prohibition of private members' Bills and amendments involving either an increase in expenditure or a decrease in revenue, the increased powers of the Government to control criticism and hostile votes in debates, and the prohibition of votes on resolutions, or on policy declarations by departmental Ministers. The effects of these measures have been variable, and some could well not survive if there were to be a return to less stable Parliamentary majorities.

Control over the Parliamentary timetable (article 48) confers real powers on the Government. The right to priority for Government Bills helps to speed up the carrying out of its programme and enables it to defer consideration of issues that it dislikes or that it fears might prove awkward. Used in conjunction with the power to rule out of order private members' Bills with financial implications, it has effectively reduced to a small trickle the floods of such Bills that were formerly introduced every session.[31] Since, however, most private members' Bills have never reached the stage of debate (and have never been expected to), the statistics so often quoted are not an accurate guide to the real degree of deprivation involved. Power over the timetable has also been used effectively, thanks to the Gaullist majority in the National Assembly, in order to give preference to the Government in other ways – for instance, to give Gaullist Questions precedence on the agenda and to keep off the agenda Questions that, for whatever reason, the Government has found it inconvenient to answer. Among devices used have been the grouping of Questions on similar topics, a logical process, but one that can involve delay, the non-availability of Ministers to answer Questions on particular days, and sometimes a delay so prolonged that by the time the reply comes, all public interest in the subject has faded. The most striking example of delay is perhaps that of Questions on the Ben Barka affair put down by four Deputies on 9 November 1965, which was replied to on 6 May 1967.[32]

The limitations of amendments with financial implications to those that 'seek to suppress or effectively to reduce expenditure and to produce or increase revenue'[33] has been more strictly applied than it was under the Fourth Republic. Apart from the fact that it is now a constitutional limitation, applying to all amendments and not only to amendments to the finance Bill, it can no longer be evaded by the 'compensatory' device adopted under the previous régime, which had meant that the Deputy could propose that real expenditure now should be compensated for by fictitious or unrealistic economies later.[34] The fact that the Finance Committee's *rapporteurs* have been, since 1964, members of the majority party has given the Government an additional advantage, in that informed debate is mainly restricted to a dialogue between the Minister and his political supporters, unlike debates under the Fourth Republic, which began, and often went on, as a duel between the Minister and his political enemies, but with the procedural cards stacked in favour of the latter. Though some lobbying certainly is carried out by pressure groups within the Finance Committee, this is after all a normal process of democratic Parliamentary government. The additional power in the hands of the Government has naturally caused frustration among the Government's opponents, but also sometimes in the ranks of the majority, for Gaullist Deputies too have often wanted concessions in the interests of constituencies or sectional interests, so that the Government has needed to use its procedural powers to control its own supporters.

Among the most important weapons in the arsenal that the Government now disposes of has been the Government's responsibility for piloting its own Bills through the Assembly and the Senate (article 42). Ministers no longer have to resort to undignified indirect methods of securing the introduction from the floor of amendments that they themselves had no right to propose. Now, the Minister can himself prevent Deputies from putting forward their own amendments, once the debate has begun, if these have not been submitted to the appropriate committee (article 44). He is also empowered to cut short the debate by insisting, when it suits him, on asking for a vote either on those parts of the Bill not yet voted, or on the whole Bill, including whatever amendments have been proposed or accepted by the Government. This procedure, known as *le vote bloqué*, or package deal, was originally described by a member of the Consultative Constitutional Committee as being intended to 'prevent cascades of confidence votes'.[35] It has turned out to be a very efficient confidence vote in itself, used to discipline the Government's own supporters more often than the opposition.[36] For the presence in the Assembly from 1962 onwards of a Government majority that could always ensure the defeat of a general motion of censure has made the procedure whereby the Government makes a Bill a question of confidence on which it would have to resign if defeated like the use of a steam hammer to crack a nut. From the Government's point of view,

> since an appeal to discipline can mobilize a majority, recourse to the provisions of article 49 ceases to be necessary. There is no point in pledging the responsibility of the Government in order to get a Bill voted, when all that is needed is to ask for a single vote, setting the ultimate limit to the concessions that the Government is prepared to make.[37]

The figures provide an eloquent demonstration of this point. In the second Parliament (1962-7), the Government pledged its responsibility only once (and in a general declaration, not on a Bill), whereas in the previous Parliament it had done so seven times. But while the *vote bloqué* was used only 23 times in the National Assembly in the first Parliament (17 in the Senate), it was used 67 times in the Assembly during the second Parliament (60 times in the Senate).[38]

Additional means of preventing Deputies from having recourse to votes, unless they were prepared to make the issue one of refusal of confidence in the Government, included the insistence, from the beginning of the first Parliament, on the inadmissibility of votes on resolutions and the consequent obligation imposed on Parliament by the ruling of the Constitutional Council to bring the Standing Orders into line with this decision. The Constitution of 1958 attempts to draw a clear distinction between the search for information and the exercise of pressure. Oral Questions, ministerial declarations of policy and debates on these are all, in the Gaullist view, essentially part of the dialogue between Government and Parliament, and as such should not be voted on with the intention merely of exerting pressure, and so undermining the authority of the Government. The decision of the Constitutional Council ruling out of order the voting of resolutions following debates on Oral Questions was based on a strict reading of the provisions of articles 49 and 50, and of articles 34, 40 and 41, according to which (a) the Constitution provides opportunities for Parliament to supervise or criticize (*contrôler l'action gouvernementale*) *only* in the conditions laid down; and (b) it provides for Parliamentary initiative *only* by means of legislation. In other words, if members of Parliament have proposals to make, they must be in the form of private members' Bills, not of resolutions.[39]

The Government's use of special powers (under article 38) to legislate by Ordinance is not an innovation of the Fifth Republic. Though now 'constitutionalized', it is essentially the same as the right of Governments of the Third Republic to govern for periods by decree-laws, and of Governments of the Fourth to use, under the law of 17 August 1948, powers of delegated legislation that the 1946 Constitution had sought to prohibit. In other words, it is a right that has been part of the Republican tradition since the end of the first world war.[40] Governments of the Fifth Republic used these powers eight times between 1960 and 1967 for periods of four months to a year or more.[41] In the political circumstances, this does not justify the conclusion that Gaullist Governments have been less able to govern than their predecessors. Two of the grants of special powers enabled the Government to deal with Algerian problems and the aftermath of the war; three authorized the Government to apply the provisions of the Rome treaty and the EEC agricultural policy, which meant adapting national legislation to the requirements of an international treaty; one was to deal with the consequences of the referendum in Somaliland on whether or not the territory should become independent. Of the remaining two, one enabled the Government to enforce the decisions taken in 1960 to deal with the entrenched rights of home distillers and the problems of alcoholism – a long-standing problem that had bedevilled Governments for years, but one that had proved intractable owing to its unpopularity with Deputies and Senators for political and electoral reasons.

The eighth grant, in 1967, and the only one that aroused any serious opposition, enabled the Government to introduce a series of economic and social reforms, including a reform of the social-security system in an Assembly in which it had only a slender majority. It was estimated by M. Pompidou that the measures would have taken from 18 months to two years longer to become law through the normal legislative process.[42] And they might even have been defeated. In this case alone, therefore, were the special powers resorted to under conditions which had been regarded by previous régimes as necessitating their use, namely, that 'Parliament had proved its incapacity to act, or else was demonstrably unable to act.'[43] Both the limitations imposed by article 38 and the comments on its use imply that it is regarded under the Fifth Republic as a normal rather than an exceptional procedure. It has been described as 'a safety mechanism intended to compensate for the incompleteness of the provisions laid down in article 34'.[44]

The Constitution defines the purpose of resort to special powers as being to enable the Government to carry out its programme, and authorizes government by Ordinance only for a 'limited period of time'. No time limit is given, but the enabling act must state in each case how long the powers are to last. In one way, however, the powers restrict Parliament

more than they have done previous Parliaments. Article 41
expressly rules out of order private Bills or amendments in
conflict with powers delegated under article 38.[45] Limitations
on the Government are imposed by virtue of the phrase 'with
a view to carrying out its programme', which make it necessary
for the powers to be renewed with a change of Government.
This limitation would not, presumably, apply to powers
granted, as were those in the law of 2 February 1960, specifically to the President of the Republic, and not to the Government. But that was an isolated case, and the constitutionality
of the specific condition that the powers should be exercised
by the President was criticized at the time.[46]

The main procedural difficulty that has arisen from the
application of article 38 has been created by the Government's
strictly literal interpretation of the constitutional requirements
(an interpretation in accord, however, with the practice of
previous Governments exercising special powers). The Ordinances, which must be agreed to by the Council of Ministers
after consultation with the Council of State, cease to be effective if a Bill to ratify them is not laid before Parliament by the
date fixed in the enabling law. Once this date is reached, those
of the Ordinances that would normally fall within the field of
law may be amended only by law. But the requirement, it will
be noted, is that the ratifying Bill must be 'laid before' Parliament, not voted by it. If the Government chooses to delay
voting the Bill, then the Ordinances remain in a curious
administrative–legislative limbo. They continue to be applied
beyond the limiting date, but without ratification, and thus
have the force of law, though without its status. Parliament
cannot amend them because they are not laws until the ratification is voted. Yet since they are not laws, they can henceforth
be challenged before the Council of State.

On occasions, the Government has delayed ratification for a
long time, and has incurred criticisms for so doing.

I know [said one Gaullist Deputy] that at each meeting of
the Conference of Presidents, the Government representative promises to study the question the following week, but

thanks to a kind of rotation of Government representatives,
the one actually present never knows what the preceding
one has promised.[47]

As a result of the Government's habit of delaying, a Socialist
Deputy sought to introduce a private Bill to make Ordinances
invalid if the ratifying Bill was not discussed within a certain
time limit. By mid 1972, this step had not been taken.[48]

RELATIONS BETWEEN GOVERNMENT AND PARLIAMENT
(iii) POLITICAL REALITIES

That these procedures have assisted the Government to govern
is incontrovertible. What is difficult to assess is the extent to
which their contribution has been decisive, or has been merely
a useful adjunct in a situation in which political factors have
been primarily responsible for Government stability and efficiency. Nor is it a simple matter to decide how far they have
enabled Governments to govern well. An attempt to make any
such assessment must form part of a general consideration of
the achievements and failures of the régime, including, along
with the effects of institutions, the influence of the evolution of
parties and the impact of events. But two direct effects of the
working of the institutions described in this chapter ought perhaps to be noted. The first is that, though defended by Michel
Debré as essential instruments for the creation of strong and
coherent government, these institutions could do their work
properly only in certain political conditions that have up to
now not existed. It is one of the axioms of democratic theory
that Governments can govern effectively and democratically
only when Oppositions can oppose, for nothing assists Parliamentary good manners so much as the political necessity to
'do as you would be done by'. On both sides of the Channel
there have been comments (and M. Debré has made some of
them) to the effect that most of the procedural restrictions on
Parliament described in this chapter are taken for granted in
the British system, in which both sides agree that a Government with a majority has the right to govern – including the

right to control the Parliamentary timetable, to retain a virtual monopoly of legislation, and a total monopoly of proposals to increase expenditure. It is possible for both sides to accept this situation, however, only because British Governments know that sooner or later they will become the Opposition. It therefore suits both sides that the Standing Orders and conventions accord generous opportunities to the Opposition both to put forward its own alternatives and to criticize the Government (including in particular the right to Parliamentary time on a number of specific occasions, of which the most important are the days following the Speech from the Throne and 26 supply days). About a third of the Parliamentary timetable is at the disposal of the Opposition.

For historical, political and temperamental reasons, French politicians rely much more on written rules than on conventions. But where, in those of the Fifth Republic, are the built-in rights for opposition parties? One reason for their absence is that the rules are designed for a quite different situation – for one in which opposition parties are strong enough to be obstructive, though not strong enough or united enough to constitute a credible alternative Government, and in which Governments are relatively weak. Throughout the Fifth Republic, Governments have been strong and oppositions weak. In the British system, Government and Opposition are rivals playing the same political game according to the same rules and, because both are strong, they do not need the rules to be either so rigid or so ungenerous. The strength of the Opposition – and even its potential strength in periods when the Government has had a very large majority – provides an incentive for mutual toleration and good manners. For instance, the Speaker is accorded a degree of discretion that allows him (with the approval of both sides) to obtain a hearing for minority opinions that is out of all proportion to their numerical strength, because each side is conscious, when in power, that it will one day need the same tolerance and good will when it becomes once again the Opposition.

French political and constitutional history has not up to now given parties on either the Government or the opposition side grounds for enough confidence in each other to enable them to dispense with written and rigid rules making sure that 'the Whig dogs' do not have the best of it. The deduction to be made from the above comparison is not, as British politicians too often suggest, that the French need a British-style two-party system. Both Michel Debré and Maurice Duverger, in their different ways, have realized that if a solution can be found, it will have to be adapted to French political habits and traditions. But it is precisely these that have helped during the Fifth Republic to intensify the domination of the majority party instead of mitigating it. The Conference of Presidents, the Parliamentary committees, the system of 'organized debates' – these have been traditionally regarded as the most democratic methods of providing for expressions of minority viewpoints, because they are based on participation in Parliamentary activities on the basis of the numerical strength of Parliamentary groups. In a multi-party system, made up of unstable or shifting majorities and minorities, with at times no discernible majority at all, these organs and procedures have achieved a fair hearing for all, though often at the expense of Governmental action. In an Assembly dominated since 1958 by a large disciplined majority supporting the Government, confronted by a number of small, disparate, opposition groups, unable to agree sufficiently among themselves to provide effective criticism, let alone to propose alternative policies, the traditional proportional principle has provided a built-in recipe for increasing the Government's domination, already provided for in the Constitution.

The most important single political reality of the Fifth Republic is not the emergence of strong Governments, but the non-emergence of strong Oppositions able to prevent the majority from doing what any majority will do if it can (and what the present opposition parties did when they were the majority), namely, to take advantage of their position. The fact that the Gaullist party has had its own problems to contend with has made it inevitable that a Gaullist-dominated Conference of Presidents should manipulate the agenda, that preference should be given to Gaullist Questions and Bills,[49] that Gaullists should hold the offices of President and *rapporteur* in the Parliamentary committees. It has been equally inevitable that divided opposition parties, reduced to Parliamentary impotence, should have failed to modernize their organization or their thinking, and continued to protest that they are the victims of unscrupulous misuse of procedural rules. The essential point that M. Michel Debré failed to realize was that this is a game that 'only two can play', in the sense that it cannot be played by one alone. As it is, the Government has been playing a new game with new rules, while the opposition parties have stuck to the old game and clamoured for the restoration of the old rules.

It is in this context that the Government's insistence from the beginning of the first Parliamentary session of the régime on preventing Deputies from voting unless they were prepared to turn out the Government appears undiscerning. It is true that the traditional habit of French members of Parliament to want to vote on all conceivable and inconceivable occasions is largely a ritual and out-dated gesture. But it could be regarded as unwise, in the Government's own interests, to afford Deputies no safety valve, no 'graduated response'.[50]

One achievement of the Gaullist governmental system has been its use by the Government to transform the heterogeneous Gaullist movement into a more efficient Parliamentary machine. During the first Parliament, there were repeated rumblings of discontent on the Government back benches, but the General's indispensability was able to hold the party together until the end of the Algerian war. From then on, the long haul of building up a real Parliamentary party was undertaken. A series of *journées d'études parlementaires* were held in different towns,[51] and, more important, regular party meetings in the Palais Bourbon were established, in which discussions with Ministers, prepared by special study groups, led to habits of constructive criticism and co-operation. There was much hard bargaining and too much independence on the back benches was prevented by the Government's use of the *vote bloqué* and by threats of refusal to endorse candidatures of recalcitrant Gaullist Deputies. Some Government concessions to

Deputies were part of the price involved in this process.[52] There was no attempt, however, until 1969, to provide for some coherent organization of the majority as such (which by then included representatives of three Parliamentary groups). On the opposition side, apart from the short-lived, limited experiment of the left-wing Federation, any realistic effort to replace the traditional multiplicity of internally divided groups by an organized 'Opposition' has been ruled out by the political atmosphere.

A political factor that has certainly affected the working of Governmental institutions, though exactly how and to what extent must remain largely a matter of conjecture, is the permanent uncertainty as to what has been, is and will be the real position of the President within the institutional framework. Is it true, as is so often alleged, that real power lies with the President and that the Government apparatus headed by the Prime Minister is no more than an elaborate façade? Both General de Gaulle and M. Pompidou have had a good deal to say on this subject, the latter both as Prime Minister and President, and so has M. Pompidou's Prime Minister, M. Chaban Delmas. The precise significance of these statements is best assessed in the light of the known actions of Presidents in office. One fact, however, may be noted here. Perhaps the most important factor making for the increased status of the Prime Minister under the Fifth Republic has been his ability to survive, thanks, it has been assumed, to a continuing majority in the National Assembly. But even with a majority, prime-ministerial longevity has not been proof against presidential action. When the first Gaullist Prime Minister, M. Michel Debré, surpassed the previous record for longevity (that of Waldeck-Rousseau in 1902), Robert Escarpit of *Le Monde* made a prophetic comment. 'In M. Debré's place', he said, 'I should not feel easy. Longevity is a disease that invariably proves fatal.'[53] It did so shortly afterwards. The President replaced M. Debré by M. Pompidou, another record-breaking Prime Minister, who, six years later, suffered the same fate at the same presidential hands.

CHAPTER V

The President

TRADITIONAL FUNCTIONS OF THE PRESIDENT

General de Gaulle began his period of office as the first President of the Fifth Republic on 8 January 1959. He was the first President since MacMahon in 1873 to have been an officer in the regular army and not to have been a member of Parliament. His 15 predecessors since 1875 had all been politicians – ten of them Presidents of one of the two Parliamentary assemblies. Almost all had been elder statesmen not in the front rank. He was to become the third President to be elected for a second septennate, and the fourth to resign voluntarily before the completion of his term of office. He remained in office longer than any of his predecessors,[1] but throughout the whole of his period of office he was a subject of political controversy such as no previous President had ever been.

His presidency, like the Constitution that he helped to frame, must be regarded as being in many ways out of line with French Republican tradition. Yet the functions of Presidents of the Fifth Republic, as defined by the Constitution of 1958, have a great deal in common with that tradition. The President carries out those formal and ceremonial functions of a Head of State that General de Gaulle dismissed disdainfully on one occasion as 'opening chrysanthemum shows'. He appoints the leading personalities of both the civil and military establishment, including Ambassadors and other representatives of France abroad. Foreign Ambassadors are accredited to him, and he receives foreign Heads of State. He is the head of the armed forces and, as such, presides over the most important defence committees. He presides over the Council of Ministers, signs the most important of the Ordinances and decrees, including all

99

those agreed on in the Council, promulgates laws, and has the right, before doing so, to request Parliament to reconsider a Bill (a request that cannot constitutionally be refused). These are all functions essentially similar to those carried out by his predecessors.[2]

In his capacity of 'protector of the independence of the judiciary' (article 64), the President of the Republic presides at meetings of the Higher Council of the Judiciary and appoints all nine of its members. This body is responsible for advising the Government on appointments to higher judicial posts and for advising the President on his exercise of the right of pardon. It also acts as a disciplinary court for judges (though in this capacity it is presided over by the First President of the Court of Cassation). In practice, the President's rôle, except in the matter of pardons, which is discussed later, is largely formal. The Vice-President, who is the Minister of Justice, can deputize for him in the Chair, and his choice of the members of the Council is limited both by the requirement of a ministerial counter-signature and by conditions laid down in the organic law of 22 December 1958, which requires him to choose seven of the nine from a panel of 27 candidates, presented by the *bureau* of the Court of Cassation and the General Assembly of the Council of State.

Traditionally, Presidents of the Republic are politically irresponsible, except on a charge of high treason, which is essentially a political offence. This remains the position of the President under the Fifth Republic. A charge of high treason (which is nowhere defined) must be supported by a vote in both Parliamentary assemblies requiring an 'absolute' majority, that is, a minimum of 50% plus one of their membership. A President is tried by a special High Court of Justice consisting exclusively of members of both Houses of Parliament.[3] His political irresponsibility is normally ensured by the requirement that his political acts must be counter-signed by the Prime Minister, and, if necessary, by other appropriate Ministers. Under the two previous régimes, all presidential acts had to be counter-signed. Presidents of the Fifth Republic are exempted from this requirement in eight specified circumstances (article 19).

A brief consideration of these eight exceptions makes it clear that, on paper, they give the President very limited powers indeed, unless he can count on the willingness of the Government and the majority of the National Assembly to back him up. The most extensive of those conferred (article 16) can be used only in a period of 'national emergency'. Two (articles 54 and 61) merely allow him to submit a Bill or a treaty to the Constitutional Council for a ruling on their constitutionality. One (article 18) allows him to communicate with the two assemblies by means of written messages. But these must be read for him in each House and are not subject to debate. They can vary from mere formal courtesies to important constitutional pronouncements, but they cannot, of course, compel either House to take any action.[4] Article 56 allows the President to appoint three of the nine (or more) members of the Constitutional Council. This could give him some influence over the composition of a body responsible for decisions on certain constitutional issues, but only as long as there is general agreement between the President and the three members appointed by at least one of the two Houses of Parliament, for the President of the Senate and the National Assembly also have the right to appoint three members each.

The remaining three powers of independent presidential action could, in certain circumstances, be of real political importance. The exercise of the first (article 8, i), which entitles him to appoint the Prime Minister, is conditional in the last resort on the support of a majority in the National Assembly. Presidents of the two previous Republics also appointed Prime Ministers. But the formal acceptance of the President's choice by a vote in the Assembly is not now a condition of the appointment (as it was constitutionally under the Fourth Republic,[5] and in practice under the Third). The fact that the Prime Minister is responsible to the Assembly ought to be in itself sufficient to deter a wise President from risking a head-on clash with Parliament by appointing an unacceptable Prime Minister.

The second of the three powers (article 11) entitles the President to grant or refuse a request for a referendum, made either by the Government (but only during Parliamentary sessions), or by the two assemblies jointly. In strict constitutional theory, therefore, he cannot decide independently to hold a referendum, and the subjects on which a referendum can be held at all are, since the member-States of the Community became independent, strictly limited to two categories. Finally, the right of the President (article 12) to dissolve the National Assembly before the end of its term of office, though its timing could be of considerable political importance, must involve something of a political gamble. For it is essentially no more than a decision to hand over to the electorate the right to settle an issue or change a majority. Once that decision has been taken, the President is constitutionally unable to use the weapon of dissolution again for a period of twelve months following the subsequent election. He is required, before announcing a dissolution, to consult both the Prime Minister and the Presidents of both Parliamentary assemblies, but, since he is not obliged to follow their advice, this condition need be no more than a formality. In the light of the restrictions on the use of the dissolution, however, it is a condition that a wise President would take seriously if he wishes to stay in office. The use of the dissolution has proved in fact unpopular in Republican history. Up to 1962, there had been only two dissolutions in 85 years. The first, decided on by the President (with the agreement of the Senate) in 1877, ultimately cost him his job, and discredited the instrument of dissolution itself for the following 60–70 years. The second, decided on by the Prime Minister in 1955, resulted in his ceasing to be Prime Minister.[6]

In addition to these eight specific opportunities for independent presidential action, the Constitution of the Fifth Republic in one or two respects allows the President more elbow room than was allowed to his predecessors. For instance, whereas Presidents receiving foreign Heads of State were formerly expected to do so in the presence of Ministers or officials (unless the Prime Minister agreed to a private interview), Presidents of the Fifth Republic can receive such guests in private. Under both the previous régimes, too, Presidents did not themselves normally negotiate treaties, although they were required to sign them. The 1946 Constitution had merely stated that 'The President of the Republic is kept informed of international agreements. He signs and ratifies treaties' (article 31). Article 8 of the Constitutional Law of 16 July 1875 had stated that 'The President negotiates and ratifies treaties', which is the phrase also used in article 52 of the present Constitution. The latter adds that he is also 'informed of the negotiation of all international agreements not subject to ratification'.

Presidents of the Fifth Republic have interpreted these provisions much more literally than their predecessors did. For instance, General de Gaulle was clearly seen to be in charge during the first and second negotiations on the British application to join the EEC. He also represented France in person at the Rome meeting of the Six in May 1967. President Pompidou attended the Hague summit conference of the Six in December 1969, and was clearly closely and actively concerned in the 1971 third round of negotiations on the British application to join the EEC.

It would be a mistake, nevertheless, to deduce too much from these changes of the presidential rôle in the field of foreign policy. For one thing, on foreign policy there has usually been complete harmony of views between the President and the Gaullist majority – and relatively little real opposition from other parties. More important in the constitutional context is the fact that Presidents have traditionally been allowed more latitude in this field than in others. Even under the Fourth Republic, which regarded any presidential initiative with suspicion, it was possible for President Auriol (who did not share the views of Governments or of the majority in the Assembly on European policy, and especially on the question of the EDC) to make speeches that diverged somewhat from the required reflection of Government opinion. And during the first thirty years or more of the Third Republic, there was a generally accepted convention that Presidents, however effaced their rôle in internal affairs, had the right to some initiative and independence in matters of foreign policy.[7] It is still, therefore, not possible to say for certain whether or not, in the long run, there will be a reversion to older habits. The special freedom accorded to General de Gaulle by virtue both of his personality and of the special circumstances in which he returned to power in 1958 may not continue to be accorded to his successors.

One point on which there appears to be some uncertainty concerns the President's traditional right of pardon (article 17). The 1958 Constitution, like the two previous ones, requires a ministerial counter-signature. In practice, Presidents seem to have shared the opinion expressed by some constitutional authorities that this right ought to be a personal presidential decision. Under the Third Republic, the Minister of Justice is said to have generally given the President in effect a blank cheque.[8] Under the Fourth, President Auriol took advice, and paid very serious attention to it, especially where the death penalty was involved, but did not have a counter-signature. The constitutionality of this procedure was, however, criticized in some quarters.[9] The authors of the 1958 Constitution have, somewhat surprisingly perhaps, gone out of their way to make it more rather than less difficult for Presidents to treat pardons as a personal right. For the organic law of 22 December 1958, on the organization of the Higher Council of the Judiciary, not only makes consultation of this Council obligatory in all cases involving the death penalty (though it is optional in others), but also specifies the need for the counter-signature of both Prime Minister and Minister of Justice, and possibly of a third Minister as well.[10] General de Gaulle seems to have followed the precedent set by President Auriol and regarded himself as bound to take advice but free to make the final decision. The required counter-signature is, therefore, automatically provided by the Minister or Ministers concerned.[11]

THE PRESIDENTIAL ELECTORAL SYSTEM

One of the most important changes in the status of the President under the Fifth Republic results from General de Gaulle's use of the powers given to him under article 11 in order to revise the presidential electoral system. Under the two previous régimes, Presidents were elected by the members of the two Parliamentary assemblies sitting together as a 'Congress' at Versailles. This system came in for a certain amount of criticism following the 1953 election, which, for purely political reasons, required no less than 13 ballots to elect as President a totally unexceptionable, conservative, elder states-man, senior Vice-President of the Senate, and a man totally unlikely to seek to play an active political rôle. The system chosen in 1958, and by which General de Gaulle was elected President on 21 December 1958, was, however, never used again. It, too, had been criticized, mainly on the grounds on which the system of election to the Senate has been criticized. For it provided for the election of the President by an electoral college of 81,764 members consisting of Deputies and Senators, together with Mayors and Councillors of local authorities, in which representatives of *communes* with populations of under 1500 constituted a clear majority.

It is possible that this predominance of small-town, conser-vative local notabilities, which, in the senatorial college,[12] has been responsible for the persistence of traditional party alignments and consequently for the failure of Gaullism to make much headway in the Senate, had some influence on the President, though the reasons that he himself gave for the change were quite different. In his broadcast of 20 September 1962, announcing the decision to hold a referendum to revise articles 6 and 7 of the Constitution, he implied that the timing of the change had been influenced by the fact that he had narrowly missed being assassinated the previous month. His positive reason for replacing the 1958 system by one in which the President is elected by universal suffrage was that his successor, whoever he might be, would not be able to count on the nationwide support that had made his own election a foregone conclusion ('determined in advance by force of circumstances'), and would, therefore, need all the authority that election by universal suffrage would confer. He returned to this theme in the weeks preceding the election.[13] In 1958,

General de Gaulle's chief spokesman on the Constitution, M. Debré, had given as one of the reasons for not choosing a system based on universal suffrage precisely the fact that it would confer on the President a widely based authority and so would be resented by Parliament.[14] In the last (posthumous) volume of his Memoirs, *l'Effort*, however, General de Gaulle states categorically (pp. 18–21) that he had intended from the first to have the Head of the State elected by universal suffrage, but had deemed it wise 'not to do everything at once', and especially not to arouse the passionate objections that, ever since Louis-Napoleon, had been the response of certain sections of opinion to anything that could be regarded as 'a plebiscite'. Nevertheless, he was, he said, determined to 'complete the edifice' before the end of his septennate by a constitutional revision providing for presidential election by universal suffrage.

The constitutional controversy aroused by the decision is discussed later in this chapter. It did not prevent the referendum of 28 October from providing the President with 62·25% of the votes cast. General de Gaulle was, therefore, re-elected for a second term by this system in 1965, and his successor was elected by it in 1969. It is a two-ballot system, which requires an absolute majority of valid votes cast to elect a candidate at the first ballot. At the second ballot, held fourteen days after the first if no candidate achieves the required majority, only two candidates may stand – the two who head the poll, or who occupy that position owing to the withdrawal after the first ballot of candidates who polled more votes. At the second ballot, a simple majority only is required. Nobody may be a candidate at the second ballot who has not polled 5% of the votes at the first.

Presidential candidates must be nominated by 100 elected representatives (members of Parliament, of the Social and Economic Council, local Councillors or Mayors), among whom must be included representatives of at least ten different *départements* or Overseas Territories. All candidates must make a deposit of 10,000 francs, which is reimbursable, together with the cost of circulars and posters, up to a maximum of

100,000 francs, to candidates who receive over 5% of the votes. The Constitutional Council is responsible for the general supervision of presidential elections (as it is of referenda and elections in general), including the investigation of any alleged irregularities (though only if the allegation is made within 48 hours and by a candidate), and for the promulgation of the result. The conduct of the campaign, which lasts fifteen days, is supervised by a special commission of five, chosen from the *Conseil d'Etat*, the *Cour des Comptes* and the *Cour de Cassation*, and which has as its main duty to ensure equality of treatment for all candidates on radio and television and to prevent any polemics from exceeding reasonable limits.[15]

The election of a President takes place not less than 20 or more than 35 days before the expiry of the term of office of the retiring President, or within the same period following a presidential vacancy caused by death, by retirement or by 'incapacity'. 'Incapacity' must be duly certified by the Constitutional Council at the request of the Government. In the case of an election caused by a presidential vacancy, the President of the Senate becomes interim President until a new President is elected.[16] In the case of an election at the end of a normal presidential term of office, that is at the end of seven years, the outgoing President remains in office until he is either re-elected or replaced.

Neither the Constitution nor the organic law regulating the conditions of election of the President specifies any qualifications required of candidates for the office of President of the French Republic. There is no reference to age, sex, the possession of civil or political rights, or even of nationality. Nor is there under the Fifth Republic any limit to the number of terms that a President may serve. Under both the previous régimes, Presidents could be re-elected only once. There is no ban on the candidature of members of families that have previously reigned in France, as imposed by the Constitutional amendment of 1884 and retained in the 1946 Constitution. Nor is there any statement in the 1958 Constitution that the office of President is incompatible with any other public office, though the previous Constitution (article 43) did include this incompatibility.

Another curious omission is that of any provision for a Vice-President. The President may (under article 21) appoint the Prime Minister to deputize for him in the committees and councils of national defence. In exceptional circumstances, the Prime Minister may be authorized to deputize for the President in the Council of Ministers, but the Constitution specifically states (article 21) that a separate authorization and a specific agenda is required on each occasion.[17]

THE PRESIDENT AS ARBITER

The functions of President of the Fifth Republic, as they have so far been described, do not seem to make the President the dominant figure that the first President claimed to be. In the Assembly debate on the censure motion condemning the President's use of the referendum in order to revise the constitutional provisions governing the election of the President, M. Paul Reynaud asked whether the new system would give General de Gaulle the powers that he had referred to in his broadcast of 20 September 1962. The Prime Minister's reply was that

> the President of the Republic will have no new powers, and those that he has, if looked at closely, are limited. If the Government refuses to support the President, he will not be able to resort to the referendum. If the National Assembly turns the Government out, the President can dissolve it, but he will have to come to terms with the fact that he cannot do so again for at least a year.
>
> In reality, the National Assembly retains, as is normal, a preponderant place in the State.[18]

This statement is not easy to reconcile with President de Gaulle's description of his own functions given only a fortnight earlier. He then claimed – and on a number of subsequent occasions made similar, and even more comprehensive claims – that

> ... the keystone of our régime is the new institution of a President of the Republic who, in the minds and hearts of

Frenchmen, is called to be Head of the State and France's guide. Far from limiting the President to the representative and advisory rôle that has hitherto been his, the Constitution now entrusts to him supremely important responsibility for the destiny of France and of the Republic.

According to the Constitution, the President is, indeed, the protector (*le garant*) of the country's independence and integrity and of respect for its treaty obligations. Which means that he is responsible for France. The President also ensures the continuity of the State and the functioning of the public authorities. Which means that he is responsible for the Republic.[19]

What General de Gaulle was doing was, in fact, summarizing the provisions of article 5 of the Constitution. But in this article, the President's functions as 'protector' (*garant*) and as arbiter are described, not defined, and neither in the article itself, nor anywhere else in the Constitution, is there any indication that it confers on him any powers whatsoever. It has often been described as one of the most important of the innovations of the 1958 Constitution, and certainly neither of its predecessors contains any such general description of the presidential function. Nevertheless, it is possible to find echoes of similar sentiments in a number of statements made by previous Presidents. President Fallières, for instance, believed that 'the President of the Republic can be arbiter and counsellor on French policy, without, however, playing an active political rôle'.[20] President Auriol considered that he had a special presidential responsibility that he described as the exercise of 'a moral authority' (*une magistrature morale*). He described himself as 'an impartial arbiter between the parties', whose duty was to maintain the Republican State by ensuring respect for the Constitution, and whose powers were 'to advise, warn and conciliate', 'to defend the State, its Constitution, its institutions and also the permanent interest of France that that State represents'.[21] In 1948, the President of the Assembly (and also the Communist Deputy, Marcel Cachin, then *doyen d'âge*) appealed to President Auriol in his capacity of 'guardian of the

Constitution' to intervene in a matter relating to Parliamentary immunity.[22] Neither they, nor the President, nor anybody else ever claimed, however, – nor did the Constitution recognize – that the duty to perform these functions gave the President any concomitant powers.

The grandiloquent, but vague, description of presidential responsibilities contained in article 5 of the 1958 Constitution did form the basis of claims on his behalf to one contingent power that the President certainly used, though its juridical validity is dubious. Its limits were stated in 1961 by the President of the Assembly, who argued that, in the absence of a clear constitutional ruling, the President, by virtue of his responsibility under article 5 to ensure respect for the Constitution and to provide by his 'arbitrament' for the regular functioning of the public authorities, had the right to give his own interpretation of constitutional requirements. Though this view was expressed in connection with a particular issue,[23] there was some support for it as a general principle. The Director of the Paris Institute of Political Studies, for instance, wrote that General de Gaulle's claim 'that it is his function to act as supreme interpreter of the Constitution' was 'in a sense recognized in article 5 of the Constitution'.[24]

The difficulty is to decide precisely in *what* sense this right could be said to exist or to be recognized. Professor Georges Vedel has described the notion of 'arbitrament' as 'the densest of the clouds that obscure the French political sky'.[25] Traditional Republican opposition opinion regarded it as implying neutrality. 'No sporting team', said M. Guy Mollet, 'chooses the captain as referee' (*comme arbitre*).[26] And in the reply to the Prime Minister's objection that politics was not sport, he added that the only acceptable definition of presidential 'arbitration' was that given by General de Gaulle himself in his speech on the Constitution on 4 September 1958 – 'the right to appeal to the judgement of the sovereign people'.[27] For Marcel Prélot, on the other hand, the term 'arbitrament' (*arbitrage*) must be understood in the sense of *arbitrium*, 'judgement, decision, the power of decision', and this, he claimed, was the sense in which General de Gaulle used it in the memoirs.[28] The official commentary on the Constitution published by the French Information Service in 1959 adopted this view. The President's mission is described as being that of an arbiter –

> but an arbiter in a positive sense. There are two ways of defining the function: an arbiter can be merely an onlooker, but he can also take decisions, make judgements (*des arbitrages*). In this Constitution, the President is not content to be an onlooker; he really decides (*c'est quelqu'un qui arbitre effectivement*) in the positive sense of the term.[29]

The commentator goes on to describe the three ways in which the President can act in this capacity. He can exercise 'moral authority', for instance, when he presides over Governmental councils and signs documents as he has traditionally done. He can make a certain number of independent decisions, as authorized by the 1958 Constitution, such as those relating to the referendum and to the dissolution of the National Assembly. And, in circumstances of extreme danger, he can take the appropriate measures, under the powers granted to him by article 16. But it is necessary, he says, to distinguish clearly between arbitrament, or arbitration, and sovereignty.

> Where the dissolution is concerned, the President of the Republic resembles (*tend à être*) a sovereign arbiter. It is generally said that sovereignty belongs to the people, who must settle (*être l'arbitre*) the great political conflicts by elections. Automatic dissolution, which means that the elected representatives bring it about, would have preserved this notion of decision (*arbitrage*) by the sovereign people, whereas it is now left to one man to take that decision.

As if appalled by what he has almost said, however, the author immediately retreats, concluding that

> This arbitral decision nevertheless does hand over the (real) decision to the people, since it is they who eventually elect the new Assembly.[30]

French constitutional exegesis is responsible for much verbiage on the theme of the President's function as an arbiter, most of it being merely repetition of these arguments about the two senses of the word. But the French political sky has been obscured by at least three additional 'clouds' of varying density. In the first place, the 1958 Constitution contains a number of ambiguities or omissions that call for interpretations. The President, however, did not limit his interpretations to these. He also interpreted, or re-interpreted, some that were, in the view of the majority of jurists and politicians, perfectly clear. In the second place, he added to the confusion and uncertainties as to what exactly was implied by the President's arbitral function by changes of emphasis and vocabulary that transformed the *arbiter* into a *guide*, and so removed him even farther from M. Guy Mollet's conception of a President-referee.[31] And third, the deliberate obscurity of the President's remote and lofty phraseology, interspersed with some surprisingly precise claims to a presidential authority embracing practically every aspect of government, not only demanded of his Prime Minister, M. Pompidou, some tricky exegetic exercises of his own, but also presented to the political leaders irritatingly conflicting images that did nothing to facilitate the solution of the problems that arose over some half-dozen or more constitutional controversies caused by presidential interpretations. When the President states in a press conference that it must be clearly understood that

> the indivisible authority of the State has been conferred wholly on the President by the people by whom he is elected, that all other authority, whether ministerial, civil, military or judicial, is conferred by him and dependent on him . . .[32]

this, if taken seriously, makes nonsense of the whole concept of the arbiter – above the battle – whether he be conceived of as referee, guide or Solomon.

CONSTITUTIONAL AMBIGUITIES AND PRESIDENTIAL INTERPRETATIONS

Before discussing the problems created by presidential interpretations of constitutional provisions, it is necessary to emphasize the contexts in which they occurred. The first was that of democratic Parliamentary government, and the second that of the political conditions during the years of General de Gaulle's presidency. All constitutions, whether written or unwritten, have to be modified in the process of application, if they are to be flexible enough to work efficiently. It is true that, under the Gaullist system, this process has often seemed to involve the establishment of unwritten rules or conventions that are in flat contradiction to the written rules as formulated in the text of the 1958 Constitution. But in a Parliamentary democracy, provided that Governments are willing to accept a *de facto* reversal of the relations between President and Prime Minister as laid down in the Constitution, and provided that Parliaments are prepared to back them up and electorates to go on returning Parliamentary majorities that will do so, the essential condition of Parliamentary government must be regarded as being fulfilled. It remains government by consent of Parliament and people. Nothing in the theory of Parliamentary government requires a country to refuse to let most of its thinking be done for it by a party, a Government or a man, provided the essential requirement of consent is met, which is that the procedures allowing Government, Parliament or electorate to change their minds are respected. It may be unwise to revise constitutions by ignoring the procedures provided, but, in these conditions, it is an unwisdom shared by President, politicians and the majority of the electorate.

The final test, therefore, of the legitimacy of General de Gaulle's unofficial constitutional revisions must be political as well as constitutional. First, it must take account of the criteria by which consent can be assumed. Napoleon III, for instance, clearly fails to pass the test. Following his *coup d'Etat* of 2 December 1851, he, like General de Gaulle, was entrusted with the responsibility for drawing up a Constitution on five conditions, and, like him, submitted the Constitution to a referendum in which a majority of the voters accepted it. But, unlike General de Gaulle, he did not provide for *free* elections, making it in practice possible for electors subsequently to withdraw their consent. Second, it must take account of what appear to be the reasons for which consent is forthcoming.

During the ten years of General de Gaulle's presidency, both Parliament and electorate had frequent opportunities to refuse their consent and both did so once. Parliament defeated the Government in October 1962, but the subsequent general election reaffirmed the electorate's support of Government and President. The electorate defeated the President in a referendum in 1969, and he promptly resigned. But prior to 1969, there had been three general elections and one presidential election, together with three referenda, and in all these the President had threatened (or promised) to resign if he did not obtain the support of the majority. The reasons for this support were undoubtedly political rather than constitutional. The majority preferred what many of them regarded as unconstitutional presidential interpretations of his rôle to the alternative of a change of President with all the political dangers that that might involve in the circumstances. Such a choice is one that any free electorate has the right to make.

The problems created by presidential interpretations of the Constitution are really of three distinct kinds. The first category concerns a number of constitutional provisions related to the rights and duties of the President in which there are real or possible ambiguities or omissions, together with some whose intentions cannot be precisely related to the President's actions, so long as these are not publicly known and Prime Ministers and Governments are prepared to underwrite them. Even Presidents of the Third and Fourth Republics had a certain degree of latitude in interpreting the limits of their right to independent action. The first President of the Fifth Republic gave himself very much more latitude and, moreover, called attention to the fact that he was doing so, by deliberately dramatizing his rôle and at times attributing to himself the responsibility not only for constitutional, but also for governmental decisions that by rights did not concern him.

Questions in this first category include, for instance, the President's right to appointment and dismissal. Has he the right to dismiss a Prime Minister, when article 8 (i) provides only for him to 'terminate his period of office on the presentation by the Prime Minister of the resignation of the Government'? What rights, if any, has the President to a say in the choice of Ministers, in view of the fact that article 8 (ii) merely states that 'he appoints and dismisses other members of the Government on the proposal of the Prime Minister'? What would happen if a President were to die or to resign between the two ballots of a presidential election?[33] Is it justifiable for the President to announce that a referendum will be held *before* he receives the official (and constitutionally obligatory) request from either the Government or the two Parliamentary assemblies? Is it constitutional for him to announce policies as his own, and to do so publicly without consulting the Government, in view of the statement in article 20 that 'the Government decides and directs the policy of the nation'?

Everybody except M. Debré agrees that the President dismissed one Prime Minister – M. Debré himself. President de Gaulle was actively concerned in the formation of Governments, as was M. Pompidou in that of 1969. Indeed, Marcel Prélot states as a fact that both appointments of Ministers and reshuffles of Governments have *always* been carried out by agreement between President and Prime Minister and that the President has exercised a real power to dismiss Ministers.[34] In 1964, in reply to a question by M. Mitterrand, M. Pompidou stated that

> France has now chosen a system midway between that of America and Britain, in which the Head of State, who inspires general policy, derives his authority from universal suffrage, but can carry out his functions only with a Government that he chooses and nominates and that can survive only if constantly assured of the confidence of the Assembly.[35]

If Prime Ministers are prepared to accept this position and to resign whenever the President asks them to,[36] then constitutional proprieties are safeguarded, even though the President himself admitted that he did not possess the right to dismiss Prime Ministers. When General de Gaulle was questioned on this point by the Consultative Constitutional Committee in August 1958, his reply was

> No, for in that case, he [i.e. the Prime Minister] could not

govern effectively. The Prime Minister is responsible to Parliament, not to the Head of the State.

On later occasions, however, he did claim the right to dismiss Prime Ministers. M. Pompidou seems to claim the same right, and his Prime Minister to accept it.[37]

Similarly, if neither Government nor Assembly objects to announcement of referenda before instead of following the Government's request for them, as required by the Constitution (and this was the position in the case of all four referenda held by General de Gaulle), the request, when made, formally regularizes the situation. And if policies are announced, as happened frequently under General de Gaulle's presidency, before the Council of Ministers has been informed,[38] Governments and legislature have the power, if they so wish, to make the President's position politically impossible. For, whatever the degree of personal power permitted to a President, while the system remains one of responsible Parliamentary government, as that of the Fifth Republic still is, in the last resort it is the will of Parliament or people that prevails. The remedy, therefore, has been and still is in the hands of Parliament and the people, and both have had frequent opportunities for expressing their opinion. But the result of elections and referenda has been to 'regularize' the situation by general consensus. The sole exception, that of 1969, resulted in the resignation of General de Gaulle precisely because the people did for once assert themselves against him.

The problems created by the second category of presidential interpretations differ from the first in degree more than in kind, and in the last resort similar arguments can be used to defend the thesis that either Parliamentary or public acceptance or both have *de facto* 'legitimized' the President's actions. They differ from the first, however, in that they are concerned with articles of the Constitution generally (and in one case traditionally) regarded as being perfectly clearly expressed, but that the President deliberately interpreted in ways that suited himself, though they were unacceptable to jurists, non-Gaullist members of Parliament, and sometimes to the Constitutional

Council and the Council of State as well. The most important controversies arose over the presidential interpretation given to provisions of articles 11, 27, 29, 30, 46 and 89. Here, critics regarded the President as having been guilty of much more serious infringements of constitutional rules.

The first, chronologically, was the question of the constitutional right of Parliament, under articles 29 and 30, to hold a special session, if requested by the Prime Minister or the majority of the members of the National Assembly. Two special sessions at the request of the Prime Minister had already been held since the end of the previous regular session. In March 1960, however, 287 Deputies signed a request for a special session to discuss Bills on agriculture that were to be tabled. In the view of Deputies ranging from conservative to Communist, the President's signature of the required decree convening Parliament should have been, in the circumstances, a mere formality, the use of the present tense being regarded as mandatory. Commenting on the constitutional position, Professor Maurice Duverger pointed out that the relevant articles in the Constitutions of the two preceding régimes had always been interpreted as requiring the convening of Parliament if the constitutional conditions had been complied with.[39] This had also appeared to be the view of M. Debré in 1958, for, in his speech to the Council of State, he had said, 'Either the Government or the majority of Parliament may *decide* to hold special sessions'[40] (author's italics). The President, however, treated himself as having the right to refuse his signature and, in a letter to the President of the National Assembly,[41] gave three reasons for his decision not to agree to the special session. These were first, that, in the conditions in which it had been requested, a meeting would be contrary to the spirit of the institutions, respect for which it was his constitutional duty to ensure (article 5 again!); second, that pressure had been brought to bear on Deputies, which in his view amounted to an infringement of the condition of article 27, prohibiting an 'imperative mandate'; and third, that the proposed Bills would in any case be ruled out of order as contrary to article 40, which prohibits private members' Bills proposing increased expenditure.

All three reasons were challenged by a number of Deputies, who argued that 'ensuring respect for the Constitution' meant being an arbiter in the sense of a referee, that is, it meant applying existing rules, not interpreting them, and that the question as to whether the Bill would be ruled out of order was irrelevant, since once the constitutional conditions had been complied with the President was constitutionally bound to permit the holding of the session. There was some support for the President's point of view from a Councillor of State who, in a letter to *Le Monde*, pointed out that the expression used in article 29: '*at the request of* (*à la demande de*) the Prime Minister or of the majority of the members of the National Assembly' must juridically imply that the person to whom the request was addressed was free to state whether or not it was valid.[42]

Though the argument that the use of the present tense was mandatory is not conclusive, it is strong. Article 44, for instance, which uses the present tense, has always been regarded as being mandatory, and well over 150 uses of this tense in the Constitution are either descriptive or mandatory, but never permissive. A more practical objection to the holding of the special session was the President's view that the whole affair was political, since the ordinary session was due to open only a fortnight later. But this was, of course, irrelevant to the constitutional issue.

The second important constitutional difference of opinion in this category concerned the use of the referendum in 1962 to revise the Constitution. In fact, only two of the four referenda held by General de Gaulle were on constitutional issues, though all four were criticized on the ground of political and constitutional morality. The two referenda on Algeria (8 January 1961 and 8 April 1962) clearly did comply with the requirements of article 11, since both provided for the organization of provisional institutions in Algeria.[43] In the view of numerous critics, including jurists as well as politicians, the referendum of October 1962 on the reform of the presidential electoral system, and that of April 1969 proposing the reform of the Senate, just as clearly did not comply with constitutional requirements, for both involved changes in the text of the Constitution, and the procedure for constitutional amendment is laid down in article 89. This provides for revision in two stages, the first being an affirmative vote in both Parliamentary assemblies – which means that no constitutional reform can be carried out in practice against the will of the Senate. The second stage is a referendum, unless the President (who requires a counter-signature in this case) decides to substitute for the referendum a combined vote of the two Houses sitting in Congress.[44] It was no doubt partly because a majority in the Senate for the proposed reform was highly doubtful that the President chose the method of the referendum under article 11, but no doubt partly also because he preferred the direct appeal to the people to dependence on Parliament.

Objections to the proposed method were, therefore, raised by members of Parliament on political as well as on constitutional grounds. There were also objections to the form in which the question was put in 1962, as there were in the case of all four referenda during General de Gaulle's presidency. There were two political objections, one relating to the method itself and one to the constitutional implications of the President's presentation of it to the electorate. Three of the four Bills submitted to referendum were 'package deals' in that they required answers to two separate questions by a single Yes or No. In the referendum of January 1961, the electorate was asked to approve the policy of self-determination for Algeria, and at the same time to agree to provisional institutions being set up by decrees made in the Council of Ministers. In that of April 1962, approval was sought for the application of the provisions of the Evian agreements, and these were to take the form of Ordinances by the President during the provisional period preceding independence.[45] The 1969 referendum asked for approval of the creation of certain regional institutions and also of a reform of both the composition and functions of the Senate, and the electorate was given no option to accept the one and refuse the other.

All four referenda were, however, objected to also on the ground that the President was asking, in effect, for a vote of confidence in himself, for he made it perfectly clear before each referendum that, if the proposals were to be defeated, he would resign. In other words, a President who was constitutionally irresponsible was asking for a vote of confidence on questions of policy, although these are entrusted by the Constitution to a Government responsible to Parliament. And he was asking for this confidence by a method which by-passed the 'constitutional public authorities', which, in two of the four cases, ought, in the opinion of many members of Parliament, to have taken the decision.

The October 1962 referendum was a 'package deal' only in that the President left no doubt in anybody's mind that he would resign if the proposals were to be defeated, but it created more hostility to the Government than had any previous issue, or than did any subsequent issue, except that of the reform of the Senate, in 1969. The Government was, indeed, defeated in the National Assembly by a motion of censure (the only successful one in 12 years), declaring it to be unconstitutional. One Minister resigned, while the President of the Senate expressed his criticisms so forcibly, and received such a striking demonstration of support in the Senate, that relations between the Elysée and the Senate remained strained for a period of years.[46] Both the Constitutional Council, unofficially, and the Council of State, officially, advised the Government that the proposed method was unconstitutional.[47] The referendum, however, gave the President his majority, mainly, though not entirely, because the Algerian problem and the danger presented by the OAS commandos were both still close enough to make it unsafe for the voters to risk the political upheaval of a presidential resignation. His majority was partly explained by the fact that, leaving out of account the question of the constitutionality of the method, the reform itself was not unpopular in the country. This was demonstrated by the rapidity with which it became generally accepted, even by members of Parliament, once it had been 'regularized' or 'legitimized' by the votes of the electorate, first in the referendum, and then in the subsequent general election, which returned a strengthened Gaullist party.[48]

In 1969, however, there was no such danger. The President was no longer indispensable, and so the proposals were defeated, bringing the President's immediate resignation. The attitude of the Senate in 1962 had no doubt strengthened the President's desire to reform it, but his views on what the composition and functions of the second Chamber ought to be had long been known, and had been clearly expressed as far back as the Bayeux speech of 1946. He then spoke of its contribution as being to 'supply the administrative qualities that a purely political college inevitably tends to neglect', adding that it would be suitable to include in the Senate 'representatives of economic, family, and intellectual organizations, in order to ensure that activities of importance within the State can make their voices heard'.[49] This semi-functional and vaguely corporatist conception of a second Chamber was hardly likely to appeal to Senators, most of whom, whether on the Right or the Left, were political traditionalists. The proposal itself was on the lines laid down at Bayeux. The combination of the Senate and the Economic and Social Council in one body, a frankly advisory, rather than subordinate, legislative organ, was, indeed, unpopular outside as well as inside the Senate. And, as in 1962, the constitutional requirements seemed clearly not to permit of a referendum under article 11. In this case, too, the Council of State was reported to have advised against this method of revision.[50]

The Government did not have an easy task in its efforts to offer a juridical defence of the referendum on the Senate. In the Senate debate, the President of the *Centre démocrate*, André Colin, reminded his colleagues of M. Pompidou's statement on the use of the referendum in 1962, when, as Prime Minister, he had also been trying to find juridical grounds on which to defend its use.

The fact that a referendum on the organization of the public authorities can be legitimate, even if it also concerns constitutional provisions [he had then said] does not imply that any provision of the Constitution can be so changed. It would not be permissible to make a revision that affected one of these public authorities without its own approval.[51]

In 1969, that was precisely what the referendum was seeking to do, for a revision introduced by the procedure laid down in article 89 would certainly have been defeated in the Senate, as the President himself had openly admitted.[52] The defeat of the proposal in the referendum, however, effectively cut short this acrimonious constitutional battle and nothing further was heard of the reform of the Senate during the following three years.

These presidential interpretations left intact the anachronism of a politically irresponsible President, who, where referenda were concerned, pledged his responsibility no less than a Prime Minister does under article 49 during the passage of a Bill through Parliament, yet who, in constitutional theory, bore no more responsibility for these measures than he did for Bills submitted to Parliament. The logical way to get rid of this anachronism would be to transform the quasi-presidentialism of the Fifth Republic into a fully presidential system, in which the President would be a responsible head of the Government as well as Head of State, as he is in the United States. So far, though there is some support for a real presidential system, it comes only from a small minority. From time to time there have, however, been suggestions that at least the time has come to repeal the law of 1881, which makes criticism of the President a criminal offence. Under the two previous régimes, when Presidents were irresponsible in practice as well as in constitutional theory, little resort was made to it.[53] But between 1958 and 1966, over 300 cases were brought. Yet the Court of Cassation rejected the view that the changed position of the President could constitute a valid defence, and ruled that

> ... any offensive or scornful expression, any defamatory imputation concerning either the conduct of the President of the Republic as Head of State, or his private life, may be regarded as an attack on his honour or his dignity, and as such constitute an offence.[54]

THE PRESIDENT'S EMERGENCY POWERS

The powers of the President under article 16 were used by General de Gaulle only once, between 23 April and 30 September 1961. This period of emergency cannot be regarded as a test-case, illustrating the opportunities or dangers of the powers (though they have been criticized more than all the others put together), because the particular emergency – a military insurrection in Algeria – was one in which the President had virtually the whole nation behind him. It lasted a relatively short time and was ended voluntarily by him, without any lessening of support for him in the country. And most of the measures taken by him to deal with the situation were generally approved as political necessities, even when, as was the position with some, their constitutional validity was open to question.

Nevertheless, these powers are extremely important and can be regarded as constituting a third series of constitutional ambiguities and disputed presidential constitutional interpretations, not only because the powers themselves were revealed to be extensive and in practice uncontrollable, but also because the complex political and constitutional issues that arose were not all cleared up. Future use of these powers, therefore, in different political circumstances, or by a President less politically secure or less scrupulous than General de Gaulle, could constitute a potential constitutional danger.

To begin with, there is the problem of deciding exactly when an emergency can constitutionally be said to exist. Article 16 postulates two conditions which must exist *simultaneously*. There must be 'an immediate and serious threat to Republican institutions, national independence, territorial integrity or the application of international agreements'. And the threat must be such that 'the regular functioning of the constitutional public authorities is interrupted'. On 23 April 1961 the first condition was evidently met, for Algeria, still constitutionally part of the French Republic, was in a state of civil war and there was a real danger that the military insurrection would spread to, or spark off disturbances in, France. But the main constitutional public authorities – President, Government and Parliament – were certainly able to function, since the normal Parliamentary session opened two days later on the appointed date.[55] This fact created a political difficulty. To wait until 'a threat to Republican institutions' had actually *interrupted* the normal functioning of the constitutional public authorities, in order to comply with the second condition of article 16, instead of taking steps to prevent the situation going from bad to worse, would have made political nonsense, and that is certainly how public opinion would have regarded delay in applying article 16.

According to the Constitution, it is for the President himself to decide when the constitutional conditions justifying the declaration of a state of emergency exist, but only after he has consulted the Prime Minister, the Presidents of the two assemblies, and the Constitutional Council. He is also required to consult the Council on the measures that he proposes to take to deal with the situation. The Council's opinion on the existence of the emergency (with reasons) must be published. It is apparently under no obligation to publish the advice (if any) given to the President on the measures that he intends to take.[56] The state of emergency must be announced to the nation by a message. And throughout the period of special powers, Parliament may meet as of right and cannot be dissolved.

The required formalities were duly carried out by the President,[57] but, by this stage, there were already at least half-a-dozen constitutional questions to which neither the Constitution nor the organic law relating to the Constitutional Council had provided answers. The opinion (*Avis*) published by the Constitutional Council, following the President's consultation of it, as required by the Constitution, described the factual circumstances and concurred with the President's view that the constitutional conditions for the application of article 16 existed. It did not give the kind of reasoned statement that could provide guidance for the future on the interpretation of the phrase 'the constitutional public authorities',[58] or on what was to be regarded as constituting their 'regular functioning'. Nor was it clear then, or has it become clear since, what the constitutional position would be if some or all of the conditions could not be met – if, for instance, Parliament, or the Constitutional Council were unable to meet,[59] or if, for some other reason, the President was unable to consult the Prime Minister or the Presidents of the two assemblies. No information has been forthcoming on the significance of the Constitutional Council's opinion regarding the measures to be taken, if, as seems clear, the President is under no obligation to take any notice of them, and if neither Parliament nor public is told what they are. The limits of the President's authority are equally undefined. Could he, for instance, suspend the application of the Constitution, or even change it?[60] The only guidance given by article 16 is that the measures taken by the President 'must be inspired by the desire to ensure to the constitutional public authorities, with the minimum of delay, the means of fulfilling their functions'. But if he is to be the sole judge of his own conduct, then there is no constitutional protection against an abusive use of his powers by the President. Nor is it clear what purpose is served by Parliament's remaining in permanent session, if the President alone is empowered to deal with the emergency.

Answers to some other questions were provided by the President's words and actions, and theories were put forward regarding some of the points not cleared up. Thus, on 25 April, the President's answer to the question regarding Parliament's function was that

the application of article 16 should not affect the work of Parliament, namely, its legislative and supervisory powers. Consequently, the relations between Government and Parliament should be normal, except in so far as measures taken by virtue of article 16 are concerned.[61]

In other words, he intended to use his powers only in areas where ordinary procedures could not be used or were too slow. But, as became apparent, President and Parliament interpreted the word 'normal' quite differently, and the result was certainly the most confused, if not the most serious, constitutional dispute during General de Gaulle's presidency. One thesis regarding the utility of the consultations of the Constitutional Council was that these were really 'for the record', that is, they could serve as evidence if the President's behaviour during a period of special powers was ever to result in his being brought before the High Court of Justice.

Parliament's right to sit throughout the emergency could also be intended to emphasize the ultimate political responsibility of Parliament, though this was certainly not the President's conception of its functions.[62]

At least a number of useful procedural precedents seem to have been established. The form in which the President's actions were taken was that of '*décisions*', published in the *Journal Officiel*. There were 18 of them, including the first announcing the application of article 16, and the last two bringing it to an end. In general they were regarded by the Council of State as belonging to the law-making field and, as such, outside the jurisdiction of the Council. Measures to apply the decisions, if taken by authorities other than the President, were regarded as being within the jurisdiction of the Council. The initial announcement by the President of his decision to apply article 16 was regarded by the Council of State as *un acte de gouvernement*, that is an inherent Governmental power. The Council of State could not, therefore, consider any challenge to its legality, or to the length of time during which the President exercised the powers. Nor could it pronounce on the question as to whether the constitutional conditions had or had not been complied with. During the period of emergency, the President was, in the view of the Council of State,

> authorized to take all measures required by the circumstances which caused it and, in particular, to exercise legislative powers as provided for by article 34 and rule-making powers as provided for by article 37 . . .[63]

A commentator described the situation in simpler terms.

> In reality [he wrote] the President of the Republic, supreme interpreter of constitutional texts that have proved full of pitfalls, could claim that all these rights [i.e. constitutional] had been suspended, except Parliament's right to meet and to bring him before the High Court of Justice on a charge of high treason.[64]

In fact, the President made no such claim. On the contrary, he claimed, with reason, that he had kept his use of special

powers 'within narrow limits'.[65] Most of the decisions were
directly concerned with suppressing the insurrection, purging
the army, the police and the public services, and setting up
special courts to try those accused of crimes in connection with
the events. There were nevertheless criticisms of him on two
counts. The first was the duration of the emergency and the
way in which it was ended. Since military resistance had
collapsed within a matter of days and no further *'décisions'* were
required from mid-June onwards, politicians began to feel by
August that there was no longer any need for the powers.
When they were ended by two *décisions* at the end of September, the first prolonging the application of some essential
security measures and the second stating simply that article 16
was no longer to be applied, there were objections from some
Deputies on the ground that measures taken under exceptional
powers ought not to be applied beyond the period of exercise
of these powers.[66] It is customary, however, for measures
taken by virtue of special powers to continue in application
after cessation of the exercise of the powers. As Maurice
Duverger commented, '. . . firemen cannot be withdrawn as
soon as a fire is extinguished; they must remain for a time to
ensure that it does not flare up again . . .'[67] In more precise
terms, the legal position is that

> An act that was valid at the time that it was carried out
> continues to produce its effects, unless a time-limit has
> been expressly stated – a civil servant who has been dismissed
> under special powers (for example, in wartime, or in a purge)
> does not go back to his post when these powers expire; valid
> acts completed during an emergency period, therefore,
> outlive the emergency.[68]

Moreover, Parliament was free, once the emergency had ended,
to pass laws putting an end to any measures that it considered
to be no longer necessary.

The second criticism resulted from a controversy between
the President and Parliament regarding the legislative rights of
the latter during the period of the emergency. Parliament
having risen on 22 July, since circumstances seemed by then

normal enough to justify this, a number of Deputies decided that a special session was necessary in September in order to introduce Bills to deal with discontent and demonstrations among farmers. The President had no power to veto this session, of course, since Parliament has the right under article 16 to sit throughout the period of its application. But the President did feel that he had the right to say what Parliament could and could not do during such a session. In a letter to the Prime Minister, he expressed the view that legislation should be restricted to 'normal sessions'. The function of Parliament during a session held as of right ought to be concerned with the emergency. Parliament was there 'to make its voice heard' or 'to support the President of the Republic and the Government' if needed, but not, of course, to legislate in the field, which, under article 16, was his responsibility. Legislation on agriculture, which had no relation to the emergency, should be deferred to the normal session (which was due to open only three weeks later).[69]

This new example of constitutional interpretation by the President – 'normal' Bills in 'normal' sessions, discussions (but no Bills) in 'abnormal' sessions – was immediately challenged by the decision of Deputies to table a motion of censure. This, too, was ruled out of order, not by the President of the Republic, but by the President of the Assembly, whose reasons were ingenious if unconvincing. They were expressed in a very involved argument, based, first, on his assumption that the President's powers under article 16, in conjunction with those that he possessed under article 5 (discussed earlier), entitle him to determine the rules governing the functioning of institutions during a period of emergency, and second, on his own interpretation of the views of the President of the Republic, as expressed in the latter's message to Parliament and letter to the Prime Minister. Since neither of these contained any reference to a possible motion of censure, and since the Constitutional Council had declared itself incompetent to give any ruling on that question,[70] the President of the Assembly felt obliged to *deduce* what he *assumed* to be the President of the Republic's interpretation of the constitutional position.

Briefly summarized, his conclusion was that,

> given the fact that the work of Parliament can be expressed
> in legislation only in normal sessions, and that the Govern-
> ment is deprived of the right ... to pledge its responsibility
> on the passage of all or part of a Bill or motion, it follows
> that, in order to ensure a fundamental balance of power, the
> Assembly cannot use the right that it possesses in normal
> circumstances ... to challenge the responsibility of the
> Government by passing a vote of censure.[71]

This argument makes no sense. Only *private members'* Bills had
been ruled out in the President's letter, and then not by a
formal *'décision'*. Nothing in the Constitution, and nothing for
that matter in either of the President's two statements, rules
out the possibility of Government Bills, Government requests
for confidence or Government defeats during a period of
emergency in which article 16 is in application. Article 16
merely prohibits the dissolution of Parliament. Nor does
anything either in the Constitution or in the President's
statements justify the conclusion of the President of the
Assembly that the right of dissolution is in some way a
constitutional concomitant of the Assembly's right to defeat
the Government.

> The Constitution [he said] gives the National Assembly
> the right to turn out the Government, at the risk of being
> itself dissolved. Since the application of article 16 rules out
> the possibility of dissolution, can the National Assembly
> retain its right without that risk?[72]

The answer to this question is that it certainly can and does.
The Constitution itself rules out a further dissolution during
the twelve months following any previous one (article 12),
but does not prohibit Government defeats during those twelve
months. It is also constitutionally possible to dissolve the
Assembly when the Government has not been defeated, as
General de Gaulle did in 1968.

It was suggested at the time that the real explanation of this
curious exercise in presidential interpretation by proxy was that

the President did not want motions of censure to be voted on while he was constitutionally unable to penalize Deputies by dissolving the Assembly, but did not want to say so, and so left the President of the Assembly to find a way out of the impasse as best he could.[73] The result was, however, to create three new unanswered constitutional queries. First, is the President's distinction (in a message, not a formal '*décision*') between Parliament's legislative powers in 'normal' and in 'special' sessions held as of right now to be regarded as constitutionally valid? Second, what constitutional validity has a ruling by the President of the Assembly – and moreover, one that the President of the Republic later repudiates, even if only unofficially? And third, what is the constitutional position regarding motions of censure in any future period of exceptional presidential powers?[74]

The original cause of the whole controversy had by then been almost forgotten. The two agricultural Bills were introduced, however, during the special session and were duly ruled out of order on perfectly normal grounds that had nothing to do either with the President's views on legislation during a special session held 'as of right' or with the question of motions of censure.[75] But the controversy had at least one positive result – perhaps even two, for it may have helped the President to decide to end the period of special powers (and thus regain his power of dissolution). It certainly helped to show up the difficulties that could arise as a consequence of the application of article 16, even in the most favourable circumstances, owing to the defective drafting of the article itself. The Algerian issue was probably unique, in that the President could count on the support of virtually the whole nation. The purpose of article 16, however, had been stated by General de Gaulle in 1958 to be to prevent a repetition of the failure of leadership that had occurred in 1940,[76] and by M. Debré as being an instrument to be used in an emergency such as a nuclear war.[77] In neither of these cases would a President necessarily be able to count on such ease of application, such a degree of general support, or such a rapid disappearance of the immediate danger. For in 1961 the military revolt had collapsed in a matter of a few days.

The constitutional uncertainties associated with the application of article 16 certainly helped to strengthen the dislike of it on the Left. The joint policy declaration published by the Communist party and the Federation of the Democratic and Socialist Left in 1968, expressly reserved the right to get rid of it.

APPEARANCE AND REALITIES OF PRESIDENTIAL POWER
(i) THE 'PERSONAL EQUATION'

Throughout the Fifth Republic, the President, Prime Ministers, Gaullist and opposition Deputies, along with political commentators of all political opinions, have been agreed that, whatever the Constitution may lay down, Government policy has been, in reality, determined by the President. Both General de Gaulle and his then Prime Minister, M. Pompidou, affirmed in 1964 that there was 'no dyarchy at the summit'[78] and this denial was repeated by the latter when he became President, and echoed, though not in such precise terms, by his Prime Minister, M. Chaban Delmas.[79] The situation, it appeared, was as it had been described by political commentators since 1959.

> Political power, no longer in the hands of Deputies, belongs to one man. Whether as Prime Minister or as President, General de Gaulle has governed since the day of his investiture on 1 June 1958 and has reigned since he entered the Elysée on 8 January 1959. . . .
> Those who feared conflict between the two heads of a bicephalous executive can rest assured: there is only one head.[80]

The President's own definition of his position in the State, in his press conference of 31 January 1964, has already been quoted. It was repeated, in essentials, in that of 27 November 1967.

> Everyone knows [he said] that the most important element in French institutions is the attribution to the Head of the State, elected by the people, of the means, together with the responsibility, of representing, emphasizing, and if necessary

imposing what is in the permanent and overriding interests of the nation, as against specific or ephemeral interests. And everyone knows that in order that policies shall reflect essentials, the President must choose the Government, determine its composition and preside over its meetings. . . .

As Head of State, the President is responsible for maintaining these institutions in the spirit and in the letter, and for directing French policy as long as he remains the sole representative of the entire French nation.[81]

Some of his supporters and critics spelled out these responsibilities in more detail. The definition of what was described as the 'presidential' or the 'reserved' sector of policy given by the then President of the National Assembly, M. Chaban Delmas, on 15 November 1959, was later described by him as being unofficial, in the sense that it was addressed by a Gaullist to a Gaullist conference, but it was none the less taken as representative, not only of what Gaullists feel should be the President's position, but also of what the majority of politicians and political scientists regard as the actual position. The limits of this presidential sector have, however, varied in practice, and not all commentators have been agreed as to where the line has been drawn at any one time.

For M. Chaban Delmas, the presidential sector comprised foreign affairs and defence (and also, at the time at which he spoke, Algerian and Community affairs). What he described as 'the open sector' comprised all the rest. In the presidential sector, the President initiated and carried out policies; in the 'open' sector the Government was both initiator and executant. As a supporter of a democratic but fully presidential system, Professor Georges Vedel naturally envisaged the President as playing a more active political rôle than had Presidents of the Third and Fourth Republics. He saw the President's field of activity, however, as consisting of three sectors – a 'reserved' sector concerned with foreign affairs and long-term defence policies; what he called a 'delegated' sector, in which control of short-term, technical matters was handed over to technicians; and a 'supervisory' sector, in which the President intervened, but only intermittently, whenever, in his view, any issue took on immediate political importance.[82]

It is now clear that the latter conception was much nearer that of President de Gaulle himself and that it allowed him in practice a degree of latitude that makes impossible any attempt to describe a clear-cut delimitation of his powers. Already in 1964, the President had reserved the right to adjust the boundaries between his field of personal action and that left to be 'managed' for him by the Government and the appropriate Ministers. But in the final volume of his Memoirs, published only after his death, he provided a detailed statement of the areas 'of greatest general importance' on which his attention was mainly concentrated. Up to 1962, these included, along with foreign policy and defence, Algeria and the Overseas Territories, questions concerning national unity, Catholic schools, the National Plan, the budget, monetary problems, agriculture, and workers' participation in industry. During the following years, this list was extended. And the varied number of councils and committees over which he presided, discussed later, made it clear that he took his responsibilities in this wide field very seriously. He also restated in this fourth volume of Memoirs his general position in terms that echoed the comprehensive claims to overall personal control made in 1964 and 1967.[83]

How much truth is there in the President's own picture of his rôle? How much allowance must be made for General de Gaulle's deliberate and continuous effort to project his image as national leader (the 'de Gaulle' whom he liked to speak of in the third person), and for the possibility that he became a victim of his own myth? There are many passages in the last complete volume of his Memoirs that could support such a conclusion: his description, for example, of meetings of the Council of Ministers, in which his constitutional function of 'presiding' was interpreted by him to mean control of the agenda, decision of all issues, and even control of the wording of the official communiqué; the mention of Cabinet committees (*Conseils restreints*) in which Ministers and high officials studied different problems *with him*; his description of his relations

with the Prime Minister, who, though given an audience once
a week to discuss the progress of affairs and invited to discuss
the business of the Council of Ministers before the weekly
meeting, took action 'on important matters only on presidential
directives', was relieved of his office at any moment thought
suitable by the President, and, while still in it, was 'authorized'
by the President to put the question of confidence in the National Assembly 'only four times in three and a half years'.[84]
Even more revelatory are the passages describing the President's own estimate of the changed political atmosphere
brought by the new system – the 'cheerful contentment' that
reigned at his New Year receptions for high officials, and also
in the *départements* that he visited. 'Everyone', he said, 'is
happy to feel that the edifice of the State now has its keystone
and pillars cemented.'[85]

This idyllic scene (General de Gaulle was writing only about
the period 1958–62) was marred apparently only by disgruntled
journalists and politicians – a 'hostile coalition' whose rancour
he bore with fortitude.[86] If it is an accurate picture of General
de Gaulle's conception of his own rôle, then it suggests certain
questions. For instance, how far was his emphasis on Parliamentary institutions during the period of his premiership and
the drawing up of the Constitution in 1958 merely a necessary
concession paid to Parliamentary representatives whose votes
he needed, both to enable him to return to power 'legitimately' and to establish the 'legitimacy' of his own leadership
during the difficult years before he had settled the Algerian
problem, restored the authority of the State and ensured the
presence of a working majority to support him in the National
Assembly?[87] Did he intend, later, instead of relying on constitutional amendment by interpretation, to transform the text
of the Constitution (as he was doing in the case of the Senate
in 1969) into something nearer his own conception of personal rule, in which the Prime Minister would be merely
'a sort of civil chief of staff',[88] and Parliament a deliberating
and legislative Chamber deprived of any real influence on
policy?[89]

The answer to these questions remains elusive for a number

of reasons, one of the most important of them being the unreliability of the evidence of General de Gaulle himself. For one thing, words were, for much of his life, his most potent political weapon. During his period of exile in London he had often had no other. During the first four years of his presidency, though politically indispensable, he was, in many fields of great importance to him, virtually impotent while the military, economic, political and international problems created by the Algerian war persisted. He was also under no illusions regarding the effort that would be made in some quarters to get rid of him once the war did end.[90] And so, while he slowly and patiently sought to find ways of ending it, he had had to use words to deceive as well as to persuade. And above all he used words to project his own image, as well as that of a France with restored power and influence in the world – an image that bore little relation to reality.

One of these words was 'legitimacy'. When he said that 'Nothing is so important as the legitimacy, the institutions and the functioning of the State',[91] the word could be interpreted in its normal sense. And he did always seek legitimacy in this sense. He categorically denied ever having any contacts with the Algerian insurrection that had been responsible for his return to power.[92] He was determined to assume office by virtue of legitimate procedures. Even when his interpretations of these were juridically questionable, he always sought plausible, if not wholly defensible, arguments to back them up, instead of deliberately flouting legality or constitutionality. But in his mind the word 'legitimacy' also meant something quite different. It was a curious, semi-mystical bond that he called a 'contract', between France and himself, in his rôle of 'de Gaulle'. He alone appeared to be qualified to determine its terms.[93] And the relationship between the two conceptions of 'legitimacy' was clearly recognizable only by him. This no doubt helps to explain why he felt able to claim that he respected 'the letter and the spirit of the Constitution'.[94] Presumably, there were occasions when his 'legitimacy' in the one sense enabled him to regard as legitimate in the other sense actions that many did not see in the same way as he did.

It is obvious that General de Gaulle's wartime experience as a rebel general had a profound influence on him, but it would be too facile an explanation to treat this as being in itself an adequate explanation of his preoccupation with 'legitimacy' in this wider meaning of the term. His constitutional battles, for instance, were fought on the basis of personal interpretations difficult to justify, except on the assumption that the President invariably knew what was right for France, which, indeed, he claimed to do. They revealed the skill with which he could manipulate words to serve his own ends. But the fact that he won them all except the last had really nothing to do with his legitimacy or with the constitutional merits of his case as he put it. Between 1958 and 1962, he won them because he was indispensable while the Algerian war lasted. As Raymond Aron noted, he did not really need the Constitution to govern at this time.[95] It is possible that his obsession with the idea of his 'legitimacy' resulted in reality from the realization that he could be sure of its recognition only in periods of national emergency. During the years of retirement from 1946 to 1958, he is reported by Jean-Raymond Tournoux to have said, 'All that I have done has been possible only because we were at war. Since then, the French have not understood.'[96] The fact that much less was heard from him about legitimacy after 1962, may well justify the comment of François Goguel and Alfred Grosser that 'People talk about "legitimacy" only in countries and at times when it is contested.'[97] For between 1963 and 1969, his authority rested firmly on solid support not only in the National Assembly but also in the country – the *pays réel* to which he so often resorted in preference to the *pays légal* – but which he eventually discovered to be more volatile and unreliable.

The real extent of his authority during the period in which there was no problem of 'legitimacy' is difficult to estimate, however, for Ministers and officials have been no more reliable than the President in their public statements. They were chosen by him primarily for their loyalty to him, as is illustrated by the following description of a meeting of the Council of Ministers:

> Opposite me sits Michel Debré. On my right I have, and always shall have, André Malraux. The presence beside me of this friend and genius, dedicated to exalted visions, seems to protect me from the commonplace. This incomparable witness has in his mind a picture of me that strengthens my resolve.[98]

Ministers' public statements on their relations with him, and especially those of M. Pompidou, his Prime Minister for over six years, were, therefore, a reflection of his own. On the other hand, statements by former office holders – after their dismissal – are suspect as not being wholly exempt from some degree of personal rancour.[99] The President's own need to appear as the guide and saviour of France often made him unable or unwilling to see what appeared to others to be obvious weaknesses in the system and illogicalities in his own arguments. He continued to assert in the last two volumes of his Memoirs, published after his resignation, that the separation of powers provided for in the 1958 Constitution was effective, especially the institution of Ministerial and Parliamentary incompatibility. Yet he had repeatedly claimed for himself the *indivisible* authority of the State and the right to appoint *all* other authorities. He had ordered Ministers to get themselves elected to Parliament, as they had done in the derided epoch of 'non-separated' powers – thus effectively depriving the theory of all credibility. Nor did it make sense to describe himself as an 'arbiter', while claiming the credit for winning the political wars, and leaving Ministers who were merely obeying his orders to bear the consequences of losing the Parliamentary battles.

APPEARANCE AND REALITIES OF PRESIDENTIAL POWER
(ii) A PROVISIONAL BALANCE SHEET

One of the weaknesses of the Fifth Republic's quasi-presidential system is the degree of secrecy that surrounded and still surrounds Governmental activities – and presidential activities too, except for those that the President deliberately chooses to highlight. The growth of decision-making in small Ministerial sub-committees (*Conseils restreints*) and in Elysée committees, together with the participation in decision-making of members of the President's private office,[100] has made it difficult for Gaullist supporters as well as opponents to discover exactly where power and responsibility lie. The growth of Cabinet committees is not, of course, restricted to France. They exist in Great Britain, and are an inevitable consequence of the increasing technicality and complexity of modern politics. But the significant difference between those of the Fifth Republic and those of Britain is that the British Prime Minister really is in charge of policy, and that he, his Ministers, and the majority in Parliament form one compact bloc, opposed by a bloc of opponents, so that far more political battles of real substance are fought out publicly in Parliament. In France, the Council of Ministers has become more and more not only a body that ratifies policies made elsewhere, but one that ratifies policies made partly in committees, which may include high officials, including those on the President's personal staff, and which are put to the Council of Ministers as virtual *faits accomplis*, subject only to the procedure outlined by the President himself, in which he listens to others and then makes up his own mind. President and Ministers, who are the real focus of political interest, are not members of the legislature. Much of the evidence regarding the reality of presidential power is, consequently, scrappy, though there is a plentiful supply of gossip and anecdote.

Gaullist personal rule certainly evolved considerably between 1958 and 1969. Under M. Debré's premiership, there were only a few Elysée committees, and these were concerned with what was then accepted as the presidential sector – the Elysée committees on defence, and those on Algerian and African affairs. In spite of his well-known opposition to the President's Algerian policy, M. Debré was given considerable scope for action, even within this sector, so much so that he was accused by the *Canard enchaîné* of sabotaging Elysée foreign policy.[101] But under the premiership of M. Pompidou the President greatly extended both the number and the scope of councils and committees. They dealt with administrative and educational reform, judicial problems, the reorganization of the Paris region, town planning, radio and television, police reform, energy policy, technological and scientific problems and economic questions, including the stabilization plan. No longer could it be said that the President was uninterested in problems of '*l'intendance*'! By 1966, this panoply of committees was described as resembling that of the White House (though the Elysée staff was certainly very much smaller than the staff of the White House), and the system as being like that of an American presidential Cabinet.

> The president [wrote Pierre Avril] meets Ministers concerned, together with high officials, and important decisions requiring detailed study are taken at that level. These are either presented later for ratification by the Council of Ministers, or else are used as a basis for policy directions to the Government, especially in the diplomatic field. It should be added that representatives of the Elysée frequently attend preparatory inter-ministerial committees meeting in the Prime Minister's office.[102]

The President himself revealed something of the scope of these activities in terms of time, when he stated in his press conference of September 1965 that, during his septennate, he had presided over 302 meetings of the Council of Ministers and 420 *Conseils restreints*. All this presidential activity resulted in a tendency for the Prime Minister to have a declining scope for independent action during M. Pompidou's premiership, counter-balanced, however, to a considerable extent by his growing political authority and more conciliatory methods both in Parliament and in the Gaullist party. The division of labour became one in which dossiers were prepared by the Prime Minister's office and then discussed and decided on in one or other of the various councils or committees. The method of work had weaknesses, however, that adversely affected Governmental efficiency. For the President's domain could be extended at any time and anywhere by personal interventions in affairs that happened to interest him, perhaps only temporarily. One result was an inevitable overlap between the by then much larger presidential staff and the ministerial departments. The latter never knew when a particular subject might suddenly become a presidential concern, or how long the President's interest would last. Nor were these sporadic interventions always effective, because, as Maurice Duverger noted, the President lacked contact with the administrative machine.[103] By this he meant, apparently, that the French administrative machine, as it has been able to do to some extent under every régime, can often succeed in practice in evading, delaying or merely burying in red tape political decisions that it dislikes.

Between 1964 and 1966, reorganization of defence responsibilities, counter-espionage and the police also came under criticism as diminishing the rôle of the Prime Minister and expanding that of the President. One of these measures, the decree of 14 January 1964 which, among other changes, provided that the President should decide when the strategic air force should be engaged, led to perhaps the best attended and certainly the most dramatic Assembly debate of the régime. In discussing an Oral Question, M. Mitterrand on the Left asked why the Government agreed to its own demotion to the 'position of a consultative committee'. M. Coste-Floret (MRP) asked who governed France, and replied to his own question – 'De Gaulle'. He then went on to give examples of the President's failure to consult Ministers, in particular before the presidential press conference of 15 May 1962, following which five MRP Ministers resigned, to criticize the growth of *Conseils restreints*, whose existence was now being discovered only thanks to casual press reports, and to ask the Prime Minister why he did not resign, since he no longer existed. Finally, he claimed that the Prime Minister had no right to sign the offending decree, since it concerned the 'fundamental principles of defence' and, as such, should have been the subject of a law, not a decree.[104]

The Prime Minister gave a soothing reply to the specific points raised, but his statement was primarily interesting in that it provided the first detailed description from the Prime Minister's angle of the relations between President and Prime

Minister under the Gaullist régime, and was clearly intended to reply to the more general criticisms of presidential power, not only on the Left, but also among Centrists like M. Coste-Floret, himself a supporter of a presidential system. M. Pompidou denied the existence of either a 'reserved domain' or a 'dyarchy'. He stated categorically that all presidential decisions were taken only after discussion, and by agreement between President and Prime Minister, and that the rôle of the Prime Minister was strengthened by his reliance on the support and confidence of both President and Assembly. The latter claim was rendered less convincing, however, by his later admission that he could not continue in office if he were to lose the President's confidence, since this obviously implied that he, and not the President, would go in such an eventuality. In the two cases of previous serious divergence between President and Prime Minister it was the President who had to resign![105]

During the debate, M. Pompidou referred to 'the prestige that the Head of State henceforth derives from his election by universal suffrage, the possibilities that he had of appealing to the people by referendum or by a dissolution . . .' which obviously raised in the minds of many Deputies and commentators a further query. What would happen if a President with this additional prestige found it impossible to find either a Prime Minister or a majority in the National Assembly to agree with him? Both legislature and President would now be able to claim that they had the support of the majority of the electorate. As Jacques Fauvet noted:

> Not only is this régime unprotected in face of such a conflict – which if it is unimaginable while the General is there is conceivable after him – but the risks of it have been increased by the election of the President by universal suffrage and for a period different from that for which the Assembly is elected.[106]

Various answers were put forward, one of which, favoured particularly by some politicians and political scientists on the Left, was to have the two elected for the same period. But this did not answer the question as to what would happen if, as is conceivable, when both President and Deputies had faced the electors together, after a dissolution, conflict persisted. For if the President had dissolved the Assembly in order to settle the issue of presidential disagreement with the majority of the Assembly, he would constitutionally be unable to dissolve it again for twelve months. The general view seemed to be that if a general election twice returned a majority unfavourable to the President he ought to resign, but this view was accompanied by some doubts as to whether a President with the possibility of submitting matters to a referendum, or, perhaps, even the temerity to use article 16, might not perhaps refuse to do this.[107] That the question was far from academic became obvious during the candidature for the presidency of M. Alain Poher, President of the Senate, in 1969. He duly produced a programme of '*grandes options*', but commentators were quick to ask the vital question, which was: 'With what majority could a President Poher hope to put such a programme into operation?', only to come up with the obvious answer, which was that, given the actual state of the parties, he (a Centrist) was virtually certain to be faced by an Assembly which would not accept it.[108]

Nor has this problem been resolved. M. Chaban Delmas, in a speech on institutions at the beginning of 1970, had to admit that

> Our Constitution has an Achilles heel. This weakness can be summed up in a word: it requires close and almost intimate relations between the President of the Republic and the Prime Minister and an almost total confidence in each other.[109]

He had apparently no suggestions to offer on the problem of confidence between President and Assembly. Maurice Duverger saw the 1962 referendum as having, so to speak, added a new dimension to the presidency. The President, he said, now enjoys not only 'legitimacy' (in the normal sense of the term), but also a 'democratic legitimacy' 'more direct than that of the Prime Minister and the Government who are elected by popular vote,

but only indirectly, through the confidence expressed in them
by the Assembly itself elected by the people'.[110] This, he felt,
created a new constitutional situation. But, up to the end of
1971, no new constitutional provisions had been produced to
deal with it. Most of the suggestions that have been made are
really no more than academic speculation. If and when answers
to the questions raised are forthcoming, they will be dictated
neither by loyalty to the Republican tradition, nor by new
constitutional provisions, but by the facts of the political
situation at the time.

In addition to these activities in the field of internal policy,
the President's rôle in foreign affairs must be taken into account
– his meetings with Heads of State, and especially his ritual two
meetings a year with the German Chancellor, his personal
conduct of negotiations of European policies, his direction of
Atlantic and defence policies and his various pronouncements
on foreign affairs in the course of his numerous visits. Well
before General de Gaulle's presidency ended, the all-embracing
nature of the presidential sector in practice had become evident.
It is less evident, however, that this degree of presidential
personal involvement in day-to-day affairs by other Presidents
will be permanently acceptable to French politicians. In spite of
reaffirmations of General de Gaulle's views on both the rôle
of the President and his relations with the Prime Minister,
made by both M. Pompidou as President, and by his Prime
Minister, M. Chaban Delmas, there were, indeed, almost
immediately, some significantly differing emphases. Whereas
General de Gaulle seemed to go out of his way to produce, as
one of his opponents put it, 'a sensation twice a year',[111]
M. Pompidou projected a more sceptical, pragmatic, conciliatory and down-to-earth image – perhaps a little too like 'the
average Frenchman on holiday'.[112] He expressed the desire
for more confidence and better collaboration between the
executive and Parliament. He admitted that where General de
Gaulle could command, he would have to persuade.

In politics, contacts, as General de Gaulle realized, can bring
political vulnerability. Moreover, M. Pompidou enjoys neither
the special personal status that gave General de Gaulle much

of his authority in the early difficult years, nor the special advantages that he derived from the political situation that made him indispensable. He cannot even pretend to be 'an arbiter', since he was for over six years head of a Government and effective leader of the majority party, under whose banner he fought elections. And the increasing rôle of politicians in the dominant Gaullist party, together with the evolution of the party itself, which is discussed in a later chapter, must sooner or later bring the normal stresses and strains that are characteristic of political parties. Even during the first year of M. Pompidou's presidency there were already rumours of tensions between the President and the Prime Minister, who was an experienced and subtle politician. They were, of course, denied, but the denials carried no more conviction than did the latter's ritual reaffirmation of the essentially subordinate rôle of the Prime Minister in the essential 'partnership' between the two[113] in the Gaullist system. This did not mean that there was likely to be a return in the near future to the Republican tradition of powerless Presidents.

One thing, indeed, that seems clear beyond all reasonable doubt is that, since 1966, non-Gaullists have been either reconciled to, or positively in favour of, the presidential system as laid down in the Constitution, in which the President is no longer 'a mute and powerless onlooker'.

> As for the President of the Republic [wrote René Pleven] even when he is no longer Charles de Gaulle, he will no longer be merely ornamental.[114]

> With a President who is less of a towering figure, and one who has a less strong personality [wrote Alfred Grosser] parties and Parliament will play a more important rôle.[115]

But he did not believe either that the President would revert to his pre-1958 position. The system of presidential election by universal suffrage is also generally popular.[116]

It does not follow, however, that there is general support for, or even knowledge of, the degree of presidential control that characterized what is sometimes called the 'reign' of

Charles de Gaulle. An opinion poll carried out in 1969 revealed that 40% of those who replied believed the Government to be responsible for general policy indications (*les grandes orientations*) and only 38% believed the President to be responsible.[117] Nor does it follow that what was accepted or tolerated under General de Gaulle's presidency will continue to be accepted under that of his successors. The greatest difficulty of all in trying to estimate what is likely to be the power of Presidents of the Fifth Republic in the political system provided for by the 1958 Constitution is the uniqueness of the first President, in his own as well as the nation's judgement. He was a unique personality who did not *come* but *returned* to power in unique circumstances. He had a unique capacity to exploit situations to his own advantage, and was, beyond all doubt, his own best public-relations officer. He had the advantage, hitherto unique in Republican history, of having for ten years a continuous working, or near-working, majority in the National Assembly. These are imponderables that are never likely to recur – or not all at once. It is understandable, therefore, that the second President of the Fifth Republic should hold office in a political atmosphere characterized by a sense of impermanence or of transition. The Constitution has been there since 1958, but the régime is still in its infancy.

PART II

Parties and Interest Groups

CHAPTER VI

The French Party System

Of the many paradoxes presented by the French party system, the most obvious, and the one most frequently commented on, is the picture that it conveys of instability, change and fluidity, combined with an obstinate, underlying stability that often amounts to ossification. Between the two world wars, there were in the French Chamber of Deputies at one time or another, eight right-wing 'tendencies', that is, opinion groups forming sometimes up to six officially recognized Parliamentary groups. Both groups and names changed frequently. There were from one to four centre-right tendencies, similarly changing their labels and composition, from one to four centre-left tendencies, and from four to six left-wing groups. During the same period, there were 41 Governments and 22 different Prime Ministers – 23 of the Governments lasted less than six months.

The picture was much the same during the eleven and a half years of the Fourth Republic. The National Assembly included some fourteen distinct political tendencies, together with a number of small fringe groups that came and went. Five called themselves left-wing; two or three belonged to the Centre-Left or the Centre; three were Gaullist; and four or five were conservative, though using labels that avoided the word. In all, during these years there were some 30 different Parliamentary group labels. There were 21 Governments and 16 different Prime Ministers (including the last Government headed by General de Gaulle). The longest period of office of any Government was thirteen and a half months, the shortest four days.[1]

The Fifth Republic brought a spectacular change. During

General de Gaulle's presidency (which was only one year shorter than the life of the Fourth Republic) the National Assembly included six groups throughout, two being right-wing or centre-right, two centre-left, and two (the Socialists and the Communists) left.[2] There were only six Governments, of which the shortest lasted fifteen months and the longest four and a half years, and only three different Prime Ministers, of whom the first remained continuously in power for three and a quarter years and the second for over six years. During these years, the composition of the Government majority remained the same (though there were minor differences in the distribution of Ministers among parties), the Gaullists remaining throughout the overwhelmingly predominant party in all Government coalitions.

This was a situation that allowed General de Gaulle to claim with some plausibility that the new institutions had provided political stability. There was certainly a general acceptance by the majority of the system and methods of the Fifth Republic. Though it was qualified on the part of the orthodox conservatives who formed part of the Government coalition by a certain number of 'ifs' and 'buts', though there were disagreements within the Gaullist party on the priority that ought to be given to different aspects of Government policy and sometimes restiveness regarding internal party discipline, these were no more than frictions between individuals or differences of opinion on tactics and organization.

General de Gaulle's political opponents, however, argued consistently up to April 1969 that the majority was held together in fact almost entirely by loyalty to him or by the recognition that his presence at the head of the State was essential to the Government's own survival. Unfortunately, the opposition parties agreed on little else, which helped to explain why, during the months following General de Gaulle's resignation, the majority did not break up. Yet though Gaullist cohesion still showed little sign of erosion even in the second year of life without de Gaulle, objective observers were still far from convinced that the political system was basically any more stable than it had ever been. In spite of the greater

Governmental stability, political affiliations in the country as a whole (as opposed to those within Parliament) underwent great changes. Within Parliament, the system of 'affiliates' – that is, of representatives regarding themselves as having, either politically or administratively, something of a 'special relationship' with a Parliamentary group – continued to encourage fluidity. Some Parliamentary groups were heterogeneous, in that they included several politically distinct (and sometimes partially hostile) tendencies, largely because, under the 1959 Parliamentary regulations, no group with fewer than 30 members had the rights and privileges of a recognized Parliamentary group. The numerous extra-Parliamentary political parties and movements of the 1960's presented, indeed, a picture of great instability, most of them being ephemeral and the precise differences between some of them being often inexplicable except within their own particular circles. The Centre remained, as usual, unable to withstand the fundamental centrifugal forces that have always made the survival of any given Centre party difficult in the short run and impossible in the long run. On the Left, the permanent controversies between Communist and non-Communist parties and movements continued unabated.

In some ways, then, French party politics under the Fifth Republic presented a much more traditional picture – that is, a picture of the continuance of a traditional instability – than that indicated merely by the diminution of the number of Parliamentary groups and the longer duration of Governments. It was still true, as Jacques Fauvet had said during the Fourth Republic, that no country had made more revolutions than France, and that none was more conservative,[3] as was borne out by the abortive revolution that did occur in 1968, for it was essentially a traditional, backward-looking revolutionary outburst. Before that, the régime had seen during its first five years two abortive insurrections (in 1960 and 1961), and a degree of violence in the following two years that could well have brought down the régime if the Government had been directed by anyone except de Gaulle.

Even looked at from the point of view of electoral statistics, the Fifth Republic appears far more like its predecessors than either General de Gaulle or his supporters cared to admit. They revealed the familiar regional political differences, Catholic and right-wing tendencies predominating in the North-West and the East, Socialist and Communist strength being mainly in the North-East and the South-West. In 1936, the Popular Front obtained over 30% of the votes in that part of France that was shortly to become the 'unoccupied' or Vichy zone. In 1849, *'la montagne'* had polled over 40% of the votes in roughly the same area. In the presidential election of 1965, the 24 *départements* in which the candidate of the left-wing parties, François Mitterrand, obtained a majority of votes were all in the former unoccupied zone, with the single exception of the one that included his own constituency (Nièvre).[4] In 1946, François Goguel had noted that, as between 1877 and 1928, the changes in the relative strengths of the right and left tendencies that he described as representing respectively *l'ordre* and *le mouvement* varied by no more than 0·5%.[5] In 1958, Raymond Aron concluded that 75% of the electors had voted along traditional lines.[6] And in 1970, a speaker at a *journée d'études* of the small group, the *Centre républicain*, expressing some scepticism regarding the practicality of proposals that had just been published with a view to reforming the Radical party, asked, 'Do not 80% of the French electors, when they find themselves in a polling booth, vote automatically as they are accustomed to?'[7]

It is traditional to explain the mixture of diversity, instability and conservatism of the French party system as being in part a consequence of France's economic self-sufficiency up to the outbreak of the second world war. This, it is claimed, enabled her to regard politics as 'a matter of individual taste rather than a vital necessity'.[8] Over-indulgence in a national predilection for argument about ideas rather than about practical policies has also been frequently cited in explanation of the survival of this attitude into an era in which politics *had* become a vital necessity, even if this fact was inadequately recognized by the majority of the politically-minded in France. Almost all political analysts emphasize the over-riding attraction, especially on the Left, of theories and doctrines, distinctions of principle and attitudes, often wholly divorced from considerations of practicality. Before the first world war, Robert de Jouvenel noted that 'in the eyes of legislators, laws are less important than resolutions'.[9] In 1932, Albert Thibaudet began his study of French political ideas with the affirmation that 'Politics are made up of ideas'.[10] The ideas themselves are, moreover, and this is particularly true of the Left, inherited from the past and continue to be subjects of political controversy long after they have ceased to be relevant to contemporary society. Jacques Fauvet describes eloquently this characteristic of French politics:

> At a time [he says] when the French Parliament was arguing passionately about the presence of crucifixes in law courts, England and Germany were debating their future in a world on the threshold of the twentieth century.[11]

The French Parliament was still behaving in this way when the twentieth century had run almost three-quarters of its course. It could be regarded merely as an amiable eccentricity that, in 1898, *La Dépêche* should still have been dating its numbers *Prairial* and *Fructidor*. It is more disturbing that some of the inadequacies of the Constitution of the Fourth Republic should result from the anxiety of the Parliamentary Commission responsible for the presentation of the draft text to the National Assembly to be faithful, not merely to the principles of the Declaration of the Rights of Man, but also to those that had inspired the revolutionary (and abortive) Constitutions of 1793.[12] It is even more disturbing that, in the 1955 election, a candidate of the small left-wing movement, *La jeune République*, should have felt it worth while to remind the electors that his party was the only one of which all the Deputies (all four!) had voted against Pétain in July 1940.[13] And it is much more disturbing still that, in 1970, a Gaullist Government with an unprecedentedly large majority in the National Assembly should have hesitated to submit to Parliament a Bill to replace the 1959 law dealing with State aid to Catholic schools, lest it should spark off among teachers and anti-clerical political movements a revival of political agitation in schools and universities over an anti-clerical issue that ought to have been dead for a quarter of a century.[14]

The fact that old quarrels, old loyalties and old attitudes have so often mattered more than current policies has helped to make French parties (particularly left-wing parties) traditionally less concerned about power than is necessary in the modern world if the democratic Parliamentary system is to survive. Some compromise is unavoidable if Governments are to be formed at all, and are to be able to survive even for a brief period. But the necessity for electoral, Parliamentary and Governmental compromise has often left intact organizational and doctrinal loyalties that have hitherto made it impossible for French parties to form themselves into coherent and lasting Government and opposition formations. Doctrinal purity has tended to be preferred to the political efficiency ('*efficacité*') that has become the watchword of the more disciplined Gaullist party.

Stability and instability, then, are really two sides of the same coin. Faced with the choice between the disciplines and compromises of power and the freedom to express traditional political attitudes and intellectual loyalties, some parties and movements can be counted on to prefer the purity of opposition to the danger of contamination by the responsibilities of government. To quote Jacques Fauvet again,

> Neither the rank and file, nor Deputies, nor even at times Ministers, feel bound by decisions of the Government that they are supposed to be supporting; they consider themselves to some extent to be at one and the same time in power and in opposition. This is true of most of the groups. Historically, the parties of the Left, which are the most disciplined, have been formed in opposition and they conserve some of their opposition mentally when they come to power.[15]

One change that has occurred under the Fifth Republic is that the most disciplined parties are no longer on the Left. It is the discipline of the Gaullist party, not the new Constitution, that has been responsible for transforming the political

life of the first twelve years of the régime from one of stable
oppositions and unstable Governments to one of stable
Governments and unstable oppositions. Whether that change
will be permanent or not will depend on the capacity of the
Gaullists to remain disciplined, and that capacity will in turn
depend on the extent to which they can transform themselves
from a *Rassemblement*, where unity comes from loyalty to a
man, into a political party with roots in the local politics of
town and country. It will depend, too, on the kind of party
they create, and on the extent to which the opposition remains
a conglomeration of disunited parties or succeeds in transforming itself into a coherent body, capable of forming a Government and anxious to do so.

THE NATURE OF A POLITICAL PARTY

To define precisely what characterizes a political party in
France is no easy task, as is shown by the number of definitions
that have been given at one time or another by political scientists. Some help to explain how the French system works, but
none is wholly satisfactory as a definition. In his book, *Le
Régime politique*, François Goguel defines a party as

> a group with organizations on local, regional and national
> levels, whose aim is to participate in the functioning of
> political institutions, to attain power, partially or wholly,
> and to promote the ideas and interests of its members.[16]

It would no doubt be a good thing if French parties were such
organizations, but the fact is that a number of what are generally regarded in France as authentic political parties do not
comply with these requirements. Some have or have had little
or no organized activity outside Parliament, and others have
more theoretical than real aims of achieving power. The French
Socialist party, to which nobody in France would deny the
title of a political party, stated categorically, following its reorganization in 1969, that power was not an immediate
priority,[17] and this attitude was by no means merely the consequence of the disintegration of the Left in the 1968 elections.

In 1947, when the Socialist party was one of the three parties
in power, and had been since 1944, its leader, Léon Blum, said:

> I have never considered that for the Socialist party the exer-
> cise of power or participation in power has become a
> necessity or even a normal situation. I consider that, although
> it is frequently imposed by circumstances, it remains some-
> thing exceptional.[18]

The Communist party, which, up to the rebirth of Gaullism in
1958, had been numerically the largest party in France for
over ten years,[19] formed part of Governmental coalitions only
during the brief post-war years from 1944 to 1947, and since
then has shown no desire to obtain power by revolution. In
Socialist dissident groups and political 'Clubs', there is also
a tendency to the kind of 'oppositionism' expressed in the
sentiments of Léon Blum, and which has been increasingly
the attitude of Socialists during the years of Gaullist rule. The
Gaullist party, on the other hand, still lacked in 1970 and 1971
the roots in local and regional politics that left-wing parties
as well as orthodox Conservatives had, though its aim of
attaining and retaining power could not be questioned.

Maurice Duverger has defined a political party as being
'above all an ideological group',[20] and also as 'a community
with a particular structure'.[21] Major parties on the Left are
certainly highly structured, having both Parliamentary and
extra-Parliamentary organs, the latter being organized on departmental and local levels and including ancillary movements
providing for participation by special categories such as
women and young people. They also have constitutions providing regular procedures for arriving at party decisions,
electing leaders, and transmitting the views of the rank and
file to the leadership. But if this description applies to the
Socialist and Communist parties, and also applied to the post-
war Christian-Democrat party, the MRP, which had a constitution and a highly-structured party organization, it is by
no means true of other parties whose status as parties would be
questioned by none. Both the Radical party and the Conservative federation of *Républicains indépendants* have always been

very loosely organized outside Parliament, relying more on Parliamentary leaders, together with committees of notabilities, to determine policy and using their apparatus of conferences and local organizations as political show-pieces. In the Radical party, the real source of power and decision has always been held to be undiscoverable, belonging in unquantifiable proportions to national leaders, Parliamentary representatives, local notabilities and a national Congress. The only certainty has been that, on most issues, the party would be divided. Nor have Radicals, *Républicains indépendants* or Gaullists had either 'mass' organizations, as Socialists and Communists understand them, or the kind of basic principles that would justify their inclusion in M. Duverger's category of 'an ideological group'. Indeed, the absence of any doctrinal basis in the Radical party has long been something on which there was general agreement inside as well as outside the Radical party, from Barrès, who, in 1893, concluded simply that: 'The Radical party has no ideal'[22] to the Radical Minister, who, according to French party mythology, when presented with a copy of Alain's *Eléments d'une doctrine radicale*, remarked with surprise: 'If we had a doctrine, we should be the first to know.'[23] On the other hand, the Gaullist party, which certainly has had neither a doctrine nor a mass membership, is a highly structured party.

If it is difficult to classify, on the basis of their structure or their ideology, the main parties that have Parliamentary groups, it is impossible to give any meaningful or coherent description of the structure of more extremist groups, whether unrepresented in Parliament or only intermittently represented by from one to half a dozen Deputies. The *Parti socialiste unifié* (PSU) has all the trappings of a left-wing party – local and factory branches, procedures for decision-making in national congresses, the democratic election of party leaders and so on. It is also an ideological party, believing in direct 'revolutionary' action among the rank and file, and from 1968 onwards attaching increasing importance to 'mass' and 'direct' action, yet also continuing to present candidates for election to Parliament and even having its own candidate in the 1969 presidential election.

It therefore satisfies a number of the requisites laid down by
François Goguel and Maurice Duverger, but not the essential
condition of the former, which is the desire to attain power.
There is a great deal of verbalism about power, but the perpetual state of schism of all the extremist groups, both on the
Right and on the Left, reduces all of them in practice to small,
quarrelling '*groupuscules*', incapable of organizing themselves
for anything more than demonstrations, peaceful or violent,
and far more occupied with fighting each other than with
fighting the system that they propose in theory to overturn.

In reality, a political party in France is a political group,
whose right to the title is recognized, implicitly or explicitly,
by other parties. It is therefore incapable of precise definition.
But there are certain criteria, both negative and positive, that
help to describe, if not to define, what is meant by a party.
There would, for example, be general, if not universal, agreement that the numerous political Clubs formed during the
Fifth Republic, and discussed in a later chapter, are not parties,
though they are often ancillaries to parties. When Maurice
Duverger maintains, for instance, that parties are '*less* definable
in terms of their programme or the class to which they belong'[24]
than they are in terms of their organization, one can only reply
that some French parties are not even *distinguishable*, much less
definable, in terms of either. Though all Parliamentary groups
are obliged to produce 'political declarations' signed by their
members (and published in the *Journal Officiel*), these are usually
couched in such vague and general terms as to be virtually
meaningless. And the so-called 'programmes' of those political
parties that do produce them are usually statements of doctrine,
general principles or pious hopes, justifying the view that
French politics represent 'a victory of the abstract over the
concrete'.[25]

French parties are certainly not 'class' parties in the sense in
which the word is often used in Britain. It is true that there are
more company directors among the members of the *Républicains indépendants* than there are in the Communist party, and
more representatives of the industrial working class in the
latter than in the former. But left-wing parties include a

number of highly articulate and often influential middle-class intellectuals, while right-wing parties include a number of representatives of the 'little man', the peasant farmer, trades-man and white-collar worker – the sectors left behind by the second industrial revolution now in process in France. It is still true, as Peter Campbell wrote in 1954, that

> No French party is controlled by one social interest or de-pends on it for the bulk of its vote in elections; similarly no social interest is to be found wholly in the ranks of one party, and, except for the industrial workers no important social interest is to be found mainly in the ranks of one party. Each party is a medley of social groups and is responsive to pressures of several kinds, even conflicting ones.[26]

All parties are subject to sectional pressures because all parties with any significant representation in Parliament con-sider that the job of the Deputy or the Senator is to look after the interests of his constituents as well as, and sometimes in preference to, the interests of party and nation. The promotion of local interests and of sectional interests within the con-stituency is encouraged by the presence in Parliament of an astonishing number of local Councillors and Mayors. In a highly centralized and over-bureaucratized State, the most effec-tive method of doing something for a locality or a particular interest is usually via the Parliamentary representative. And the more unstable the Government, the more it is liable to be subjected to pressure on behalf of such interests. But even the most stable Government expects pressure from Deputies, because electors expect their Deputy or their Senator to act in this way on their behalf. Gaullist candidates and rep-resentatives have been no less anxious than others to draw the attention of their electors to what they could do or have done on behalf of the constituency. To have a Mayor who is also a Minister (not excluding the Prime Minister) is a valuable advantage to any municipality.[27] Sectional interests are more obvious in right-wing parties, because some of them have tended to choose titles indicative of such interests, particu-larly those of the peasant farmer.[28] But usually the sectional interests cut across party divisions, sometimes being expressed in the form of Parliamentary 'intergroups'. In the 1956 National Assembly, one short-lived group, that of the Poujadists, constituted in itself a pressure group on behalf of small tradesmen, rather than a political party.[29]

TWO 'TEMPERAMENTS' – LEFT AND RIGHT

Throughout the history of French political parties, the most meaningful distinction between them has been that between the Right and Left. It is no less difficult to define the distinction than it is to define what precisely constitutes a political party, but, at least until recent years, the division, however 'arbitrary, ill-defined and porous'[30] it might be, was in practice easily recognized by the French themselves, who either still believed in it, or at least paid lip-service to it. Here again, a great many attempts have been made to provide definitions, most of them being unhelpful and some positively misleading. M. Mitterrand's definition of the Left as 'the enormous mass of men and women who are dependent on others'[31] can be dismissed out of hand, since it is obvious that almost as many of these vote for the Right as for the Left. Albert Thibaudet's definition:

> The Right has its mind on what it owns; the Left has its mind on what others own[32]

ignores the number of peasant owners in the South-West and elsewhere who vote Communist, as well as the Radicals who, though demonstrably on the Left as he himself convincingly shows, do often have 'their pocket-books on the Right'. An avowed member of the Right recently redefined Right and Left as being for him essentially attitudes of mind.

> The Right means consciousness of the discomfort and difficulty of life, having the courage to live – and die. It involves a certain pessimism about human nature, refusal to compromise, satisfaction in doing one's duty, even if this has its unrealistic side. The Left believes that liberty is all-powerful, all-knowing and all-embracing. The Right recognizes the power of things, and especially of heredity.[33]

It would be possible to challenge every one of these points (though each has some truth in it), because this is a subjective definition, based on feeling. Many definitions of the Left by those who feel themselves part of it are no less subjective.

Here, too, however, it is possible to describe where it is impossible to define. To be Left – and it is essential to begin with the Left, because much of the Right represents a reaction from the Left – is, above all, to have not only a certain attitude of mind, but also certain political principles that are both more and less than a philosophy. They are more, because the principles have been built up over the years and are inextricably intermingled with loyalties and phobias formed by past political battles. They are less than a philosophy, because so many of the habits and attitudes have become symbols without relevance to modern political problems. To be Left is first of all to remember, to look backwards, but to look no farther back than to the French Revolution, and to see that through something of a sentimental haze.

What this means in real terms is that to be Left is essentially to *feel* Left, to be able to accept spontaneously, unquestioningly and unthinkingly that certain attitudes are right and proper and even praiseworthy, while others are no less certainly wrong and wrong-headed. The Radical philosopher, Alain, has described this essential Leftism unforgettably.

> When [he said] I am asked whether the division between men of the Right and men of the Left still has any meaning, my first thought is that the man who asks such a question is certainly not a man of the Left.[34]

This instinctive Leftness would almost be the intellectual (though not the moral) equivalent of Goering's Nazi instinct to reach for his gun at the mention of the word culture, were it not that one of the most powerful and authentic left-wing attitudes is also the belief in reason, the reason of the ordinary individual. It is

> the conviction that it is reasonable to appeal to the judgement and the critical spirit of the individual and that,

consequently, the people can and must be consulted on how they are governed: the Left believes sincerely in universal suffrage.[35]

It may be argued that this belief is no monopoly of the Left and that the expression of it was one of the secrets of the successful dominance of public opinion by the personality of General de Gaulle. A 'man of the Left' would argue that the Gaullist appeals to the people were not genuine consultations, in that the dice were always loaded in such a way that (up to the last referendum in 1969) the people could safely be counted on to come down on his side. But it is still undeniable that many men of the Left did support General de Gaulle, at least in part, precisely because he proclaimed his faith in universal suffrage.

One left-wing conviction shared by the Right is that the majority of the French people find the Left more acceptable than the Right, though the sentiment is less precise than Barrès' famous dictum that 'France is Radical'. This Left orientation – or 'sinistrism' – of opinion helps to account for a certain defensiveness on the Right, of which one expression is the avoidance of the word 'Right' as far as possible in whatever political label a right-wing party or movement may choose. Not since the right-wing majority of 1919 in the Chamber of Deputies has any Parliamentary group described itself as 'Right', with the exception of a short-lived three-member group (M. Tixier-Vignancour's *Rassemblement national*, or *Nouvelle Droite*') in the National Assembly of 1956. 'The great success of the Left', said Maurice Duverger, 'is to have given the Right a bad conscience.'[36] 'Independent', 'moderate', 'liberal', 'Republican', 'social' – all these and other adjectives are called in, either separately or in combination, as descriptions of conservative parties and groups. This 'sinistrism' also affects the Left, and so Centre parties often describe themselves as Left, Radical or near-Radical parties as Socialist-Radical or Socialist-Republican, and so on.

It is when it comes to defining what the Left stands for in contemporary politics that the problems come thick and fast. It is much easier to describe what it does not stand for. In spite of Communist (and sometimes Socialist) platform oratory, it is not a class concept, as has already been said. Nor does the Left have any common ideological principles. Communists are, of course, Marxist, but there have always been dissident Marxists, more preoccupied with controversies with other Marxists than with the struggle against the ostensible common enemy, capitalism. The Socialist party's attachment to Marxism is highly eclectic, and sometimes consists of little more than lip-service paid to theories that no longer have any relevance to practical politics. Radicals and progressive Catholics (the former MRP) are not Marxist. Indeed, quarrels over Marxism are among the most permanent divisive factors on the Left.

Nor is it possible any longer to classify Right and Left on the basis of François Goguel's thirty-year-old distinction between the forces of order and those of movement.[37] On the one hand, different elements of the Left have come to advocate 'movement' in so many bitterly contested directions that they have become immobile – imprisoned in a traditional jargon that nobody dares to abandon because it has become one of the accepted symbols of Leftness. It is even truer of the Socialist and Communist parties under the Fifth Republic than it was under the Fourth that they have been rendered impotent by 'a political agitation which exhausts itself in ideology, the revolutionary ideology of a conservative country'.[38] 'Progress', or 'movement', has become, for much of the French Left (as it has, indeed, for the Left in other European countries), associated more and more with protest, whether protest in political opposition in Parliament, or in the more recent form of the sterile demonstrations that have come to dominate student left-wing movements, and the token strikes that have come to be used more and more frequently by trade-union elements on the Left. In France, such strikes usually prelude agreements reached with the employers (including the State) with the help and co-operation of the Government, and without any discernible influence of political attitudes on the Left.

There is, however, considerable 'movement' on the side of what the Left regards as constituting the forces of 'order'. It was General de Gaulle who more than anyone else drew the attention of the French public to the changing relations of capital and labour in the modern world, and to the need for what he called '*les grandes mutations*' – the wholesale changes in social and economic organization called for by the advent of the technological age. The fashionable slogan of 'participation' is by no means a monopoly of the Left. It is the Gaullists who have preached the principle (however lukewarm their applications of it in practice), while it is the trade unions that have been suspicious of it – no less suspicious of it, indeed, than the more reactionary employers.

The attitudes of parties towards the ideas of democracy and equality afford no more guidance regarding the distinction today between Left and Right. Today, all parties with any real influence in French political life are democratic. 'No speaker has ever mounted the rostrum in the National Assembly', says Jacques Fauvet, 'and said: I am not a democrat.'[39] Only among the small, extreme-right and extreme-left fringe groups is there either an anti-democratic or an anti-Parliamentary approach. And the extreme left-wing parties are careful to use all the emotive, democratic phrases in the propaganda in favour of direct militant action to which they resort. The Communist party, described in 1951 by Jacques Fauvet as being 'not a party like the others',[40] is reproached today by dissident violent groups, particularly by Maoists, with being indistinguishable from other parties, in that it uses democratic processes, tries to restrict strikes to industrial objectives, and is visibly neither expecting nor working for a Communist revolution in France in any foreseeable future. The Communist objective, as presented to the nineteenth party Congress in 1970, was the achievement through the ballot box of 'an advanced democracy and a Socialist France'.

Parties of the Left frequently assert their belief in equality, their rejection of a 'natural right' to property and the need to justify the right to property on social grounds. But statements of principle in constitutional texts and party constitutions and declarations are one thing and specific programmes another. In practice, both Socialist and Communist Parliamentary representatives have sought to protect the interests of small-scale property owners, especially small-scale farmers, as enthusiastically as they have denounced, in principle, the large-scale industrialist and the capitalist system. Nor is it accurate to say, as Charles Morazé does, that 'In the twentieth century, France thinks that the solemn proclamation of a right is a guarantee of its enforcement.' It is, on the contrary, precisely because nobody is under that illusion that it is safe to make the declarations of principle! The Socialist revolution, like the renunciation of sin, is more comfortably contemplated from a safe distance.

What has, in the past, helped to differentiate Left and Right is the belief of the former that the State ought to be the instrument of 'movement', of social and political change. But there are wide differences between left-wing parties on this point, and today there is no longer any clear-cut difference between left and right parties in their attitudes towards the State. The Communist list of projected 'nationalizations' is far longer than that of the Socialists. The Radicals have always been tepid about nationalization (except in the field of education). And the confused babble of comment that greeted the more utopian sections of the document produced in 1970 by the new secretary-general of the Radical party as a blueprint for the revival of the Radical party left no illusions regarding the scepticism with which critics as well as admirers envisaged the likelihood of its provisions ever being put into practice.

There has always been, too, a striking ambivalence about Socialist and Communist attitudes towards the State, a combination of the collectivist approach that looks towards the State as an agent of the people's will, and the individualist dislike of the State as an expression of '*étatisme*', of bureaucratic control. Charles Morazé explains this ambivalence but does not really succeed in explaining it away.

> The great majority of Frenchmen [he says] have two political personalities. On the one hand, there is the citizen who sees the State as himself, and on the other the subject who sees the State as other people – the rich or the Government. The first accepts certain sacrifices. . . . the other demands subsidies or protection.[41]

The truth of this view is exemplified in both right- and left-wing politics today. Both believe in practice in State intervention on behalf of the citizen. The Right traditionally believed in such intervention in the interests of producers; the Left believed in it in order to protect 'the masses'. Today, both sides see the State as an essential element in the application of economic planning, the need for which is generally accepted. Nevertheless, there is still a conflict between them.

The longest-lived and most easily recognizable distinction between Right and Left – apart from their attitudes to the French Revolution – has been the clerical issue. The Left is traditionally anti-clerical, believing that the Republic should neither allow Catholicism any right of expression within a State-controlled education system, nor subsidize Catholic schools outside it. Today, this issue remains one of the most important of the Left's symbolic reflexes, though it has become largely unreal. And precisely because of its symbolic nature, it is still potentially capable of sparking off very real political controversies.

One important change since the early 1950s that is likely to prove irreversible has been the introduction of a regular system of aid to Catholic schools, involving association of some with the State and the partial integration of others. Another is the development of what was originally a predominantly Catholic trade-union Confederation into an authentically left, and even to some extent revolutionary, movement. While the movement called itself the *Confédération française des Travailleurs chrétiens* (CFTC) and was associated in the minds of the public with the predominantly Catholic party, the MRP, both bodies continued to be somewhat suspect to the traditional Left, as being likely to put their Catholic loyalties before their loyalties to the workers. The development in the 1950s of the Worker–Priest movement, the CFTC's record in the defence of wage claims, its decision in 1964 to drop the denominational adjective and to call itself the *Confédération française démocratique du Travail* (CFDT),[42] and the increasing militancy in the 1960s of certain elements on the Left of the movement – all these combined to dissipate suspicion and to give it a reputation of authentic

Leftness. In 1970, it could no longer be said with the confidence expressed by André Siegfried in the 1930s that 'no militant of the Left has learned to believe that the Church can sincerely work for the Republic'.[43]

Almost the only generalization that can be made about the Left with confidence today is that it is antagonistic to the Right, even though it is often far from clear what the antagonism is really about. As has already been said, on some social and economic issues the MRP under the Fourth Republic and the Gaullists under the Fifth have been farther to the left than the orthodox left-wing parties and trade-union movements, in the sense that they have been readier to try to move with the times. In foreign policy, other divisions cut across the Left–Right division, the Communists being in a number of ways closer to the Gaullists than to either Atlanticists or 'Europeans' on the Left. The gap between Right and Left has been further narrowed by the *de facto* disinclination of the Left to make any considerable extension of the public sector a real political issue, and by the genuine left-wing elements in Gaullist membership as well as in its social and economic policies.

There remains, however, the difference of 'temperament', of emphasis and approach, perpetuated by history and habits. As a general rule, the Right is without the passion for theorizing and systematizing that distinguishes the Left. Its supporters are less interested in general ideas and symbols than in specific sectional and material claims. Where the Left looks to the State in theory, but regards it in practice with suspicion, the Right objects in principle to State control but in practice counts on State aid in the form of subsidies or protection for different sectors of the economy, whether farmers or small-scale wine-growers in the South, large-scale beetroot-growers in the North, or industrialists in need of capital or of special measures to render them less vulnerable to foreign competition. The Left, too, as has been said, often exercises sectional pressures, but the pressure of the Right tends to be more specifically and more nakedly economic, whereas, on the Left, there is almost always some social or political top dressing.

In 1945, André Siegfried wrote that 'on the Right the

conviction reigns that the mass is stupid and wicked. (Your people, said Hamilton to Jefferson, is a great beast.)'[44] This was no longer true in the 1960s. Much of General de Gaulle's appeal was deliberately made, as he himself claimed, to 'the man in the *Métro*' – the little man, and the small, independent and inherently conservative provincial tradesman. Even Pierre Poujade himself was claiming to be a Gaullist in 1968. Among orthodox conservatives and particularly big business elements, there was, on the other hand, considerable wariness regarding General de Gaulle's dangerously 'progressive' ideas about profit sharing and class collaboration.

This may merely amount to saying that Gaullism is *sui generis* and does not fit into the traditional pattern of French political opinion. But there is no doubt that for the more moderate elements of the orthodox Right, it is near enough to the Right for prolonged co-operation between the two to be possible. There is no doubt either that the active members of the parties of the Left, as opposed to the a-political man in the street, regard Gaullism as being on the Right, in spite of the areas in which there is some convergence of opinion. For the Left there are two, if not three, Rights: the traditional Right, represented by the *Républicains indépendants*; the Centre, including some Radicals, some former members of the now defunct MRP, together with some dissident conservatives; and the majority of the Gaullists.

If there is more than one Right, just as there is more than one Left, the relationship between the parties regarded by the Left as belonging to the Right is more remote than that between different left-wing tendencies. There is far less controversy, because there is no ideological passion. But there is also less sense of belonging to the same political 'family', however deep the rifts between different tendencies may be. In spite of the failure (at the end of ten years of talks) of Socialists and Communists to achieve any lasting co-operation, much less an agreed policy, there are still many Frenchmen on the Left who cannot give up the dream of a united Left including the Communists, some day, some year – or some century!

The French political system is, then, permanently bipolarized in the sense that, however little this may correspond to reality, the feeling of being either on the Left or not on the Left persists. That it does is borne out by the permanently un-stable position of what is called the Centre. It is not always possible to identify where it begins and ends, much less to de-fine what Centrism is. It is not in fact 'the seat of all contradic-tion and all intrigues'.[45] It is rather a collection of politicians who are in a fundamentally impossible situation. The Centre groups claim at one and the same time to have a more 'human face' than the Right in social and economic matters and a more idealistic face in matters of foreign policy (though this rarely counts much at elections). They have a more tolerant face than the Left in matters involving religion and are less toler-ant of co-operation between Communist and non-Communist parties. They are suspect to both sides on precisely these grounds, yet have no positive bond to unite them, and so tend permanently to split into Centre–Right and Centre–Left ten-dencies, thus strengthening the traditional Left–Right axis.

On the Parliamentary plane, the Left–Right dichotomy is permanently blurred by the pressures imposed by political and Parliamentary facts, as well as by the individualism of French politicians. The semicircular Parliamentary seating arrange-ment and the system of 'affiliates' to Parliamentary groups enable 'fringe' groups and individual members to combine with parties to the extent that suits them, and so to play a more important rôle than is played by the ordinary maverick back-bencher in a system of highly disciplined parties such as the British. The unwillingness of parties to combine to fight elections on Governmental policies is accompanied by the habit of concluding *ad hoc* or traditional electoral alliances on a local constituency basis that does not commit the partners to any lasting co-operation. New problems create conflicts that tend to cut across traditional dividing lines – old-fashioned versus modern economic policies, large-scale management techniques versus small-scale one-man businesses. There is a growing gulf between rich and poor, between industrial and agricultural workers on the one hand, and employers on the other, between old-fashioned politics and what is often called the new thinking of the younger generation, or the '*nouvelles couches*' – whose new thoughts often turn out to be merely old dreams in even more extravagantly impractical dress. All these new factors have combined during the Gaullist régime to make the future evolution of the French party system a matter of conjecture.

CHAPTER VII

The Parliamentary Parties
(i) Left and Left-Centre

THE SIX PARLIAMENTARY 'FAMILIES'

French Parliamentary parties can be classified on the basis of the factors determining the constitution of Governmental and opposition groupings, as well as on the basis of the political principles underlying the thinking of the different groups. In neither case do the divisions coincide necessarily with those separating Parliamentary groups found in the legislature at any given moment. In the early 1930s, Albert Thibaudet identified six distinct 'political ideologies': traditionalism; liberalism (in the French sense of the word – liberalism in the British sense of the word has played no identifiable rôle in French political life); industrialism;[1] social Catholicism; Radicalism and Jacobinism – the latter being a part of the former; and Socialism. There were at that time some fourteen Parliamentary groups in the Chamber of Deputies. In the 1950s, Jacques Fauvet also distinguished six political 'tendencies', which he described as being those of authoritarianism, conservatism, liberalism, Catholic democracy, Socialism and Communism.[2] There were at that time ten distinct Parliamentary groups in the National Assembly. Guy Mollet and François Mitterrand, both practical left-wing politicians concerned more with problems of Governmental and opposition combinations than with ideas, distinguished four main political 'families' – the Right, the Centre–Right, the Centre–Left and the Left, the two middle groupings representing respectively 'liberal' and sometimes Socialist or Socialistic democrats. The leader of the *Centre démocrate* formed under the Fifth Republic, M. Lecanuet, also identified four main tendencies represented in Parliament –

Gaullist, Centre, non-Communist, and Communist Left. For M. Pompidou, the four main political divisions were Gaullism and Communism, Left and Right. But he subdivided both Left and Right, the former into the nostalgic, the utopian, and the reactionary Left, the latter into the European and the nationalist Right. M. Giscard d'Estaing saw five main divisions, Communist and non-Communist Left, Centre, and moderate and extremist Right.[3]

It is possible to quarrel with all these classifications on one ground or another. But whether or not the different political movements can best be divided into four, five or six 'families', Parliamentary groups have certainly tended since the war to reduce themselves for practical purposes, either by alliances in Governments or in opposition, or by 'affiliation' of smaller movements or larger ones, into six main divisions. Indeed, there have been since 1920 a Communist, a Socialist and a Radical Left, a moderate and a more reactionary Right, and an often amorphous and heterogeneous Centre that tended permanently to be eroded on both fringes.

The frontiers between them have, however, varied from one period to another and sometimes from one issue to another. For instance, throughout the Third Republic and some of the Fourth, the Radical party remained politically on the Left but economically on the Centre or Right, because it rejected the collectivist tendencies of Socialists and Communists. But in an age of economic planning and massive Governmental intervention in economic affairs, this issue of free enterprise versus nationalization has become largely unreal. Both Thibaudet and Jacques Fauvet regarded 'Social' or 'Christian' democracy as a special category, and throughout the Third and Fourth Republics there was at least one Parliamentary group whose distinguishing characteristic was loyalty to Catholicism. But, during the Third Republic, except for the small *Jeune République*, social Catholicism was regarded (and regarded itself) as belonging to the Centre, whilst during the Fourth Republic it regarded itself as belonging to the Left. During the Fifth Republic, after some years as part of a Centre grouping, 'social' or 'Christian' democracy ceased to be the distinguishing characteristic of any single Parliamentary grouping or extra-Parliamentary party. Gaullism had two separate existences as a Parliamentary or would-be Parliamentary movement after the war, but, by 1954, had become a small group regarded by most of the Left as part of the Right, and by the Right as belonging to the Centre. The Radical party had by 1956 split into three groups, of which two were regarded by the Left as belonging to the Centre. By 1962, the Radical party seemed almost to have disappeared as a Parliamentary force, while the Gaullists had become the dominant party, but one which was regarded by many of its members as not being on the Right, a view shared by the right-wing party led by M. Giscard d'Estaing, which, nevertheless, formed part of the Gaullist Governmental majority.

During the 1960s, three significant strands of opinion placed themselves almost or wholly outside the Parliamentary framework. They were the increasingly numerous small extremist movements on both right and left, the dissident Socialist party called the *Parti socialiste unifié* (which by then had one foot in and one foot outside the Parliamentary camp, in that sections of it were more and more seeking to co-operate with extremist groups), and the political Clubs that claimed to represent new thinking, but which for a time avoided involvement in the regular machinery of parties and Parliament, though without condemning the Parliamentary system itself.

This chapter and the following one are concerned only with the Parliamentary 'hexagon' as Henri Queuille called it, which includes Communism; Socialism; Radicalism (very much in decline, but seeking to make a come-back); a Centre made up of disparate elements stretching from Christian-Democrats constituting the rump of the former Christian-Democrat party, the MRP, to right-wing Radicals and moderate Conservatives; Gaullism; and the conservative *Républicains indépendants*, led by M. Giscard d'Estaing. All six have a certain number of characteristics in common. They are all 'families', in the sense, first, that they have near and distant relations belonging to associated or fringe groups or even to rival groups, some of them outside Parliament, and second, that family feuds are frequent. 'Looked at closely', concluded Alfred Grosser, 'each is more like the Atrides than a Corsican clan.'[4] But all of them accept in practice, even if not in theory, the use of Parliamentary methods of Government as the means of obtaining their political ends. All regard themselves as being Republican and democratic. And all, at least from 1965 onwards, were prepared to use the 1958 Constitution as the agreed framework for political institutions.

All of them also have in common (the Gaullists to a lesser extent than the others) the inheritance of certain attitudes from the past that they have too often found it impossible to adapt to changed circumstances. Much of both Thibaudet's and Jacques Fauvet's analysis remains, in other words, truer today than it ought to be. The main purpose of these two chapters is to analyse briefly their attempts under the Fifth Republic to make themselves effective organs of Parliamentary government, and to try to assess the extent of, and the reasons for, their success or failure. It is an attempt to describe political ideas and attitudes in terms of party policies and tactics, rather than to provide a detailed picture of either party structures or the distribution of party strengths in different regions.[5]

COMMUNISM

Though the French Communist party dates only from the end of 1920, and never attracted more than 15% of the votes up to the 1939 war, it was from the end of the war up to 1958 the largest party in France, polling between five and five and a half million votes. Only in 1946 was its vote surpassed by that of any other party, and then for only a few months. Between 1958 and 1968 its vote was surpassed only by that of the Gaullists. Only once did it fall below four million, though it only once (in 1967) reached five million.[6] Communist strength in the National Assembly showed much greater variations, since party strengths were sometimes greatly affected by the working of different electoral systems. The highest number of Communist Deputies was 183 (in 1946) elected by proportional representation (the system that, comprehensibly, the Communists have always advocated), and the lowest was 10, elected in 1958 by the single-member system with two ballots. In the 1967 election, the number of Communist Deputies rose from 34 to 73, but this was due to an electoral understanding with the Socialists more than to an increase of voting strength. Party membership remained steady, except for a brief period immediately following the war, when the Communist leadership claimed 800,000 members, and for a few months, a million. Since then, according to official party statements, membership has been round about 400,000.[7]

Since its foundation, the Communist party has been with two brief intervals an opposition party. From 1936 to 1937 it supported the Popular Front Government of Radicals and Socialists (though without holding office in it) and from 1944 to 1947 Communist Ministers were included in all Governments except the brief interim Socialist Government of December 1946. As a general rule, the party refused to vote for all other Governments when the latter asked for the confidence of the National Assembly on taking office, and voted for all motions of censure.[8]

During the last years of the Fourth Republic a number of factors combined to create difficulties for the Communist party. In the first place, the period of economic prosperity and industrial peace that followed on the introduction from 1953 onwards of long-term wage agreements in some of the larger and more strike-prone industries with dominant Communist trade unions, placed the party on the defensive by depriving it of one of its major attractions – the opportunities for exploiting economic grievances. The main Communist-dominated trade-union paper *Le Peuple* was, indeed, reduced to trying to prove to its readers, with the aid of complicated statistics, that they were in reality less well off than they thought – the obvious improvements being in the Communist view merely *relative* – and that the situation was, in accordance with orthodox Marxist doctrine, one of 'absolute impoverishment' (*la paupérisation absolue*).[9] Second, as the most Stalinist party in Europe, the French Communist party found the period of de-Stalinization following the XXth Soviet Congress of

1956 a very painful process, and it was not until 1961 that the Communist leader, Maurice Thorez, could bring himself to stress the 'crimes' of Stalin. Third, the Hungarian revolt of 1956 shook the faith of many working-class members as well as of a significant section of the more articulate intellectual fellow-travellers, who found it difficult to stomach the fact that Soviet guns had been used against Hungarian workers.[10] Fourth, the Algerian problem found the Communist party hesitant and unsure of itself. Communist leaders (in spite of what they claimed later) never came out openly either for or against the continuance of some form of French Algeria, but concentrated their activities as far as possible on the organization of 'peace movements', in which they could combine the objectives of peace in Algeria with hostility to French nuclear policies.[11] And lastly, the period was one of acute internal dissension from 1952 onwards, and prominent Communist leaders who were expelled from the party or its leading organs lost little time in publishing damaging attacks on the leadership.[12]

When General de Gaulle returned to power in 1958, the party touched its lowest electoral level, and the party leaders themselves estimated that about a million and a half Communists had voted for him.[13] Recovery was slow, though the party found popular causes in opposition to police and army treatment of Algerian nationalists and of French sympathizers with them, and later in opposition to the activities of the OAS. But the Berlin air-lift and the Cuban crisis left the Communists more than usually vulnerable to Guy Mollet's often quoted accusation that they were 'not so much on the Left as in the East'. The early 1960s, too, were years of increasing prosperity, and it was not until 1963, with the miners' strike of March, that a strike of any serious proportions took place. The party's situation in Parliament was, moreover, disastrous. Not only were Communist Deputies reduced to ten,[14] but the Standing Orders of the National Assembly as well as the Constitution no longer made possible the kind of permanent obstruction of Parliamentary business that had been a familiar Communist tactic under the Fourth Republic. In the circumstances, there was only one thing to do. The Communists adopted their traditional weakness response: 'if you can't beat them, join them!' and advocated unity of the Left, and this they continued to do consistently throughout the 1960s and into the 1970s.

If this was the only policy that made electoral sense, it did not make political sense. From 1964 to 1971 the only perceptible result of hours of meetings with Socialist delegates to discuss the terms on which united action could be based was the familiar understanding at the second ballot that had been an electoral tradition even under the Third Republic. The party's fortunes varied considerably, however, during these years. From 1962 to 1967 there was a slow recovery of the votes lost in 1958, and from 1965 to 1967 the chances of something more than electoral alliance, though falling short of Socialist–Communist unity, seemed for a time relatively bright. But with the students' and workers' 'revolution' of May 1968, the party once again ran into a period of difficulty.

The improvement (or apparent improvement as it turned out) in Socialist–Communist relations coincided with the failure in June 1965 of the bid made by the leader of the Socialist Parliamentary group, M. Gaston Defferre, to be the presidential candidate of the Left. The Communist party had objected to M. Defferre as being insufficiently anti-clerical, not interested enough in the policy of nationalization, and too anxious to win support from sections of the Centre parties.[15] He was also an enthusiastic 'European', and the Communist party disliked the EEC and regarded the Franco-German treaty as 'an alliance directed against the Socialist countries'.[16] M. Defferre had openly attacked the Communist policy of 'national independence' as being dangerously like Gaullism. 'If, as I believe', he had said, 'the Communists have become Gaullists, then they can vote for de Gaulle. At the present moment they are adopting some queer attitudes.'[17]

M. Defferre had also deplored the lack of democracy within the Communist party. In practice, though the Communists accepted M. François Mitterrand as a more suitable presidential candidate of the united Left, he did not make any more concessions to them than his predecessor had done. However,

by 1967 the Communists had made some significant concessions to the Socialists in the interests of unity. M. Waldeck
Rochet, who had become the leader in 1964 only a few weeks
before the death of Maurice Thorez, conceded Communist
recognition of the existence of the EEC (though the Communist party hoped to change its 'capitalist' organization).[18]
The Communists also agreed to recognise the principle of a
plurality of parties under Socialism,[19] to accept the responsibilities of power together with the Socialists, and to guarantee
to Catholics the maintenance of individual liberties.[20] They
also abandoned the demand for a change in the Constitution
as a prior condition of a common Socialist–Communist programme.[21]

In spite of these concessions, M. Waldeck Rochet was compelled to admit, in January 1968, that the achievement of
unity would still take a long time.[22] The party's recovery was
also taking a long time. Though there was a slight improvement in recruitment from 1964–5 onwards, and a slight increase in Communist votes in the 1965 municipal elections,
there were already signs that reviving interest was taking the
form of demands (mainly from teachers and students) for freer
discussion inside the party. These were already leading to prolonged debates in the student movement on the merits of
'polycentrism'[23] and were destined to lead to more serious
trouble later. There were, indeed, signs of trouble on both the
party's right and left wings. There were already small dissident
revolutionary groups (mainly among students), but in 1966
there was for the first time public criticism of Moscow from
the most orthodox of Communists, when Louis Aragon published a protest against the verdict in the trial of Daniel and
Siniavsky.[24]

From 1968 onwards, the Communist party steadily lost
ground. The May events increased its internal difficulties,
since the leadership had to regain control over the spontaneous
factory groups, or *'groupuscules'*, that had supported the revolutionary students. Communist attempts, first to contain the
movement, and then to use it to step up the pressure for a
united left-wing programme, both failed. At first, there were

Communist attacks on leftist 'adventurers', described as 'false revolutionaries who must be shown up'.²⁵ But events moved too fast, and, by 18 May, the Communists were calling for 'a Government of the people and of democratic union'.²⁶ The Communist-dominated trade-union confederation, the CGT, took part in the marches and demonstrations, but tried as far as possible to restrict the slogans to general support for 'power to the workers' or to specific demands, such as the recognition of trade-union rights in factories, and a forty-hour week.²⁷ They realized that a massive reaction of public opinion in favour of order was likely to produce anti-Communist repercussions, and so were careful, in the election campaign, to wave the tricolour as well as the red flag, and to disavow any connection with the black flag of anarchism.²⁸ They also appealed specifically for order and for working-class discipline. 'We are acting within a framework of legality', said Madame Vaillant-Couturier, a veteran and impeccably orthodox Communist, 'in the certainty that we are defending the interests of the French people.'²⁹

In the event, the party fell between two stools. The Gaullist landslide certainly affected all parties. But the public found the Gaullists more credible defenders of order than the Communist party, while a number of sympathizers with the revolutionaries, particularly among the younger electors, found the Communists no longer credible as revolutionaries. Although the elections showed a slight increase in the Communist vote over the country as a whole, it fell in almost half the *départements*.³⁰

The second blow to the party fortunes was the Soviet invasion of Czechoslovakia, only two months after the election. This was not just Hungary all over again, but a similar shock in a very different climate. In 1956, the French Communist party had still been one in which Stalinist discipline could be maintained, even if only at the cost of successive witch-hunts and expulsions. In 1968, 'polycentrism' was acceptable to many French Communists, and belief in a Czech 'Socialism with a human face' and a Roumanian road to Socialism was widespread. For the first time in the history of the French Communist party, the leadership openly proclaimed its lack of solidarity with the Soviet Union. It is true that the first statement expressing 'surprise and reprobation'[31] was later watered down somewhat (though the party never specifically withdrew it) and that it was speedily followed by the decision not to take any action that might affect the party's relations with the Soviet Union. This was not enough to appease some of the older stalwarts who remained firmly pro-Soviet and opposed to any protest.[32] On the other hand, some of the prominent members more favourable to a greater degree of independence of the Soviet Union – in particular, Louis Aragon and Roger Garaudy – continued to condemn the Soviet action. The leadership was faced with 'opportunist' deviations from both sides!

By 1970, therefore, the French Communist party was facing three major problems. The first was that of its own unity. The resignation in October 1968 from the political bureau of a veteran such as Madame Jeanette Vermeersch, the long-drawn-out public debate first on the Garaudy and then on the Tillon affair, followed by the expulsion of M. Garaudy from the political bureau and the Central Committee in February 1970, and the later expulsion of both from their 'cells', did nothing to improve matters. Nor did the revelations of both 'rebels' on the internal affairs of the party and the unreliability of some of its information do anything to improve the party's image. The second problem was that of the containment of revolutionary leftists, whose verbal attacks were as often directed against the Communist party as against 'bourgeois' society. Their activities were helping to disintegrate the main students' union as well as creating trouble in factories between Communist and CFDT trade-union confederations. And the third problem was the absence of any positive policy capable of reviving rank-and-file interest. At the end of 1969, the acting secretary-general, Georges Marchais, himself had to admit that membership of party cells was falling.[33]

By 1972, the position was, if anything, worse. The Socialist party, under its new leader, M. François Mitterrand, had put off the resumption of Socialist–Communist talks on a joint Governmental programme until the Spring of 1972, by which time both Communist and Socialist parties had produced their own programmes independently. The Communist programme, published in October 1971, contained no spectacular new proposals, but neither did it make any concessions on the outstanding points of disagreement between the two parties. Further talks, therefore, seemed bound to be even more of a deaf men's dialogue than earlier ones had been.

In his study of the Gaullist party, published in 1970, Jean Charlot concluded that

> up to now, only the Communist party has been able to evolve an anti-Gaullist strategy, instead of being content to react as best it can to events.[34]

An anti-Gaullist strategy, however, was not enough. The Communists had, in fact, put all their eggs in one basket – unity of the Left. They had no success and they had no alternative strategy. Indeed, in some ways, they seemed farther away from their goal of a united Left than they had been five or six years earlier. In 1965, Communists, Radicals and Socialists had at least managed to agree on a common left-wing presidential candidate. In 1969, they could not even do that, and so two Communists and two Socialists (three, if the Defferre–Mendès France tandem is counted as two) confronted the electors separately. In February 1970, the nineteenth French Communist party Congress endorsed the official policy of 'an advanced democracy and a peaceful passage to Socialism', an objective in itself sufficiently unrevolutionary to be acceptable to even the most timid member of the non-Communist Left.[35] But the Socialist 'comrades' to whom the Communists appealed for support were by that time far too busy quarrelling amongst themselves (on how best to approach the problem of obtaining a united Left, among other things) to be any more interested in this appeal than they had been in previous ones.

The dilemma of the Communist party in 1971 was that, in its quest for unity, it had ceased to be a credible revolutionary party for many elements among its own clientèle. It had become 'a party like the others', but without being any *more* credible to its non-revolutionary would-be partners as a protagonist of 'advanced democracy' and 'the peaceful passage to Socialism'. The non-Communist Left had, after all, vivid memories of former attempts to work with the Communist party! In such circumstances, it is not easy to explain in a few words the persistence of the Communist appeal for at least four million French electors. But two dominant elements in that appeal at least are obvious. First, a great deal of it is almost wholly nostalgic. It is part of that combination of essential political conservatism and revolutionary romanticism that characterizes French left-wing politics in general, with the difference that – as André Siegfried had noted in some profound pages thirty or forty years earlier – the Communist party proclaims itself as the *most* Left and as such is the most attractive.[36] In this capacity it supplies to intellectuals the doctrinal wholeness, the systematic analysis, the philosophical basis, the political universalism that have for so long formed the traditional framework of the political ideas of the Left. To the working class, as well as to intellectuals, it supplies too the familiar Republican, Revolutionary and Marxist vocabulary. Indeed, it supplies precisely the same brand of 'pseudo-revolutionary verbiage' that the official Communist party rightly accuses the 'leftist' dissident movements of supplying. Nowadays the latter are more attractive to some of the younger elements because they do sometimes produce at least mini-pseudo-revolutions, whereas official Communist vocabulary is no longer intended to have this effect.

In his *Caliban parle*, published in 1928, Jean Guéhenno has given an unforgettable portrait of the French left-wing revolutionary as a permanent victim of the 'establishment'. In a moment of truth, his Caliban admits that he is

the maker and the dupe of revolutions. That is my destiny. . . . I ensure the victory of others, but am never myself the victor. When the revolution is over, I am still at the door of the palace, like a dismissed domestic servant. . . . It's always the same. When I've torn up the paving stones, manned the barricades, occupied the Central Post Office, put to flight, merely by showing my face, the Prefect of Police and the

Minister of the Interior, and flown the flag of the new system from the tops of public buildings, a gentleman followed by a number of prominent personalities, comes up to me, shakes me by the hand, makes a speech about my traditional qualities and then, to the strains of the national anthem, leads me gently to the door with copious advice on the desirability of my going peacefully home. [37]

In 1968, the basic difference between the revolutionary extremists and the orthodox Communist party was that the latter had long since recognized the fact that the French workers did not want real revolution, while the former clung to the fiction of the workers as the revolutionary 'victim' of the bourgeoisie.

The second dominant appeal of the French Communist party is the hold that it has on the working class, by virtue of its disciplined and effective organization for action, whether in the field of industrial negotiation with employers' organizations or in the field of strikes and political or industrial demonstrations. The intellectual may be satisfied with gestures and symbolic pseudo-revolutionary outbursts. The workers can also expect to obtain practical benefits in the shape of wage increases that the Communist party and the Communist trade-union organization, the CGT, (in practice a subsidiary of the party) are far better organized to obtain than are the other left-wing parties and trade unions. And even when the latter succeed, as they sometimes do, in taking the lead, the Communists are usually able to steal a good deal of their thunder and take much of the credit. Their efficiency is, ironically, one of the main obstacles to the achievement of closer relations with parties and trade unions on the non-Communist Left, whom long experience has taught to be wary of Communist 'comradeship', precisely because it risks becoming a Communist take-over. The French Communist party has, too, a considerable peasant vote in some regions, which is rare among Communist parties in developed countries.

There is, however, no guarantee that this appeal will be as strong in the political climate of the 1970s. Even behind the iron curtain, the undemocratic organization of Communist parties is coming under fire. In France, it has already been a major cause of friction. A tightly controlled, vertical structure and communications, together with party decisions and elections in which there is no real opposition and which are a foregone conclusion, are ceasing to be acceptable in an age in which there is a general demand, particularly among the younger generation, for more opportunities for rank-and-file members, as well as for ordinary citizens, to have a say, and perhaps a share, in the running of affairs that concern them. It is doubtful whether the French Communist party will be able to retain its hold on the working class without relaxing discipline much more than its leaders seem prepared to do, and indeed, perhaps more than they can afford to do, without threatening the entire internal discipline on which much of their former militancy has depended.

SOCIALISM

Throughout General de Gaulle's presidency, the French Socialist party was dominated by two incompatible obsessions: the first was the belief in the need for a Socialist–Communist understanding or, failing that, for Socialist–Communist electoral agreements in order to defeat Gaullism; the second was the belief that Gaullism could be defeated only by a combination of the Centre and the non-Communist Left. The Socialist dilemma was twofold. First, neither of these alliances was likely to be stronger numerically than the Gaullist forces, yet a condition of each was the non-inclusion of one of the partners of the other. The Centre was uneasy at the prospect of an alliance including Communists, while an alliance between Socialists and Centre parties alienated both the Communist party and sections of the Socialist party. Second, even if an electoral coalition stretching from Centre to Communists could have succeeded in winning an election, the victors would have found it impossible to agree on a Governmental programme.

In these circumstances, it is not surprising that the history of the Socialist party during these years should be one of in-

creasing ineffectiveness and decline. There were also more profound causes of weakness in French Socialism. Though the
idea has a long history going back to. the late years of the
eighteenth century, and a number of Socialist movements were
already in existence by the 1880s, they were from the start
divided, and the whole history of the Socialist movement has
been one of repeated attempts and failures to prevent internal
divisions from becoming a dominant preoccupation or resulting (as they have done) in disruption and impotence. This basic
weakness creates a special problem for the Parliamentary
group. There were Socialists in the French Parliament by 1881.
In 1903, six rival Socialist parties were reduced to two, and in
1905 a single unified party was finally created, though not
without the arbitration of the Socialist International. Its title,
Section française de l'Internationale ouvrière (SFIO), did at least
survive intact up to 1969, but it was never a united party.
Throughout these years, its divisions ranged from near-
anarchism and Marxist authoritarianism to a democratic and
humanist conception of Socialism that recognized affinities
with other democratic parties. The permanence of divisions
meant that a democratic party organization had to recognize
organized minorities and provide for the regular expression
of their points of view. Once a Parliamentary party has the
prospect of participating in Government, it is inevitably
weakened both by a party organization that reflects division
instead of decision, and by the difficulties that this situation
creates in the relations between the Parliamentary organization
and the party executive.

In its sixty-seven years of existence up to 1972, the party
went through five distinct stages. During the Third Republic,
it gained ground until, in 1919 and 1924, it had over 100
Deputies in the Chamber, and 144 in 1936, when Socialists
and Radicals formed a Popular Front Government. By then
Socialists had already replaced Radicals as the strongest party
on the Left. The war, however, found the party divided, as it
did other parties. It nevertheless emerged from the occupation
as a resistance party of great prestige and influence, increased
by the fact that, for some years following the war, both the

Radical and conservative parties remained in a state of relative weakness, having been even more dislocated by the wartime problems created by collaboration with the Germans or with the Vichy Government. A new party, the predominantly Catholic MRP, had, however, rapidly established itself as a third left-wing party and MRP, Socialists and Communists between them held three-quarters of the seats in the 1945 provisional Assembly. The Socialists occupied the key position, in that their support was indispensable to the formation of all Governments. This remained largely true even after 1947, when the Communist party went into opposition and the Radicals were beginning to recover some of their pre-war strength. Socialists were, in fact, represented in all Governments of the Fourth Republic except those between February 1950 and July 1956 and General de Gaulle's Government in June 1958. Between 1944 and 1947 they were the essential link between the Communists and the MRP; and from 1951 onwards, with a permanent Communist opposition of between 150 and 180 and a Gaullist opposition of about 120 between 1951 and 1953, the remaining conservative, Centre and Radical groups could govern only with the co-operation, or at least the support, of the Socialist group in the National Assembly.

From 1947 onwards, however, the position of the Socialists became progressively more difficult. Compelled to accept, either directly or indirectly, the responsibilities of government, they were less well placed to compete for working-class votes with a Communist party which, being permanently in opposition, was not called on to apply the policies it defended in election campaigns and in Parliamentary debates. The presence of the MRP on its right worsened the position of the Socialist party in at least two ways. To co-operate with a pro-Catholic party which favoured State aid to Catholic schools, and one, moreover, whose supporters still included a number of Gaullist sympathizers, was to hand over valuable propaganda assets to the Communists. The latter could appear as the defenders of both traditional left-wing anti-clericalism and working-class interests, undiluted by association with a partially 'bourgeois' party. Yet the more the Socialists were driven to assert their left-wing and Marxist principles in order to keep up with the Communists, the more they alienated possible sympathizers on their right, particularly among the MRP, whose co-operation in Governments was essential to them. For the MRP's social policies were in the main well to the left of those of the Radical party, the Socialist party's traditional governmental partner. In any case, it was not until the early 1950s that the Radical party's Parliamentary representation came near to equalling that of the MRP, by then already in decline.

Throughout the remaining years of the Fourth Republic, the Socialist party entered on a third stage in which it never regained the attraction that it had had during the immediate post-war years. It was further weakened in 1958, when General de Gaulle returned to power, by the formation of the dissident Socialist *Parti socialiste autonome* (PSA),[38] which meant that henceforth it had to face the risk of being outflanked by two parties on its left. What it lost in membership it might have gained in cohesion – since the elements forming the dissident party were among the least amenable to party discipline – if it had not been for the fact that the party itself was divided on both constitutional and political issues.

As it was, the evolution of the Socialist party during this third phase, which lasted well into the Fifth Republic, continued to be downhill all the way.[39] The 1958 policy of 'constructive opposition' involved support for General de Gaulle on Algeria, but the opportunities for effective opposition on anything else were limited both by the fall in Socialist and Communist representation in the 1958 Assembly and by the provisions of the new Constitution restricting opportunities for effective opposition in debate. The party was reluctant to regard the Constitution as anything but a temporary concession to General de Gaulle and, therefore, wasted a great deal of time in theoretical discussions on the kind of Constitution that ought to replace it, once it was safe to defeat Gaullism. It also fell back on that traditional Socialist occupation in times of defeat – the reconsideration of its Marxist principles. The net result was that it gave an impression of contracting out of practical politics and retiring happily to traditional opposition tactics and sterile doctrinal family disagreements. The 1962 election revealed the inability of the opposition parties to combine beyond the point of saying 'No' to de Gaulle.[40] The party leaders were conscious of ageing membership, yet unable to discover how to make the party attractive to the young.

It was the approach of the 1965 presidential election that galvanized it into action and marked the beginning of the fourth stage in its evolution, characterized at first by a recovery of both energy and optimism, if not of numerical strength. The decision of the leader of the Socialist Parliamentary group, Gaston Defferre, to present himself as the potential Parliamentary candidate of a united non-Communist Left was officially endorsed at the beginning of 1964, and from then until the breakdown of the attempt in June 1965 there were at least positive and practical problems to argue about. The problems were, indeed, many and difficult to resolve, and those that concerned the Federation of the Left, proposed by M. Defferre and later achieved by M. Mitterrand, are discussed briefly later. For the Socialist party itself, there were also a number of major difficulties. The party was not agreed on what the political rôle of a non-Gaullist President ought to be, and this led to familiar constitutional theorizing, in the course of which M. Defferre seemed at times unsure of himself and failed to reassure his fellow Socialists.[41] There was a division between those Socialists who really wanted the association to be between what they regarded as 'like-minded' organizations, that is, Socialists and associated trade unions and political Clubs, those who believed that it could not succeed without some understanding with the Communists, those who were hostile to any understanding with the Communists, and those who feared that M. Defferre's plan for association with non-Socialist and non-Communist parties would undermine the undenominational character of State education.[42] The inclusion of the MRP was particularly feared as being likely to weaken the Federation's 'Socialist' content.

The upshot of it all was that at a meeting of the Socialist National Council (18-19 July 1965), the party decided by 2998 votes to 2053 to entrust M. Guy Mollet with the task of setting up a different kind of federation, restricted to members of the 'Socialist family', a decision which did nothing to improve relations between Molletists and Defferrists within the party.[43] The Federation of the Democratic and Socialist Left, set up in the autumn of 1965, with François Mitterrand as its President, aroused much less dissension in the party, and certainly helped to increase Socialist Parliamentary representation in the elections of 1967. But it, in turn, broke up after the 1968 elections, because it had already lost its immediate *raison d'être*, which was to defeat the Gaullists in that election. From 1969, the party entered on a fifth phase, heralded by prolonged discussions. A new Socialist party[44] came officially into existence on 4 May, though it was not until the constitutive conference the following July that its precise aims and organizations were decided. Circumstances were not auspicious since, in the meantime, the new party had had to choose a presidential candidate, and disagreements over both candidate and policies recalled the bad old days and ways of the deceased party to an extent that justified the impression that little had changed except the name.

The conference of July 1969, indeed, already revealed major and complex divisions of opinion.[45] There was agreement that the new Socialist party must condemn capitalism, be reserved towards the Communist party, and oppose Centrism, but it was left to a later conference to work out the political implications of these general principles. The inclusion in the party of Alain Savary's *Union des Clubs pour le Renouveau de la Gauche* (UCRG) and some members of other political Clubs created political as well as administrative difficulties, because most of the Clubs wanted an understanding not only with the Communist party, but also with the PSU, formerly the PSA. Some members had refused to be represented at the conference at all, because they were apprehensive (probably justifiably) lest their organizations should lose their identity within a monolithic party.

A number of decisions were finally reached. The emphasis was henceforth to be on collective leadership. The secretary-general of the old SFIO was, therefore, replaced by a 'first secretary' who was to be regarded as a spokesman, but not as party leader. The *comité directeur* chosen by conference was retained. Since the pursuit of power was not to be regarded as an absolute priority in the Socialist party there were to be no alliances with 'political forces representing capitalism', which meant no alliances with Centre parties. This was exactly one month after the party had advised its members to vote at the second ballot in the presidential elections for the Centre candidate, Alain Poher. Its major aim was to be 'the union of the Left' (which was precisely what it had failed to achieve during the previous seven years). This union must be based on a programme inspired by Socialist principles. Yet the choice of partners must not be made on the basis of past political divisions.[46]

Relations with the Communist party were to be discussed in a public debate on the methods by which capitalist forces were to be opposed and the transition to Socialism brought about. It was to be a debate undertaken with no undue readiness to condone Communist errors (*sans complaisance*) and without any prior implications regarding Communist attitudes towards current problems in Eastern Europe. The party's attitude to sympathizers with 'leftist' views was to be 'neither negative nor paternalistic', but was also to be '*sans complaisance*'. Trade unions were to remain independent of the party, but the latter was to try to convince them that their ends would be achieved only within a Socialist framework that it was their duty to help to create.

The new first secretary, Alain Savary,[47] summed up the party's immediate tasks as being the achievement of Socialist co-operation, the unity of the Left and the adoption of methods making possible a Socialist majority. The continuing and over-riding preoccupation with questions of internal organization and of relations with other left-wing parties would, in itself, have necessarily reduced questions of Socialist policy to second place, even if these had not been rendered even less attractive by the Left's permanent state of ineffectual opposition throughout the Fifth Republic, by the extent of sympathy in Socialist circles (and even more in Communist circles) for certain aspects of Gaullist foreign policy, and by the obvious and irreconcilable conflicts between Socialist and Communist policies.

On the policies of *détente* with the Eastern bloc, American withdrawal from Vietnam, and French withdrawal from NATO, the Socialists' only real quarrel with Gaullism was about methods. The official Socialist policy of simultaneous dissolution of both the NATO and Warsaw alliances was no more than a pious hope; indeed, it was not even that, but merely a device to provide a verbal compromise that might be acceptable to both Socialists and Communists. In principle, the Socialists opposed the Gaullist policy of 'national independence', which the Communists accepted. They believed that the French nuclear deterrent should be 'European', while the Communists wanted it to be abolished.[48] They were in favour of British membership of the Common Market, though not prepared to press for any easier conditions than those imposed by the French Government.[49] Nor were they prepared to accept the stringent conditions put forward by the Communist party.[50] They remained faithful to the idea of political unity in a supranational 'Europe' and fearful of the influence of Gaullist nationalism on Germany. 'The Rhône', said Guy Mollet, 'is not a credible barrier against the contagion of nationalism'. The Communists, however, shared General de Gaulle's belief in national sovereignty.

In internal policy, successive party declarations did no more than repeat earlier statements on familiar themes, such as

i) the need for constitutional and legal measures to protect civic rights and political liberties, including the suppression of special courts, improvements in the position of women, recognition of the rights of trade unions in factories, more freedom of the press and radio, greater independence of local administration from the centralizing control of Paris, and the revision of some articles of the Constitution in order to restore some of its past authority to Parliament;[51]

ii) the need for economic and social reforms aiming at greater citizen participation, increased purchasing power through better wages, salaries and pensions, reforms of the social-security system, the creation of new jobs, the reduction of hours of work, a lower retirement age, equality of opportunity in education, increased State expenditure on housing, the prevention of speculation in building land, the nationalization of merchant banks, armament and space industries;

iii) the need to democratize French planning;

iv) the need for workers' control in nationalized sectors and the right of workers to increased supervision of the running of industries in the private sector. . . .

This list is merely a brief summary of the 120 social and economic reforms put forward in the 1968 joint declaration of the Federation of the Democratic and Socialist Left and the Communist party, described by a prominent Socialist as being characterized by 'a degree of verbalism that has nothing revolutionary about it'.[52] The 'plan for Socialist action', accepted unanimously at the constitutive Congress of the new party, held in July 1969, was briefer than the federal programme of the previous year, but even more ambitious.[53] It was followed by an 'action programme', adopted in June 1970, which contained no surprises. The only real change was that 43 Socialist and 13 Radical Deputies in the National Assembly sat, from October 1969 onwards, as two separate organizations, though not as two separate groups, since the Radicals, not having the requisite number of members to form a Parliamentary group, became 'affiliates' of the Socialist party 'for administrative purposes'. The change was, therefore, minimal. For the rest, the same faces were seen and the same voices heard on Socialist platforms, advocating the same policies, even if some had moved up and others down in the party hierarchy.[54] In October 1969, *Le Monde*'s political correspondent reported that

The Socialists are still proposing an ideological debate with the PSU, which is of little interest to the Communist party. The PSU still doubts the utility of party 'summit talks', and the *Convention des Institutions républicaines* [CIR] has decided to go its own way.

Each of the left-wing organizations is camping firmly on its own ground.[55]

By the end of 1971, there had been more profound changes in Socialist party organization, but these did nothing to make the ostensible objectives of the Socialist party look any less remote. In 1969 and 1970, the inclusion in the reorganized party of a number of leftward-looking and individualistic political Clubs had been feared by some Socialists as being likely to undermine still further whatever cohesion still existed in the party. In 1970, it seemed as if this process had already begun. At the end of 1969, André Chandernagor, a Socialist Deputy who had always regarded the pursuit of unity with the Communists as both undesirable and unrealistic, had formed *Démocratie socialiste*, a movement including Radicals and Centrists as well as Socialists. It was not intended to form a splinter party, though it was doubtful whether a split could be prevented.[56] A small dissident Socialist party (*Le Parti démocrate socialiste indépendant*) in sympathy with M. Chandernagor's views was formed a few months later.[57] The powerful Nord and Bouches-du-Rhône federations were known to include a number of opponents of the official party policy of *rapprochement* with the Communist party.[58]

The further step taken in 1971 towards what it was hoped would be a more united Socialist party was the unification of the party, as reconstituted in 1969, with M. Mitterrand's CIR. This involved a hard-fought debate on the reorganization of the party's governing bodies. Alain Savary was replaced as first secretary by François Mitterrand – only three days after the latter had become a member of the party.

The immediate changes were not such as to encourage confidence in the prospects of the 1971 'Socialist party'. First, the party returned to the habit that M. Mollet had succeeded in eradicating, namely, that of providing for the proportional representation of organized minorities in its governing bodies. Second, so closely fought were the battles in the Congress that it was thanks only to an improbable alliance between M. Mitterrand's leftward-looking CIR and the more 'conservative' federations of the Nord and Bouches-du-Rhône, that he obtained a majority. In reality, what separated the two dominant groups – that led by M. Mitterrand and supported by MM. Defferre and Mauroy, and that led by MM. Mollet and Savary and supported by M. Poperen – was personalities more than policies, and the differences concerned party organization more than attitudes to the Communist party and left-wing unity, on which their differences were tactical only. The only immediately perceptible consequences of this further party reorganization were the election of a far more heterogeneous directing committee and bureau, what looked like the definitive relegation of M. Mollet to a back seat, and the postponement of a resumption of talks with the Communist party for nine months. It was a fragile and improbable base from which to build up the new left-wing dynamic that the party was ostensibly seeking.[59] It was an even more improbable base from which to negotiate a joint Socialist–Communist programme, since the new party spent the following nine months gestating its own party programme, to be submitted to a party convention (after having been considered by the departmental federations) in March 1972. Communists and Socialists would both then, presumably, be in the unpromising situation of being committed to their own programmes, incorporating decisions on, for instance, workers' control (*autogestion*), foreign policy, including nuclear defence, education and politics – on all of which the two parties were in disagreement with each other as well as with the PSU. It could hardly be expected, therefore, that 1972 would be the year of left-wing unity. But if unity was an ever-receding goal, it was still an ever-present preoccupation that, more than anything else, prevented the party from concentrating on the vital problem of making itself more attractive to the electors.

RADICALISM

Though the Radicals never succeeded under the Fifth Republic in attaining the requisite number of Deputies to constitute an official Parliamentary group, there are a number of reasons for

continuing to include them among the six Parliamentary
'families'. Radicals continued to play a rôle in local politics
and in the Senate, and their importance in the controversies
of the Left was out of all proportion to the party's numerical
strength. Whatever the future of Radicalism, it will still be
essential for a long time to come to take account of the past
political influence of Radicalism in order to understand the
politics of the Left. General de Gaulle is reported to have said
that everyone in France had been, was, or would be a Gaullist,
a remark that was wholly inaccurate. But few politicians and
political parties of the Left and Centre–Left have escaped the
influence of Radicalism, that is of certain Radical attitudes
shared also by a number of groups with which the Radical party
has at one time or another been in alliance.

The Socialist-Radical party, or *Le Parti républicain-radical et
radical-socialiste* to give its full name, is the oldest of all French
political parties. Formed in 1901, it quickly became the largest
and most important party in the Chamber of Deputies. It was
never Socialist, and differed from the other left-wing parties in
being highly individualistic and very loosely organized. It was
always a party of local notabilities, of committees, of local
party organizations enjoying a high degree of autonomy, not a
mass party. It has never claimed to be based on any political
ideology, but its strong Republicanism, anti-clericalism, belief in universal suffrage, and in the equal right of all citizens
to a State-controlled education have given it an unchallenge-
able place on the Left, in spite of an individualistic economic
conservatism that made it equally out of touch with the
nationalizing enthusiasm of the Socialist and Communist
parties in the 1940s and with their emphasis on mass action in
the 1960s. Its greatest period was in the early years of the
century, when it achieved the separation of Church and State
and a comprehensive State educational system. By 1936, though
it could still command 23% of the votes and had over 100
Deputies, it had already been overtaken by the Socialist party.

The position of the Radicals, on the right of the Left and the
left of the Right, made them essentially a Government party,
whereas, as has already been said, the history of both Socialist

and Communist parties is predominantly one of political opposition. Of the 41 Governments formed between the wars, Radical Prime Ministers headed 18, and their attachment to the Constitution that the majority was anxious to change in 1945 increased their post-war unpopularity as the party that, in the view of many Frenchmen, was associated more than any other with the policies and the failures of the Third Republic. In 1945, with only 29 Deputies, the Radical party was the smallest of the post-war parties, yet even during these years of post-war weakness it was not without influence. Of the 21 Governments of the Fourth Republic, ten were headed by Radical Prime Ministers, and two by the like-minded Left-Centre party with which it was closely associated, the *Union démocratique et socialiste de la Résistance* (UDSR).[60] Between 1947 and 1953, both Parliamentary assemblies were presided over by Radicals.[61] The Radical group in the Senate, the *Gauche démocratique*, was in 1948 the largest group in that House and, even in 1958, when the strength of the Radicals in the National Assembly had declined to 23 and their share of the vote had fallen to 11%, the Radical group in the Senate was still second only to the conservative *Indépendants*.

The party was much weakened during the later years of the Fourth Republic by its own internal quarrels which led to a series of splits. For two years, following the retirement of M. Herriot from the presidency of the party, M. Mendès France, as its effective leader, tried to transform it into a disciplined party, with a programme supported by its united votes. This attempt failed, and though the elections of 1956 revealed considerable support for M. Mendès France, particularly among the the younger sections of the electorate,[62] the bitter hostility to his plans from sections of his own party led to the formation in 1956 of two separate dissident Radical groups, the *Rassemblement des Gauches républicaines* (RGR) formed by Edgar Faure, and the *Centre républicain* led by André Morice. The former did not survive the events of 1958. The latter, whose members were in favour of keeping Algeria French, voted for General de Gaulle and the new Constitution and continued to exist in the Fifth Republic, but remained small and almost wholly extra-Parliamentary. In 1958, M. Mendès France himself left the party and, with a few supporters, contested the election of 1958 as part of the *Union des Forces démocratiques* which opposed General de Gaulle and the new Constitution.

Between 1958 and 1970, the Radical party remained consistently in opposition.[63] During these years, it went through three distinct phases. The first, which lasted up to about 1964, was one of great difficulty. The older leaders – Edouard Herriot, Edouard Daladier, Henri Queuille, René Mayer – had gone, and the younger generation – Félix Gaillard, Maurice Faure, Maurice Bourgès-Maunoury, René Billères – were rivals and often differed greatly on policies.[64] Edgar Faure did not return to the Radical fold until 1961 and he remained in it for only a few years. In 1962, the Radicals polled only 8% of the vote, though they formed with members of other small groups, including the rump of the UDSR, a heterogeneous group of some 40 Deputies.[65] This was essentially a period of convalescence.

The second period, from 1964 to 1968, was that of association and ultimately, in 1966, federation, with the Socialist party as a member of the Federation of the Democratic and Socialist Left – an association in which Radicals were not merely uneasy allies of the Socialists, but also divided among themselves about the desirability of the whole idea. Sections led by Félix Gaillard and Maurice Bourgès-Maunoury wanted to give priority to the problem of unity within the party; sections led by Maurice Faure and René Billères were conscious of the need to seek strength through association with other parties, but divided as to where to look for partners. The former favoured *rapprochement* with the Centre, and in particular with the MRP, while the latter was drawn to the Socialist party. Though the Billères view prevailed, the Radicals were never happy as the allies of a party that was liable to become an ally of the Communist party. There was also strong objection from the Radicals to the proposals for an immediate move towards fusion within the Federation, that were put forward at the beginning of 1968. The party finally decided in favour of 'an association of a confederal type'[66] and of collaboration with 'Republicans belonging to the opposition', by which was meant, of course, with Centre parties, a course to which the Socialist party was becoming steadily more opposed. In November 1968, by which time the Federation was already dead, the Radical Congress reaffirmed these decisions, and decided merely to accept 'administrative affiliation' of the 13 Radical Deputies with the Socialist group in the National Assembly, a procedure that was mutually convenient, but involved no political commitment of any kind to the Socialists.

By this time, the Radical party had reached its lowest ebb. There was talk of 'the total indifference of public opinion towards Radicals' and of disagreements between local federations and active Radical party workers.[67] In October 1969, Jean-Jacques Servan-Schreiber, then editor of *l'Express*, an influential weekly with *Mendésiste* sympathies, was made secretary-general of the party and given the task of producing within 100 days proposals for its reorganization and modernization. The party had entered a third phase of would-be Radical renewal, which proved eventful if nothing else. A year later, it could certainly not be said that there was public indifference towards Radicalism – or at least not towards the Radical secretary-general. His 197-page manifesto, *Ciel et Terre*, was duly published on 28 January 1970, three months after his appointment. Its claim to give Radicalism a new image was based essentially on four main innovations designed to reconcile the Radical party's acceptance of a competitive, market economy with the intention to deal in a humane way with the problems of the new industrial age. First, capitalist concerns were to stand on their own feet and were thus, within a period of five years, to stop counting on subsidies except for special purposes, such as research and development. Second, measures were to be taken to lessen social differences, and these would include the replacement of military service by a form of social service, and increased provision for deprived children, women and the old. Third, hereditary privilege would be ended, first by the abolition of inherited wealth, except for small family estates on which death duties would cease to be paid, and by taxes on wealth. And fourth, regionalism would be developed as a means of democratizing the centres of decision-making.

The report certainly created a great deal of interest, some admiration, but more criticism. The main comments were that it was a diagnosis, but not a cure;[68] that it was an expression of hopes rather than a statement of policies;[69] that it was either impossibly utopian or merely a 'gimmick';[70] that it would be impossible to apply the proposals relating to inheritance without bringing a financial crisis;[71] and that, either the new Radical secretary-general had chosen the wrong party, or the party had chosen the wrong secretary-general,[72] since the Radical party would never accept such a plan. In fact, the special Radical Congress held to consider it did accept it in principle,[73] though the President, Félix Gaillard, was certainly opposed to it.

The secretary-general's ideas were, however, overshadowed during the following months by the interest aroused by his methods in a quite different field. In June, he successfully contested a by-election in Nancy, in a spectacular American-style campaign based almost entirely on local issues. He was, in his own words, offering himself as an 'Ambassador for Lorraine'. In September, he unsuccessfully contested a by-election in Bordeaux, in which he opposed the Prime Minister, M. Chaban Delmas, who was also Mayor of Bordeaux. Since neither the Prime Minister nor the Radical secretary-general and Deputy for Nancy intended to sit for Bordeaux if elected (for the office of Prime Minister was constitutionally incompatible with membership of the National Assembly, and M. Servan-Schreiber was ineligible to sit for Bordeaux while remaining as he said he would do, the Deputy for Nancy) the purposes of the contest were clearly propagandist. The Prime Minister obtained a striking vote of confidence in Gaullist policies, while his most spectacular opponent[74] obtained a no less striking vote of no confidence, at the cost of dividing still more the Left, whose unity he was in theory there to promote. But he did obtain a vast amount of publicity, not all of it favourable, and it was comprehensible in the circumstances that there should have been frequent allegations that personal publicity had been his main aim.[75]

When the shouting died down, it was difficult to see in what way either *Ciel et Terre* or the activities of the Radical secretary-general[76] were likely to bring about a Radical revival. His election as President of the party by the 1971 Congress threatened, indeed, to produce a split. A fortnight later (on 3 November), the Radical party and the *Centre démocrate*, led by M. Lecanuet, announced that they had united to form the *Mouvement réformateur*, whose main purpose would be to co-ordinate electoral strategy. It became immediately clear that the two leaders, as well as the rank and file of the Radical party, disagreed on electoral strategy. The rift between the section of the Radical party led by the outgoing President and the rest widened. When the two parties ratified the agreement regarding the *Mouvement réformateur*, it was far from clear what exactly was being ratified. The future of Radicalism remained, therefore, in some doubt, as it had been throughout the Fifth Republic.

THE LESSONS OF THE FEDERAL INTERLUDE

The actual experiment of limited federation between Socialists, Radicals and a number of political Clubs, which lasted only from 10 September 1966 to the summer of 1968, arose from the ashes of the abortive Defferre attempt between 1964 and 1965 to organize a widely based non-Communist federation. It differed from that attempt, however, in ruling out from the start any effort to attract the support of Centre parties. The main difficulty, and that on which the Defferre plan had eventually foundered, had been that of finding any basis on which the MRP and the Communists could agree. The Socialist party would not give up the idea of Socialist–Communist alliance, though, as has already been said, the prospect of any Socialist–Communist understanding, other than electoral, was always remote.[77] All that the relentless Socialist pursuit of this will-o'-the-wisp really achieved was, therefore, to make their Radical partners in the new Federation wary and lukewarm from the outset. This fact, together with the problems introduced by the presence within it of some of the political Clubs, and the divisions within the Socialist party itself on the evolution of the Federation, never justified much optimism regarding its survival.

Since the Mitterrandist Federation included neither Centre, PSU nor Communists, it was, on the face of it, a much more homogeneous organization than its Defferrist predecessor, though it was, of necessity, dominated by the Socialists. Divided internally as it was, it involved in reality nothing more than the constitution of a single Parliamentary group in the 1967 National Assembly, together with an electoral alliance of the traditional kind with both Communists and PSU, in which its position was strengthened by the fact that it could negotiate as a single entity. Since it left virtually no trace, the experiment was not in itself important, and the facts of its brief life can be summarized in a few paragraphs. It does, however, provide a striking illustration of the fundamental difficulties and fundamental weakness of the French non-Communist Left.

Following the breakdown of M. Defferre's proposed *'grande federation'*, on 18 June 1965, the Socialist party had agreed in principle to form a Socialist-based democratic federation, and this, duly created on 10 September, provided in its Constitution for a careful weighting of the representation of its three 'families'.[78] The achievement of the single left-wing candidate, François Mitterrand, in obtaining 32% of the vote at the first ballot of the presidential election raised unduly hopes of left-wing co-operation, as did the Federation's success in increasing the representation of the non-Communist Left in the general election of 1967. But this was due to an electoral alliance with both the Communist party and the PSU, which included no provisions for a common programme either in Government or in opposition.[79] Thus the Gaullist majority, though so reduced as to be statistically almost non-existent, remained safe from political challenge during the fifteen months that elapsed before the following election, after which the Federation broke up.

A number of policy documents were produced by the Federation, on electoral tactics, on proposals for economic and social reforms, the defence of individual liberties, and so on, which did no more than reaffirm the general principles laid down in its constitutive Charter in July 1966.[80] Two agreements were reached with the Communist party. The first, on 20 December 1966, provided for the traditional alliance of left-wing parties at the second ballot. It was the first positive agreement between Radicals, Socialists and Communists since 1945, but it fell far short of the common programme and common candidates at the first ballot that would have justified some belief in the possible achievement of the unity of the Left. The second agreement was the declaration of 24 February 1968, described as a joint declaration by the Federation and the Communist party, though it was, in reality, a declaration of agreement on some questions of general principle, accompanied by a statement of their specific disagreements on numerous questions of both internal and external policy.[81] If evidence had still been needed of the impossibility of achieving an agreed political programme, this document provided it.

The reduction of the combined left-wing representation in the 1968 National Assembly to under 100[82] reduced the Left as a whole to Parliamentary impotence. The Radicals, who had been uneasy for some time, and who particularly disliked agreements with the Communists, officially buried the Federation at their annual conference the following autumn. The Federation had presented them with four main problems. First, they did not want to be automatically committed to vote for left-wing candidates at the second ballot, but wanted their local party federations to have a voice in determining electoral tactics.[83] Second, they were divided on the question of contacts with the Centre. Third, they did not want a common platform, since they refused to compromise on questions such as their fidelity to the Atlantic alliance, Europe and political democracy. And finally, they were suspicious of Socialist plans for the future of the Federation, and hostile to M. Mitterrand's CIR. In other words, they remained Radicals, resistant to discipline, particularly that imposed by national executives. They therefore proposed to substitute for the Federation a loose form of 'confederal' co-operation that would preserve their traditional freedom of action. The Socialists retreated no less happily into the close family relationship that many of them had wanted all along – a reorganized Socialist party that would accept (that is, absorb) any Radicals or members of the Clubs prepared to agree to its terms.

Whether the Federation achieved anything positive is debatable. It made an attempt to recognize and remedy the Left's perennial inability to discipline its minorities in order to present a coherent Governmental programme to the electorate. But the attempt did not succeed. The *'contre-gouvernement'* formed by M. Mitterrand in 1966 never looked remotely like a real shadow Cabinet, nor even like the 'good public relations gimmick' that the Gaullists saw it as.[84] Two political facts help to explain the defeat. The first was the electoral conservatism of the parties of the Left and the political dilemmas that it created throughout the Fifth Republic.

> The tragedy of the Federation [wrote Jacques Fauvet in May 1966] is that it has no electoral future except with the help of the votes supplied by M. Waldeck Rochet and no governmental future except with the votes supplied by M. Lecanuet. Its temptation is to evade this difficulty by refusing, or alternatively accepting, a commitment to both – in other words, by refusing to choose between them.[85]

The inability of parties of the Left to persuade the electors to change their habits was in great measure due to the second political fact, which was the unwillingness (or inability) of party leaders to change the characteristics that more than anything else alienated precisely the sections of the public that they hoped to attract. The experiment of the Federation only underlined what had been clear during all the years of talk about unity, which was that each party, and each section within divided parties, was in favour of unity only on its own terms. But so permanent and deeply rooted were their divisions that the organization of the Federation itself simply provided an additional subject of division, and an additional arena for carrying on old disputes. This was a game that appealed only to those playing it, as General de Gaulle had not failed to realize when he so frequently castigated the traditional parties for their addiction to 'party games'.[86] The game itself was an eccentric kind of political musical chairs in which the number of players and chairs remained unchanged, because when it came to the point no player was prepared to accept the removal of his own chair. For the Federation ever to have had a chance of becoming an integrated body, there would have had to be real compromises, not merely verbal declarations of intention. By the beginning of 1972, left-wing unity seemed more remote than at any time during the twelve years of the régime. The Gaullists were well aware, even if their opponents were not, that the divisions and uncertainties of the non-Communist opposition were among their own most powerful political assets.

CHAPTER VIII

The Parliamentary Parties
(ii) The Centre and the Right

THE CENTRE

According to Jean Charlot, 'Centrism' has no specific characteristics and, for most people, is identified with the policy of
European unification. It is, in any case, off-centre, being
nearer to Gaullism than to the Left, and lacks the main attraction of Gaullism, which is the confidence it creates in its
capacity to ensure political stability.[1] Maurice Duverger sees
'Centrists' as people who cannot agree whether it is better to try
to influence Gaullism from the inside or to oppose it from the
outside.[2] Centrists themselves emphasize their unwillingness
to pose their problem in that way. Where the aim of Gaullism
is to create a political bi-polarization that reduces political
choice effectively to the alternatives of Gaullism or a Left of
which the Communists would be the dominant element, their
aim is a tri-partite division, and the search, not merely for a
French, but for a 'European' majority 'made up of those who
are neither revolutionaries nor conservatives'.[3]

These three descriptions of the Centre all illustrate the main
difficulty in attempting to analyse its significance in French
politics. It is not a political party, but a reaction from the
French Left–Right dichotomy. It is a body of people united by
the desire not to be swallowed up by either. It is compelled,
therefore, to swim perpetually against both political currents.[4]
For not only is the Left–Right axis a deeply rooted feature in
French politics – however little its survival may be justified by
the facts – but there is also an inherent bi-polarity in the democratic political process, to the extent that it requires a division
into Government and Opposition and that it requires answers

of Yes or No to specific questions. Centre groups that play any active part are, therefore, compelled to lean either one way or the other, at the risk of splitting into a Centre–Right and a Centre–Left. The attempt of Centre parties under the Fifth Republic to avoid this dilemma by defining their function as being 'to become a majority' (*une formation centriste à vocation majoritaire*) can be regarded only as escapism in a political situation in which this objective is both statistically and politically impossible of attainment. If consideration of the Centre were to be limited to its evolution between 1958 and 1970, it would indeed be tempting to dismiss it out of hand as being politically irrelevant.

Centre parties have, however, had a long history, largely bound up with the fortunes of Catholic democracy, whose spirit, like that of Radicalism, has at times been very important in French politics and may be so again. The rôle of the Christian-democrat MRP in the early years of the Fourth Republic was extremely important. At that stage, many of the members of the MRP would have rejected the view that the party belonged to the Centre. In the context of Parliamentary party politics, however, the Centre can be defined for practical purposes as including, not merely those parties or groups that do not regard themselves as belonging to either Right or Left, but also those that neither Right nor Left will acknowledge as belonging to their own side. And the MRP was always in a situation in which it was wholly accepted by neither Right nor Left.

Formed during the war as a resistance movement, it was a direct descendant of the Christian democrat movements and parties of the Third Republic. It emerged from the war as a large party, characterized by democratic Republicanism and inspired by Catholic principles, though with a far from exclusively Catholic membership. Its main strength was and remained, however, in the traditional Catholic strongholds in Eastern and Western France. Its political programme was one of social reform, but it was non-Marxist and opposed to doctrinaire collectivism. During the early post-war years, when the traditional parties of the non-Marxist Left, the Radicals in particular, as well as the moderate Right, were disorganized and to a greater or lesser extent discredited, the MRP attracted many people, particularly among resisters who were seeking a 'new look' in politics, yet were neither Socialist nor anti-Gaullist.

In 1945, the MRP had 150 Deputies, and in 1946, with 169, for a few months ousted the Communist party from first place. It seemed for a time likely to take the place of the Radicals as a party forming a hinge between the moderate Right and the anti-clerical Left. In its organization it resembled the Left more than the Right, being a disciplined party with a democratic constitution and institutions providing for regular contacts between leaders and rank-and-file, including also contacts with a strong trade-union movement going back to 1919, which was also predominantly Catholic. Yet the party's electoral fortunes waned rapidly and, although it provided three of the Fourth Republic's Prime Ministers and controlled the Ministry of Foreign Affairs continuously in 14 of its 20 Governments up to May 1958,[5] by 1952, its representation in the National Assembly had fallen to 84, and by 1963, it had only 34 Deputies.[6]

The failure of the MRP to consolidate its post-war position was attributable to a number of factors. First, it did not fit – and did not want to fit – into the traditional Left–Right framework, which, whatever the MRP's desires, was still a political reality in the minds of politicians. And for different reasons it was unacceptable to both Right and Left. It was not strictly speaking a religious party, but was inspired by religious ideas and had a largely Catholic membership, a fact which was, in itself, sufficient to alienate the Left. But its social policies were also suspect, because they were not based, as were those of the Left, on a class ideology (though the party did recognize the existence of a class struggle),[7] but on the requirements of Christian morality. All these facts combined to prevent it from securing a firm place in the highly traditional world of local politics, which provides the most stable basis for political survival in France. Second, much of its support in the early post-war years was a consequence of the special conditions of the period. As the Right and the Radicals recovered their strength, they also recovered some of their clientèle that had temporarily found a home in the MRP. And third, with the formation of the Gaullist party in 1947, a number of those who were either Gaullist at heart, or who merely disliked the traditional parties, deserted the MRP for the Gaullist RPF. In the 1951 election, which was the first that the RPF contested, the MRP lost half its votes and 58 seats, and its share of the poll fell from 25% to 13%. The RPF obtained 21% of the votes. Fourth, as the only party wholeheartedly committed from the start to the idea of European unification, the MRP became identified with the policy of a supra-national Europe. And since all parties (except the Communists, who opposed the whole idea of closer relations between the countries of Western Europe) were divided on the issue, the MRP could not be expected not to lose some support. Finally, by remaining uneasily poised between Government and opposition up to 1962, when the Left had gone into opposition – even if it was still 'constructive opposition' – from the end of 1958 onwards, the MRP was already acquiring the reputation of Centrism, even although there continued to be electoral alliances with the Socialists in some constituencies.[8]

From 1962, therefore, the MRP was not merely in decline, but already in something of a political limbo.[9] Both the 1962 and the 1963 party conferences approved the idea that the MRP should be a Centrist formation 'aiming at becoming a majority party'. If this phrase had any meaning at all, it could only imply either willingness to co-operate with some elements on its right, or alternatively a quite unrealistic optimism regarding the likelihood of a major change in the electoral situation. As it was, the MRP was not even close enough to the non-Communist Left to make more than a lukewarm and critical approach to the Defferre proposals for a *grande fédération*. Its Centrist orientation was intensified in April 1964, when the president of the MRP, M. Lecanuet, and the president of the *Rassemblement démocratique*, M. Maurice Faure, formed a *comité de liaison des démocrates*, which was joined by the small right-wing Radical party, the *Centre républicain*, and the independent conservative *Centre national des Indépendants* (CNI); and still more in 1965, when the Defferre plan for a federation broke down, largely owing to disagreements with the MRP. Although the specific objections of the MRP were to the Socialist party's attitude to co-operation with the Communists, to its support for nationalization and to the perennial problem of the relations between the State and Catholic schools, there was in reality present in the minds of some members of the MRP a great reluctance to cut themselves off from the moderate Right.[10] In 1965, the Centre had its own presidential candidate, M. Lecanuet, who stood at the first ballot in opposition to the single left-wing candidate, François Mitterrand.

On the strength of his achievement of 16% of the poll at the first ballot, M. Lecanuet launched, in January 1966, the *Centre démocrate*, a movement intended to build up the image of a more dynamic MRP with a wider appeal. The 'wider appeal' was in part prevented by the Radical party decision not to allow its members to join the *Centre démocrate*. Nevertheless, by April the movement claimed to have 50,000 members. Many of these, however, were conservatives, though M. Lecanuet denied that it was a right-wing organization.[11] But his hopes of 100 members in the following Assembly were disappointed, since the 1967 elections gave them in fact only 27. By that time, the movement clearly included three conflicting tendencies. There were those, such as Maurice Schumann, who believed that the party should co-operate with the Gaullists; those, like M. Pflimlin, who at least did not want to cut the party irretrievably off from the Gaullists; and those, led by M. Lecanuet, who, though anti-Gaullist, were still prepared in principle to consider the possibility of joining a Gaullist Government on certain conditions. In fact, the conditions laid down by M. Lecanuet would have ruled out that possibility since they postulated an agreed social programme, an undertaking that France would remain in NATO after 1969, and approval of the policy of European unification.[12]

By this time, however, it mattered little whether the conditions for entering a Gaullist Government were realistic or not, for the Centre had already virtually ceased to exist as a political force. The 1967 elections dealt the final death blow to the MRP. Even in Alsace, traditionally an MRP stronghold, all 13 seats went to the Gaullists.[13] The following statement, made by a member of the directing committee of the MRP after the elections, summed up the situation:

> The *Centre démocrate* is politically dead already; it has failed because its programme is, like its members, too disparate and contradictory.[14]

On 13 September 1967, the MRP decided to cease political activity, and this decision was ratified the following February by the resignation of the secretary-general, Joseph Fontanet.[15] The Centre entered on a new phase, but without any real hope of a revival. A new Parliamentary group, *Progrès et Démocratie moderne* (PDM), replaced the former *Centre démocrate*, whose president, Jacques Duhamel, had been a member of the *Rassemblement démocratique*. The group was divided from its inception. A more conservative right wing, led by René Pleven and Jacques Duhamel, believed that the Centre should work with the Gaullist majority, but be less subservient than the Giscardian allies. The Giscardian '*Oui mais*', said the latter in a radio interview, always turned out in practice to be '*Mais oui!*'[16] The former MRP tendency, led by M. Lecanuet, was more hesitant, and a number of Deputies elected with the aid of left-wing votes did not want to be cut off from the Federation. The *Centre démocrate* continued in existence, but in spite of a plan for its revival, published in February 1968, remained divided into left and right wings that found it difficult to live together.[17]

In the 1968 National Assembly, of the 33 members of the PDM group, no less than 15 had the support of UDR votes, and nine owed their election to these. The Centre was moving towards the Centre–Right. In July 1969, three members of the Centre who had supported M. Pompidou's candidature in the presidential election joined the Government. A new Centre group, the *Centre Démocratie et Progrès* (CDP), was formed to represent those Deputies in favour of participation in the Government. But no evidence was forthcoming that, any more than the Giscardian representatives in the Government, the Centre Ministers were able to influence the by then over-whelming Gaullist majority. To form part of the Government perhaps gave both allies the semblance of a function. Their participation was useful to the Gaullists because it gave them the opportunity to appear to be representing the majority of the nation and isolated the left-wing opposition parties. But in reality the Gaullists could comfortably withstand any conceivable challenge from Parliament without the help of either ally. The position of the Centre in the 1969 referendum on the reform of the Senate and regional decentralization had provided an illuminating illustration of the real extent of disintegration of the Centre. The PDM group had been divided, and so members of the group had been finally left free to vote as they chose. The three Centre leaders who were shortly to join the Government had all been opposed to the terms of the Bill. The Centre's divisions by now rivalled the traditional divisions within the Radical party!

The circumstances in which Radicals and Centrists agreed to form the *Mouvement réformateur* in October 1971 revealed the impossibility of uniting two parties so profoundly divided. There was immediately increased dissension both within and between them on the objectives and methods of the new movement. It was, moreover, becoming less and less easy to distinguish the policies of the Centre from those of the moderate Right – on foreign policy, for instance, economic policies, the position of private schools, the Constitution. At the *Journée d'Etudes*, held in October 1971 by the governmental CDP (the seventh since the group's formation in 1969), it was still not clear exactly what it stood for. Its existence was defended by M. Jacques Duhamel as 'a third element of the majority', but its contribution in that capacity was described only as 'something indefinable and yet essential'. On the other hand, the efforts of the opposition wing, the *Centre démocrate* movement, led by M. Jean Lecanuet, to distinguish itself from both Right and Left, were not much happier. The 'vocation' of the Centre, said M. Lecanuet at the National Convention at Nantes at the beginning of October 1971, was to constitute 'a force looking to the Left, but not turning its back on the Right' (*ouverte sur notre gauche, mais qui ne se ferme pas à droite*).[18] It has been shown only too often in French political history that to the extent to which the Centre approaches the Left it is *ipso facto* alienated from the Right and vice versa. Yet to face both ways risks the disintegration of the Centre.

Two further developments on the Centre front ought perhaps to be mentioned briefly. Though the primary aim of M. Jacques Soustelle in forming the movement *Progrès et Liberté* in 1971 (which was soon joined by the small *Centre républicain* (ex-right-wing Radical) party) was undoubtedly to assist his passage back into the mainstream of French politics, he was appealing specifically to Centrists and reformists. And his expressed objective, too, was to form the basis of 'a new majority in favour of a new policy' – a policy not easily distinguishable from that of the main Centre organizations. The second development was the formation in December 1971 by some 80 Deputies and Senators of the *Union parlemantaire du Centre*, which included representatives of the small rump of non-governmental *Indépendants*, the CNI. By 1972, the Centre's quest for unity had, like that of the Left, produced only additional quarrels and additional organizations.

In spite of its political impotence, however, the Centre could take courage from the fact that it remained electorally attractive to some 10% of the voters. Who were they? On the evidence mainly of opinion polls, they included older ex-liberals, often local notabilities, who disliked Gaullist 'authoritarian' methods; younger professional people, often professed 'supranationalists'; social reformers, who were mainly middle-class, individualistic, pragmatic and tolerant, and, therefore, disliked both personal and party rule and Communist working-class dogma. Like the supporters of the British Liberal party, they represented the eternal search for a middle way, a 'third force'. But their problem was that, when it came to policies, they tended to see different middle ways. The French Centre, concluded Alain Duhamel, includes three Centres, 'the French Centrist temperament, the residual Centrism of the real Centre, and the potential Centrism of the third force'.[19]

THE GAULLIST PARTY

The Gaullist party has inherited the quality formerly attributed by Jacques Fauvet to the Communist party: it is not – or at least not yet – a party like the others. It belongs to neither the traditional Right nor the traditional Left. As a Parliamentary party, it has had a brief and discontinuous past, throughout the whole of which it was a reflection of the purposes and views of one dominating personality. It has thus been without the historical shackles – the backward-looking reflexes – that play so large a part in determining the political reactions of the older parties. And in 1970, when it had been for twelve years uninterruptedly a Government party, it was still only just beginning to look forward confidently to a Parliamentary future.[20]

The movement formed in 1958 on General de Gaulle's return to power was, in fact, the third Gaullist movement since the war. There had been a small Gaullist Union in 1946 that shared the General's hostility to the 1946 Constitution. In 1947, General de Gaulle formed the *Rassemblement du Peuple français* (RPF), a mass organization that remained extra-Parliamentary until 1951, when 21% of the voters (over four million) returned 120 RPF Deputies. For two years, the RPF constituted the largest group in the National Assembly. Its members sat on the extreme Right, though this was against their will, and they persistently denied being a conservative group. They were anti-Communist (this was the period when General de Gaulle consistently described the Communists as '*séparatistes*'),[21] opposed both to the Constitution – which they regarded as a recipe for weak government – and to the party system – referred to pejoratively by General de Gaulle as '*le système*' or '*le régime des partis*'. The movement had its own party organizations, however, including national conferences, described then as later as '*Assises nationales*'. Gaullists were also opposed to anti-clericalism and so were classed automatically by all left-wing parties as being on the Right, merely by virtue of the fact that they favoured State aid to Catholic Schools.[22]

The movement's positive programme consisted of

i) fidelity to General de Gaulle and, in particular, to the constitutional principles expressed in his Bayeux speech;[23]
ii) belief in a national foreign policy and opposition to European integration and therefore especially to the proposal for a European Defence Community from 1950 onwards;[24] and
iii) the belief that the class war could be ended by giving workers a stake in industry – the system described in the 1950s as '*l'association capital-travail*'.

This last policy was also, of course, regarded unanimously in left-wing circles as an expression of right-wing attitudes – even of neo-corporatism.[25] In reality, of course, Gaullism was not, and has never been, concerned with ideological principles.

Though Gaullist Ministers were included in several Governments of the Fourth Republic,[26] this took place only after Gaullism as such had officially ceased to exist. Between 1953 and 1958, the movement disintegrated even more rapidly than it had grown up. In 1953, the General dissociated himself from the Parliamentary group, which soon became a leaderless and largely purposeless rump, whose members called themselves Social Republicans. From 1955 onwards, the national movement was to all intents and purposes dissolved.[27] General de Gaulle made no political statements for the following three years. The third Gaullist movement, formed when he returned to power in 1958 – the *Union pour la nouvelle République* (UNR) – was a heterogeneous body,[28] 234 of whose members became Deputies in the election held in October of that year. If the period of wartime Gaullism is taken into account, however, this was not merely the third Gaullist Parliamentary party, but the third generation of Gaullism. M. Pompidou saw Gaullism as having a history of thirty years, during which it had moved 'from the heroic Gaullism of 1940 to the militant Gaullism of 1947, and then to Governmental Gaullism in 1958'.[29]

Power brought with it new requirements, among which one of the most important was to create a majority party strong enough and united enough to support a stable Government. This meant to begin with that a number of members of the UNR who had joined it primarily in order to ensure that Algeria remained French had to go as soon as the way to a solution of the Algerian problem was clear. It meant, too, that the party would have to decide what its function was to be, in addition to keeping a Gaullist Government in power, and on this point there were major divisions within it. There were those, like the 1959 secretary-general, Albert Chalandon, who believed that it ought to be a party of '*cadres*', that is of a managerial or technocratic élite entrusted with the carrying out of General de Gaulle's policies. There were others who were convinced that Gaullism would be unable to remain a Governmental party and would be unable to survive in the absence of General de Gaulle, unless it developed the electoral and propagandist machinery of a modern mass party. To some extent these two tendencies continued to co-exist within the Gaullist movement, though the first rapidly declined in importance, and finally, during the premiership of M. Pompidou, became no more than a relatively uninfluential minority.

There was also a division of opinion between those, on the one hand, who believed in Gaullism, either as an instrument of a strong foreign policy or as a force making for economic progress and political stability, and those, on the other hand, for whom one of its main purposes was seen as being to supply an economic and social dynamism that demanded new approaches to problems of industrial and social relations. In 1959, a number of Gaullists formed the *Union démocratique du Travail* (UDT) which, though outside the framework of the UNR, was Gaullist, and accepted the need to work within the framework of the Constitution of the Fifth Republic. This group, together with a number of like-minded groups, was particularly anxious to recruit support from the French Left, and to avoid the assimilation of Gaullism to conservatism. In 1962, the UDT fused with the UNR (not without some misgivings), and so the UNR–UDT faced the first critical election following the end of the Algerian war, at least as a cohesive body, though still without a generally accepted policy.[30]

This first period of Governmental Gaullism was essentially one of preparation, since French politics was dominated by the Algerian problem. The second phase, from 1962 to 1968, saw the emergence of Gaullism as a potential majority party in normal circumstances. It no longer owed its position to the threat of civil war, though it still owed much of its prestige to the continued presence at the head of the State of General de Gaulle. It is possible to regard these six years throughout which Georges Pompidou remained Prime Minister (thus establishing an all-time Republican record for longevity) as constituting in reality two distinct phases, because in 1962 public opinion had not yet returned to normal. Three-quarters of a million French settlers who had left Algeria had still to be absorbed; the OAS was still a potential danger; the army had still to be reorganized and to return to its traditional position of subordination to the State. It was not really until 1965, when General de Gaulle had been re-elected President for a second term, and by universal suffrage, that Gaullists could begin to take for granted their permanent existence as a party.

During these six years, up to the May revolution of 1968, the Gaullist party became identified with certain predominating attitudes. First, it set out to build up the image of itself as a practical party. Its watchword was efficiency (*'l'efficacité'*), regarded by its opponents as a synonym for technocracy. Its internal programme was concerned with administrative and regional reform, improvement in the running of the social-security system, the continuation and extension of industrial and agricultural modernization. Second, the desire for Gaullism not to be regarded as synonymous with conservatism became more identified with social policies and, from 1967 onwards, with a modest application of the Gaullist ideas for profit-sharing in industry.

Our programme [said a prominent Gaullist Minister in 1963] must owe as much to the Left as to the Right; to the Left its social generosity; to the Right its emphasis on the nation.[31]

This preoccupation with 'Centrism' was exemplified by the

UNR's change in the seating arrangements in the National Assembly following the Gaullist victory in the 1962 elections. Opposition parties were banished to the back rows, while serried ranks of Gaullists filled the front rows from right to left. A third attitude was the implicit understanding by which the party left the direction of foreign affairs to the President. In 1959, M. Chaban Delmas did, in fact, make an explicit statement that not merely foreign affairs, but also questions of defence and Community affairs belonged to a 'reserved domain' which remained the exclusive responsibility of the President.[32] This certainly continued to be the accepted practice throughout the presidency of General de Gaulle.

One important change was the gradual evolution of the party's Parliamentary group into something more like a conventional Parliamentary party. In 1962, *The Times* had referred to the Gaullists as 'more a claque than a party'.[33] And certainly the strength and cohesion of the Parliamentary group were mainly ensured by restricting its functions as far as possible to those of advice and assent, instead of encouraging its participation in decision-making. Recurrent outbursts of discontent on the part of backbenchers went some way towards modifying the view expressed by *The Times*, but it needed more than mini-revolts to invalidate it. There was evidence during the Parliament of 1962–8 of attempts to improve working relationships between the group and the Government – the creation of specialized committees of Deputies, in particular (though these were not always made use of), but the most that could be said was that those Deputies who so desired had the opportunity to exercise 'a non-negligible influence on Governmental action'.[34]

Relations between the leaders and the Parliamentary party on the one hand and the rank and file of the party on the other left even more to be desired. In his study of Gaullism, published in 1967, Jean Charlot notes the evolution of the party as being '. . . at first a Ministerial team, then a Central Committee for the selection of candidates, then the largest group in Parliament, and – at last – a party'.[35] If the UNR became a party in electoral and Parliamentary terms during the 1962–7 Parliament, it

was not until 1968 that the problem of transforming the
movement itself into a party was seriously tackled. In 1963,
one of the most percipient of Gaullist critics had described
Gaullism as a heterogeneous *Rassemblement* with rival leaders.
'Its methods', he said, 'are elementary and often criticizable.
Divided between *de facto* Bonapartism and verbal leftism and
with a conservative electorate, its disequilibrium is uncon-
testable.'[36] Plans to improve its methods – through the
organization of departmental parties, better training of local
party administrators, and greatly improved contacts with
trade-union and professional organizations at *journées d'études*
and round-table discussions – met with only moderate success.
The results of local elections showed, too, that by 1967 the
party had still a long way to go in order to achieve its goal of
establishing strong local roots.[37]

The Lille *'Assises'* of November 1967 mark the beginning
of a third period of Governmental Gaullism. From 1968
onwards, a determined effort was undertaken to create a strong
and well-organized national party. Party structure was reorganized, particularly with a view to improving contacts
between the Government and the Parliamentary group and
also between leaders (whether in the Government or in Parliament) and the rank and file of the party, and especially between
Paris and provincial centres. At Lille, too, M. Pompidou
emphasized the need for the party to look ahead and to ensure
its own survival by attracting and giving more responsibilities
to younger members. The party sought to give itself a new
image by adopting a new name (not without opposition from
the older, 'unconditional' Gaullists), a new statement of basic
principles, and a new secretary-general, not, this time, a
'historic' Gaullist, whose loyalty to the party went back to 1940,
but a young and dynamic Deputy, Robert Poujade, who had
been only twelve in 1940. The old controversy, never really
resolved, between supporters of a party of *'cadres'* and a mass
party, was at least side-stepped by an approach that concentrated attention on the primary need to produce a powerful
machine in support of a majority party.

The chief ways in which the party – now calling itself the

Union des Démocrates pour la Ve République (UDV^{e}R) – endeavoured to rejuvenate itself from 1968 onwards were:

i) by providing for regional representation in the *bureau politique* of the Parliamentary group and for organization of the party outside Parliament on both a constituency and a regional basis, with regional Councils and regional *journées d'études*;[38]

ii) by widening the party's basis through the association within the party organization of personalities of the Fourth Republic and left-wing Gaullists, without integrating them in the party;[39]

iii) by the decision to place more emphasis on measures to achieve 'participation'; and

iv) by attempts to appeal more to the young, and to modern conceptions of progress.[40]

If the party's desired image was clear, the clarity of its political objectives was less obvious. The six objectives of the UDV^{e}R were defined at Lille as being democracy, new ideas, expansion, revivification, efficiency, and the putting down of local roots.[41] These were not new, most of them were not exclusive to Gaullists, and they were considerably less precise than the official declaration of principles of the Parliamentary group published in the Spring of 1967, which also noted six objectives. These were: to preserve the institutions of the Republic; to create a 'true social democracy by means of structural reforms, security of employment, a better standard of income . . .' and so on; to continue the policy of expansion on the basis of the National Plan; to continue to provide aid to under-developed countries; to defend national independence, by protecting France's power within a united Europe which would 'respect the responsibilities of nation States'; and finally to develop East–West relations in order to ensure a durable peace.[42]

Jean Charlot described the Lille 'message' as being more like British Conservatism than traditional Gaullism.[43] Gaullist

pragmatism, lack of ideological content and even opportunism
are certainly characteristics shared by the British Conservative
party. But the emphasis on 'participation' and the regionalism
of Gaullism, as expressed in 1969 in the Bill defeated in the
referendum, were specifically French, though neither was
exclusively Gaullist. Regionalism has been a recurrent phenomenon in French politics, but though frequently preached has
rarely been practised, and has never succeeded in beginning to
breach the fortifications of French centralized administration.
If this ceases to be true in the 1970s, the climate engendered by
the May events of 1968 may have more to do with the change
than the dynamism or efficiency of Gaullism. For the student
revolution followed so close on the heels of the Lille decisions[44]
that it is impossible to assess the extent to which either was the
real source of the new spirit.

The May–June events both helped and hindered Gaullism.
One – very minor – Gaullist casualty was the new party name,
which, after the elections, became the *Union des Démocrates pour
la République* (UDR).[45] The immediate effect of the revolution
was to shake Gaullist confidence. M. Pompidou's concessions
to trade-union demands, General de Gaulle's silence at first,
and then his apparent lack of authority when he did speak, his
sudden and unexplained absence from Paris – all these did not
square well with the Gaullist image of dynamism and vigour,
while the continued disorder and violence seemed likely to put
an end to the campaign to present Gaullism as a force for
efficiency, order and stability before it had got off the ground.
But the public's early tolerance for, and even sympathy with,
the students soon gave way to irritation and anger in the face
of what looked like purposeless destructiveness. General de
Gaulle's second broadcast on 30 May, announcing the dissolution of the National Assembly and the holding of elections,
was followed by a massive demonstration of public support
(much of it expressive of relief at the President's habitual tone
of confident authority). The divisions, hesitations and mistaken
tactics of the Left offered no credible alternative to Gaullism,
and so, whether or not the ensuing electoral landslide was the
expression of fear of disorder rather than of enthusiasm for

Gaullism, the result was a rapid increase in the number of members of the party.[46]

The election was followed, however, by the passage of the law providing for the reform of university education (one of the main planks of the supporters of 'participation'), which revealed a noticeable lack of enthusiasm on the right of the party, on the ground that the reforms went too far, and by provisions for an extension of workers' participation in industry, which aroused hostility on the left of the party, on the ground that they did not go far enough.[47] In 1969, the UDT decided to return to its original independence of the UDR, not only for this reason, but also because it disapproved of the policy decided on at Lille and blamed M. Pompidou, both for betraying Gaullist principles by turning the movement into a political party, and also for his pronounced anti-Communism during the election campaign, which they regarded as likely to defeat the party's efforts to win over elements on the Left.[48] The continuing disruption of universities (and disturbances also in some secondary schools) during the 1968–9 session (and to a lesser extent during the following session), the grievances of students and parents caused by the upheaval of a too rapidly improvised and inadequately financed university reform, the political feelings aroused by the terms of the so-called 'anti-smashers'' Bill, and by the apparent consignment to a legislative limbo of the Bill on regionalism – all these, combined with the country's economic problems, made the beginning of the 1970s inevitably a testing time for the Gaullist party.[49] It had also at that time to learn to adapt itself to living without President de Gaulle and with President Pompidou.

By the 1970s, the party could at least claim three major achievements. It had succeeded in obtaining general acceptance for the Gaullist Constitution. Even the Communists were merely suggesting the revision of specific articles and were not really making an issue of that degree of revision. Second, there was no serious opposition to the main principles of Gaullist foreign policy, and certainly no alternative policy attracting attention, much less enthusiasm. And third, the party structure was becoming generally accepted as an alternative bond to that supplied by loyalty to the personality of General de Gaulle.

This is not to say that the future of Gaullism was assured. Even the achievements could be questioned. The first two were certainly due to General de Gaulle rather than to the party, while the strength of the party, as judged by election results, could be attributed more to outside circumstances – fear of disorder and the disintegration of the Left – than to a permanent implantation of Gaullism. Would party cohesion stand up to a continuation of the strains such as those imposed by the May events and their consequences? What exactly did the party stand for? Its claim to be nationalist and pragmatic could be matched by the *Républicains indépendants* who, under the leadership of Valéry Giscard d'Estaing, were also seeking to create a more modern image. It certainly could not claim to be fundamentally any more united than other Republican parties, whose unity had succumbed in face either of the responsibilities of office, or of lack of responsibility created by absence from office.

GAULLIST ASSOCIATIONS AND MOVEMENTS OUTSIDE THE UDR

Gaullist movements outside the main party fall into two quite separate categories. Some are little more than agents of the central Gaullist organization and do not differ essentially from the ancillary movements of other political parties. Others are independent, in the sense that they determine their own policies, and do not always agree with those of the Government party. But they do not constitute in any meaningful sense opposition parties. Extremist left-wing or right-wing parties oppose the policies of orthodox left-wing or right-wing parties, and in most cases the system of Parliamentary government itself. The extremist Left, for instance, is more opposed to the Communist party than to 'bourgeois' parties. But all Gaullist movements share a common loyalty to General de Gaulle and to Gaullist principles as defined by him. They all consider themselves as belonging to the Gaullist 'family', and as having the duty to work for Gaullism. They are not 'sleeping partners' as are some of the Socialist Clubs, which consider their function to be to act as 'think tanks' or even as academic seminars, without any responsibility for mundane jobs such as trying to win elections. Some of the independent Gaullist movements, indeed, consider themselves to be more accurate interpreters of the true milk of the Gaullist word than the Gaullist party itself.

These groups are worth some consideration, in the first place because they are so numerous. In his study of Gaullism, Jean Charlot estimated that there were upwards of thirty of them, but he was including groups associated with Governmental partners not themselves Gaullist. They are, however, perpetually changing, and there is considerable overlapping between them. These are, of course, characteristics common to most French fringe parties. But in the case of the Gaullist party, which is still not quite a party like the others, and whose principles and aims are less clearly defined, it is perhaps more difficult to follow the relations between the Gaullist party and bodies which, though not satellites, are still closer to it than, say, dissident Socialist movements are to the Socialist party.

i) Ancillary organizations

There were, in 1970, about half-a-dozen of these, carrying out functions similar to those carried out by ancillary organs of any political party – for instance, Clubs providing information, undertaking research or organizing meetings, such as the *Centre d'Information civique*, the *Service d'Action civique* and the *Clubs Ve République* (*Nouvelle Frontière*). There are organizations concerned with special problems such as the *Union des Jeunes pour le Progrès* (UJP), the *Centre féminin d'Etudes et d'Information*, *l'Université moderne*. The last mentioned was formed in 1965, but from 1968 onwards considered its special function to be to follow the development of university reform. In this category the largest movement, and the one most in the public eye, is the UJP, which, in the 1967 elections, had four candidates endorsed by the party (though none was elected). It claimed to have 4000 members in 1967 and 7300 in May 1968. Its action was hampered by personal quarrels resulting in the formation, after General de Gaulle's resignation, of two rival movements – the Club *Jeune France*, and the *Front des jeunes Progressistes*.

ii) Action committees

Some of these are intermittent, and exist mainly to help in Gaullist election campaigns; the *Comité d'Action pour la Ve République*, for instance, had the job of endorsing Gaullist candidatures for the 1967 elections; the RPF, though it claims to be still in existence, seems to be dormant; *l'Association pour le Soutien du Général de Gaulle* (Pierre Lefranc) and *l'Association pour la Ve République* (André Malraux) have both been concerned mainly with electoral activities. The *Comité de Défense de la République* (CDR) had more energetic conceptions of action and was criticized in 1969 even within the Gaullist movement. The Caen and the Dijon organizations quarrelled with Gaullist personalities in the *départements* and Edgar Faure, in an acrimonious dispute with the CDR for the Côte d'Or, referred to its behaviour as being like Fascism in its early stages. Created in June 1968 to help to maintain 'Republican order', different departmental CDR behaved in very different ways. At their National Congress in May 1971, the CDR were preoccupied with the problem of subversion, in particular with left-wing disorders in the universities. The movement then claimed 50,000 members.

iii) Gaullist fidelity

In June 1969, a Gaullist organization, *Présence et Action du Gaullisme*, was formed to defend the spirit of Gaullism. This movement, which had a Parliamentary 'subgroup', *l'Amicale parlementaire*, consisting of some forty Deputies, including MM. Couve de Murville and Messmer, was reputed to be secretly under the direction of M. Debré, and represented the 'conservative' viewpoint of those for whom 'life stopped with General de Gaulle's resignation'.[50] After a period of inactivity, it was revived in 1970, when it described its aims as being outside the framework of day-to-day politics. Since it represented the purest Gaullist orthodoxy, it had the official approval of the party leaders. It had no connection with the so-called 'unconditional' Gaullism of the Gaullist Left.

iv) The Gaullist Left

The label *Gaullistes de Gauche* has covered a bewildering variety of organizations. They have shared with each other a general acceptance of Gaullist foreign policy, but a critical attitude to its economic and social policies, and a fear of being absorbed in a monolithic party in Governmental harness with a traditional conservative party. The most influential of them, and the earliest, except for the *Centre de la Réforme républicaine* (CRR), is the *Union démocratique du Travail* (UDT), officially formed on 14 April 1959, when the CRR merged with it, except for a number of dissidents who ultimately merged with the *Convention de la Gauche Vᵉ République* (see below, v). Its most prominent leaders, Louis Vallon and Réne Capitant, were not merely left-wing but also 'unconditional' Gaullists, who refused to attend the 1967 Lille conference because they did not want to see the movement transformed into a political party. They had also come to see in the proposals for workers' participation put forward by Marcel Loichot and described by some as 'pan-capitalism', *the* solution to the problem of industrial relations. This plan was, however, too Socialistic to be acceptable to the Government. The UDT, which had been integrated in the Gaullist party from 1962, resumed its independence of the UDR in September 1969, following General de Gaulle's resignation. Two dissident movements formed a few months earlier, the *Union populaire progressiste*, which included members of the team of journalists on *Notre République*, together with the *Union gaulliste populaire*, formed by René Capitant, then rejoined the UDT. In 1962, when it had merged with the UNR, the UDT had had about 5000 members, of whom two-thirds were in the Paris region. In 1969, its weekly *Notre République* claimed a circulation of 8900 – though without stating how many copies were distributed free! In spite of its social progressivism[51] (it saw in the Loichot proposals for participation a method by which workers could become majority shareholders in 25 years), it was politically conservative in the sense that René Capitant and his supporters did not want to look ahead at all. 'As long as de Gaulle is there', he wrote in *Notre République* (10 November 1967), 'we have nothing to fear. ...'

Le Front du Progrès, formed in 1964 and led by Jacques Dauer, include dex-*Mendésistes* and some Socialists. It sought to be a hinge between majority and opposition, and resisted absorption in the UDR. It largely shared the UDT's general social approach.

Le Front travailliste, formed in 1965 by ex-members of the UDT, Radicals, ex-Radicals and some Socialists, also resisted absorption into the UDT. Its leader, Yves Morandat, a war-time resister with a trade-union background, feared UDT association with the Giscardian conservatives and even resigned as president of the movement on this issue. He thought that the result of the alliance would be that 'the French waggon would be hitched to the American tank', and France would be involved in American quarrels.[52] The movement eventually joined the *Union de la Gauche Vᵉ République* (see below, v).

The *Groupe des 29*, formed after the presidential election of 1965, was more a Club than a party, and a number of its members also belonged to other groups (for instance, Yves Morandat, André Philip, Jacques Dauer). It also included two prominent fellow travellers, Emmanuel d'Astier de la Vigerie and a former secretary-general of the CGT, Pierre Le Brun. Its main emphasis was on support for General de Gaulle's foreign policy, particularly the withdrawal from NATO and the search for *rapprochement* with the USSR. It was self-consciously left-wing, anxious to prove that it was possible for 'the Left to be Gaullist with a good conscience' and to persuade the Gaullist party to be more Left. It supported the Vallon position on participation. The movement eventually joined the federation, the *Union de la Gauche Vᵉ République* (see below, v).

v) The Federation of left-wing Gaullist movements
In 1966, two established and three smaller left-wing movements formed the *Convention de la Gauche Vᵉ République*, led by

Philippe Dechartre. The member movements were the CRR, the *Front du Progrès*, the *Association nouveau régime*, *Clubs Vᵉ République* and the *Centre Jules Vallès*. The Convention reached an agreement with the UDT in the election of 1967 and a number of its members stood as candidates endorsed by the UDT. Its political manifesto of 21 June 1967 stressed the need for European independence of the USA, support for the election of the President by universal suffrage, and the reform of the Senate along Gaullist semi-functional lines. It also advocated increased powers to works committees in industry and better conditions for shop stewards.

Although it retained a separate existence, the movement considered itself as part of the majority and three of its members held ministerial office in the 1967 Government. The *Front du Progrès* became estranged from it in the autumn of 1967, and when the *Convention* reorganized itself under the name of *Union de la Gauche Vᵉ République* in September 1967, remained outside. Three new movements joined it (the *Groupe des 29*, the *Association radicale pour la Vᵉ République* and the *Mouvement pour un Ordre social nouveau*).

In November 1969, the *Union de la Gauche Vᵉ République* federated with two other left-wing Gaullist movements, *Démocratie et Travail* and the *Front travailliste*. Far from heralding greater unity, this federation was confronted by a rival left-wing Gaullist federation within a year of General de Gaulle's death.

GAULLISM AFTER DE GAULLE

The resignation of General de Gaulle in 1969, and his death in November 1970, were bound to create uncertainties, even if they did not threaten the unity of the Gaullist movement. Even before his resignation, at least four distinct (and sometimes overlapping) kinds of Gaullism were discernible in the movement. There was, first, what Pierre Viansson-Ponté called 'the Gaullism of the General'[53] – that of the 'unconditional' loyalists, such as Michel Debré, Pierre Messmer, Maurice Couve de Murville – which, by the end of the 1960s, was already becoming conservative, in the sense that it was almost wholly backward-looking. These Gaullists had always relied exclusively on the General for inspiration, leadership and orders. They regarded themselves as the true 'heirs' of Gaullism and criticized Gaullist policies when, in their view, they deviated from what General de Gaulle would have done. In February 1967, Christian Fouchet and the General's brother-in-law, Jacques Vendroux, had already left the UDR, because it was not 'Gaullist' enough for them, though they continued to vote with the majority in the National Assembly. Another Gaullist Deputy left the UDR in December 1970, and in November 1971, Jean-Marcel Jeanneney, a former Gaullist Minister who had been closely associated with the General's plans for regional and Senate reform, also resigned, having publicly stated that he did not believe in 'Gaullism without de Gaulle'.

The second kind of Gaullism was that which Maurice Duverger called 'the institutional Gaullists'.[54] This was unquestionably the strongest element and had rapidly become the new seat of orthodoxy. It consisted of those who, like the President and his Prime Minister, were counting on the development of party structures to provide the necessary cement to compensate for the absence of de Gaulle. Though both men continued to pay lip-service to General de Gaulle's conception of Gaullism as a movement or a *Rassemblement* rather than a party, in reality, under their leadership it had acquired the structures of a political party better organized than most. Its new and active secretary-general, René Tomasini, had toured the country in a successful recruitment drive, and the party could consequently claim in 1971 to have 200,000 members (that is to have doubled its membership in a few years). The links between the Parliamentary group and the Government were becoming stronger. There was a strong sense among rank and file Deputies of the need for political cohesion and party discipline.

Nevertheless, there were still many influential institutional Gaullists who were anxious that the party should retain its general appeal to Frenchmen as well as its party appeal, and that it should stand for 'A Republic of realities', as that most loyal of Gaullists, Lucien Neuwirth, put it. What the majority of the party stood for was well summed up in presidential press conferences, prime-ministerial declarations and statements by orthodox party spokesmen. It added up to moderate, cautious and practical conservative reformism.

> Gaullism [said Alexandre Sanguinetti at Toulouse in February 1971] means legislative institutions subordinate to the executive and the primacy of an executive directed by the Head of the State. Gaullism also means economic freedom – a third way between wholehearted capitalism and wholehearted collectivism. . . . In foreign policy, Gaullism means national independence and the progressive creation of Europe to the point at which it becomes conscious of itself as one country (*une patrie*). . . . Finally, Gaullism means a constant attempt to develop French industrial strength.[55]

This was altogether too prosaic and unambitious to satisfy 'unconditional' Gaullists such as Jean-Marcel Jeanneney, for whom the cautious rightward tendency of post-Gaullism was seen as a betrayal. But if orthodox Gaullism was to remain the dominant element of a cohesive majority party, then some concessions to more conservative opinion in the ranks was essential. There were 'Jacobins' such as M. Debré, for whom any concept of regionalism that involved real local government was anathema, defenders of order and discipline, for whom the Faure law providing for more autonomy in universities looked like the road to anarchy, and business men and employers, for whom the kind of 'participation' envisaged by some of de Gaulle's more enthusiastic supporters looked like the road to Socialism. There was a real danger that, if forced to choose between the more progressive of Gaullist social policies and orthodox conservatism, they would prefer the latter. Just as there was a danger that, if the procedures of Parliamentary democracy appeared too slow and clumsy, the party, instead of improving them, might succumb to the appeal of more technocratic and bureaucratic systems of government.

The technocrats or would-be technocrats constituted the

third strand of Gaullism. Some of the more left-wing Gaullists specifically feared the development of technocratic tendencies in the party. In November 1971, David Rousset, a left-wing Gaullist who voted with the Gaullist Parliamentary group, though he was not a member of the UDR, severed his links with the group, precisely because he saw it already as a 'spreading bureaucracy' that had deserted Gaullist policies of 'participation' in favour of '*le capitalisme de grand'père*'.

The fourth strand was made up of the semi-autonomous collection of small left-wing Gaullist organizations, increasingly critical of the rightward drift of the UDR in the two years following General de Gaulle's resignation. Even so loyal a Gaullist as Léo Hamon, who, though a Minister, was still associated with the left-wing Gaullist movement *Démocratie et Travail* and had belonged to the UDT, found the Government's achievements between 1969 and 1971, though considerable, somewhat uninspired. 'In 1969', he said, 'the French had heard enough talk about large ideas. In 1971, they would have liked to hear more.'[56]

The future of the left-wing Gaullists was becoming, indeed, increasingly problematical. In April 1971, Gilbert Grandval, also a former member of the UDT, tried to bring seven of these small movements into a single organization. He succeeded (though only with some difficulty) in uniting four of them – the *Front du Progrès* (Jacques Dauer), the *Union gaulliste populaire* (Hugo Bonneville), the *Front des jeunes progressistes* (Dominique Gallet) and the *Union populaire progressiste* (Jacques Debû-Bridel) in the *Union travailliste*, of which he became the President at the Unity Congress held at Toulon at the beginning of October. The movement's aim was, as stated by M. Grandval to the press on 28 September, to be independent of the UDR, in the sense of an equal partner within the majority.

The movements constituting the *Union travailliste* were closer in approach to the 'unconditional' than to the institutional Gaullists. They were not in reality united, and their representativity was contested by the three movements that remained outside. These three – the *Union de la Gauche V*[e]

République (Philippe Dechartre), *Démocratie et Travail* and some members of the divided *Front travailliste* (Yves Morandat) – united, in November 1971, with Edgar Faure's *Comité d'Etudes pour un nouveau Contrat social* to form the *Mouvement pour le Socialisme par la participation*. Its President was General Pierre Billotte and its honorary President, M. Faure.

The differences between the two were personal as well as political. The latter was closer to the orthodox majority of the UDR (indeed, M. Dechartre and M. Hamon were both Ministers), and M. Hamon declared at the time of the Unity Congress of the Grandval movements: 'We are quite happy behind MM. Pompidou and Chaban Delmas.' The professed aim of both 'Unions' was to unite the Gaullist Left, an objective as unlikely to be achieved as the unity of the orthodox parties of the opposition Left. Perhaps more politically significant than the creation of either movement was the declaration by M. Faure, on 12 May 1971, that he intended to be a candidate in the presidential election of 1976.

These different strands of Gaullism – integrationist or loyalist, institutionalist, technocratic and social reformist – whether based on faith, reason, or merely on political opportunism – all represented potentialities for discord. For the paradox of the Gaullism of the early 1970s was that, having ensured its own survival by adopting the methods advocated by M. Pompidou and his supporters, it had become a political party that was no longer insulated by the presence of a national danger or a national saviour from the centrifugal tendencies characteristic of French political parties. General de Gaulle's disappearance meant that the party had to answer a number of questions for itself that could not be squarely posed before. Was Gaullism to be a party of the Right or of the Centre? Was left-wing Gaullism to be a part of it or had it any real future at all without General de Gaulle? Would the cohesion of the Parliamentary party break down as it had done in the 1950s, owing to different electoral pressures, or perhaps owing to the ambitions of rival leaders? Would the Gaullist party have entered on a new phase by the time the Deputies elected in 1968 had to face the electorate again?

CONSERVATISM

French Conservatism has traditionally been made up of a number of groups, characterized by inability to combine with each other, or to impose discipline within groups. The post-war years saw the failure to survive of the hoped-for single, strong conservative group, the *Parti Républicain de la Liberté* (PRL). In 1949, remnants of this group, together with two others – the *Républicains indépendants* and the *Groupe d'Action paysanne* – formed a loose federation called at first the *Centre national des Indépendants* (CNI), then the *Centre national des Indépendants et Paysans* (CNIP), and in February 1967 the *Fédération des Républicains indépendants*. The founder of the party in its post-1949 form, Roger Duchet, a Paris Senator, was its first secretary-general, and it included a number of elder statesmen – Antoine Pinay, René Coty and Paul Reynaud. It was intended to strengthen the Right against both the Left and the two-year-old RPF, which was attracting support in conservative circles. In 1958, the Pinay and Duchet sections disagreed on the question of support for General de Gaulle and on his Algerian policy. The more moderate majority supported General de Gaulle, though often reluctantly, but disliked his hostility to the idea of European integration and to NATO and was suspicious of the more progressive aspects of Gaullist social policy.

In 1959, the CNIP was represented in the National Assembly by 129 Deputies. The organization of the party in the country was one that relied on the support of local Councillors, Mayors and other notabilities rather than on mass appeal and it was, indeed, little more than a Parliamentary group plus an electoral organization and a national Congress – though it did hold periodic small meetings, such as *journées d'études*, to discuss political problems. In the 1962 election its numbers were drastically reduced to under 50. It then divided into a minority that joined the Centre group in the National Assembly and retained the name *Centre national des Indépendants*, while the majority of 32 Deputies, led by M. Giscard d'Estaing, formed a Parliamentary group, the *Républicains indépendants*. This group supported the Gaullist Government, in which its members continued to be represented. By 1969 their numbers had doubled, but since the party fought elections as part of the majority, its own electoral strength was impossible to assess with any accuracy.

Like conservative parties in previous régimes, the *Républicains indépendants* have had no co-ordinated policy and no real control over their members. From 1966 onward, Mr. Giscard d'Estaing set up a series of provincial Clubs entitled *Perspectives et Réalités*, with the aim of maintaining and strengthening the party's identity. In accordance with the party's political habits, members were drawn mainly from industry and the liberal professions, and the Clubs were not intended to be anything like a political movement, but were rather auxiliary 'think-shops', without any discernible influence on decision-making within the party. The fact that M. Giscard d'Estaing actively encouraged them and attended many of their meetings could well be explained as part of a campaign, not merely to keep the party identity intact, but also to strengthen his own position as its leader.[57] By the end of 1968 there were 38 of these Clubs and by 1969 there were 50, claiming some 3500 members.[58] At the end of 1969 a separate youth movement, the *Jeunes Républicains indépendants* (JRI) was organized and formed a *Centre d'Etude des jeunes Républicains et Démocrates*, aiming at appealing to a wider circle of opinion, including Radicals.

Though the *Républicains indépendants* have never had a precise programme, their political attitudes have traditionally included opposition to State control of industry, to anti-clericalism and to Communism. Their positive policies have included support for European integration, Western solidarity in the Atlantic alliance and the continuance, alongside modern-ized agriculture, of the traditional small-farm economy that has always involved in practice generous State aid to un-economic 'family' concerns. In terms of policies, it is not easy to draw a clear line between *Indépendants* and right-wing Radicals. During the war, there was rather more collabora-tion with the Vichy Government by *Indépendants* than by Radicals; the former had never been anti-clerical and so were positively in favour of some form of State aid to Catholic schools in the 1950s. The main difference has been the kind of positive attachment to political democracy that made Radicals consciously identify themselves with an egalitarian educational policy, a Republicanism stemming from the principles of the Declaration of the Rights of Man, and an anti-clericalism that (though steadily declining in strength) still theoretically entitles Radicals to call themselves Left. Neither *Indépendants* nor Radicals, however, have ever recovered their pre-war political prestige, though both retained a strong influence in local politics. Both were, under the Fourth Republic, characterized by a high degree of individualism and consequently had Parliamentary parties constantly divided. Under the Fifth Republic, the indiscipline in the ranks of the *Républicains indépendants* was, however, severely curbed by the obligations imposed by their coalition with the Gaullists.

The main differences between Gaullists and *Républicains indépendants* in the 1960s were, first, the lack of real opposition to '*le système*' on the part of the latter. They were a product of it and retained a more traditional Parliamentary approach. They were, for instance, suspicious of the Gaullist belief in bi-polarization, and disliked both Gaullist presidentialism[59] and the Gaullist attitude to the question of the need for 'dialogue' between Government and Parliament.[60] Second, *Républicains indépendants* have always been regarded as '*libéraux*', that is, disbelievers in State intervention in the economic field. Much of this attitude has been eroded by the working of successive National Economic Plans. But if they accepted State intervention pragmatically, as an economic necessity, they never developed any of the Gaullist enthusiasm for it as an instrument to be used in the service of a strong State.[61] Third, they supported the idea of European supra-nationalism and the Atlantic alliance, though they shared Gaullist fears of American economic domination, and expressed cautious support for the principle of British membership of the EEC. Whether this 'support' was ever worth much in practice it is difficult to say, since they envisaged conditions much the same as those desired by the Gaullists. Fourth, the nature of their support for Gaullism was essentially critical. They were never more than fellow-travellers. This absence of 'unconditionalism' was spectacularly reaffirmed by M. Giscard d'Estaing in January 1967 when he described his party's attitude to the Gaullist party as being one of 'Yes – but'.[62] The precise weight to be attached to the 'but' was never made clear, and the statement was no doubt a declaration of intent rather than of policy, an expression of the desire to keep options open and to avoid being swallowed up by Gaullism.

Up to General de Gaulle's departure – and indeed beyond – the criticisms were more evident in terms of electoral declarations than in matters of Governmental policy. The party often felt, with some justification, that it was being treated as a poor relation, and its bargaining position was seriously weakened by the Gaullist electoral victory of 1968. But during the period of 1965 to 1968, when M. Giscard d'Estaing was out of office, he did, on a number of occasions, take an independent line, objecting, for instance, to General de Gaulle's anti-Americanism, his conception of neutrality in the Middle East, support of French-Canadian separatism, and use of personal power to carry out policies without adequate consultation of either Parliament or Cabinet. He specifically objected, too, to the use of special powers to reform the social-security services.[63] In view of the traditional heterogeneity and indiscipline of French conservative parties, however, it is difficult to be sure how far his view represented a general opinion in the party, and how far, as a young and ambitious politician, his attitudes were dictated by considerations regarding the possibilities of a future bid for power. His strength lay in his youth, his ability and his political experience, and in the continued rôle of conservatives in local politics. His weaknesses were that he was not sufficiently Gaullist to be acceptable to the UDR, yet not sufficiently opposed to it to provide a credible alternative, and that he had to rely on a party whose image, in spite of his attempts to rejuvenate and modernize it, was associated in people's minds with policies and even more with economic attitudes more reactionary than his own. In 1971, the position of the *Républicains indépendants* could best be described as a consistent and cautious policy of 'wait and see'.

CHAPTER IX

Extra-Parliamentary Political Groups

THE EXTREME RIGHT AND THE EXTREME LEFT

The foregoing picture of six Parliamentary planets, each with its satellites, would give a totally misleading impression of French political opinion without some attempt to describe the ferment on the extreme Right and Left, always potentially present, and from time to time becoming active and menacing as it did during and following the May 'students' revolution' of 1968. Extremist parties and groups have a long history in France, and some of these have existed longer than influential Parliamentary parties. They are far more difficult to describe summarily, owing to their much greater fluidity, to the impermanence of particular groups, and to the partial clandestinity of much of their activity. But whether they are on the Right or on the Left, extremist political organizations have a certain number of characteristics in common, not the least important of which is the extent to which each side feeds on its opposition to the other. Thus, Right and Left extremism tend to flourish and have their periods of quiescence together.

Since the first world war, there have been four main periods of extremist activity. The first was in the decade leading to the second world war, when Fascist and para-military leagues opposed both the Republican régime and the parties of the Left. The second was during the first half of the Fourth Republic, when intense Communist militancy followed the breakdown of the left-wing tripartite coalition that had formed the first post-war Governments. The waves of Communist-led strikes on both political and industrial issues between 1947 and 1951 threatened the stability of the régime as well as the economic and political recovery of the country, and helped to en-

courage, alongside the growth of a powerful Gaullist movement, whose main platform was anti-Communism and opposition to the régime, the formation of a number of extreme
nationalist groups. The third was in the early 1960s, at the
height of the Algerian war, when there was a proliferation of
activist movements on the extreme Right, including the OAS,
whose clandestine commandos threatened the breakdown of
law and order in their attempt to prevent the Government
from agreeing to Algeria's independence. And the fourth was
the left-wing movement of discontent with the organization of
French society and, in particular, with the organization of the
educational system of universities that culminated in the outburst of violence in May 1968 and led, among other things, to
a proliferation of new extremist movements on both Right
and Left, whose clashes were threatening by the 1970s to make
university life untenable in Paris and in some parts of the
provinces. Some left-wing extremists – though still only small
minority groups – had even extended their distinctive violence
to sections of society outside the university.

Whether on the Right or the Left, these movements almost
defy classification and analysis. They are small, often no more
than small coteries, whose formation and activity may be
almost entirely the work of one person or a handful of people.
They give no membership figures. Some are semi-clandestine.
Some are really no more than nostalgic, backward-looking
seminars or protest movements. Others are mainly engaged in
direct and sometimes violent political action. All of them are
perpetually splitting and re-forming, and have periodicals that
appear, disappear and are revived under new names. A description of the organization and ramifications of the different
movements at any one time would almost certainly be inaccurate within a period of months, if not weeks, even if it were
possible to obtain sufficient reliable information to guarantee
accuracy in the first place. There is thus no means of knowing
how far the rivalries, conflicts and arguments of, say, 1966
to 1971 will still be those of 1972 to 1975. For example, once
the Algerian war was ended, little more was heard of most of
the extreme Right organizations of the early 1960s, until the

events of 1968 led to the formation of new movements, some with new leaders, some including personalities who had been active half-a-dozen years earlier.

What does emerge from an attempt to follow the activities of extremist movements over a period of years is at least an impression of the extent to which they resemble each other and the extent to which they remain basically the same, or change their attitudes on certain issues. Whether they are right- or left-wing, they agree in rejecting the Parliamentary system as it exists – though some use the machinery of Parliamentary elections. They agree in advocating, to a greater or lesser degree, forms of direct action – though some restrict this to verbalism or to demonstrations, while others form real commandos and set about destroying society, or at least disrupting some of its normal activities. They are alike too in being almost entirely negative in their political approach. Though each side rejects the assumptions and ideas of the other, the positive content of their thinking is almost equally minimal. Objectives are usually vague and unrealistic, often indeed totally absent, attacks on unacceptable policies or physical attacks on the holders of them appearing to the attackers to constitute sufficient programmes in themselves.

There are none the less important differences between the two sides as well as differences between recent and earlier manifestations of right-wing and left-wing extremism. With one or two well-known exceptions (the OAS and *Occident* in particular), right-wing movements under the Fifth Republic have been, or at least were up to 1971, less violent than the active protagonists of violence on the Left, and showed little desire to transform the will to destroy into a generalized political theory. They also had less influence on, and were less attractive to, students, among whom both extremist movements recruited most of their support. And whereas the most militant of the left-wing extremists moved even farther away from the orthodox left-wing parties than earlier movements had done, some of the right-wing ideas came closer to those of orthodox parties, not all of them on the Right. Some right-wing movements, for instance, adopted certain Gaullist ideas, or at least absorbed fashionable words and phrases such as *'participation'*, *'contestation'*, *'concertation'* – the fashionable panaceas of the late 1960s. And few right-wing movements showed any real Fascist tendencies.[1]

RIGHT-WING EXTREMIST MOVEMENTS

The most influential of the right-wing organizations up to 1968, M. Tixier-Vignancour's *Alliance républicaine pour les Libertés et le Progrès*, provides an illustration of the difficulty of laying down hard and fast rules on the line dividing extremist from orthodox right-wing opinion, and also of determining exactly what any extreme right-wing movement really stands for, in view of its rapid changes of organization or leadership or both. Formed on 23 January 1966, after M. Tixier-Vignancour's campaign as a presidential candidate in 1965, it was really the successor of an earlier movement, the *Rassemblement national*, formed by him in the 1950s, but now minus the issue of Algerian independence and plus that of the welfare of the million or so French Algerian victims of it who had settled in France. Its unity was challenged even before it had taken shape, and a rival movement created by a former Poujadist Deputy, M. Le Pen, who vigorously denied that his movement was a 'breakaway', accused M. Tixier-Vignancour of calling him a Fascist, and contested the election of 1967 at the head of a group then entitled *Rassemblement européen de la Liberté*.[2]

On paper, the distinction between the two movements was difficult to pinpoint. Both were anti-Gaullist, both professed to be 'European', though opposed to supra-nationalism. The differences were, in fact, mainly personal – the hostility of the two leaders to each other – together with the kind of aura created by the association with one or other movement of certain personalities and political viewpoints. For instance, though the movement led by M. Le Pen included a number of members not hitherto associated with the Right, its secretary-general, Dominique Venner, had been a member of the extreme Right group *Jeune Nation*, dissolved by the Government in 1958, and had served a sentence for crimes against the authority of the State. It included some former members of the FEN (*Fédération des Etudiants nationalistes*) and of *Europe-Action*, formed in 1960 by François Sidos, another member of *Jeune Nation*.[3]

M. Tixier-Vignancour's movement was supported by a heterogeneous collection of reluctant nationalists, ex-Pétainists, former supporters of *Algérie française* and ex-Algerian settlers repatriated to France.[4] He himself, however, never advocated direct action, nor was he anti-Parliamentary. He described himself as a Republican who accepted the 1958 Constitution,[5] advocated fidelity to the Atlantic Alliance, defended free enterprise – what he called '*le capitalisme populaire*' (whatever that might mean) – was anti-Communist and supported compensation for Algerian settlers and a general amnesty for all who had been imprisoned for their activities during the Algerian war.[6] When General de Gaulle himself amnestied the most notorious of the activist leaders in June 1968, M. Tixier-Vignancour rallied to Gaullism and declared himself a supporter of M. Pompidou in 1969.[7] Little has been heard subsequently about either movement. Neither contested the election of 1968, and neither attracted any attention during or after the May events. Since the dominant preoccupation of both was opposition to General de Gaulle's Algerian policies, their *raison-d'être*, except as potential rallying points for sectional discontent, would seem to have largely disappeared with the amnesty and with the measures taken in 1969–70 to deal as far as possible with the grievances associated with the problems of compensation for expropriated settlers.

Of the movements that were active or in the news from 1968 onwards, it is possible to distinguish three main categories. First, there were those that existed as vehicles for the expression of nationalist ideas. This is one of the permanent manifestations of right-wing extremism, and the oldest of the movements, *La Restauration nationale*, claims to be the only right-wing movement whose existence in the university goes back to 1906.[8] It aims to be a centre of royalist propaganda, carrying on the Maurrassian tradition of the *Action française*, and its paper, *Aspects de la France*, retains both the initials and the out-

look of the former paper, *l'Action française*. It supports, for
example, decentralization and autonomous universities, fears
social disorder and dreams of a 'popular monarchy'.[9] The movement is anti-Parliamentary, anti-Communist, and opposed to
what it describes as 'the pot-bellied, adipose and scurvy
bourgeoisie' (*la bourgeoisie ventrue, adipeuse et pelliculaire*). It was
opposed to General de Gaulle, tepidly in favour of M. Tixier-
Vignancour (though only as a lesser evil, and owing to his
record as a supporter of *Algérie française*), opposed to 'the Europe of the Euromaniacs', to a 'technocratic civilization', and
during the 1969 presidential election was more anti-Poher than
anti-Pompidou, because the former was the more 'European'.
It believed, however, that France ought to remain in the
Atlantic Alliance, and ought to co-operate with both the Six
and Great Britain. This last-mentioned belief appears to have
been almost its sole contribution to a positive programme. It
was hostile to the whole machinery of orthodox politics. 'We
are not interested in electoral matters', it declared, 'and feel
no need to choose between two forms of Republic.'[10]

Two other nationalist groups ought perhaps to be mentioned. They are *L'Œuvre française*, founded by Pierre Sidos,
who belonged to that section of the extreme Right that
'denounces pell-mell Zionism, Marxism and Gaullism and
advocates a régime traditionally nationalist, deriving its principles from the works of Barrès, Maurras, Drumont and Brasil-
lach'.[11] This attitude is essentially one of ossified fidelity to the
past. The principles described as animating the most recent
nationalist group, the *Parti national populaire français*, formed
only in January 1970, have not yet been clearly enough defined
to be regarded as looking anywhere in particular. It described
itself as being in favour of 'French renaissance', of 'evolu-
tionary nationalism' and of 'European civilization'.[12]

A second category of right-wing formation was, at least in
theory, less exclusively concerned with the past, and has tried
to achieve some kind of synthesis between traditional views
and those that became fashionable from May 1968 onwards.
Pour une jeune Europe, which includes some nationalist students
from the FEN and some from the activist movement, *Occident*,

was among these. So was the *Mouvement jeune Révolution* (MJR),
which was opposed to Gaullist policies of university reform
(as, indeed, was *La Restauration nationale*, seeing them as inevitably productive of social disorder, which it especially
feared). *Jeune Révolution*, though naturally anti-Communist like
all extreme right-wing movements, was not violently anti-Left.
Formed by a former OAS group, its action has been mainly
clandestine, but it had a doctrine of sorts, compounded of
opposition to capitalism as well as to Marxist internationalism
and of support for a kind of Europeanism that would take
account of the special characteristics of different regions. It
sought to attract the young in particular.

What in 1970 seemed likely to become the most important –
and some feared the most sinister – of the movements in this
category, *l'Ordre nouveau*, was formed at the beginning of 1970.
It attracted more immediate publicity than any other of the
extreme right-wing movements and was admitted by several of
the extremist leaders to be 'the only significant' (*sérieux*) movement on the extreme Right.[13] It was founded by Jean Galvaire,
a teacher in the Law Faculty in Paris and formerly secretary-
general of M. Tixier-Vignancour's *Alliance républicaine*. *L'Ordre
nouveau* (which should not be confused with the movement of
the same name created before the war by, among others,
Robert Aron) also described itself as 'European' in the sense
that it wanted a 'multinational' Europe that would be a new
country stretching from the Atlantic to the Eastern marches.[14]

Any resemblance between this Europe and General de
Gaulle's Europe 'from the Atlantic to the Urals' can be immediately ruled out. *L'Ordre nouveau* lost no time in making
itself *persona non grata* to the Gaullist authorities by trying, in
February 1970, to organize meetings in Paris on a 'European'
level. Representatives were invited from the German NPD,
the Italian Social Movement, and the movement described as
'neo-Swedish'. The result was an outcry from the Left and
threatened clashes with extreme Left movements. There were
accusations that the movement was Fascist, and the upshot was
that the Government banned the meeting. M. Galvaire, in a
press conference, denied being either Fascist or Nazi, but

admitted to being a revolutionary who rejected existing society (though he apparently felt no desire to fight on any barricades). He described the movement as non-violent, though admitted that some of its supporters had resorted to violence. Its immediate objectives were to 'prevent the proliferation of Leftism', and its long-term objectives were 'the gradual conquest of power . . . by the procedures of Parliamentary democracy'.[15] Beyond this the party's aims and doctrine (if it had any) were far from clear. Some of its members came from the *Groupe Union-Droit* (GUD), whose main target was Leftists in the Paris Law Faculty. Its vocabulary included phrases about 'social justice' and 'neo-patriotism', but what exactly was new about it had still to emerge.

The third category, which overlaps with the others, was made up of movements whose sole, or predominating, purpose was to combat leftism, and especially the extreme left-wing militant movements in the Paris universities. Some, like GUD, recruited members mainly from a specific faculty, and their main interest was to oppose the university reforms introduced after the May events by Edgar Faure's *loi d'orientation de l'enseignement supérieur*, voted at the end of 1968, and painfully and slowly put into application over the following two years. *Action nationaliste*, for instance, though claiming to consist of militant nationalists and not merely of anti-Marxist activists, was largely recruited among students of the Institute of Political Science and was violently anti-American, seeking to liberate France from 'foreign parties and the power of financiers'. The movement best-known for its anti-Marxist activism, *Défense de l'Occident*, claimed to be neo-Fascist, though denied that its own brand had any relation to past types of Fascism. It was certainly 'activist', and when dissolved by the Government in November 1968 was stated by the Minister of the Interior to have been responsible for a number of violent incidents since its foundation in 1964. According to the editor of *Aspects de la France*, who repudiated any direct relation with it, its main object was to drive the Marxists out of university life.[16]

What will remain of these right-wing organizations in a few

years is anybody's guess. Their future will no doubt depend in part on the general political situation in France and in part on the evolution of political opinion in the universities. While they remain active, however, their main practical achievement will no doubt be, as it has been, to add fuel to the flames on the extreme Left.

LEFT-WING EXTREMIST GROUPS

The extreme Left presented a more serious problem to the authorities and constituted an even more divided, confused, unrealistic and fantasy-ridden collection of groups, '*groupuscules*', and periodicals, whose action ranged, and still ranges, from what are little more than academic discussions of different applications of Marxist doctrine to the organization of veritable commandos with the avowed aim of destroying universities as the first step to the destruction of French society. For some, the 'bourgeoisie' (never coherently defined) remains the main enemy. For others, the French Communist party has now taken its place, being regarded as the arch-betrayer of the working class. The Communist party leadership has been comprehensibly no less concerned than have other parties in France with the need to bring these extremist left-wing movements under control, since, though right-wing opposition often strengthens the Communist party, dissident Communist movements indubitably weaken it.

Out of the welter of confusion created by and continuing after the student 'revolution', some general characteristics of the extreme Left do emerge. Not that its positive aims have been any clearer than those of their opponents on the Right; but this is nothing new. French left-wing thought has always indulged freely in the romantic, revolutionary play-acting that has been among the less useful heritages of the French Revolution. The most vociferous demands for solidarity with 'the workers' (or more usually 'the masses') have come from the numerous middle-class intellectuals who have constituted the driving force in the elaboration of revolutionary theories, and have done most to maintain the unending quarrels between revolutionary theorists that have helped to make the French Left increasingly divided and impotent.

The new factor in the first decade of the Fifth Republic was that the student population in Paris – the traditional hunting-ground of romantic revolutionaries – had more than doubled, and with a speed that no Government could have kept pace with. Students, and particularly in Paris, have always played an active part in both left- and right-wing politics. But in the 1960s they had real practical grievances to add to their theoretical constructions, with the result that the traditional talk was accompanied by action, though often by action that had no more relevance to these problems than French left-wing theorizing has ever had to political realities.

The extreme Left can be divided into three distinct groups of movements, though the distinction is often blurred in practice by overlapping, as well as by the confusion created by the constant splits and re-formation of groups, and the appearance, disappearance and reconstitution of periodicals associated with different organizations. Each approach, or complex of approaches, constitutes, not a picture, but an incomplete jigsaw of allied or rival organizations, whose doctrinal position is as hazy as that of all the others.[17] The oldest tradition, that of anarchism, is naturally the most diffuse and has always presented a spectacle of almost inextricable confusion. It derives essentially from the belief, shared by some late eighteenth-century reformers, in the possibility of creating a harmonious society, in which the individual would be free to be himself, without the restraints imposed by the machinery of the State. But anarchists have always disagreed both on the extent to which some forms of social organizations are necessary or desirable, and also on the extent to which their propaganda methods should include violence. Some believe only in non-violent action, and have, therefore, resisted the obligation of military service. Others have advocated violence ('propaganda by deed') and, towards the end of the nineteenth century, were responsible for a number of bomb-throwing incidents.

Present-day anarchist movements are distinguished by two main approaches. There are the extreme individualists, for whom action is seen as something spontaneous, and who, therefore, reject in principle both political leadership and all large-scale organization. This traditional form of anarchism has generally been anti-Marxist. Marx himself had found anarchists his main enemies in the First International, and the orthodox French Communist party has continued to be hostile to them as a potential threat to their own tightly knit and disciplined organizations, based on collective controls and popularly accepted leadership. Under the Fifth Republic, the school of thought emphasizing spontaneity was represented in the 1960s mainly by such movements as the *Fédération anarchiste*, publishing *Le Monde libertaire*, a journal that in its present form dates from 1953. As its name indicates, the anarchist federation does believe in organization, at least to the extent of advocating an international federation of anarchists. It was joined in 1961 by a section of the *Groupe d'Action révolutionnaire*, formed in 1956. An opposing section of the latter movement, calling itself anarcho-Communist, formed a separate group, *Noir et Rouge*, of which Daniel Cohn-Bendit was a member until he formed, in 1968, with 142 students then occupying the Arts Faculty of the University of Nanterre, the *Mouvement du 22 mars*. Since the dissolution of the *Mouvement du 22 mars* in June 1968, as a result of its activities in the students' May revolution, *Noir et Rouge* appears to have worked with a movement called *Information et Correspondance ouvrière* (ICO), which denounces trade unions as 'conservative'.[18]

The second approach, that of anarcho-syndicalism, opposes 'spontaneity', believing not only that some common ground can and should be found between anarchism and Marxism, but also that organized trade unions provide the only effective framework for revolutionary action. It has been represented mainly by the *Organisation révolutionnaire anarchiste* (ORA), a movement created in 1967 by the union of a number of small local groups and related to other small groups formed in 1968. Revolutionary syndicalism need not, of course, be anarchist, and a number of its organizations have not been anarchist. In practice, however, the two approaches overlap, since both believe in trade unions as the basic unit of society and of both industrial and political action. The main expression of revolutionary syndicalism, *la Révolution prolétarienne*, publishing a monthly with the same title, was founded in 1925 by a minority section of the CGT.

It was estimated in 1959–60 that there were then in France some 15,000 anarchists. Any figure must be treated with caution, however, for diffused as they were, both doctrinally and geographically, their rôle in trade unions and in relation to the Left generally was normally no more than that of a minor, disruptive irritant. There were two brief periods of revival of activity, in 1956 and in 1968, but the impetus was rapidly exhausted, and the activities of anarchists in 1968 and since were soon eclipsed by the more modern forms of violent extremism deriving from the theories of Communist China.

The second tradition on the extreme Left, that of Trotskyism, has a long history of successive crises and schisms, on personal as well as on doctrinal grounds. The *Parti communiste internationaliste*, originally the most important movement, was formed in 1936 as a movement farther to the Left than the Communist party, joined the Fourth International, and immediately split. Some of its members joined the left wing of the Socialist party, the workers' and peasants' group led by Marceau Pivert, who was for many years one of the more colourful leaders on the extreme left of the Socialist federation of the Paris region. A number of Trotskyist candidates stood in the elections of 1945 and 1946, though none were elected. The movement then split into supporters and opponents of the Fourth International, some believing that the Communist party should be fought, others that it should be infiltrated.

The situation became doubly confused when, to the divisions created by previous feuds and schisms, there were added new ones arising from the creation and subsequent dissolution of Trotskyist movements supporting the students' revolution in 1968, and their re-formation or re-alignment under other names. But, at the beginning of the 1970s, there were four main distinguishable tendencies. First, there was the *Organisation Trotskiste* publishing a periodical, *La Vérité*. This tendency (*Lambertiste*)[19] was in favour of reconstituting the Fourth

International. It was joined by the student movement, the FER (*Fédération des Etudiants révolutionnaires*), dissolved in June 1968, and associated with two other student Trotskyist movements, the AES (*Alliance des Etudiants pour le Socialisme*) and the AJS (*Alliance des Jeunes pour le Socialisme*), which, in 1970, was well on the way to gaining control of what used to be the most important student union, the UNEF (*Union nationale des Etudiants de France*).[20] Each has its own periodical.

The second Trotskyist tendency, that of *La Ligue communiste*, founded in 1969 by Alain Krivine, one of the leaders of the student revolution and a presidential candidate in that year, published a weekly, *Rouge*, and represented the section (*Frankiste*), which considered itself to be the authentic representative in France of the Fourth International. It included the JCR (*Jeunesse communiste révolutionnaire*), formed in 1966 by students expelled from the Communist party and dissolved by the Government in 1968.

The third tendency (*Pabliste*), represented by the *Alliance marxiste révolutionnaire*, resulted from the schism of 1955 when Pablo, or Michel Raptis, was expelled. He believed in workers' control (*autogestion*) and the need to infiltrate existing mass movements.[21] The fourth tendency, represented by *Lutte ouvrière*, publishing a periodical with the same name, was active in factories after 1968, and had formed upwards of 100 groups by 1970. It was then considering union with the *Ligue communiste*, though the two movements were not agreed on the form that the union should take. An agreement on partial fusion was finally reached on 7 January 1971.

The official *raison d'être* of Trotskyism, the need to restore to Communism the original purity of doctrine before the Stalinist epoch, to admit of no compromise with 'State capitalism, party bureaucracy and the 'nationalist' attitude of Soviet Communism',[22] has long since been submerged in the flood of conflicting interpretations, never-ending dissensions, and theoretical arguments in the continually changing movements and their publications. The only real links between these small, rival tendencies have been, first, their common hostility to orthodox Communism and second, their common attraction for some sections of the trade-union movements, and in particular, for the youth sections of Socialist and Communist parties[23] and student organizations. They have constituted a permanent, potentially disruptive influence.

The most serious political threat to the régime between 1968 and 1970 came from neither of these two traditional minority extremist movements, but from the third, and most recent, the Maoist movement. This, too, includes a number of different organizations, frequently divided, splitting and reforming themselves, each claiming to represent the purest form of Marxist–Leninism. The Maoists have been essentially action groups, violently opposed to the existing system. Where Trotskyists have preferred to infiltrate other left-wing organizations, Maoists believe in destructive revolutionary action by the rank and file. They were among the active organizers of the May revolution, and commandos of their organizations continued to disrupt university life during the following two sessions. They also believed in direct action elsewhere.

Up to 1968, there were three main Maoist movements. The first, formed in 1964 as a group sympathetic to Communist China, was the *Fédération des Cercles marxistes-léninistes*, which published, from 1965, the periodical *Humanité nouvelle*.[24] In 1966, this group became the *Mouvement communiste de France (marxiste-léniniste)* and in 1967, the *Parti communiste marxiste-léniniste de France*. It was dissolved by the Government in June 1968. The second, the *Centre marxiste-léniniste de France*, formed in 1965, was hostile to the Chinese 'cultural revolution'; and a majority even approved of General de Gaulle's candidature in the presidential election of 1965. This movement was not dissolved in 1968, but split, some members (mainly from the Rhônes–Alpes region) forming a separate organization called *Voix prolétarienne*. The third, represented by the *Union des Jeunesses communistes marxistes-léninistes* (UJCML) was formed by members of the *Ecole normale supérieure* and published the *Cahiers marxistes-léninistes*. It consisted mainly of Marxist theorists who were former members of the Communist Students Union and had been either expelled or had left the movement in 1966. The UJCML was dissolved in June 1968.

Since 1968, the dissolved movements[25] have re-formed themselves into two main organizations. The first, calling itself the *avant-garde révolutionnaire*, formed the *Front uni*, a body expressing in the main student opinion, publishing a paper called *Humanité rouge* and advocating a united front against what it called 'the Fascist régime'. It was less aggressive than the second, *la Gauche prolétarienne*, one of whose leaders, Alain Geismar, a young university teacher and the former secretary-general of the left-wing association of university teachers, was among the most active of the 1968 student revolutionary leaders. This movement published *La Cause du Peuple*,[26] whose editor, Jean-Pierre le Dantec, was arrested in March 1970 on charges of provocation to arson, murder and theft, and of crimes against the security of the State.[27] *La Gauche prolétarienne* (which was dissolved in May 1970) included members not only of the former *Union des jeunesses marxistes-léninistes*, but also of the *Mouvement du 22 mars*, both dissolved in June 1968. It had a 'parallel' organization, *la nouvelle Résistance populaire*, which carried out commando activities, was anti-police, and was opposed to the orthodox Communist party and the Communist-dominated trade-union confederation, both of which were accused of collaboration with the bourgeoisie. Though this movement, too, originated as a student organization, it has also included outside members, particularly among immigrant workers. *La nouvelle Résistance populaire* was attacked by the PSU organ, *Tribune socialiste*, as being a purely destructive guerilla movement 'with a populist ideology of anarchistic implications'.[28]

The former leader of the *Mouvement du 22 mars*, Daniel Cohn-Bendit, certainly consistently defended destructive violence for its own sake as an expression of revolutionary anarchism, and this is also the Maoist position. In May 1968, Daniel Cohn-Bendit had claimed to be seeking 'a temporary rupture in the cohesion of the system' and had seen the future as a series of revolutions that would fail, in the sense that they would not in themselves bring a new society, but would merely destroy the existing system of law and order.[29] In defending the Maoist active position in 1970, Jean-Paul Sartre (not himself a Maoist, but an admitted sympathizer) affirmed his solidarity with the actions of M. Le Dantec and with all actions (such as those then *sub judice*) that wanted to extend existing violence to the masses in order to emphasize its revolutionary nature.[30]

By the spring of 1970 the Government had a real battle on its hands in order to protect not merely the State educational system, but also private citizens peacefully engaged in lawful business, from attacks by Maoist commandos who might happen to have taken it into their heads to regard them as symbolic of the 'bourgeoisie' or of 'capitalism'. Though in all cases the violence was the work of small – often very small – bands, it was enough to cause a great deal of damage and the disruption of a considerable amount of university work.[31] There was never any likelihood that it would bring 'the revolution' any nearer, or indeed any evidence that the Maoists wanted a real revolution.

Perhaps the most striking illustration of the futility and hypocrisy, or alternatively the fantasies, involved in some of these exploits was the attack on 8 May 1970 on the well-known luxury Paris foodstore of Fauchon. A twenty-year-old sociology student admitted the offence and justified it on the ground that it was 'a political operation intended to restore these expensive preserves to the poor'. Her father defended her action as being 'illegal, but inspired by a noble cause'. The facts established at the trial showed that employees of the store had been physically assaulted (presumably they did not count for Maoists as authentic 'workers'!) and quantities of bottles of spirits and preserved fruit had been smashed, instead of being 'distributed to the poor'. Though the offence was punishable by a term of imprisonment of up to five years, the defendant was given only a thirteen-month sentence, together with a fine of 3000 francs to cover some of the damage. Nevertheless, there was something of an outcry in left-wing circles, by no means limited to members of extremist movements. For instance, the argument of the prosecuting Counsel that the action was puerile as well as illegal cut no ice at all with M. Jean-Paul Sartre, and the fact that *innocent* workers had been physically attacked by young people whose working-class *bona fides* were, to say the least, doubtful also left him cold. In a long article,[32] he placed the blame on the social system which, he said, constituted 'a permanent oppression that in itself calls forth popular violence'. The authors of the offence were, he went on, merely 'refusing to accept bourgeois legality'.

This was a traditional, romantic French left-wing reaction. What matters still to many people on the Left, not all of whom are rebellious students, is the gesture, not the facts. What matters is neither logic nor political morality, but the sentimental legend of 'the sacred right of revolution', or of a 'right to freedom of opinion' invoked to justify illegality, the refusal to others of the same rights, and physical violence towards those whose opinions are subjectively and arbitrarily classed as 'bourgeois' or 'reactionary'. These windmills that the Don Quixotes of the extreme Left have invented to tilt at, without risk to themselves or to their (objectively) bourgeois way of life, are the stuff of which Fascism, not a Socialist revolution, is made. But the immediate effect of the measures taken by the Government was to stimulate a kind of implicit (where it was not explicit) solidarity of the extremist and non-extremist Left, because no French left-wing party can afford to allow itself to be 'outflanked on the Left' on a matter involving what is claimed as 'Socialist' or 'revolutionary' action.

It is not being suggested that the measures themselves were not in many respects criticizable, or that the police were not guilty themselves of acts of violence, and sometimes of indiscriminate violence. But there is no doubt whatsoever that one of the main Maoist aims was precisely to provoke the police to a point at which some such reaction would be unavoidable. They were able to do this with relative impunity owing to the traditional right (recognized by the law and vigorously defended on the Left) of universities to exclude the police from their premises. One result was to intensify the already bad relations between the Left and the police, inherited from the period of the Algerian war.

In 1970, it sometimes seemed as if the Left as a whole was withdrawing into a fantasy world, characterized by old-fashioned, sentimental reactions towards violence and by the propagation of political ideas more suited to the conditions of 1870 than to those of 1970. There was, however, one significant exception. The Communists had their own internal quarrels, and their own objections to the existing system. But they were carrying on at least two battles with their feet firmly on the ground; the battle for improved wages and conditions, and the battle to prevent Maoists, Trotskyists and anarchists from infiltrating or weakening their own organizations, and from making the educational system unworkable.[33]

THE CASE OF THE PSU

The evolution of the PSU during the first ten years of the Fifth Republic makes it something of a special case. It originally occupied a position on the Left analagous in some respects to that of M. Tixier-Vignancour's *Alliance républicaine* on the Right. Both were essentially opposition or protest movements, recruiting support among minority elements and on the margin between Parliamentary and extremist groups. Both were intermittently represented in the National Assembly, but only by one or two Deputies.[34] Up to 1968, the PSU certainly behaved like a Parliamentary party. It contested elections, seemed likely sooner or later to rejoin the Socialist party, and represented the traditional theoretical, doctrinaire and dissident leftism that is endemic in French politics. Its persistent attraction for middle-class and highly articulate intellectuals, indeed, gave it an importance in left-wing circles out of all proportion to its numbers, which were small, and to its impact on policies, which was nil. It was revolutionary, but so (in theory) are the Socialist and Communist parties, and like theirs, its revolutionary ardour was of the armchair variety and limited to talk. It was certainly highly unlikely that a politician of the stature of Pierre Mendès France would have agreed to be associated with it if it had been anything more revolutionary than a splinter party claiming to be more authentically 'left' than the others. He joined it in September 1958, with supporters of his small *Centre d'Action démocratique*, and remained a member up to 1968, in theory at least. Though an ex-Prime Minister, and by far the most outstanding personality in the PSU, he never in fact played any active rôle in it or appeared to have any influence on it, or indeed any contacts with it. In the press conferences that he gave from time to time during these years, he always seemed to be speaking entirely for himself.

The May revolution was, however, a traumatic experience for the PSU and transformed it (or sections of it, for it was never unanimous about anything) into an organization characterized by acute political schizophrenia. Its leaders continued to quarrel about their relations with other (Parliamentary) left-wing parties, while expressing their disbelief in the possibility of attaining their ends by Parliamentary means, and advocating 'direct democracy' and co-operation with left-wing extremist groups. It was already rumoured that M. Mendès France was about to resign from the PSU before his surprising declaration (on 28 May, at the height of the student revolt) that he would not refuse the responsibility of trying to form a Government at the request of a united Left. Though he did appear, for a brief moment, to sympathize with the revolutionary movement, he in fact resigned from the PSU later in 1968, and supported the Socialist presidential candidate, Gaston Defferre, the following year. Meanwhile the secretary-general of the PSU continued to tolerate the Parliamentary system to the extent both of standing as a presidential candidate and getting himself elected to the National Assembly (the only PSU representative in the 1968 Assembly). But the party's increasingly active co-operation – or more accurately perhaps, expressed desire for co-operation – with anti-Parliamentary and violent extremists would seem to justify the view that, from 1968 onwards, it should be regarded as an extremist rather than as a Parliamentary party.

When it was formed in September 1958, the *Parti socialiste autonome* (PSA), as it was then called, consisted of a minority of Socialists opposed to the new régime and to the 'constructive opposition' to it advocated by the majority leader, Guy Mollet. His policy was, of course, dictated by the overriding need to prevent a civil war in France over Algeria, and was inspired by the hope that, after the failure of six successive Governments to deal with the problem during the past four years, General de Gaulle might be able to find a way of ending the Algerian war. In April 1960, having been joined by some small heterogeneous left-wing groups, including mainly ex-Communists and intellectual fellow-travellers, the PSA changed its name to PSU (*Parti socialiste unifié*), a striking misnomer for a party whose history has been one of permanent disunity and recurrent schism. There was talk of reunification with the Socialist party for some years, but nothing came of it, partly, no doubt, owing to the personal hostility of some of its members to Guy Mollet, but also owing to its uncompromising hostility to the régime (at a time when the Socialists were beginning to be reconciled to it), to its unrelenting advocacy of common action (on its own terms) with the Communists,[35] and especially owing to its anti-Atlanticism and unending internal quarrels. By 1961, it had already developed its own minority section; by 1963, it consisted of five or six discernible rival sections.

During these years its membership remained roughly stable at around 15,000,[36] and its vote varied from 0·8% of the votes cast in the election of 1958 to 3·94% of the votes cast in 1968. At its peak, therefore, it never polled more than 10% of the total left-wing vote.[37] Most of its members were in the Paris region and it was estimated in June 1969 that a third of them were academics. It opposed the two attempts by the Socialist party to create a Federation of the non-Communist Left, objecting to Gaston Defferre's proposed '*grande fédération*', on the ground that he was seeking support from the Centre (and especially from the MRP),[38] and to François Mitterrand's proposed '*contre-gouvernement*', on the ground that it made him a prisoner of the Socialist and Radical parties.[39] It did, however, accept the terms of the electoral alliance concluded by the Communist party and the non-Communist Federation of the Left in December 1966, though it regarded the latter as constituting an association between technocracy and international cartels and held, contrary to the belief of the rest of the non-

Communist Left, that France ought not to renew her membership of the Atlantic Alliance in 1969.[40]

The first major split in the PSU occurred in 1965, when some
of its leading members formed, along with a number of
political Clubs, the *Union des Clubs pour le Renouveau de la
Gauche* (UCRG), under the leadership of Alain Savary.[41]
Divisions became pronounced again following the election.
They culminated in the breakaway, in October 1967, of a minority under the leadership of Jean Poperen, which was in
favour of association with, though not of membership of, the
Federation of the Democratic and Socialist Left. This minority
took the title of *Union des Groupes et Clubs socialistes* (UGCS).
Both breakaway groups believed in the need for some formula
permitting co-operation with the Federation of the Left.

By this time, it had become impossible to envisage any
partner acceptable to the PSU in its theoretical campaign for
united action by the Left, and one prominent member of the
party put the issue squarely to the delegates at the party Congress in 1967.

> We want unity on the Left [he said], but on condition that it
> is not unity with the Communist party, the Socialists, the
> Radicals – perhaps not even with members of the *Convention*.
> With whom, then, are we proposing to unite? . . . The PSU,
> in its pure and solitary ivory tower, cannot defeat Gaullism
> by itself.[42]

The immediate effect of the May revolution was a rise in
PSU membership, but at the cost of a vital change in the party's
political complexion. The sympathy expressed by the PSU for
the student revolt, its encouragement of the setting up of
Comités d'Action populaire, its emphasis on the need for direct
government by workers, peasants, universities or regions,[43]
naturally attracted to it a number of revolutionaries for whom
the traditional parties, and the Communist party even more
perhaps than the others, had become so many expressions of
co-operation with the 'bourgeoisie'. At the PSU's sixth Congress in March 1969, it was stated that 42% of its members
had joined the party since 1968, and that, of these, three-

quarters had not previously been members of any political party. If the old hands were content to go on with the familiar exercise of revolutionary games theories, this would not do for the new, and mainly youthful, revolutionary members. The PSU was therefore faced with a serious problem of revolutionary tactics on which it was, as usual, hopelessly divided. There were those who wanted it to retain its autonomy, but to 'discuss' common action with the Communist party; those who believed that this was impossible and wanted the party to commit itself frankly to co-operation with the left-wing extremist movements; and those who occupied various intermediary positions, inspired by the desire to maintain contact with the revolutionary groups without actually severing their relationship with traditional parties.[44]

Divisions on these issues led to the formation of yet another breakaway movement in 1969, the *Centre d'Etudes et d'Initiatives révolutionnaires* (CEIR), led by Marc Heurgon, which rejected 'reformism', described itself as a movement of 'militant Communists', and advocated contacts with extremist parties in Italy.[45] The movement was joined by several members of Marxist–Leninist groups.

In practice, the decision by the secretary-general, Michel Rocard, in 1969, to take the battle for Socialism on to the factory floor, and to make it a condition of working with other parties that they should not *a priori* rule out co-operation with the left-wing extremists, helped to resolve the tactical dilemma, though the decision itself constituted an object-lesson in the political unrealism of French intellectual left-wing revolutionary attitudes. For the immediate effect was to anger 'the masses', with whom the PSU was seeking to work. Both Communist and non-Communist trade-union leaders objected to what they regarded as an attempt to impose PSU political leadership in factories, in defiance of the half-century-old tradition of trade-union independence of political parties.[46] Moreover, the PSU's belief in 'direct democracy' and its interpretation of 'participation' were rejected by the overwhelming majority of the organized workers. The Communist party was, indeed, determined to keep industrial action within the existing framework and had no sympathy whatsoever with the idea of government by 'the masses'.[47] The policy only revealed once again how minimal were the PSU's contacts with the workers, and how out of touch with twentieth-century realities was its conservative ideology of the class struggle.[48]

After twelve years of existence, and perpetual splits, the PSU had effectively ensured its own non-credibility in the eyes of all its potential allies and brought open hostility from some. In the words of one of the more revolutionary members of its political bureau,[49] it was unable to go beyond verbalism in its campaign. A Maoist weekly described it as 'a by-product of a debased form of Marxism'.[50] Unfortunately for the efficacity of French left-wing politics, it was precisely its unrealism that constituted its main attraction. Political unrealism, endemic doctrinal bickering, old-fashioned Socialist ideology and revolutionary play-acting exercise a force of attraction precisely because they are intellectual attitudes divorced from practical political action. It is impossible to understand French politics unless adequate account is taken of this fact, a fact exemplified day after day by the inclusion in the serious and more intellectual French press and periodicals of long accounts of the thoughts, decisions and quarrels of innumerable small left-wing groups. They are news, and they interest those large sections of opinion – particularly of intellectual, middle-class opinion – for whom politics means first and foremost an intellectual exercise involving symbolic and ritual gestures – for whom resolutions are still more important than programmes.

THE POLITICAL CLUBS

In a report on an intellectual 'round table' discussion on 'the consumer society, its ills and its cures', a political commentator remarked in May 1970 that

> Colloquia, seminars, round tables on the future of society are increasing. They are frequently attended by the same men – members of the 'intelligentsia', economists, industrialists, high civil servants, teachers . . . etc.[51]

The most depressing feature about the above comment is that it could equally well have been made at almost any moment during the previous seven years. If the most disquieting development of the extreme Left and the extreme Right was their defence of, and actual resort to, violence, and if that of the PSU was its intellectual flirtation with violence, the most disquieting development on the non-extremist Left was the growing tendency to sit back and concentrate on intellectual analyses unaccompanied by any sense of personal responsibility for participation in the political process. At the beginning of the régime, the orthodox Left, conscious of its unattractiveness to the public, its ageing membership and falling numbers, had set out to appeal to what were generally described as '*les nouvelles couches*', that is, to the younger generation and to sectors of opinion outside parties. Unfortunately they had nothing new to offer and the 'new thinking' was, therefore, conducted in organizations reluctant to be associated with party politics.

During the first half of the 1960s, some 120 or more political Clubs came into existence in Paris and the provinces. Most of them were small, with memberships of 500 or, perhaps, 1000. They were predominantly middle-class, with a high percentage of intellectuals and civil servants.[52] Though critical of both the Fourth and Fifth Republics, they were not systematically opposed to the latter. Nor were they rivals of the established parties, because they were generally uninterested in them. They were small coteries, interested primarily in political discussion and debate, and though most of them had recognizable political affiliations,[53] or at least predilections, they remained aloof from the machinery of party politics and for the most part uninterested in elections or in the machinery of obtaining power. Their interests were in such topics as the principles of Republican democracy, the development of Europe, the recovery of citizenship and constitutional reform, and their aim was

> to encourage the birth of a new political generation by appealing to those who, for the most part, have held aloof from politics.[54]

To set out to revolutionize a political system by holding academic seminars preaching detachment from the regular machinery of politics to an audience that has hitherto shown little or no interest in politics may seem an original kind of non-revolutionary non-activity. But the Clubs held no brief for Gaullist 'efficiency'. Their idea was to re-educate society by some process of osmosis, that is by the gradual percolation of their new thinking to parties from which they themselves would remain aloof. Their specific rôle was

> to be a centre of study and a pressure group that refuses participation [i.e. in party politics] but seeks to create the conditions in which participation would be possible.[55]

It is evident that this tendency to opt out of practical politics and engage in research and analysis without any personal sense of involvement was hardly likely to appeal to politicians who, however unrealistic their policies might be, were nevertheless brought into contact with some political realities by the obligations of party and electoral activities. Nor were they likely to welcome education by a self-appointed élite, described by one prominent Socialist as 'at heart, merely Romantics, with no contacts with the masses, too many leaders and no rank and file'.[56] In any case, the disagreements and lack of homogeneity among the Clubs would in themselves have prevented them from having any real influence. The would-be educators were themselves sufferers from the disease of '*a-politization*' that they sought to cure, and their ideas tended too often to be merely utopian, though some felt apparently that this was as it should be.

Somewhere between 1964 and 1966, a number of the Clubs began to seek closer links with political parties. In 1964, a certain number formed the CIR, which, by 1966, had become to all intents and purposes a political party,[57] since it had joined the Federation of the Democratic and Socialist Left and was regularly represented on its governing body. There was much disagreement among the Clubs on the questions of relations with the Federation. The *Club Jean Moulin*, for instance, eventually refused to join it on the ground that the function of the Clubs was to constitute an élite, 'a kind of aristocracy, not subject to partisan obligations'.[58] There was a real fear on the part of some that to join the Federation would be to accept integration in precisely the kind of party organization that they regarded it as their duty to reject.[59]

In the following years, two developments affected the position of the Clubs. The first was that the 'Club' habit spread to the orthodox parties and even to some trade unions. These set up their own Clubs, not to carry out 'non-partisan' research, but for the most part to act as party satellites or spearheads intended to attract new members.[60] The second development resulted directly from the decision of the *Convention* to join the Federation and to contest the elections in 1967 as part of it. Sixteen members were elected and sat in the National Assembly as part of the single Parliamentary group constituted by the Federation. In the elections the following year, all but their leader, M. Mitterrand, were defeated. It was clear henceforth that the only road back to active politics was via membership of the Socialist party, then in process of reorganization. As was natural, the Clubs were split on this issue. The *Club Jean Moulin, Objectif 1972*, and the *Convention* itself eventually opted to stay outside, while M. Savary's UCRG joined the Socialist party, and M. Savary himself became 'first secretary' and spokesman. Some members of the *Convention* also decided to join, as did a section of the members of the *Union des Groupes et Clubs socialistes* (UGCS) led by Jean Poperen.[61]

In a country less addicted than France to the perennial creation and re-formation of small left-wing splinter groups and movements, the situation of the Clubs in 1970 would have justified a prediction that their vogue was over. In France, such a prediction would be rash. The president of the *Club des Jacobins*, M. Charles Hernu, expressed the opinion that 'when parties are in crisis Clubs flourish',[62] and if that is so, then political Clubs could well continue to be born and reborn for a long time to come. Agreed only on the vaguest of aims, they always interpret these in many different ways, with the result that splits and the formation of new movements become inevitable. For instance, M. Poperen's membership of the new

'Socialist party' did not prevent him from announcing the formation of a new Club of his own, and the *Convention* set up its own Club for research and information.[63]

In reality, the political Clubs of the 1960s (and presumably of the 1970s) do not represent 'new thinking' as they claim or hope to do. They constitute a very old approach to politics. They represent that combination of intellectualism, universalism and individualism that has characterized French reformist and revolutionary politics since the eighteenth century, and that, perhaps more than anything else, has helped to prevent the consolidation of stable and disciplined democratic parties.

CHAPTER X

Interest Groups and Politics

INTEREST GROUPS IN THE FRENCH SYSTEM

One of the functions of parties in all democratic systems is to represent local and sectional interests. This has always been especially important in France, owing partly to the weakness and instability of Governments, and partly to the weakness of parties as formulators of realistic Governmental policies, whether in Government or in opposition. Whether or not the existence of a highly centralized and powerful bureaucratic administrative machine has been primarily due to the weakness and divisions of parties, or whether its existence enabled parties to be irresponsible with impunity, the fact remained that the real source of power, under both the Third and Fourth Republics, lay in Parliament, not the Government. Too often the most effective way for an individual or group to cut through the jungle of administrative procedures, delays and red tape was to find a Deputy who would approach the Minister directly. When Government majorities were precarious, the power that individual Deputies wielded could often be considerable.

One of the consequences of this situation has been the high proportion of Parliamentary representatives who normally combine the functions of local and national representative. But the fact that Deputies have been accustomed to act as spokesmen for the local interests of the municipality of which they were Mayors or the *départements* of which they were Councillors does not mean, of course, that pressure groups have not been numerous and active, and some of them very powerful. In his pioneering study on pressure groups, published in 1957, Jean Meynaud lists some three hundred of them,[1] ranging from industrial giants to small societies that could not hope to be more than study groups without any real influence. The powerful groups undoubtedly do bring pressure to bear directly on Governments, but since, like lightning, they take the shortest route, they may choose to act through Parliament, when Parliament appears stronger than Governments, or may bring pressure on both. Some interests have been openly represented in Parliamentary 'intergroups', cutting across parties. Among these have been groups to defend the interests of farmers, winegrowers, home distillers, Catholic schools, ex-servicemen, and so on.

All this does not mean, as is sometimes alleged, that in France parties *are* pressure groups, but rather that the line between their political and pressure-group activities is more difficult to draw than in the case of systems like those of Britain, where both parties and Governments are normally strong and have relatively coherent policies. Jean Meynaud accepts the classic criteria for identifying interest and pressure groups. These are: the possession of a common interest; the use of collective action to further it; and the choice of action in the form of pressure on decision-making bodies, rather than of effort to obtain political power directly. The third condition alone rules out political parties, whose action, whether on behalf of interests or of principles, is (at least in theory) directly related to the hope of obtaining power. But, as has been pointed out earlier, the power motive is conspicuously absent in some French political parties. There is therefore a certain overlap between the functions of parties and those of pressure groups.

There is often an overlap between the fields of action of different interest groups. These are ideological (including moral), economic (including sectional and professional), and political. But the Deputy who belongs to a left-wing ideological party manages to combine his political theories with practical action on behalf of local interests, both collective and individual, while the trade-unionist manages similarly to combine his practical economic objectives with a great deal of political and ideological theorizing. It is significant that, though there has been a complete organizational separation between political parties and trade-union movements in France since the Amiens Charter of 1906,[2] political preoccupations and political ideology in trade-union movements have been far more important than they are in British trade unions, of which most of the larger ones are directly affiliated to the Labour party and directly represented on the party's executive.

Nevertheless, though there is an overlap of attitudes and functions, political parties and trade unions in France do have recognizably different rôles to play. Nothing brings this out better than the example of the Poujadist group in Parliament from 1956 to 1958. Though members of this group openly acted as spokesmen for a pressure group of tradesmen and craftsmen, the *Union de Défense des Commerçants et Artisans* (UDCA), in their capacity as Deputies they also had decided views on other subjects. They were, in particular, ardent supporters of the policy of keeping Algeria French, a subject totally unrelated to the fortunes of the UDCA. Nor do French trade unions, however deeply interested in and divided on political issues they may be, treat these as parties do. Even the Communist-dominated trade-union movement, the CGT, though it remains so faithful in practice to Communist political directives as to make its claim to 'independence' of the Communist party a meaningless fiction, plays a quite different rôle in French political life from that played by the Communist party. Parties and trade-union movements have different functions and different emphases. Communist trade-union leaders, in particular, have expressed themselves very plainly on this point.[3]

The demotion of Parliament under the Fifth Republic and the emergence of Governments with a stable majority in the National Assembly have helped to weaken the impact of direct pressure on Deputies and of Deputies on Governments. But there is still a strong conviction among political parties (Gaullists not excepted) that the road to political victory is smoother, and the victory more permanent, for candidates who have strong roots in local political life and for Deputies who pay attention to the personal and material interests of their constituents.[4] And the dependence of all candidates except those in large cities on a politically significant farmers' vote has meant that Governments have always been peculiarly vulnerable to pressure from farming interests. General de Gaulle's ability to resist them in 1960 was in great part the consequence of the special circumstance of his indispensability while the Algerian problem existed. But even this did not enable the Government to avoid making concessions when farmers resorted to a long campaign of direct action.

The difference between the situation under the Fourth Republic and that under the Fifth is really only one of degree.[5] The balance has shifted somewhat from direct pressure through Parliament to direct pressure on Governments, because Governments are now the more powerful of the two. This means that even less is known than before about the real strength of pressure groups. For by its nature, direct pressure through Parliament is more open, and therefore more subject to counter-pressures. Its long-term political effects can be serious, in particular its disintegrating effect on the functioning of the party system. But Parliamentary intergroups cutting across parties can sometimes be resisted by determined Governments, since the different organizations can to some extent cancel each other out. The pressure was much harder to resist within the legislative committees which, under the Fourth Republic, were often packed with supporters of certain economic vested interests. Under the Fifth Republic, with fewer and larger committees, this pressure has been more difficult to organize.

No attempt can be made, within the scope of this book, to give anything like a complete picture of the range of French pressure groups. Their numbers are considerable and their activities complex and varied. Within the framework of the three categories mentioned, it is possible to divide and subdivide them almost *ad infinitum*. 'Ideological' groups include those with religious, political, politico-religious preoccupations; influential groups and small coteries; long-lived groups and ephemeral ones. Economic and professional groups include industrial and farming organizations, workers' and employers' organizations (some of which are also defending religious or anti-clerical interests), and organizations representing large-scale and small-scale industries. Even those that appear on the surface to be homogeneous and non-political prove in reality to be highly complex. For instance, the powerful ex-servicemen's lobby includes associations with differing political opinions and concerned with different ex-servicemen's problems. All that can be attempted in a single chapter is to discuss briefly the most important of those interest groups that have, or have had, the most evident direct impact on politics, and to try to show what they regard themselves as standing for and how they are related to each other.[6]

IDEOLOGICAL AND MORAL INTEREST GROUPS

Of the ideological and moral interest groups, undoubtedly the most politically influential have been those concerned with the rôle of Catholicism in politics. There are a host of Catholic associations representing employers, women, youth, trade-unionists, farmers, students, and so on. On the other hand, there are powerful organizations opposed to the political influence of Catholicism, some of which – freemasonry, for instance – have probably at times been suspected of having more influence than they really had, because of the secrecy surrounding their activities. Of the organizations defending the principle of non-denominational education, the oldest, the *Ligue de l'Enseignement*, goes back to the second Empire. There are also associations of the parents of children in State schools. Similarly, those who support the continued existence of Catholic schools have their own interest groups, including associations of parents of children in independent schools (virtually all of which are Catholic). In all, Jean Meynaud lists at least twenty associations promoting either Catholic, anti-clerical or Protestant interests.

Except in periods in which there is intense political controversy on this issue (as there was in 1951 and again in 1959), when their activity flares up afresh, the influence of these groups may be regarded as weakening. M. Debré's 1959 legislation provided some alleviation of the most pressing problems of the Catholic schools and created a framework in which both sides could gradually become resigned to co-existence. But it would be rash to assume as yet that the problem will never again be a subject of acute political controversy. In 1971, the immediate response to the Government's inclusion of the amendment to the Debré law on the agenda for the April Parliamentary session was a revival of pressures from opponents of State aid to Catholic schools. Though small in extent, it was nevertheless symptomatic. It included a brief strike called in a lycée, a Communist attack in *l'Humanité*, describing the fight for *l'école laique* as not merely historically important, but an aspect of the class struggle, and proposals for a strike against the measure, put forward by some CGT and CFDT teachers' unions.[7]

Among other organizations in this category that have been politically influential are those defending moral and individual rights. Though there are associations in favour of pacifism and moral rearmament and opposed to the existence of an independent French nuclear deterrent, these issues have never had anything like the political importance that they have had in Great Britain. The most politically influential has probably been the left-wing *Ligue des Droits de l'Homme*, founded in 1898 at the time of the Dreyfus affair. In addition to its defence of individual rights, it has been opposed to clericalism and racialism, including anti-Semitism. But its heyday was in the 1930s when it could claim to have a Parliamentary 'intergroup' of 200 Deputies and Senators. Nowadays, though it issues declarations from time to time, it is difficult to feel that these carry any real political weight, even inside left-wing circles. There are, of course, a number of other interest groups that could be included in this category, but they are too heterogeneous, and in many cases too small and ephemeral to be discussed in a book primarily concerned with politics.

ECONOMIC INTEREST GROUPS (i) TRADE UNIONS

By far the most important economic interest groups are the trade-union movements and the employers' associations.

Trade unions have had a difficult history in France. The persistence of fears of them inspired by the survival of Rousseauistic
doctrines regarding the conflict between particular interests
and the general interests of the community, theories of economic liberalism, and the strength of employers' hostility to trade
unions have all contributed to their difficulties. In 1791, the
Loi le Chapelier forbade all associations, whether of employers
or of workers.[8] Under Napoleon, severe penalties were imposed
on labour organizations. And though, from about 1855,
Napoleon III tended increasingly to tolerate trade-union
activity, and lifted the legal ban on strikes in 1864, it was not
until 1884 that the Third Republic legalized freedom of
association, and then only subject to conditions unacceptable
to many trade unions. In 1895, a federation of all major trade
unions, the *Confédération générale du Travail* (CGT), was formed,
but in 1920 it was officially dissolved, following an abortive
general strike. In practice it continued to exist, and by 1936
trade unions had become generally accepted as responsible
bodies, able to negotiate collective agreements, and as partners
in machinery for conciliation and arbitration in industry. From
1946 onwards, their representatives became an important
element of the quasi-parliamentary Economic Council. The
right to strike was constitutionally recognized, even though it
was limited in practice by restrictions on the right of civil
servants to strike, and also by some voluntary agreements in
which unions undertook not to strike for a certain period in
return for certain benefits.

More and more, trade unions have come to accept the need
for practical co-operation with the State (in spite of the
opposition of dissident or potentially dissident revolutionary
Trotskyist or anarchist elements). For instance, the social-
security system, built up after the war, has always been administered by elected bodies representing mainly the major
trade-union movements, the State intervening only to amend
the rules and to provide subsidies. Trade-unionists are also
represented on the governing bodies of nationalized industries,
on the Economic and Social Council, on committees responsible for drawing up the national economic plans, and on the

economic advisory bodies set up under the 1964 law creating economic regions.

Throughout their existence, however, French trade unions have been weakened by a number of factors. First, they have always been strongly influenced by political issues and have been, like political parties, both politically and ideologically divided. They have always included – alongside reformists mainly concerned with the practical job of trying to better the condition of the working classes – anarcho-syndicalist and other revolutionary elements, preaching (though usually without practising) direct action, including the general strike, together with Marxist Socialists, primarily interested in theories of the class struggle. In 1921, following the Socialist party split into a Socialist and a Communist party, the CGT also split into two rival confederations, the majority remaining the CGT and the minority becoming the Communist-dominated *Confédération générale du Travail unitaire* (CGTU), which became affiliated to the Red International. Except for two brief periods, one before the war (1935–9) and one just after (1944–7), when there was an uneasy reconciliation between the two, they have remained rivals. After the 1947 break, however, it was the Communist-dominated movement that was the stronger and that retained the traditional title of CGT, together with the CGT premises and periodical (*Le Peuple*), while the non-Communist federation called itself CGT-FO (*Force ouvrière*). The return to France of Alsace-Lorraine in 1919 made many Rhineland Catholic trade-unionists into Frenchmen. From then onwards, therefore, there also existed a predominantly Catholic trade-union movement, the *Confédération française des Travailleurs chrétiens* (CFTC).[9] In 1964, this also split, the majority adopting a non-denominational position and thus changing its name to *Confédération française démocratique du Travail* (CFDT), while the minority movement retained the old name and the original fidelity to Catholicism. There are also trade-union movements, mainly of teachers, students and *cadres* (managerial staffs), which remain independent of all these four.[10]

For purposes of industrial bargaining, the only organizations that really count are the CGT, CGT–FO, CFDT, and CGC (the

Confédération générale des Cadres),[11] which is, of course, a white-collar organization. But the fact that there are four main movements with conflicting interests, three of which are rivals, clearly weakens the impact of trade unions as interest groups. They are also weak because, in addition to their divisions, all of them are relatively small. Membership varies greatly and, as in the case of French political parties, is extremely difficult to estimate accurately, since the figures given by each organization regularly inflate its own strength and deflate that of its rivals.

What is certain is that, in comparison, say, with the figures for British trade-union membership, membership is not only small but has declined considerably since the immediate post-war years. In 1920, the CGT had over two million members. At the time of the Popular Front in 1936, it claimed (but for a brief period only) to have five million, and just after the second world war, six million. In the 1970s it is doubtful whether the CGT, which is the largest and best organized, has more than a million and a half, and the FO and CFDT more than a million between them.[12] But whatever the precise figures may be, the fact that only between two and three million of France's thirteen million workers are organized helps to cancel out some of the advantages of the more rational structure of French trade unions, as compared with those of Great Britain. They are in the main organized on the basis of industrial unionism and so, though they have their own internal problems, they have fewer of the who-does-what disputes that occur so often in Britain.[13]

Another factor making for trade-union weakness is the hostility that the unions have always encountered from the employers. This has always been much stronger than that encountered by British unions. For instance, even in 1968 the unions were still campaigning for the recognition by employers of the right of union officials to carry on union business in the firm's time. (This was one of the demands put forward in the Grenelle negotiations that took place during the May events.)

French union structure is much less centralized than that of British trade unions, and that, too, makes for weakness in

financial resources and in action. All three main workers'
confederations have a similar structure. The central body, the
confederation, includes all organs belonging respectively to the
CGT, FO and CFDT. Each individual union within it has
both a vertical and a horizontal structure. The former is the
national Federation, headed by a national executive, representing the basic local units – the local branches, as they are called
in Britain, *les syndicats* as they are called in France.[14] The
different nomenclature is indicative of a real difference of
relationship between the grass roots and the national organization. In France, the relationship is federal and the member
unions have far more autonomy (including financial autonomy)
than exists in the more centralized British system. The horizontal organization is the *union départementale*, a federation of all
unions belonging to the same confederation within the
geographical area of the *département*. The main function of these
bodies is as propaganda agents. Jean-Daniel Reynaud describes
their secretaries as 'Prefects of an inadequately centralized
Government, having the varied functions of Prefects, but
without Prefectoral authority'.[15] The confederation is essentially a co-ordinating rather than a governing body and all of
them have little in the way of financial resources. Strikes are
therefore a luxury that they can normally not indulge in, except
for very short periods, unless they can rely on enough support
to turn them into mini-general strikes.[16]

By far the greatest weakness is, however, the divorce
between trade unions and political parties. This is, of course,
largely theoretical where the Communist confederation is
concerned, but is real in the case of the other two. It helps to
weaken both unions and parties for, as Jean Meynaud points
out, 'the total separation of trade unions from politics is a myth,
once the Government's aim is to control the level of wages and
to influence by its policies the distribution of the national
income'.[17] The fact that there is *de facto* harmony between the
Communist party and the Communist-dominated CGT gives
this movement a built-in advantage over the others. It is larger,
richer, and can always rely on the backing of the Communist
party. Even so, it has normally preferred the short 'token',

'lightning' or 'rolling' strike to a strike of any length, and normally seeks the support of the other two confederations. Only in 1936, 1947 and 1948, and 1968, has there been anything like a partial general strike of any duration, and all these had strong political motives.[18]

During the quarter of a century from the end of the second world war, the relations of the three confederations to each other and to political and economic issues have changed a good deal. The two that could logically have been expected to have most in common, the CGT and the FO, have remained frozen in traditional attitudes, the latter in particular expressing Socialistic views familiar in the 1930s and in the post-war trade-union heyday. The FO, for instance, has continued to support the principles of nationalization. It has been in favour of the *comités d'entreprise*, created after the war, and then seen as an introduction to trade-union participation in management. It has reaffirmed the principle of the class struggle, though without much conviction. In practice, the CGT–FO unions, up to 1970, represented predominantly workers in the public sector.[19] The CGT has reflected faithfully the political pre-occupations of the Communist party and orthodox Marxist ideology, at the same time regarding itself as the spearhead of the defence of workers' material interests, a combination that has sometimes involved the movement in some curious intellectual convolutions, such as the attempt, in 1955, to prove that, in spite of all the CGT's efforts, workers were bound to get poorer.[20] The theme of working-class unity has been persistent, but unaccompanied by any evidence of progress towards the objective. Indeed, in its policy statement, the FO Congress of 1966 reaffirmed the movement's rejection of unity with the CGT and its belief in a united Europe, to which the CGT was, of course, opposed.[21]

Even before the 1968 'revolution', there were increasing stresses within the Communist-dominated CGT (as there were in the Communist party) owing to the growing demand for opportunities for the expression of differing opinions. But the 1968 strike movement revealed the extent to which undisciplined forms of 'leftism' were taking hold among the rank and file. The CFDT was even more infiltrated by 'leftist' elements, because it showed more sympathy with the strikers than did the other two confederations. During the previous years, following the CFDT's abandonment of the denominational adjective, there had been attempts at rapprochement between CFDT and CGT. An agreement between them was signed in 1965, but it was purely tactical and its results proved disappointing. It produced few joint lists in the elections to the administrative body of the social-security services.[22] It did not prevent the CFDT from making proposals for closer relations with the non-Communist Left, and did not prevent growing divergence between the two movements on political issues – on Vietnam, for instance, on economic policy, on Israel, on the 1967 reforms of the social-security services and on strikes in the public service, which the CGT approved and the CFDT opposed.

It looked as if, with the cement of Catholicism gone, the CFDT was seeking to substitute a Socialist cement, which might perhaps help to explain its more sympathetic attitude to the 1968 revolutionary students and strikers.[23] The consequences were predictable. The influx of new members to the CFDT, mainly young revolutionaries,[24] created internal dissensions and widened the rift between the CFDT and the two more traditionally minded rival movements, at a time when the CGT was concentrating on trying to restore the discipline in its ranks that had been threatened by the 'spontaneous' strike movements in 1968. At its 35th Congress in May 1970, the CFDT used the phrase '*la lutte des classes*' for the first time.[25] But the CGT was at that time advocating 'democratic, mass and class trade unionism', which meant unity and no freedom for organized minorities (*tendances*) and, for the first time since 1936, ended its own Congress with the singing of the Marseillaise as well as of the Internationale.[26] The CGT was also more interested in concrete wage demands than in ideological debates about the future of society, and its secretary-general said so in no uncertain terms. He described the leftist trend in the CFDT as 'revolutionary infantilism, suitable to a reformist Utopia or to anarcho-syndicalists'.

We prefer [he said] to stick to our own conception of a democratic, mass and class trade-union movement, working for the general interests and class solidarity of all workers. . . . By definition, the trade union cannot be a political *avant-garde*; its specific vocation is to recognize and defend all the interests of all workers, irrespective of their political opinions and religious beliefs.[27]

By then, the CFDT was becoming belatedly aware of the dangers to its own unity presented by the new revolutionary elements. The reduction to total impotence of what had been the main student union, the *Union nationale des Etudiants de France* (UNEF), owing to its degeneration into an arena for quarrelling extremist factions (among which the Communists looked like old-fashioned democrats), constituted a salutary warning. So did the quarrels with the PSU, whose post-1968 enthusiasm for revolutionary action on the factory floor was resented by both CFDT and CGT, neither of which welcomed the PSU's self-appointed mission of 'leadership' in what they regarded as their exclusive domain.[28] The post-1968 period therefore saw a tightening of trade-union ranks, both CGT and FO reaffirming the traditional belief in total independence from all political parties. Like the political parties, the trade-union movements have seemed to be agreed only in the defence of conservative and backward-looking attitudes, and have been equally unable to provide any unity of action between themselves going beyond tactical alliances on immediate objectives. It is ironical that what new thinking there has been has been restricted to the CFDT, where it has been productive of more rather than less dissension, and of attitudes even less relevant to the needs of the twentieth century than those of the rival movements.

ECONOMIC INTEREST GROUPS
(ii) EMPLOYERS' ORGANIZATIONS

Employers' organizations became active early in the twentieth century, in response to strikes and to the growth of trade unions. The main employers' confederation, the *Confédération*

générale de la Production française (CGPF), dates from 1919.
Reconstituted after the second world war, and known since
1946 as the *Conseil national du Patronat français* (CNPF),[29] it
represents mainly employers in the larger industrial concerns –
mining, engineering, chemical, building, textiles, etc.

Employers' organizations have gone through four distinct
stages. Between 1929 and 1936 they were dominated by a few
very powerful interests, such as the *Comité des Forges* and the
Comité des Houillères, employers in the chemical and insurance
industries, firms often with interlocking interests and inter-
married families, described loosely in Socialist literature of the
1930s as 'the 200 families'. The second period, from 1936 to
1939, was characterized by hostility both to trade unions and
to the Popular Front of 1936 to 1938, by considerable sympathy
for 'appeasement' in foreign policy, and by the extension of the
organization to include a greater number of smaller industries.
During the third period, the war years of 1940 to 1944,
considerable numbers of the employing classes not only
complied with, but also agreed with, the partially corporatist
system introduced by the Vichy Government. As a consequence
the right-wing parties with which most of them were associated
were decimated and politically discredited during the first
post-war years. General de Gaulle is said to have remarked to
a number of employers whom he received on his return to France
after the liberation, that he had not seen any of them in London,
adding: 'Well, after all, you are not in jail.' Whether apocryphal
or not, the story was apparently well known and did nothing
to increase his popularity with members of the employers'
organizations.[30]

The fourth period, from 1946 onwards, saw the growth and
development of the present highly complex organization,
which includes both vertical federations of industries and
regional trade associations, each represented in the National
Council, the CNPF. This is a loose confederation, within which
member organizations retain a large degree of autonomy. It
exercises, indeed, no real discipline, although its decisions are
in general respected by members. Some of the affiliated organizations are half in and half out, in that they have their own

national, regional and confederal organs and act as independent pressure groups. Thus, for instance, the *Confédération générale des petites et moyennes Entreprises* (CGPME), created in 1936 and reorganized after the war, has been affiliated to the CNPF since 1954. Yet its interests are very different from those of the large-scale industries. The essential characteristic of the CGPME is the membership of the small or medium-sized firm in which there is personal involvement of the owner – either family concerns, or those small enough (say with 30–50 employees) for there to be direct contacts between employers and personnel. The Poujadist UDCA has a similar clientèle to that of the CGPME, but is not affiliated to the CNPF. Commerce, too, is both in and out, having its own organizations, in which national and regional federations form a *Confédération nationale du Commerce*, which is itself represented in the CNPF.[31] Some 150 to 200 local Chambers of Commerce are wholly outside the CNPF.

Another separate employers' organization, also partly in and partly outside the CNPF, but with a more progressive image than that of the CNPF, is the *Centre des jeunes Patrons* (CJP), formed in 1938. It had strong Catholic sympathies and became in the post-war years the spokesman of the more dynamic and modernistic employers. It also recruited younger employers controlling smaller concerns, including family businesses. Whereas the CNPF claims to represent concerns employing six million workers, the CJP probably represents only about four to five thousand concerns employing some quarter of a million workers. It has been nevertheless an influential movement and has its own policies. A movement with similar views to those of the CJP, though smaller and somewhat more conservative, is the *Centre français du Patronat chrétien* (CFPC), formed in 1926, but not affiliated to the CNPF. The *Association des Cadres dirigeants de l'Industrie* (ACADI), which includes representatives of big businesses, is also outside the CNPF.

The great range of both political and economic interests represented in the CNPF, together with its decentralization, means that it represents divided interests and so, if it sought to act directly as a pressure group, would have to exercise

contradictory pressures. It prefers to co-ordinate the industrial
and commercial interests represented within it, leaving direct
action to its member associations, and concentrating on
subsidizing publications that give information, or on exercising
a discreet, indirect influence on specific issues.

During the Fourth Republic, there were accusations in
Parliament that the CNPF was subsidizing Parliamentary
candidatures and, after the 1951 elections, a list of 160 Deputies
believed to have benefited from CNPF funds was circulated.[32]
In his study of employers' organizations, published in 1957,
Henry Ehrmann refers to such allegations as being highly
speculative, since, while election expenses remain (as they are
in France) uncontrolled and not liable to disclosure, there is
bound to be a good deal of speculation and 'political mythology'
about them. The accusation that some Deputies were, in effect,
agents of the CNPF is categorically denied by Jean Meynaud,
who points out that the elections of 1951 and 1956 did not
return to the National Assembly more than 40 industrialists,
heads of employers' organizations, or of large limited companies
or financial concerns. He concludes that

> for twenty years, at least, the holders of economic power
> in France have rarely been representatives in Parliament.
> Their influence in Parliament is perhaps great, but, if so,
> it is exercised indirectly.[33]

It would be naïve to assume that such influence by means of
financial resources did not exist and equally naïve to see it as a
monopoly of big business and the political Right. French
politics have a long history of political scandals and allegations
of financial corruption, by no means limited to representatives
of the Right. All that can be said with any degree of certainty
about the situation under the Fifth Republic, as compared with
that under the Fourth, is that the business lobbies have traditionally preferred to work through individuals or loosely
organized conservative parties, rather than through large
disciplined parties such as the Gaullist party. A strong Government under General de Gaulle was certainly not welcomed by
them, for they regarded him with suspicion as something of a

revolutionary – as, indeed, he regarded himself. How far they found it easier to influence the various advisory organs, such as the organs of the Plan and the Economic and Social Council, under a régime which permitted and indeed encouraged contacts between departmental technocrats and industrialists, must remain a matter of speculation until more evidence is available. But if such contacts *were* influential, they were also available to interests on the Left, and especially to the representatives of trade unions, whom General de Gaulle never regarded with the scorn that he reserved for representatives of political parties. Gaullist policies for 'associating' workers with management certainly encountered hostility from the more conservative employers, but also from trade unionists who agreed with each other on that if on nothing else.[34]

The diversity within the CNPF did not prevent a periodic expression of the general principles to which its members subscribed. Under the Fifth Republic it has evolved into an organization in favour of economic growth and competitiveness, in face of the challenge of the Common Market. It has also become resigned to acceptance of some degree of social co-operation. But its economic outlook remained for a long time unshakeably conservative. What was called the 'Employers' Charter', published by the CNPF in 1965, was generally criticized as evidence that the employers were still living in the nineteenth century, though it is perhaps going too far to describe it as expressing 'rock-ribbed economic liberalism'.[35] Of its fourteen points, some could certainly be classed in that category – its profession of faith in competition, profits, monetary stability, freedom from too much State intervention, for instance. Others were indicative of some change of attitude, for instance, acceptance of the right to work, of the need for better social conditions and vocational training. The CGC commented that it was not entirely negative![36]

It failed, however, to satisfy the younger and more go-ahead employers associated with the CJP, some of whom went much farther, insisting on the need for full employment, participation of personnel in management, recognition of the need for factory branches of trade unions and for monthly payment of

workers.[37] By 1968, some sections of the CNPF were convinced of the need for managerial reforms and had set up a
study group to make proposals. Though this caused disagreements within the movement, by 1970 reforms were in fact
taking place, and a small minority of members had formed
themselves into a kind of ginger group, called *Entreprises et
Progrès*.[38]

ECONOMIC INTEREST GROUPS (iii) FARMERS AND THE
SMALL MAN – FRUSTRATION AND DIRECT ACTION

If, under the Fifth Republic, the large industrial organizations
of employers were moving hesitantly into the twentieth century,
organizations of small farmers and small tradesmen were
seeking obstinately to remain in the nineteenth. When farmers'
associations began to be formed in 1884, they represented
mainly landed interests, sometimes inspired by Catholic
paternalism. The requirements of modernization after 1944,
and the acceleration of the exodus from the land after the
creation of the European Economic Community, created two
rural Frances. On the one hand, there were the large-scale,
prosperous farms of the North and North-East; on the other,
the under-developed regions of Brittany, the South and the
South-West, where representatives of small, uneconomic,
family farmers, small shopkeepers, small wine-growers fought
an obstinate rearguard action for survival, based on the
traditional methods of subsidies, tax concessions and price
supports. The Fifth Republic, faced with the problems of farm
surpluses and competition in the Common Market, could no
longer afford the luxury of these economic laggards, yet their
pressure remained strong because their rapid elimination was
politically, socially and humanly impossible.

The result was two developments in the organization of
interest groups: increasing dissension within associations
representing, in particular, farming interests, and an increasing
tendency to resort to direct and sometimes violent action.

After the second world war, a determined effort had been
made to create a single peasant-farmers' union, the *Confédération*

générale de l'Agriculture (CGA), intended to be a rural counterpart of the CGT. It failed, owing to conflict between Right and Left and between non-Catholics and Catholics, and by the 1950s had become no more than a pressure group within the by then dominant farmers' association, the *Fédération nationale des Syndicats d'Exploitants agricoles* (FNSEA).[39] Both this organization and the Parliamentary intergroup, the *Amicale parlementaire agricole et rurale* (APAR) were dominated by conservative elements, and most of the lobbying benefited the larger farms.[40] More and more the FNSEA came to rely on collaboration with the Government and the traditional supports, though it half encouraged and half sponsored direct action as well. It had at first been strengthened by the revival in the 1950s of the Chambers of Agriculture in the *départements*, forming the *Assemblée permanente des Présidents de Chambre d'Agriculture* (APPCA), but the two bodies rapidly became rivals, and by 1960 the latter was claiming the exclusive right to negotiate with the Government on behalf of agriculture.

It was among the younger farmers, many inspired by Catholicism and prepared for new ideas and new methods, that Gaullist Governments found their main support in the 1960s. Many of them were in favour of technocratic planning and direct access to Government departments. They were prepared, therefore, to accept the kind of long-term measures envisaged in the 1960 *loi d'orientation*. By 1962, a number had joined the numerous *Centres d'Etudes techniques agricoles* (CETA), set up first in 1945. The same elements, many of them former members of the Catholic farmers' youth organization, the *Jeunesses agricoles catholiques* (JAC),[41] had formed in 1957 a progressive wing of the FNSEA, the *Centre national des jeunes Agriculteurs* (CNJA), and the inevitable struggle had developed between conservative and reforming elements and between conventional lobbying methods and the newer technological approach. The CNJA regarded existing farming methods and attitudes as ossified. Many were thinking along lines of collective ownership and co-operative methods among smaller and medium concerns in order to make them more productive.

Both conventional and modern approaches were, however,

defeated by the pace of economic change in the 1960s. What was
necessary was the elimination of a third of the cultivatable land,
of large areas of wine cultivation in the South, and of thousands
of small and uneconomic retail businesses. Price supports and
tax concessions merely kept the small concerns marginally alive,
while supplying the more prosperous concerns with 'two
Cadillacs instead of one'.[42] Even the more modern technological approach could do no more than retard temporarily an
inevitable evolution, of which farmers and small businessmen
were the inevitable victims. The result was that interest groups
representing these threatened sectors of the economy felt
themselves increasingly driven to resort to direct action,
sometimes including violence.

The habit of recourse to direct action was, of course, not
new. The 1950s had seen demonstrations by farmers and
Poujadists, and there was already a consciousness of community
of interests between the small farmer and the small tradesman,
both threatened with extinction by modernization. Between
1960 and 1964, and again from 1967 to 1969, this 'Poujadism
of the Fifth Republic' doubly weakened the organizations
representing the small man. It increased the dissensions within
them, because they were divided on the desirability of direct
action, yet afraid of being outdone in militancy by rival
organizations. And it led to a growing importance of organizations that placed their main emphasis on direct action.

Among those that appeared most frequently in press accounts
of demonstrations and violence were the *Union nationale des
Travailleurs indépendants* (UNATI) and the *Comité d'Information
et de Défense* (CID) which was the readier of the two to resort
to violence.[43] Their main activities were demonstrations and
road blocks involving clashes with the police, carried out in
provincial towns in the regions most directly threatened by
modernization. Their main demands were quite simply for the
easing of their burdens of taxation and social-security contributions, and for limitation of the competition of supermarkets.

In *La Ve République*, published in 1959, Maurice Duverger
noted the decline of parties and the increasing influence of
pressure groups from 1951 onwards. He attributed this

evolution to the weakness of the party system, the increased discipline of employers' organizations, the stronger representation of agricultural interests and the better organization of small tradesmen in the CGPME.[44] A decade later parties were still declining, but the interest groups, including trade unions, had been themselves weakened by their own divisions and internal dissensions. Those representing the small man were fighting a rearguard action with the only weapons that they had, which were their electoral strength and the possibility of exploiting it by mass action. They resorted to the streets, because their organizations had not been created to deal with the situation that confronted them. The result was to create something of a vicious circle, for Governments could not afford to satisfy their demands, yet disorder and violence made some concessions politically unavoidable. As one grower put it:

> We are acting like the fellagas in Algeria. We shall form commandos against stocks of imported fruit and vegetables, because we have noted that only such methods pay.[45]

POLITICS AND DIRECT ACTION IN TEACHERS' AND STUDENT UNIONS

Farmers and small tradesmen have regarded themselves as being a-political, because they act purely in defence of sectional interests. The organizations representing teachers and students were also created to defend sectional interests and continue to regard this as their function. They, too, have resorted to direct action, including violence, not merely in the 'students' and workers' revolution' of May 1968, but intermittently ever since. And educational and political pretexts for action have become so inextricable that it is virtually impossible to give any coherent résumé of their activities.

The events of May 1968 belong to the political history of the 1960s and not to a brief summary of the political rôle of interest groups. But the attitude to it of the most important of the student and teachers' unions provides an object lesson to interest groups on how to achieve self-destruction by confusing legitimate professional objectives and political symbols. There had been a background of unrest in both schools and universities for some time before the outbreak of the May movement, owing to the failure of Governments to cope with the consequences of the enormous increase in the secondary school and university population between 1962 and 1968.[46] The basic professional grievances were lack of adequate buildings, qualified staff, and equipment; a rigid State control that encouraged uniformity and conservatism, both in teaching and in curricula; and an open-entry system in the universities that led to over-crowded, ill-prepared and ill-taught first year student classes with a drop-out rate of up to 50%. The addition of two sets of extraneous political preoccupations helped to make the May events what they were, and also helped to make the educational unions the political battle-field that they have become.

First, genuine educational grievances were fitted into a framework of traditional political left-wing attitudes. Romantic egalitarianism required hostility (on political, not educational, grounds) to the Government's decision to abandon the open-entry system in 1969. The teachers' and student unions thus sacrificed educational efficiency to political ideology. They objected on political grounds to the presence of police on the university campus, thus rendering the problem of maintaining order insoluble.[47] In both student and teachers' unions there were expressions of romantic revolutionary theories, linking educational reform with the destruction of capitalism, which led to what the French described as *l'aspect folklorique* of the May revolution – its barricades, its calls for solidarity of students and workers, its unending debates on theories of *contestation, confrontation, autogestion, conflits de classes* and *conflits de générations*.

Second, and perhaps in the long run more dangerous to the future of the educational unions, there was the use of the student movement by outside elements seeking to further their own interests rather than those of the schools or the universities. Divided though the trade-union movements might be, they were at least agreed on one thing. *They* were not seeking to destroy capitalist society, but to extract from it a larger share of its benefits. But trade-union leaders were prepared to go some way with the student 'revolution', in order to use it to increase their own pressure on the Government for increased wages. Left-wing parties were prepared to use a potential insurrection to discredit the Government and perhaps improve their own slim chances of returning to power. And Maoist and anarchist groups used the revolutionary slogans in order to infiltrate and disrupt rival trade unions and political parties.

This is the context in which the activities, or rather the impotence, of educational unions between 1968 and 1971 must be seen, and particularly the most important of them, the *Union nationale des Etudiants de France* (UNEF) and the *Syndicat national de l'Enseignement supérieur* (SNE–sup, the most influential of the university teachers' unions), both of which played a leading rôle in the May 'revolution'. UNEF had already had a stormy history of political controversy during the Fourth Republic, and the involvement of its more left-wing members in the politics of the Algerian war had led to a split in 1961, when a more moderate wing formed the *Fédération nationale des Etudiants de France* (FNEF). During the 1968 'revolution', its leaders, and in particular its then secretary-general, Jacques Sauvageot, preached the need for solidarity of students with 'peasants and workers'[48] and the 'democratization of education', which for them meant opening universities to all – apparently irrespective of their possession or lack of academic qualifications. 'Only the transformation to a Socialist society', it was claimed, could 'democratize education', by which was understood the establishment of autonomous universities run by committees of staff and students.[49]

The history of UNEF following the May 'events' was one of progressive disintegration. The majority felt themselves to be close to the PSU (which, of course, meant that they were in perpetual disagreement with each other); the minority was divided into Trotskyists, mainly of the AJS brand,[50] and Communists, who formed a movement called *UNEF-Renouveau*, which wanted to concentrate on educational issues and leave politics to the political parties. At its 1970 Congress (the 58th), PSU members of UNEF wanted to co-operate with Maoists, Maoists wanted the Communists thrown out of UNEF, and the only discernible point of agreement was the decision at intervals to stand and sing the Internationale.[51] By the end of the year, a provisional executive of PSU members with Maoist support had lost all control, and most of the UNEF members had either gone over to the 'leftists' or joined *UNEF–Renouveau*. In ten years, political quarrels and the disruptive tactics of 'leftism' had atomized the movement. In 1960, when France had 300,000 students, UNEF claimed a membership of 100,000. In 1970–1, when France had over 600,000 students, it claimed only 30,000, and they were divided and impotent. The more moderate FNEF claimed a membership of 50,000.[52]

The main university teachers' organization, SNE–sup, represented mainly teachers in arts and sciences and claimed a membership of 5981 in March 1969, that is about a fifth of the total number of teachers in higher education. Its secretary-general in 1968, Alain Geismar, was the leader of the then leftist majority and one of the leading university revolutionaries.[53] In 1968, its leaders had been calling, like those of UNEF, for universities open to all, and refusing to abandon the 'open entry' principle in favour of the selective principle that the Government proposed to introduce. In 1969, however, the 'leftist' majority of the previous three years disappeared, and was replaced by one representing the Communist party and the traditional Left.

Other teachers' organizations included the *Syndicat général de l'Education nationale* (SGEN), representing secondary-school teachers and claiming some 45,000 members. It reflected the views of the CFDT, to which it was affiliated, in that it adopted the slogans of May 1968 on self-government and solidarity with the working classes, and in that a minority had moved farther to the Left, without, however, accepting either the violence or the destructiveness of the extremists. On the other hand, the *Syndicat national de l'Enseignement du second Degré* (SNES), which included some 66,000 members and was Communist-dominated, had three left-wing minorities –

Trotskyist, anarcho-syndicalist and PSU. Of the organizations representing the secondary-modern and primary teachers, the *Syndicat national des Collèges* (SNC) formed in 1960, claimed to represent about half of the teachers in the *Collèges d'Enseignement général*, and the *Syndicat national des Instituteurs* (SNI), claimed to represent the other half and most of the primary teachers.[54] Both were predominantly interested in professional questions, though the second had had a Communist minority, *Unité et Action*, since 1967, and a small 'leftist' syndicalist minority after May 1968.

On educational policy, and in particular on the law voted in 1968 following the May events, teachers' and student unions were hopelessly divided. All of them were in favour of autonomous universities and student participation, which was what the law claimed to establish, but virtually all were dissatisfied with it. UNEF opposed it altogether from the start and boycotted the elections for student representatives, on the ground that the law made none of the changes desired by the UNEF, either in the educational or in the social system.[55] The FNEF, though disliking the law and regarding the so-called autonomy as 'a farce', tried at first to co-operate, but by 1970 had also opted out and decided not to join in the election of permanent student representatives.[56] Of the main student unions, only the Communist-dominated *UNEF–Renouveau* decided, in spite of its belief that the law was inadequate, to try to make it work, and to participate in the student elections.

The persistent ferment in the universities would alone have prevented the law from working properly, even if it had not in itself constituted a major and controversial university upheaval. As it was, between 1969 and 1971 there were constant disturbances in some universities (mainly in Paris and Nanterre) caused by extremist left-wing commandos. They involved attacks on administrative personnel and offices, destruction of premises, clashes with right-wing student organizations and with the police. Work was also frequently disrupted by strikes, often on trivial issues such as ministerial decisions on examinations, the marking system and so on. Any pretext sparked off some kind of protest, irrespective of whether it was relevant or logical.

> There is protest [wrote an experienced observer] against selection and against a decline in standards, against anarchy and against authority, against inaction and against reforms, against centralization and against ministerial weakness.[57]

What had happened was that students' and teachers' organizations – or at least the great majority – had ceased to be effective representatives of educational interests and had become purely political bodies. It has often been stressed that the trouble-makers never amounted to more than 5 to 10% of the university population, and that political activism had a long history in French universities, being regarded as part of the democratic right of freedom of opinion. But the situation between 1969 and 1971 was abnormal in two respects. First, previous users of the right had not sought systematically to destroy the universities as a prelude to the destruction of society. And second, never before had the organized representatives of educational interests been so riven with factions. A great deal of the disturbance was between militants of different factions, using educational pretexts to support conflicting interpretations of equally intolerant anti-capitalist political objectives. Meanwhile, what was called 'the silent majority', the 90% who wanted to get on with their academic work, were frustrated by the educational inadequacies that had become merely instruments in the political battles of the various representative organizations. Without effective leadership, they proved easy victims to calls for solidarity by activists, particularly when left-wing political slogans were being paraded – opposition to selection, for instance, or to the presence of police on the campus, or to anything the activists called 'repression'. The result was, in the words of one Paris professor, that the minority refused to obey laws that it disliked, while the majority refused to permit the application of the normal penalties for illegality.[58]

The direct action of farmers and small tradesmen was a simple and pathetic attempt to put the clock back. That of the university activists was a complex, unco-ordinated and chaotic series of political campaigns to put a lot of different clocks both back and forward at the same time. In 1970, SNE–sup protested against reports of violence in some universities, on the ground that they presented the universities to the public as 'a world of irresponsible and absurd violence'.[59] That is what they were in danger of becoming. Both universities and rural interest groups, and even the main trade-union confederations themselves, were also presenting to the public a picture of 'irresponsible and absurd' conflicts within and between themselves. In the circumstances, it would hardly be surprising if, as was frequently alleged, the more powerful interest groups, that were content to get on quietly with the traditional job of protecting their own interests instead of playing at politics or going in for violence, were to have more success than they had had under the previous régime.

CHAPTER XI

Prospect: The Régime and the Parties

Though the Constitution of the Fifth Republic showed itself to be in many respects a more workable instrument than its opponents had at first believed that it could be, the régime still appeared, in the early years of the 1970s, essentially fragile. General de Gaulle had wanted to rely on institutions, his own leadership, and the support of the general public, as the basis on which to build a strong and stable France. Without him, Gaullists and their supporters seemed to be basing their confidence in the régime's capacity to survive on the ability of the Gaullist party to adapt itself empirically to new situations, and in particular on its ability to create new political habits, as a result of the continued disintegration of the opposition parties. In some ways, the Gaullist party had revealed itself as being one of progress as well as of order – and certainly too progressive for some of its conservative allies in the Government.[1] It had surmounted the initial obstacle to any fundamental change in the French party structure, which was the difficulty of creating a single dominant party. Its leaders were hoping, therefore, to be able to combine under the Gaullist banner both the traditional principles – that of 'movement' as well as of 'order'. Even as far back as 1963, when General de Gaulle was still to be President for a further six years, Gaullist leaders had shared the optimism of Roger Frey, who had predicted that

> an intelligent and pragmatic party, with the help of a majority electoral system, and an expanding economy, can remain in power, even when the circumstances to which it owed its victory have changed.[2]

In 1971, those circumstances were seen to have been primarily three – the existence of the Algerian deadlock, the availability and the personality of General de Gaulle, and the fears of public disorder aroused by the strikes and violence of the 1968 events. Many non-Gaullists doubted whether the fortunes of the party could be maintained in the absence of any such apparent direct threat to the régime or to public order. Yet the progressive disintegration of the opposition parties made it increasingly difficult to suggest a credible alternative to Gaullism. An opposition, wrote Maurice Duverger in February 1971, needs 'clarity and an unbreakable, solid front'.[3] Twelve years after the formation of the Fifth Republic, the conflicting opposition groups, in a state of 'atomized, leaderless and spineless ruin',[4] possessed neither. The Centre was incurably divided, with only the dream of a united Europe as an unrealistic substitute for a policy. The Radicals had half-heartedly accepted a utopian programme that nobody either inside or outside the party really believed in or was prepared to try to apply in any foreseeable future. The Socialists, who, on the basis of electoral statistics, must necessarily form the core of any concerted opposition grouping, were locked in old and new family quarrels, still pursuing the endlessly retreating objective of unity of action with the Communist party – an objective that, if achieved, would alienate the support of other parties no less essential to any electoral victory. Fringe Socialist movements and some trade-union movements were at one and the same time flirting with extremist elements and talking about unity with the Communist party, which regarded the elimination of extremist threats to discipline in their own ranks as priority number one.

Nor was the Gaullist front itself characterized either by clarity or by unbreakable solidity. The leadership had to protect itself against repeated tendencies on the part of various left-wing Gaullist groups to try to assure some independent existence for themselves. Though, unlike all other political parties, the Gaullists had their feet firmly on the ground, their eyes were perhaps too firmly fixed on the ground as well. With the exception of the small and ever dwindling band of uncritical worshippers at the shrine of de Gaulle, the party lacked both the dynamism that comes from the possession of a political philosophy or from a coherent political programme, and the cement that other parties derived from involvement in politics at the grass-roots level. 'Efficiency', or '*efficacité*', may be useful as a criterion by which to judge the practicability of short-term policies, but a would-be party of movement needs to have some idea of the direction in which it wants to move. President Pompidou's timid regionalism, the Prime Minister's vaguely liberal aspirations, summed up in the phrase 'the new society', seemed inadequate inspirations to hold the party together, and likely to be even less convincing to the electorate as evidence of progressivism.

The increased attraction among sections of the Left of attitudes of protest and '*contestation*', the persistence of splinter groups within the traditional parties, and the apparent spread of conservative and technocratic inertia in the Government ranks constitute a political climate in which the Fifth Republic may be subjected to considerable stresses and strains. The Third Republic collapsed owing to defeat in war. The Fourth committed suicide owing to its inability to come to terms in time with the problems of decolonization. The Fifth spent the first twelve years of its existence in endeavouring to make France strong, to make Europe safe for France, and to ensure France's prosperity in the European Common Market. Whether these efforts were likely to lead to success or failure in the 1970s is a question to which provisional answers can be suggested only in the light of the policies pursued and the problems encountered by Governments and parties during the 1960s.

A note on the *Conseil d'Etat*

Neither the 1958 Constitution nor its two predecessors include any description of the functions of the *Conseil d'Etat*. The 1946 Constitution, indeed, makes no mention of it at all, while that of 1875 refers only incidentally to Councillors of State. The 1958 Constitution does, however, mention the new functions of the Council resulting from the restriction of the 'domain of law' and the extension of rule-making, but takes for granted, as do the two previous Republican Constitutions, the normal functions of the Council that have been carried on throughout all three régimes. In fact, as will be clear to readers of the foregoing pages, the Council of State plays a vital rôle in the working of political institutions, and the fact that it has proved necessary to refer to it a number of times makes it advisable to give a brief summary of what the Council is and of the framework within which it operates.

The main reason for the omission from constitutional texts of all but the barest mention of the Council is the French theory of the separation of powers. The Council of State is not a constitutional organ, but an administrative organ. Though its origins go back to the *Conseil du Roi* of the *ancien régime*, in its present form it dates from 1799. The Constitution of that year – the Year VIII – (article 53) merely states that 'under the direction of the Consuls a Council of State draws up Government Bills (*projets de loi*) and Government decrees (*règlements d'administration publique*) and resolves difficulties that arise in the administrative field'. The framework within which it works is laid down by a law of 1945, modified from time to time to take account of changes in, for instance, the scope of its activity or the conditions of its recruitment.

The Council of State has two important functions. The first is as the Government's chief adviser on legislation and its application. All Government Bills and all important decrees must be submitted to it. It considers their drafting, their practicability and their relation to existing legislation and administration. It also advises Government departments on administrative problems, advises the Government on the interpretation of obscure or conflicting regulations, and is sometimes asked to advise the Government on the interpretation of constitutional provisions. It may take the initiative in proposing administrative reforms and may also suggest legislation, though it has used this latter right only once (in 1948). It is also, apart from the Minister of the Interior, the main organ of administrative control and supervision of local authorities. It may be called on to advise on the legality of administrative acts of the Prefect or the Mayor, to authorize *communes* to merge with or separate from others, to approve the conditions in which local services can be provided, and so on. Its duties also include pronouncing on the legality of the acts of local authorities. It may, for instance, disallow decisions by a local authority on the ground that such decisions are not within its competence, or intervene if a local council is not carrying out as intended the functions laid down in decrees.

In its tutelary rôle in relation to local authorities, the Council of State's ability to pronounce on the expediency as well as on the legality of certain acts and policies has enabled it to develop, within the framework decided by the law, policies of its own. In its capacity as adviser to Governments, it has acquired great prestige. Governments are not obliged to follow its advice, but under the Third and Fourth Republics they almost always did. That advice is never officially made public, though in fact, it often becomes known.

The Council of State thus has not only an influential rôle, but also one that can be politically important, and this is particularly evident in the exercise of its second function as the apex of the system of administrative law. By virtue of the French theory of the separation of powers, the acts of officials in the exercise of their duties cannot be challenged in the ordinary courts, as this would be considered as interference by the judiciary in the administrative sphere. There has therefore grown up, side by side with the judicial system, a parallel system of administrative courts, in which citizens and public authorities can seek redress for wrongful actions committed by officials in the course of their duty. Nowadays, 24 local administrative tribunals hear some nine-tenths of these cases, the Council of State acting as a court of appeal. But where important decisions are concerned, including, for example, cases against a Government department, or in which more than one local tribunal is concerned, the Council of State remains the court of first instance.

The judicial function of the Council of State has been for a century or more of great and growing importance. Although the Council has four sections concerned with its administrative functions and only one section (the *section du contentieux*) concerned with its judicial functions, the last is by far the most powerful. Yet members of the Council, though they are judges in administrative matters, remain administrators and so do not enjoy, in theory, the security of tenure possessed by judges in the ordinary courts. In theory, they are liable to dismissal at the Government's pleasure. In practice, however, they enjoy unchallenged security. Towards the end of the nineteenth century, the British constitutional lawyer, A. V. Dicey, regarded French administrative courts with some suspicion as being liable to be over-sympathetic to the Government. This may have been true at one time, but it soon ceased to be so, and Dicey later changed his opinion on this point. Long before the end of the Third Republic, the Council had built up, on the basis of its pragmatic methods of extensive enquiry into the facts and collegiate responsibility for decision, a body of case-law that it uses for its own guidance, without allowing it to become a strait-jacket. It had also acquired a reputation for integrity, impartiality and independence that made it generally regarded as

> the great protector of the rights of property and of the rights of the individual against the State; the great redresser of wrongs committed by the State.
> (Joseph Barthélemy, *Le Gouvernement de la France*, Paris, Payot, 1930, p. 206.)

The administrative courts do not merely annul administrative acts, from those of Minister to Mayor, on the ground that they are *ultra vires*. They also protect the citizen from the use of administrative powers that, even when within the bounds of technical legality, have, in the judgement of the Council, been used for purposes that the legislator did not intend. This check on the misuse of powers (*détournement de pouvoirs*) is, indeed, one of the most effective of the Council's methods of protecting individuals from executive encroachments and bureaucratic rule.

During the past thirty years or so, the Council has greatly extended the scope of its protection of individual liberties by its broadening of the criteria of legality to include unwritten 'general principles of law'. In many cases, these are deduced from the constitutional rights enumerated in the preambles of both the 1946 and

1958 Constitutions, both of which reaffirm the principles laid down in the 1789 Declaration of the Rights of Man and the Citizen. These general principles, mentioned in Chapter I, take into account the right to equality before the law, freedom of speech, assembly and opinion, the right to natural justice, which implies the right to be heard, and the right not to be subjected to retroactive legislation. This wider scope does, of course, give the Council of State great political influence, or potential political influence, since it implies the right of administrative courts to interpret more freely what does and does not constitute legality. It also creates problems, for administrative courts must always take care not to lose sight of the other aspect of their duty, which is to ensure the continuity and proper working of the public services and the maintenance of public order. To balance these conflicting claims can sometimes be a delicate and complex operation.

Though, as has been said, Governments are not obliged to follow the advice of the administrative sections of the Council of State, one of the main reasons why they have generally done so in practice is the possibility that failure to follow it may involve Ministers and civil servants in actions in the administrative courts, and so may result in their ultimately being compelled to do so. For an aggrieved citizen or organization can challenge the legality of Government acts, and an executive authority that ignores a decision of the Council is acting illegally. But since the administrative courts have no agents through which to impose compliance with their decisions, they rely, in the last resort, on the willingness of the executive to respect those decisions. Some Government departments are slow to comply with the Council's requirements. Failure to do so is, however, in itself an offence, and this fact, together with the Government's respect for and need of the administrative courts – for these are equally vigilant in their protection of Ministers and civil servants from unjustified attacks by the public – generally ensures compliance with its rulings. Administrative courts work, however, within two major limits. The law is supreme and remains outside the jurisdiction of the Council of State. Any interpretation by the Council can therefore be over-ruled by a new law. The administrative courts also consider actions constituting an inherent condition of the exercise of executive power (including the small number of acts sometimes described as *actes de gouvernement*) as being outside their jurisdiction.

Under the Fifth Republic, the Council has not hesitated to annul executive acts carried out under special powers granted to the President. Thus while, as stated in Chapter V, *décisions* taken by the President under article 16 were regarded by the Council of State as having the status of law and so as outside their jurisdiction, the measures taken to apply such decisions were executive in nature, and therefore came within their jurisdiction. Some were successfully challenged in administrative courts on the ground that, at the time the specific measures were taken, the state of emergency was not such as to justify them. The Council of State also declared illegal (*Arrêt Canal* of 21 October 1962) a special Military Court of Justice, created by an Ordinance made by General de Gaulle under special powers granted to him by referendum the previous April. The Council's objection was not to the creation of a special court, but to the fact that the court in question was constituted in such a way as to deprive those convicted by it of their right of appeal, which, in the Council's view, was required by the 'general principles of law'. The first reaction of the Government was to legalize the court by law, thus placing the matter outside the jurisdiction of the Council of State. Shortly afterwards, however, the court was replaced by one whose procedure did comply with the Council's requirements.

Clearly, decisions of this kind, together with those involving estimates of the extent to which an official has faithfully carried out the intentions of Parliament or has overstepped the legal bounds of discretion, leave room for some degree of subjectivity in interpretation and so cannot be free from political implications. General de Gaulle certainly regarded the Council as being at times politically biased (*v. Mémoires d'Espoir*, vol. I, p. 298). One result of this view was a reform of 1963 that made some minor changes in the organization and working of the Council, mainly in order to provide for more systematic contacts between the administrative and judicial sections, and for some limit to the period for which a Councillor may, during his career, be 'detached' from service within the Council of State and seconded for service outside, usually in some important advisory or executive capacity, either in a Government department, or as part of a Minister's *cabinet*.

In reality, this process of 'detachment', together with the Council's custom of recruiting a proportion of its members from outside – usually eminent personalities with political experience or with experience in the higher ranks of the administration – though it may risk some degree of 'politicization', helps to provide the

Council with a continuous supply of new blood and varied expertise, which goes far to prevent the equally serious risk that it might come to look at administrative problems from an ivory tower. One of the great strengths of the Council of State as the supreme organ of the system of administrative law is precisely its great expertise in the field of administration.

During the first twelve years of the Fifth Republic, the Council's position changed in three ways. First, its advice was ignored in several important matters, already mentioned in Chapters III and V. Second, the Council became (under article 37) officially responsible, for the first time in its history, for advice on the *constitutionality*, and not merely the *legality*, of certain procedures (in conditions already described in Chapter III). Third, and much more important, the Council's scope of activity has been greatly widened by the enlargement of the rule-making sphere under article 37. For this brings within the jurisdiction of the Council of State a number of administrative acts which are based, not on law, but on the Government's constitutional right to take certain measures by decree, instead of, as hitherto, by law. In other words, these measures become liable to review by the administrative courts, if challenged by individuals or bodies considering themselves to have been wrongfully injured by them. That the Council's interpretation of the requirements of the 'general principles of law' might henceforth create difficulties for Governments is indicated by the following statement regarding the situation under the Fifth Republic, expressed by the *commissaire du gouvernement* in June 1959. He said that the Government was still subject to

> general principles of law, properly so-called, either included in declarations of rights or deduced by judges from these declarations. Among these fundamental principles, on which our political régime is based, must be included the equality of citizens, guarantees of essential liberties, the separation of powers, the principle of *stare decisis* (*l'autorité de la chose jugée*), the non-retroactivity of Governmental acts, the sanctity of established rights (*des droits acquis*), the citizen's right to challenge Governmental acts. . . . There must be included, on the other hand, the principle of the continuity of the public services essential to the life of the nation.

'These principles', concluded the *commissaire du gouvernement*, 'are binding on the rule-making authority, even when it is not limited by law.' (*Les Grands Arrêts de la Jurisprudence administrative*, No. 100, pp. 471–2.)

It is a formidable list, though it must be remembered that the *commissaire du gouvernement* is in no sense a spokesman for the Government, and that his opinions, though influential, are not always accepted by the Council. The fact remains, however, that the application of the 1958 Constitution could considerably increase the scope of the Council of State's rôle, and so its capacity to decide or to influence the interpretation, not only of the law, but also of the Constitution.

The French Constitution of 4 October 1958[*]

The French people solemnly proclaim their attachment to the Rights of Man and to the principles of national sovereignty as defined by the Declaration of 1789, confirmed and completed by the Preamble to the Constitution of 1946.

By virtue of these principles and of that of the free determination of peoples, the Republic offers to those Overseas territories which express a desire to accept membership of them new institutions founded on the common ideal of liberty, equality and fraternity and conceived with a view to their democratic evolution.

Article 1. The Republic and those peoples of the Overseas territories who, by an act of free determination, adopt the present Constitution set up a Community.

The Community is founded upon the equality and solidarity of the peoples composing it.

TITLE I

Sovereignty

Article 2. France is an indivisible, secular, democratic and social Republic. It ensures the equality before the law of all citizens, without distinction of origin, race or religion. It respects all beliefs.

The national emblem is the tricolour flag, blue, white and red.

The national anthem is the '*Marseillaise*'.

The motto of the Republic is 'Liberty, Equality, Fraternity'.

Its principle is government of the people, by the people, for the people.

[*] This translation is by William Pickles and is taken from his *French Constitution of October 4th, 1958* (Stevens, London, 1960). The three subsequent formal amendments have been incorporated in this text.

Article 3. National sovereignty belongs to the people, who exercise it through their representatives and by way of referendum.

No section of the people and no individual may claim to exercise it.

The suffrage may be direct or indirect in conditions provided for by the Constitution. It is in all cases universal, equal and secret. The right to vote, in conditions laid down by law, is enjoyed by all French nationals of either sex who are of age and in full possession of their civil and political rights.

Article 4. Parties and political groups play a part in the exercise of the right to vote. The right to form parties and their freedom of action are unrestricted. They must respect the principles of national sovereignty and of democracy.

TITLE II

The President of the Republic

Article 5. The President of the Republic endeavours to ensure respect for the Constitution. He provides, by his arbitration, for the regular functioning of the public authorities and the continuity of the State.

He is the protector of the independence of the nation, of the integrity of its territory, of respect for treaties and Community agreements.

Article 6. The President of the Republic is elected for seven years by direct universal suffrage. The methods of application of the present article are determined by an organic law.

Article 7. The President is elected by an absolute majority of valid votes cast. If this is not obtained at the first ballot, a second ballot is held on the second Sunday following the first ballot. The only candidates allowed at the second ballot – after the withdrawal, if this happens, of those with more votes – are the two who had most votes at the first ballot.

Voting begins at the time fixed by the Government.

The election of the new President takes place not less than twenty and not more than thirty-five days before the expiry of the existing President's term of office.

If, for whatever reason, the Presidency of the Republic falls vacant, or if the incapacity of the President has been certified by the Constitutional Council, at the request of the Government and by an absolute majority of the Council's members, the functions of the President, except those provided for by articles 11 and 12 below, are performed temporarily by the President of the Senate, or, should he be prevented from performing these functions, by the Government.

When a vacancy occurs, or when the incapacity is certified by the Constitutional Council to be permanent, and unless *force majeure* has been certified by the Constitutional Council, the election of a new President takes place not less than twenty and not more than thirty-five days after the opening of the vacancy or the declaration of the permanence of the incapacity.

During a Presidential vacancy, or during the period between the declaration of the permanence of a President's incapacity and the election of his successor, articles 49, 50, and 89 of the Constitution may not be brought into application.*

Article 8. The President of the Republic appoints the Prime Minister. He terminates his period of office on the presentation by the Prime Minister of the resignation of the Government.

He appoints and dismisses the other members of the Government on the proposal of the Prime Minister.

Article 9. The President of the Republic presides over the Council of Ministers.

Article 10. The President of the Republic promulgates laws within the fortnight following their final adoption and transmission to the Government.

Before the end of this period, he may ask Parliament to reconsider the whole law or specified articles. This reconsideration cannot be refused.

Article 11. On the proposal of the Government during Parliamentary sessions, or on the joint proposal of the two Assemblies, published in the *Journal Officiel*, the President of the Republic may submit

---

*Articles 6 and 7 are given above as revised by the referendum of 28 October 1962. The main provisions of the original text of article 6 are as follows:

Article 6. The President of the Republic is elected for seven years by an electoral college which includes the members of Parliament, of the Departmental Councils, and of the Assemblies of Overseas Territories, in addition to the elected representatives of the Municipal Councils. . . .

[Then followed detailed provisions for the representation of Municipal Councils.]

In the Overseas Territories of the Republic, the electoral college also includes representatives elected by the Councils of the administrative entities, in the conditions laid down in an organic law.

The representation of member States of the Community in the college electing the President of the Republic is determined by agreement between the Republic and the member States of the Community.

The methods of application of the present article are determined by an organic law.

to a referendum any Government Bill dealing with the organization of the public authorities, approving a Community agreement, or authorizing the ratification of a treaty which, although not in conflict with the Constitution, would affect the working of institutions.

If the result of the referendum is favourable to the adoption of the Bill, the President of the Republic promulgates it within the time-limit laid down in the preceding article.

Article 12. The President of the Republic may pronounce the dissolution of the National Assembly, after consulting the Prime Minister and the Presidents of the assemblies.

A general election takes place not less than twenty and not more than forty days after the dissolution.

The National Assembly meets as of right on the second Thursday following its election. If this meeting takes place outside the periods fixed for ordinary sessions, a session opens as of right for a period of a fortnight.

No new dissolution may take place during the year following these elections.

Article 13. The President of the Republic signs such ordinances and decrees as have been considered by the Council of Ministers. He appoints to the civil and military posts of the State. Councillors of State, the Grand Chancellor of the Legion of Honour, Ambassadors and Envoys Extraordinary, Senior Councillors of the Court of Accounts, Prefects, Government representatives in Overseas Territories, General Officers, Flag Officers, Air-Marshals, Rectors of Academies and *directeurs* of Government departments are appointed in the Council of Ministers. An organic law determines the other appointments to be made in the Council of Ministers, as also the conditions in which the appointing power of the President of the Republic may be delegated by him and be exercised in his name.

Article 14. The President of the Republic accredits Ambassadors and Envoys Extraordinary to foreign powers; foreign Ambassadors and Envoys Extraordinary are accredited to him.

Article 15. The President of the Republic is head of the armed forces. He presides over the Higher Councils and Committees of National Defence.

Article 16. When there exists a serious and immediate threat to the institutions of the Republic, the independence of the Nation, the integrity of its territory or the fulfilment of its international obligations, and the regular functioning of the constitutional public authorities has been interrupted, the President of the Republic takes the measures required by the circumstances, after consulting officially the Prime Minister, the Presidents of the Assemblies and the Constitutional Council.

He informs the Nation of these matters by a message.

These measures must be inspired by the desire to ensure to the constitutional public authorities, with the minimum of delay, the means of fulfilling their functions. The Constitutional Council is consulted about them.

Parliaments meet as of right.

The National Assembly cannot be dissolved during the [period of] exercise of the exceptional powers.

Article 17. The President of the Republic has the right of pardon.

Article 18. The President of the Republic communicates with the two assemblies of Parliament by means of messages which are read for him and on which there is no debate.

If Parliament is not in session, it is specially summoned for this purpose.

Article 19. The acts of the President of the Republic other than those provided for in Articles 8 (*para.* 1), 11, 12, 16, 18, 54, 56 and 61 are countersigned by the Prime Minister and, where necessary, by the appropriate Ministers.

TITLE III

The Government

Article 20. The Government decides and directs the policy of the nation. It has at its disposal the administration and the armed forces.

It is responsible to Parliament in the conditions and in accordance with the procedures laid down in Articles 49 and 50.

Article 21. The Prime Minister is in general charge of the work of the Government. He is responsible for National Defence. He ensures the execution of laws. Except as provided for under Article 13, he exercises rule-making power and appoints to civil and military posts.

He may delegate certain of his powers to the Ministers.

He deputizes for the President of the Republic, when necessary, as Chairman of the Councils and Committees referred to in Article 15.

In exceptional circumstances, he may deputize for him as Chairman of the Council of Ministers, by virtue of an explicit delegation of authority and with a specific agenda.

Article 22. The acts of the Prime Minister are countersigned, where necessary, by the Ministers responsible for their execution.

Article 23. Membership of the Government is incompatible with that of Parliament, with the representation of any trade or professional organization on the national level, with any professional activity or public employment.

An organic law lays down the conditions in which the holders of the above offices, functions or employments are to be replaced.

Members of Parliament are replaced in the manner laid down in Article 25.

TITLE IV

Parliament

Article 24. Parliament is composed of the National Assembly and the Senate. The Deputies of the National Assembly are elected by direct, universal suffrage.

The Senate is elected by indirect suffrage. It represents the territorial entities of the Republic. French citizens resident abroad are represented in the Senate.

Article 25. An organic law determines the length of life of each assembly, the number of its members, the payment made to them, the rules concerning qualification for and disqualification from election and the incompatibility of certain functions with membership of Parliament.

This organic law also determines the manner of election of those who, in the event of a vacancy, replace Deputies and Senators until the next election, general or partial, to the assembly in which the vacancy occurs.

Article 26. No member of Parliament may be prosecuted, sought out, arrested, held in custody or tried on account of opinions expressed or votes cast by him in the exercise of his functions.

No member of Parliament may be prosecuted or arrested on account of any crime or misdemeanour during a parliamentary session, without the consent of the assembly of which he is a member, except when the member is arrested *flagrante delicto*.

Members of Parliament may be arrested when Parliament is not in session only with the authorization of the *bureau* of the assembly of which they are members, except when the arrest is *flagrante delicto*, when the prosecution has [already] been authorized or the final sentence pronounced.

Members are released from custody or their prosecution is suspended if the assembly of which they are members so demands.

Article 27. Any specific instruction to a member of Parliament [from an outside body] is null and void.

The member's right to vote belongs to him alone.

The (*sic*) organic law may authorize the delegation of the right to vote in exceptional circumstances. In these cases, no member may cast more than one delegated vote.

Article 28. Parliament meets as of right in two ordinary sessions per year.

The first session begins on October 2nd and lasts 80 days.

The second session begins on April 2nd; it may not last more than 90 days. If October 2nd or April 2nd is a public holiday, the session begins on the first following workday.

Article 29. At the request of the Prime Minister or of the majority of the members of the National Assembly, Parliament meets in special session, with a specified agenda.

When the special session is held at the request of members of the National Assembly, the closure decree is read as soon as Parliament has completed the agenda for which it was called and at most twelve days after its meeting.

Only the Prime Minister can ask for a new session before the end of the month following the date of the closure decree.

Article 30. Except when Parliament meets as of right, special sessions are opened and closed by decree of the President of the Republic.

Article 31. Members of the Government have access to both assemblies. They are heard when they so request.

They may be assisted by Government commissioners.

Article 32. The President of the National Assembly is elected for the life of each Parliament. The President of the Senate is elected after each partial renewal.

Article 33. The sittings of both assemblies are public. A full report of debates is published in the *Journal Officiel*.

Each assembly may meet in secret session at the request of the Prime Minister or of one-tenth of its members.

Relations between Parliament and Government

Article 34. Laws are voted by Parliament.

Laws determine the rules concerning:

civic rights and the fundamental guarantees of the public liberties of the citizen; the obligations of citizens, as regards their persons and property, for purposes of national defence;

the nationality, status and legal capacity of persons, property in marriage, inheritance and gifts;

the definitions of crimes and misdemeanors and of the penalties applicable to them; criminal procedure, amnesty, the creation of new orders of jurisdiction and the statute of the judiciary;

the basis of assessment, rate and methods of collection of taxes of all kinds; the currency system.

Laws determine also the rules concerning:

the electoral system for Parliamentary and local assemblies;

the creation of categories of public corporation;

the fundamental guarantees of civil servants and members of the armed forces;

nationalizations and the transfer of property from the public to the private sectors.

Laws determine the fundamental principles:

of the general organization of national defence;

of the free administration of local entities, of their powers and of their resources;

of education;

of the law of property, of real-property rights and of civil and commercial contract;

of labour law, trade-union law and social security.

Finance laws determine the resources and obligations of the State, in the manner and with the reservations provided for in an organic law.

Programme-laws determine the purposes of the social and economic action of the State.

The provisions of the present article may be completed and more closely defined by an organic law.

Article 35. Declarations of war are authorized by Parliament.

Article 36. A state of siege is decreed in the Council of Ministers. Its prolongation beyond twelve days can be authorized only by Parliament.

Article 37. Matters other than those regulated by laws fall within the field of rule-making.

Documents in the form of laws, but dealing with matters falling within the rule-making field, may be modified by decree issued after consultation with the Council of State. Such of these documents as come into existence after the coming into force of the present Constitution may be modified by decree only if the Constitutional Council has declared them to be within the rule-making sphere, by virtue of the previous paragraph.

Article 38. With a view to carrying out its programme, the Government may seek the authorization of Parliament, for a limited period of time, to issue ordinances regulating matters normally falling within the field of law-making.

The ordinances are made in the Council of Ministers after consultation with the Council of State. They come into force upon publication, but cease to be effective if the Bill ratifying them is not laid before Parliament by the date fixed by the enabling Act.

At the expiration of the period mentioned in paragraph 1 of this Article, the ordinances may be modified only by law, as regards matters falling within the field of law.

Article 39. Legislative initiative is exercised by the Prime Minister and by members of Parliament.

Government Bills are considered in the Council of Ministers, after consultation with the Council of State and laid before one of the two assemblies. Finance Bills are submitted first to the National Assembly.

Article 40. Private members' Bills, resolutions and amendments which, if passed, would reduce public revenues or create or increase charges on the revenue are out of order.

Article 41. If, in the course of legislative procedure, it becomes apparent that a private member's proposal or amendment does not fall within the field of law-making, or is in conflict with powers delegated by virtue of Article 38, the Government may demand that it be declared out of order.

In the event of disagreement between the Government and the President of the assembly concerned, the Constitutional Council gives a ruling, at the request of either party, within a week.

Article 42. Government Bills are discussed, in the assembly to which they are first submitted, on the basis of the Government's text.

An assembly debating a Bill transmitted from the other assembly discusses it on the basis of the text transmitted to it.

Article 43. Government and private members' Bills are sent, at the request of the Government, or of the assembly then discussing them, to Commissions specially appointed for this purpose.

Bills of either type for which such a request has not been made are sent to one of the permanent Commissions, the number of which is limited to six for each assembly.

Article 44. Members of Parliament and the Government have the right of amendment.

When the debate has begun, the Government may object to the discussion of any amendment which has not previously been submitted to the Commission.

If the Government so requests, the assembly concerned accepts or rejects by a single vote the whole or part of the Bill or motion under discussion, together with such amendments as have been proposed or accepted by the Government.

Article 45. Every Government or private member's Bill is discussed successively in the two assemblies with a view to agreement on identical versions.

When, as a result of disagreement between the two assemblies, a Bill has not been passed after two readings in each assembly, or, if the Government has declared the Bill urgent, after a single reading by each assembly, the Prime Minister is entitled to have the Bill sent to a joint Committee composed of equal numbers from the two assemblies, with the task of finding agreed versions of the provisions in dispute.

The version prepared by the joint Committee may be submitted by the Government to the assemblies for their approval. No amendment may be accepted without the agreement of the Government.

If the joint Committee does not produce an agreed version, or if the version agreed is not approved as provided for in the preceding paragraph, the Government may ask the National Assembly, after one more reading by the National Assembly and by the Senate, to decide the matter. In this case, the National Assembly may adopt either the version prepared by the joint Committee or the last version passed by itself, modified, if necessary, by one or any of the amendments passed by the Senate.

Article 46. Laws to which the Constitution gives the status of organic laws are passed or amended in the following conditions.

The Bill, whether Government or private member's, is not debated or voted on in the first assembly in which it is introduced until a fortnight after its introduction.

The procedure of Article 45 applies. Nevertheless, if the two assemblies fail to agree, the Bill may become law only if it is passed at its final reading in the National Assembly by an absolute majority of its members.

Organic laws relating to the Senate must be passed in the same terms by both assemblies.

Organic laws may be promulgated only when the Constitutional Council has certified their conformity with the Constitution.

Article 47. An organic law lays down the conditions in which Parliament votes Finance Bills.

If the National Assembly has not concluded its first reading within forty days from the introduction of the Bill, the Government sends the Bill to the Senate, which must reach a decision within a fortnight. Subsequent procedure is that provided for in Article 45.

If Parliament has reached no decision within seventy days, the provisions of the Bill may be put into force by ordinance.

If the Finance Bill determining revenue and expenditure for the financial year has not been introduced in time to be promulgated before the beginning of the financial year, the Government asks Parliament, as a matter of urgency, for authorization to levy the taxes, and allocates by decree the sums necessary for continuing services.

The time limits fixed by the present article are suspended when Parliament is not in session.

The Court of Accounts assists Parliament and the Government to supervise the application of Finance Acts.

Article 48. The agenda of the assemblies gives priority, in the order determined by the Government, to the discussion of Government Bills and private members' Bills accepted by the Government.

Priority is given at one sitting per week to the questions of members of Parliament and the replies of the Government.

Article 49. The Prime Minister, after deliberation in the Council of Ministers, pledges the responsibility of the Government before the National Assembly, on its programme or, if it be so decided, on a general declaration of policy.

The National Assembly challenges the responsibility of the Government by passing a vote of censure. A censure motion is in order only if it is signed by at least one-tenth of the members of the

National Assembly. The vote may not take place until forty-eight hours after its introduction. Only votes in favour of the censure motion are counted, and the motion is carried only if it receives the votes of the majority of the members of the Assembly. If the censure motion is rejected, its signatories may not propose a further one during the same session, except in the case provided for in the next paragraph.

The Prime Minister may, after deliberation in the Council of Ministers, pledge the responsibility of the Government before the National Assembly on the passing of all or part of a Bill or a motion. In this case, the Bill or part of Bill or motion is regarded as having been passed, unless a censure motion, put down within the following twenty-four hours, is passed in the conditions provided for in the previous paragraph.

The Prime Minister is entitled to seek the approval of the Senate for a general statement of policy.

Article 50. When the National Assembly passes a motion of censure or rejects the Government's programme or a general statement of Government policy, the Prime Minister must tender to the President of the Republic the resignation of the Government.

Article 51. The closure of ordinary or special sessions is automatically postponed, if need be, in order to permit the application of the provisions of Article 49.

TITLE VI

Treaties and international agreements

Article 52. The President of the Republic negotiates and ratifies treaties.

He is informed of the negotiation of any international agreement not subject to ratification.

Article 53. Peace treaties, commercial treaties, treaties or agreements concerning international organization, those which involve the State in financial obligations, modify the provisions of the law, concern personal status or involve the cession, exchange or addition of territory may be ratified or approved only by virtue of a law.

They take effect only after having been ratified or approved.

No cession, exchange or addition of territory is valid without the consent of the populations concerned.

Article 54. If the Constitutional Council, consulted by the President of the Republic, the Prime Minister or the President of either assembly, has declared that an international obligation includes a clause contrary to the Constitution, authorization to ratify or approve it may be accorded only after revision of the Constitution.

Article 55. Treaties or agreements regularly ratified or approved have, from the time of publication, an authority superior to that of laws, provided, in the case of each agreement or treaty, that it is applied by the other party.

TITLE VII

The Constitutional Council

Article 56. The Constitutional Council has nine members, whose term of office lasts for nine years and is not renewable. Its members are appointed by thirds every three years. Three members are nominated by the President of the Republic, three by the President of the National Assembly, three by the President of the Senate.

In addition to the nine members provided for above, former Presidents of the Republic are *ex officio* life-members of the Constitutional Council.

The President is appointed by the President of the Republic. He has a casting vote.

Article 57. The functions of a member of the Constitutional Council are incompatible with those of a Minister or member of Parliament.

Other positions incompatible with membership of the Council are listed in an organic law.

Article 58. The Constitutional Council supervises the election of the President of the Republic, with a view to ensuring its regularity.

It investigates objections and proclaims the results.

Article 59. The Constitutional Council decides, in disputed cases, on the regularity of the election of Deputies and Senators.

Article 60. The Constitutional Council supervises the conduct of referenda with a view to ensuring their regularity, and proclaims the results.

Article 61. Organic laws, before their promulgation, and the rules of procedure of the Parliamentary assemblies, before their application, must be submitted to the Constitutional Council, which pronounces on their conformity with the Constitution.

For the same purpose, [ordinary] laws may be submitted to the Constitutional Council, before their promulgation, by the President of the Republic, the Prime Minister or the President of either assembly.

In the cases provided for in the two preceding paragraphs, the Constitutional Council decides within a month. At the request of the Government, however, if the matter is urgent, this period may be reduced to a week.

In these above-mentioned cases, reference to the Constitutional Council prolongs the period allowed for promulgation.

Article 62. A provision declared unconstitutional may not be promulgated or applied.

Decisions of the Constitutional Council are not subject to appeal. They are binding on public authorities and on all administrative and judicial authorities.

Article 63. An organic law lays down the organization and methods of working of the Constitutional Council, the procedures to be followed in referring matters to it and in particular the time-limits within which disputes may be laid before it.

TITLE VIII

The Judicial Authority

Article 64. The President of the Republic is the protector of the independence of the judicial authority.

He is assisted by the Higher Council of the Judiciary.

An organic law regulates the position of the Judiciary. Judges are irremovable.

Article 65. The Higher Council of the Judiciary is presided over by the President of the Republic. The Minister of Justice is *ex officio* its Vice-President. He may deputize for the President of the Republic.

The Higher Council has in addition nine members appointed by the President of the Republic in the conditions laid down by an organic law.

The Higher Council of the Judiciary submits nominations for appointments to the supreme Court of Appeal (*Cour de Cassation*) and to the posts of First President of Assize Courts (*Cours d'Appel*). It gives its opinion, in conditions laid down by the organic law, on the proposals of the Minister of Justice concerning the appointment of other Judges. It is consulted on reprieves in conditions laid down by an organic law.

The Higher Council of the Judiciary sits as the Disciplinary Council for Judges. It is then presided over by the First President of the *Cour de Cassation*.

Article 66. None may be arbitrarily detained.

The judicial authority, guardian of the liberty of the individual, ensures respect for this principle in conditions determined by the law.

The High Court of Justice

Article 67. A High Court of Justice is instituted.

It is composed of members elected, from their own numbers and in equal parts, by the National Assembly and the Senate, after each election to these assemblies. It elects its President from among its members.

An organic law determines the composition of the High Court, its rules of operation and the procedure applicable before it.

Article 68. The President of the Republic is responsible for actions performed in the carrying out of his duties only in case of high treason. He can be indicted only by identical motions passed by the two assemblies in open ballot and by an absolute majority of their members; he is tried by the High Court of Justice.

Members of the Government are penally responsible for actions performed in the carrying out of their duties and classed as crimes or misdemeanors at the time when they were committed. The procedure set out above is applicable to them and to their accomplices in cases of plotting against the security of the State. In the cases provided for in this paragraph, the High Court is bound by the definitions of the crimes and misdemeanours and by the rules as to penalties to be found in the criminal laws in force at the times when the actions were performed.

The Economic and Social Council

Article 69. The Economic and Social Council gives its opinion, at the request of the Government, on such Government Bills, draft ordinances, draft decrees and private members' Bills as are submitted to it.

A member of the Economic and Social Council may be appointed by the Council to appear before the parliamentary assemblies and forward the opinion of the Council on Bills submitted to it.

Article 70. The Economic and Social Council may also be consulted by the Government on any economic or social problem concerning the Republic or the Community. Any plan or pro-gramme-Bill of economic or social character is submitted to it for its opinion.

Article 71. The composition of the Economic and Social Council and its methods of work are laid down in an organic law.

Territorial entities

Article 72. The territorial entities of the Republic are the *communes*, the *départements* and the Overseas Territories. Any other territorial entity is created by law.

These entities are freely administered by elected councils in con-ditions laid down by law.

In the *départements* and Territories, the Government delegate is responsible for the interests of the nation, supervises the adminis-tration and ensures the observance of the law.

Article 73. The status as defined by law and the administrative organization of the Overseas *départements* may be modified by mea-sures intended to adapt them to local conditions.

Article 74. The Overseas Territories of the Republic have a special organization which takes account of the interests of each within the framework of the general interests of the Republic. This organiza-tion is laid down and modified by law, after consultation with the Territorial Assembly of the Territory concerned.

Article 75. Citizens of the Republic who do not enjoy ordinary civil status, the only status to which Article 34 may be construed as re-ferring, keep their personal status so long as they have not re-nounced it.

Article 76. Overseas Territories may keep their status within the Republic. If they express the desire to do so, by a decision of their Territorial Assembly, within the period fixed by Article 91, para. 1, they become either Overseas *départements* or, grouped together or separately, member States of the Community.

The Community

Article 77. In the Community established by the present Constitu-tion, the States enjoy autonomy; they administer themselves and manage their own affairs, freely and democratically.

There is in the Community only one citizenship.

All citizens are equal before the law, whatever their origin, race or religion. They have the same duties.

Article 78. The field of competence of the Community includes foreign policy, defence, currency, common economic and financial policy and policy concerning strategic raw materials.

It also includes, in the absence of a special agreement to the contrary, supervision of justice, higher education, the general organization of external and common transport, and telecommunications.

Special agreements may establish other common fields of competence or provide for any transfer of competence from the Community to one of its members.

Article 79. The member States come within the provisions of Article 77 as soon as they have made the choice provided for in Article 76.

Until the coming into force of the measures necessary for the application of the present Title, matters of common competence will be dealt with by the Republic.

Article 80. The President of the Republic presides over and represents the Community.

The latter has as its organs an Executive Council, a Senate and a Court of Arbitration.

Article 81. The member States of the Community take part in the election of the President in the conditions provided for in Article 6.

The President of the Republic, in his capacity of President of the Community, is represented in each State of the Community.

Article 82. The Executive Council of the Community is presided over by the President of the Community. It is composed of the Prime Minister of the Republic, the Heads of Government of each of the member States, and the Ministers made responsible, on behalf of the Community, for common affairs.

The Executive Council organizes governmental and administrative co-operation between the members of the Community.

The organization and methods of work of the Executive Council are determined by an organic law.

Article 83. The Senate of the Community is composed of delegates chosen from among their own number by the Parliament of the Republic and the legislative assemblies of the other members. The number of delegates from each State is fixed in a manner which takes account of its population and of the responsibilities which it assumes within the Community.

It holds two sessions a year, which are opened and closed by the President of the Community and may not last longer than one month each.

At the request of the President, it discusses common economic and financial policy, before the Parliament of the Republic and, in appropriate circumstances, the legislative assemblies of other members of the Community pass laws in this field.

The Senate of the Community considers the acts, international agreements, and treaties referred to in Articles 35 and 53, where these involve obligations for the Community.

It takes binding decisions in the fields in which power has been delegated to it by the legislative assemblies of members of the Community. The decisions are promulgated in the States concerned in the same way as the laws of the territories.

An organic law determines its composition and the rules under which it functions.

Article 84. A Court of Arbitration of the Community gives rulings on disputes between members of the Community.

Its composition and powers are determined by an organic law.

Article 85. Notwithstanding the procedure provided for in Article 89, the provisions of the present Title concerning the functioning of the common institutions of the Community are revised by laws couched in the same terms passed by the Parliament of the Republic and by the Senate of the Community.

*The provisions of the present Title can also be revised by agreements concluded between all the States of the Community; the new provisions are applied in the conditions laid down by the Constitution of each State.**

Article 86. A change of the status of a member State of the Community may be requested either by the Republic, or by a resolution of the legislative assembly of the State concerned, confirmed by a local referendum, organized and supervised by the institutions of the Community. The methods by which the change of status is made are determined by an agreement approved by the Parliament of the Republic and the legislative assembly concerned.

In the same manner, a member State of the Community may become independent. It thereby ceases to belong to the Community.

A member State of the Community may also become independent, by means of agreements, without thereby ceasing to form part of the Community.

An independent State, not being a member of the Community, can

* Additions made by the revision of 4 June 1960 are given in italics.

join the Community, by means of agreements, without thereby ceasing to be independent.

*The position of these States within the Community is determined by the agreements referred to in the preceding paragraphs and, where appropriate, by the agreements for this purpose provided for by paragraph 2 of Article 85.**

Article 87. Special agreements concluded in application of the present title require the approval of the Parliament of the Republic and of the legislative assembly concerned.

TITLE XIII

Agreements of association

Article 88. The Republic or the Community may conclude agreements with States desiring to form an association with either, in order to develop their civilizations.

TITLE XIV

Revision

Article 89. The right to propose amendments to the Constitution belongs concurrently to the President of the Republic, on the proposal of the Prime Minister, and to members of Parliament.

The amending Bill, Government or private member's, must be passed by the two assemblies in identical terms. The amendment becomes effective when it has been approved by referendum.

However, a Governmental amending Bill is not submitted to a referendum when the President of the Republic decides to submit it to Parliament, meeting as Congress; in this case the amendment is accepted only if it obtains a majority of three-fifths of the votes cast. The Bureau of the Congress is that of the National Assembly.

The amendment procedure may not be initiated or pursued when the integrity of the territory is under attack.

The Republican form of government is not subject to revision.

TITLE XV

Temporary dispositions

Article 90. The ordinary session of Parliament is suspended. The term of office of the members of the present National Assembly will

* Additions made by the revision of 4 June 1968 are given in italics.

expire on the day the Assembly elected by virtue of the present Constitution meets.

Until this meeting, only the Government has authority to summon Parliament.

The term of office of the members of the Assembly of the French Union will expire at the same time as the term of the members of the present National Assembly.

Article 91. The institutions of the Republic provided for in the present Constitution will be set up within a period of four months from the day of its promulgation.

This period is extended to six months for the institutions of the Community.

The powers of the present President of the Republic will expire only on the proclamation of the results of the election provided for in Articles 6 and 7 of the present Constitution.

The member States of the Community will take part in this first election in conditions appropriate to their status at the date of the promulgation of the Constitution.

The established authorities will continue to exercise their functions in these States in accordance with the laws and other instruments applicable on the date at which the Constitution enters into force, until the installation of the authorities provided for by their new form of government.

Until its constitution has been finally determined, the Senate consists of the present members of the Council of the Republic. The organic laws which will determine the final constitution of the Senate must come into existence before 31 July 1959.

The powers conferred on the Constitutional Council by Articles 58 and 59 of the Constitution will be exercised, until the installation of the Council, by a Commission composed of the Vice-President of the Council of State as chairman, the First President of the *Cour de Cassation* and the First President of the Court of Accounts.

The peoples of the member States of the Community continue to be represented in Parliament until the coming into force of the measures necessary for the application of Title XII.

Article 92. The legislative measures necessary for the installation of the institutions and, until that installation, for the functioning of the public authorities, will be taken in the Council of Ministers, after consultation with the Council of State, by ordinances have the force of law.

During the period prescribed in the first paragraph of Article 91 the Government is authorized to determine, by ordinances having the force of law and issued in the same form, the electoral system for the assemblies provided for by the Constitution.

During the same period and in the same conditions, the Government may also take, on any subject, such measures as it may consider necessary to the life of the nation, the protection of the citizens or the preservation of freedom.

The present law will be applied as the Constitution of the Republic and of the Community.

Notes

PART I

1. Pierre Viansson-Ponté, 'L'année zéro de l'après-gaullisme', *Le Monde*, 5-6 October 1969.

2. *v.* Maurice Duverger's description of it as '*Orléaniste*' in *La Vᵉ République* (Paris, Presses universitaires de France, 1959), pp. 195-6, and in *Revue Française de Science politique* (March, 1959).

3. René Capitant, in his preface to Léo Hamon, *De Gaulle dans la République* (Paris, Plon, 1958), described it as 'the worst-drafted in French constitutional history'.

4. *v.* for example, the following declaration, published in the MRP paper *Témoignage chrétien* on 5 May 1962: 'Everything indicates that the Gaullist régime will not survive its inventor. The Constitution, constantly violated, will never be permanently acceptable . . .'

It must be remembered that the MRP was by no means wholeheartedly opposed either to Gaullism or to presidential methods. cf. the prediction in *Le Monde*, 2 June 1962:

> His mission is coming to an end. Apart from the fact that it was entrusted to him by the country, there were no rival candidates for the job, least of all among the politicians. The situation is different now. The politicians whom he has ousted feel themselves to be better qualified than he is to rebuild France, defend the Republic and Europe.

5. *v.* 'Constitution du 3 septembre, 1791', Titre VII, articles 1-8, in H. Duguit, H. Monnier, R. Bonnard, G. Berlia, *Les Constitutions et les principales lois politiques de la France depuis 1789* (Paris, Librairie générale de droit et de jurisprudence, 1951), p. 31.

The actual revision was to be carried out by a fourth Parliament elected for that sole purpose, following agreement by its three predecessors. At least, the authors of the Constitution had rejected the proposal of one of its more enthusiastic supporters to make amendment impossible for 30 years! By that time, the 1791 Constitution, which lasted for 10 months, had been followed by eight others.

6. The precise number of Constitutions that France has had can be debated interminably, because the calculation can be based on a number of different criteria. There were, in fact, 19 written Constitutions between 1789 and 1959, but six of them were never actually applied (the two 1793 Constitutions, the 1814 'Senatorial' Constitution, the Vichy 'Constitutional Acts', the Imperial Constitution of May 1970, and the rejected draft of 1946). There were, however, in addition to written Constitutions that actually came into force, a number of provisional régimes, based on no written text (those of 1792–5, 1848, 1870–5, 1940–4 and 1944–6). Some Constitutions lasted only a very short time (that of 1815, for instance, lasted only 21 days). There were also a number of constitutional amendments, some of which (the 1869 amendments to the Constitution of the Second Empire, for example, which were not applied) really amounted almost to a change of régime, while some changes of régime involved hardly more than constitutional amendments. Of the 13 written Constitutions that are considered to have established new régimes, three were Monarchic (1791, 1814, 1830); two were dictatorial (1799, 1802); three were Imperial (1804, 1815, 1852); and five were Republican (1795, 1848, 1875, 1946 and 1958).

7. The Constitution of 1795 produced an alternative set of rights and duties of the citizen, with a strong emphasis on duties. (*v.* Duguit, *et al.*, op. cit., pp. 73–5.)

8. *Manuel de Droit constitutionnel* (Paris, Anciennes Maisons Thorin et Fontemoing, E. de Bossard, Editeur, 1923), p. 218.

9. *v.* for a later view on the extent to which Duguit's opinion is valid, Maxime Letourneur,

. . . in spite of the contrary opinion expressed by Duguit, whose views on this point are idealistic but not in accord with the present position of French law, the Declaration of 1789 contains only principles of natural law – principles that it would be certainly desirable to see adopted by legislators, which are a guide to them, and consequently to judges, but which have in themselves no positive validity . . .

'Les "Principes généraux du Droit" dans la jurisprudence du Conseil d'Etat', in *Conseil d'Etat, Etudes et Documents* (Fascicule 5, Paris, Imprimerie nationale, 1951), p. 28.

10. *Institutions politiques et Droit constitutionnel* (Paris, Dalloz, 1957), p. 283.

11. Debate of 28 August 1946.

12. Maxime Letourneur in article mentioned above, note 9.

13. Quoted in Marcel Prélot, op. cit., p. 283.

14. *v. Arrêt Dehaene*, in H. Long, P. Weil, G. Braibant, *Les grands Arrêts de la jurisprudence administrative* (Paris, Sirey, 1969, No. 79). This decision specifically states that, in the absence of a law to regulate strikes, the constitutional right must be recognized, to the extent that it does not conflict with measures taken by the Government to maintain public order. It also states that the laws of 27 December 1947 and 29 September 1948, which prohibited strikes by the police and security police, could not be regarded as constituting the 'general rules' referred to in the paragraph of the Preamble of the Constitution relating to the right to strike.

v. also Robert Pelloux, *Le citoyen devant l'Etat* (Que Sais-je?, Paris, Presses universitaires de France, 1955), p. 31:

> ... the phrase relating to the right to strike has been responsible for a change in the case law relating to the effect of strikes on the contract of service, and for the recognition by administrative courts of the legality of strikes by civil servants, subject to a number of limitations.

15. (i) Le Président Bouffandeau on the occasion of the 150th anniversary of the *Conseil d'Etat*, quoted by Maxime Letourneur, op. cit., p. 19. (ii) ibid., p. 24.

16. *v. Arrêt Canal* (Long *et al.*, op. cit., No. 105), *Arrêt Barel* (No. 92), in which a ministerial decision to refuse five students permission to sit for an examination for the National School of Administration was annulled by the *Conseil d'Etat*, in the absence of sufficient evidence as to the Minister's lack of political bias. In their *Observations* on the case, the authors specifically refer to the 1789 Declaration of Rights and the Preamble of the 1946 Constitution, adding: '... *ces textes ont valeur de principes généraux du droit supérieure à celle de tout acte de l'éxécutif.*'

On the Constitutional Council's rejection of a Government Bill in July 1971, on the ground that its provisions conflicted with rights recognized in the 1789 Declaration, see Chapter III, note 32.

17. *v.* Duguit *et al.*, op. cit., pp. 10, 81, 217, 304.

18. The phrase is that of Georges Burdeau in his study of the Constitution in *La Revue française de Science politique*, March 1959, p. 88.

19. Marcel Prélot, *Pour comprendre la nouvelle Constitution* (Paris, Editions le Centurion, 1958), pp. 70–1.

20. Nor was any attempt made to ensure that parties conformed to these requirements. For instance, the Constitutional Council refused to approve the original draft of article 19 of the National Assembly's Standing Orders, which would have authorized the Assembly's bureau to refuse to accept the declaration of a Parliamentary group, if this appeared to be contrary to the provisions of article 4. (*v*. Marcel Prélot, *Institutions politiques et Droit constitutionnel*, Paris, Dalloz, 1969, pp. 614–15.)

21. Quoted in Roger Pinto, *Eléments de Droit constitutionnel* (Morel et Corduant, Lille, 1952), p. 328.

22. Edouard Herriot during the debates on the rejected first draft of the 1946 Constitution.

23. Speech at Bône, on 5 June 1958, in which he said: '*Tout ce qui est à la tête de l'Etat et du pays doit être renouvelé. J'ai reçu mandat de le faire.*' M. Debré, the most ardent of Gaullists was, as *Garde des Sceaux*, one of the most important contributors to the Constitutional provisions. He referred frequently in speeches to the need for a powerful President of the Republic. *v*. in particular his speech to the *Conseil d'Etat*, published in *La Revue française de Science politique*, March, 1959, p. 22. 'The President of our Republic cannot be merely the head of the State who appoints the Prime Minister, as he is in all Parliamentary régimes. . . . In our France, where internal political divisions are so important, he is the highest judge of the national interest.' This reflects General de Gaulle's sentiments as expressed in his Bayeux speech. *v*. also, Pierre Viansson-Ponté, in *Histoire de la République gaullienne* (Paris, Fayard, 1970, Vol. I, p. 64), where he attributes specifically to the President the responsibility not only for article 16 but also for the other new constitutional powers of the President, discussed in Chapter 5.

24. Professor Maurice Duverger claimed that only three Constitutions had included this rare combination – the Weimar Constitution of the 1930s, the Austrian Constitution of 1951 and the Finnish Constitution (*v*. 'Les Institutions après de Gaulle', in *Le Monde*, 26 November 1969).

25. Ibid.

26. Ibid.

27. Press Conference of 2 July 1970.

28. *v.* pp. 84–8 and 91.

29. Among measures under consideration by the last two Governments of the Fourth Republic, and actually under discussion in May 1958, were: a reduction in the length of Parliamentary sessions; the authorization of legislation by decree – technically unconstitutional under article 13 of the 1946 Constitution; the attempt to ensure that Governments lasted throughout the Parliament, by making Government defeats dependent on the availability of an alternative majority, able to form a Government.

30. Constitution of 1791, Chapter II, Section 1, article 3.

31. The Consultative Constitutional Committee did, however, suggest an amendment by which, (a) in conformity with traditional practice, Ministers could be appointed from either inside or outside Parliament, and (b) during their period of office, they should cease to be members of political parties, should engage in no party-political activities, and should be suspended from membership of Parliament. Since Ministers' opinions would be known and their eventual return to both party politics and the National Assembly taken for granted, this seemed, on the face of it, politically pointless and would have deprived the Government of a sizeable number of votes, if no 'substitutes' were to replace Ministers. The amendment was rejected. (*v.* Prélot, *Pour comprendre la nouvelle Constitution*, p. 91.)

32. The provisions entitling Ministers to attend debates and to speak in either assembly enabled Léon Blum to appoint three junior women Ministers in the 1936 Popular Front Government, although, at that time, women did not have the vote and were not allowed to stand for Parliament.

33. *v.* articles 56–63 of the Constitution and organic law of 7 November 1958 (Ordinance No. 58–1067).

34. Perhaps the most striking instance of political bias was that of 1877, when 71 minority Deputies were unseated, but none belonging to the majority (Republican) party. (*v.* D. W. Brogan, *The Development of Modern France*, London, Hamish Hamilton, 1940, p. 141.) More recent examples are those of 1951 (on which *v.* Dorothy Pickles, *French Politics: the First Years of the Fourth Republic*, London, Royal Institute of International Affairs, 1953, pp. 288–9), and 1956, when a number of Poujadist Deputies were unseated, for valid reasons, but following a debate in which the influence of political preoccupations was clearly evident (*v. Année politique*, 1956, pp. 24–6).

35. *v. Journal Officiel*, 25 January 1972. As originally voted on 20 December 1971, the Bill had included provisions enabling the assembly concerned to authorize exceptions to certain of the new 'incompatibilities', in accordance with rules laid down in its own Standing Orders, or alternatively to hand over responsibility for decisions to the Constitutional Council. These parts of the Bill were declared to be unconstitutional, however, by the Council itself, which is required to pronounce on the conformity with the Constitution of organic laws. Since the Constitution, in article 25, requires the provisions on incompatibility to be applied by an organic law, the National Assembly and the Senate cannot, in the view of the Constitutional Council, exercise any *discretion* in the matter. The law, therefore, omits these unconstitutional articles and substitutes for them procedures as laid down in the 1961 law. The effect of the ruling was to restrict the scope of the new 'incompatibilities'. For criticisms of the original provisions and text of the ruling of the Constitutional Council *v. Le Monde*, 22, 23–4, and 26 January 1972.

36. Article 73 provides for 'adaptations' of their legislative régime or administrative organization that may be necessitated by their particular situation. No mention is made of possible accession to independence. Since they retain the status that they had under the Fourth Republic, they can, of course, take advantage of the possibilities for partial self-government offered by the 'framework-law' of 1956. This provided for Governmental Councils elected by the Territorial assemblies in Overseas Territories; for the extension of the powers of these assemblies, mainly in matters of local concern; for universal suffrage and a common electoral roll which already existed in most; and for Africanization of the administration. But it still left in French hands the responsibility for foreign affairs, justice, defence, the protection of individual liberties, communications, finance and higher education. The Territories were (and have remained) poor and economically dependent on France. Their number has been increased to six by the addition of Wallis and Futuna, but only in New Caledonia (and to a lesser extent in French Somaliland – renamed 'Territory of the Afars and Issas') has there been any serious agitation in favour of independence.

37. Although the Community, as provided for by the Constitution, was, in effect, dead from 1961 onwards, the post-independence relationship of the 12 States with France has been close. They all signed agreements for co-operation in the field of foreign policy,

economic and financial policy, and in some cases defence agreements. All obtained preferences for their exports in French markets
and accord French exports preference in their own. They became
'associated' with the Common Market under a five-year Convention,
signed at Yaoundé in 1963, and renewed in 1969. They all receive
technical and educational aid.

38. For instance, the report of 1947–9 claimed that upwards of
half of the Council's recommendations had been 'wholly or partially taken into consideration'. In reality, as its members were well
aware, even this degree of attention was mainly reserved for questions submitted by the Government. Very little attention was paid
to reports submitted by the Council on its own initiative and it was
hardly ever consulted by the Government on Bills.

39. The Economic and Social Council of the Fifth Republic
represents similar professional interests, but includes 200 members,
as against 169 members of the Economic Council. Under the Fourth
Republic, except for the ten representatives of '*la pensée française*'
and a handful of representatives of housing, savings, tourism and
export industries who were chosen by the Government, members
of the Economic Council were chosen to represent specified trade
unions and employers and professional organizations. Of the
members of the Economic and Social Council, one-third (64) are
nominated by the Government. They include 15 economic, social
and cultural representatives, 25 persons with special knowledge of
overseas social and economic problems, 10 representatives of the
economic and social activities of the overseas *départements*, and 10
representing in the main the interests noted above. There is no
special representation of '*la pensée française*'. Additional members of
sections, co-opted for their special experience, are also chosen by
the Government.

40. Article 89 requires unilateral action by the French Parliament, and this, of course, was unacceptable to the African States.
A referendum was out of the question, since it would have been
impossible not to provide for Algerian participation. Since the
Algerian nationalists were at that time fighting for their own independence, this was both practically impossible and politically undesirable. The Government, therefore, decided to give political
common sense priority over strict constitutional propriety. The
Conseil d'Etat view (ignored by the Government) was that the procedure adopted was, strictly speaking, unconstitutional. (*v.* Prélot,
Droit constitutionnel, 1969, p. 585.)

41. Parliamentary sessions originally lasted from the first Tuesday in October to the third Friday of December, and from the last Tuesday in April for a period not exceeding 90 days. Following the 1963 revision, Parliament meets on the 2nd October for 80 days, and on the 2nd April for 90 days. If these dates coincide with a public holiday, the session begins the following day.

42. *v. Demain la République* (Paris, Julliard, 1958), p. 70. M. Duverger states categorically that the aim of this system is 'to obtain, by constitutional devices, the result achieved in Great Britain by the working of two disciplined parties'. To a British political scientist, it seems that he under-estimates the ability of French politicians to get round constitutional rules that they dislike! Constitutions can strengthen or weaken political forces; it is doubtful, to put it mildly, whether they can create political habits.

43. Quoted in *Esope*, 15 May 1965.

44. On presidentialism in the 1950s see François Goguel in *Revue française de Science politique*, July–September 1956.

45. Presidential *'grandes options'* were laid down both by M. Gaston Defferre, in 1964, when he was hoping to be the presidential candidate of a united non-Communist Left in the 1965 elections, and by M. Alain Poher, when he opposed M. Georges Pompidou in the 1969 presidential election. For M. Gaston Defferre, these involved the expression of a general political attitude. In a speech at Clermont-Ferrand (*Le Monde*, 13 October 1964), he described these as including the belief in State independence of pressure groups; the need to give priority to national education and to principles of social and economic justice; the belief in planning in a climate of economic expansion and in a politically united Europe that would be a partner and not a vassal of the United States, and non-belief in the need for an independent nuclear deterrent. In other words, his *'grandes options'* were a faithful expression of current French Socialist party attitudes! M. Poher's *'grandes options'* similarly expressed the pre-occupations of Centrist parties (in particular, their Europeanism).

46. Some critics of the idea of *'grandes options'* pointed out an additional difficulty, namely, that if President and Assembly were required to face the electors together, then the absence of both at the same time was hardly likely to increase political stability.

47. The weakness of this system is, of course, the difficulty of ensuring that the alternative majority is not based merely on a formula of words intended to achieve office, but without any real agreement on positive Governmental policies.

48. *v. La République moderne* (Paris, Gallimard, 1962), Chapter IV.

CHAPTER II

1. The electoral system of the Third Republic was laid down in two organic laws, one of 2 August 1875 on the election of Senators, the other of 30 November 1875 on the election of Deputies. The electoral system of the Fourth Republic was laid down in the law of 5 October 1946, on the election of Deputies in the law of 27 October 1946, used for the first election of Councillors of the Republic, and that of 23 September 1948, which replaced it for subsequent Senatorial elections.

2. For a brief account of the systems put forward on the first date, *v.* the author's *French Politics: the first years of the Fourth Republic*, 1953, p. 131. On the controversy in 1955 see *Année politique*, 1955, pp. 82–90.

3. Ordinance No. 58-945 of 13 October 1958, completed by Ordinance No. 58-1015 of 29 October 1958 and by three other Ordinances, provided the electoral laws governing elections to the National Assembly. They were not organic laws and are, therefore, amendable by the ordinary legislative procedure. Ordinance No. 58-1065 of 7 November 1958, which lays down the composition of the National Assembly, the length of sessions, the length of life of Parliaments, and the conditions for replacing Deputies by substitutes, is an organic law and so amendment requires the special procedure laid down by article 46 of the Constitution. Similarly, the Ordinance of 15 November 1958, determining the composition, length of sessions and rules for the renewal of the Senate (No. 58-1097) is an organic law, while that of the same date (No. 58-1098), governing the rules for election to the Senate, is not.

4. The five systems used since 1875 are: (i) the single-member system with two ballots (1876–81; 1889–1914; 1928–36); (ii) proportional representation (1945 and two elections in 1946); (iii) a quasi-proportional system (1919 and 1924); (iv) a different quasi-proportional system (1951 and 1956); (v) a majority system with list voting, used only once (1885).

For a description of the working of these systems, see Peter Campbell, *French Electoral Systems and Elections since 1789* (London, Faber & Faber, second edition, 1965).

5. *v.* article 24 of the Constitution of 1848, article 36 of the

Constitution of 14 January 1852, article 1 of the Constitution of 1875, article 47 of the defeated draft Constitution of 1946, article 3 of the Constitution of the Fourth Republic, and article 24 of the Constitution of 1958.

6. Direct universal (male) suffrage, though introduced in 1848, was modified in 1850.

7. In 1936, Guiana and Senegal had one Deputy each but were not represented in the Senate. Cochin-China and the Indian establishments were each represented by one Deputy, but the second had no Senator. Algeria had ten Deputies and three Senators. Apart from the 'old colonies', the only voters of non-European origin were the handful of 'assimilated' persons granted French citizenship. In Algeria, these included, from 1870 onwards, the non-European Jewish Algerian population. In all, overseas representation during the Third Republic, including that of Algeria, amounted to 20 Deputies and 7 Senators, out of a total of 618 Deputies and 312 Senators. The total overseas population was then in the neighbourhood of 70 millions as against a French population of some 40 millions. But there was, at that date, no real movement in favour of the suffrage among the 20 million or so Africans under French rule. The Protectorates (Morocco, Tunisia, and Indo-China except for Cochin-China), accounting for about half of the total overseas population, were never candidates for assimilation in the French Republic. Though prepared at first to accept 'association' with France on the basis of national Governments, by the 1940s they had strong nationalist movements, as, by then, had Algeria. Nationalism in the African Territories did not become a real force until after 1958.

8. *v. Le Monde*, 12 December 1970.

9. The proportion has varied since 1946 between 68·72% and 82·7%. In all but one election, over 75% voted.

10. An exception was made in January 1956, when election day fell on New Year's Day. In order to avoid an election on a public holiday, it was held the following day.

11. The other two specified cases are those of the Deputy's appointment to the Constitutional Council, or his acceptance of a Governmental mission lasting more than six months.

12. This meant at first, in the case of substitutes in the Senate, until the next partial renewal. The law of 18 July 1962 provided that they should hold office for the full period for which the Senators whom they were replacing would have sat.

13. The Ordinance of 29 October 1958 is quite specific on this point: 'A candidate cannot present at the second ballot a substitute whose name does not figure on his declaration of candidature at the first ballot.'

14. The sixth substitute (for M. Couve de Murville) refused to resign, and so the latter had to find another constituency. On the problems created by the 'incompatibility' rule, see Chapter IV.

15. From 1962 to 1967, there were only 482 Deputies, of whom 465 sat for metropolitan France. The transformation of the two *départements* of the Paris region (Seine and Seine-et-Oise) into seven *départements* made 95 in all and increased the total representation to 487. That of the seven *départements* of the Paris region rose from 73 to 78. Of these, 47 sit for the new *départements* and 31, as before, for Paris.

16. Originally, the Overseas Territories elected their representatives at a single ballot. This was changed by the law of 29 December 1966, which substituted the two-ballot system, as in metropolitan France, except for the two-member constituency of the Comoro Archipelago, where there is one ballot and list-voting, without either '*panachage*' (mixing names from different lists), or the expression of preferences. (*v.* Electoral Law No. 66-1034, *Journal Officiel*, 30 December 1966.)

17. In 1968, the smallest constituencies were Wallis and Futuna (electorate 3–4000), St. Pierre and Miquelon (under 3000), and Guiana (14–15,000). The largest were Essonne (3), Bouches-du-Rhône (10), and Rhône (6), all of which had over 100,000. In 1967, 378 of the 470 metropolitan constituencies had electorates of between 45,000 and 75,000.

18. In 1958, only 39 candidates were elected at the first ballot; in 1962, 96; in 1967, 72; and in 1968, 154. The situation was similar under the Third Republic. In 1928, 1932 and 1936, between two-thirds and three-fifths of the constituencies in metropolitan France failed to elect a candidate at the first ballot.

19. The law of 29 December 1966 raised the percentage of the vote required to qualify a candidate to stand at the second ballot from five to ten.

20. The organic laws on which the electoral code is based do not specifically mention the case of a Deputy's right to stand in a second constituency, but only the case of a member of one assembly elected to the other, in which case, since no one individual can be both a Deputy and a Senator (article 9 of Ordinance No. 58-998

of 24 October 1958), membership of the one is automatically terminated by election to the other. A Deputy who actually occupied two seats would be infringing the rule (article L.O. 119 of the electoral Code) laying down the number of Deputies and of constituencies. It was suggested by the President of the National Assembly, in September 1970, that the electoral code should be amended so as to make it obligatory for a Deputy or Senator standing as a candidate for another constituency to resign the first seat before contesting the second. (*v. Le Monde*, 22 September 1970.)

21. In the original text of the Ordinance, the figure given is 100,000 francs. This meant 'old francs'. The new franc, equivalent to 100 old francs, was introduced at the beginning of 1960.

22. Provision of article 2 of the Electoral Law of 29 December 1966 (Law No. 66-1022, *Journal Officiel*, 30 December 1966).

In the 1967 election, groups represented in the National Assembly were allowed, in all, three hours before the first and one and a half hours before the second ballot, to be divided equally between Government and non-Government parties. The apportionment of time as between parties within the Government or the opposition was left to the presidents of the groups, or, failing agreement, to the bureau of the National Assembly. In addition, any political organization contesting the election which presented 75 candidates at the first ballot, but was not eligible under these rules (i.e. a party not represented in the National Assembly), was entitled to a total of seven minutes before the first, and five minutes before the second ballot. Television and radio broadcasts were to be simultaneous.

For the detailed working out of these rules for the 1967 election, *v. Le Monde*, 6 and 29–30 January 1967.

23. In the 1936 elections and the three elections immediately following the second world war, the proportion of voters ranged from 78% to 84%, but the political conditions in all these cases were exceptional, as they were also in 1958 and 1968. The election of 1962 could be regarded as the first to be held in normal circumstances since 1932.

24. For details on the conditions governing postal and proxy voting, *v.* Marcel Prélot, *Institutions politiques et droit constitutionnel* (Paris, Dalloz, 1969), pp. 643–6.

25. Quoted in *Le Monde*, 19–20 March 1967.

26. *v. Journal Officiel*, 26 January 1968, decision of the Constitutional Council, annulling the election at Bastia of 12 March 1967, at which M. Faggianelli was elected.

A number of comments on the situation in Corsica were less inhibited. Reporting the by-election in the same constituency, as a result of this decision, a writer in *Le Monde* spoke of '6000 ghosts in Bastia', adding that a similar situation had existed in 1958, when there were 3400 in the town of Bastia alone, and that in the country regions the problem of these 'ghost voters' was even greater. 'In some villages of 700 inhabitants', he wrote, 'there are 2000 electors on the register.' (*Le Monde*, 20 April 1968). An article in *Le Monde*, 8 July, on corrupt practices in Corsica stated that, with a population of 212,000, the island had 185,000 electors on the register, which showed a disproportion unique in France.

27. Of these, 3497 are Deputies or members of the *Conseils généraux* of the *départements*. (*v.* Maurice Duverger, *Institutions politiques et Droit constitutionnel*, Paris, Presses universitaires de France, 1970, p. 627, and Prélot, *Institutions politiques*, 1969, p. 650.)

28. As constituted in 1958, the Senate numbered 307 members, of whom 255 represented metropolitan France, 7 the Overseas *départements*, 5 the Overseas Territories, 6 French residents abroad, and 34 the Algerian and Saharan *départements*. With Algerian independence the last mentioned ceased to exist and the Senators were reduced to 273, increased to 274 by the representation of Wallis and Futuna by one Senator after it became an Overseas Territory in 1961. In 1967, 9 additional Senators for the six *départements* created from the former *départements* of Seine and Seine-et-Oise brought the number to 283. This administrative change increased the representation of the Paris region in the Senate from 30 to 39.

29. The system is that of list-voting, with distribution of seats by quotient in the first place, seats remaining unallocated going to the list with the 'highest average' vote per seat. This so-called 'highest average' system tilts the balance in favour of large, disciplined parties. The 'highest remainder' system has the opposite effect. The former was used in elections to the National Assembly in 1946, the latter in the 1951 and 1955 elections, but only in the Paris region. For a description of these two systems *v.* Peter Campbell, op. cit., pp. 111–14.

According to the Ordinance No. 58-1098 of November 1958 (*Journal Officiel*, 16 November 1958), article 26, only *départements* with five or more Senators elect them by proportional representation. Three of the Paris *départements* to which the system applies have fewer than five Senators, however. These are Essonne, Val d'Oise and Yvelines, formerly part of the *département* of Seine-et-Oise, which had eight Senators. After the reorganization in 1967, these *départements* retained the system that they had formerly qualified for.

30. *v.* Ordinance No. 59-260 of 4 February 1959, articles 13–18. Candidates must either have sat in the French Parliament or be qualified to sit by virtue of their residence or activities (article 15).

31. In 1959, all Senators were elected at the same time. A third (Series A), including Senators of *départements* listed alphabetically from Ain to Indre (together with a third of the overseas Senators), sat for three years; a third (Series B), including *départements* from Indre-et-Loire to Pyrénées Orientales, together with a third of overseas Senators, sat for six years; Series C, from Bas-Rhin to Yonne, together with the 30 Senators for the Paris region and the remaining third of overseas Senators, sat for the full nine years. Elections were held in 1962, 1965, 1968 and 1971.

32. *v.* Duverger, *Institutions politiques*, p. 627.

33. *v.* Speech to the *Conseil d'Etat*, on 8 August 1958, reprinted in *Revue française de Science politique*, March 1959, p. 24.

34. Professor Maurice Duverger has been among the most enthusiastic supporters of this theory.

35. It has been estimated that between 1919 and 1957, the average life of Governments was six and a half months in assemblies elected by proportional or quasi-proportional systems, and five months in those elected by majority systems. (*v.* M. Massenet, *L'Angoisse au Pouvoir*, Paris, Plon, 1959, p. 5.) This is hardly a fair comparison, since there were seven elections on proportional or quasi-proportional systems during this period, and only three on the majority system. If only the period between the wars is considered, then, of 39 effective Governments (i.e. excluding two Prime Ministers who held office for under a week), 14 held office in the two Assemblies elected by a quasi-proportional system, and 25 in the three Assemblies elected on the majority system. The first period covered the nine years from 1919 to 1928 and the second the eleven years up to the outbreak of war.

36. From 1917 to 1924, Right–Centre Governments had an average life of eleven months; the 1924-8 and 1936-40 Left or Left–Centre Governments had an average life of eight months; the 1946-51 Left–Centre coalitions (from 1947 excluding the Communists) had an average life of seven and a half months; and the 1951-5 Right–Centre Governments had an average life of eight

months; the 1956–8 Centre–Left coalitions had an average life of eight and a half months. During this period four different electoral systems were used.

37. The Treaty of Rome, for instance, was seen, under the Fourth Republic, as a strait-jacket to force Europe into an economically and politically integrated system, and, to begin with, as a method of forcing France herself to accept the disciplines necessary for this to become possible. Under the Fifth Republic it was used as a conscious instrument of French interests, in order to force France's partners to accept her conditions on a number of issues, but mainly on the agricultural policy of the Common Market.

CHAPTER III

1. *Le Figaro*, 30 July 1958.

2. Georges Galichon, 'Aspects de la procédure législative en France' in *Le Travail parlementaire en France et à l'Etranger* (Paris, Presses universitaires de France, 1955), p. 126.

3. This belief has led Republicans at times to prefer a unicameral legislature in which the popularly elected Chamber has no rival. It has also led them to feel that constitution-making is a matter for Parliaments rather than Governments. For instance, it led Edgar Faure in May 1955 to declare that 'the Government hesitates to intervene in the debate, since it does not want to create the impression that the Government is encroaching on the prerogatives of the Assembly'. (*Journal Officiel*, 25 May 1955.) In 1958, some members of the Assembly Committee objected to the Government's proposal to revise article 90 of the Constitution. M. Gaillard, the Prime Minister, replied that he had regarded himself as having the authorization of the Assembly. In other words, he did not question the principle.

4. Quoted in H. Duguit, H. Monnier, R. Bonnard and G. Berlia, *Les Constitutions et les principales Lois politiques de la France depuis 1789* (Paris, Librairie générale de droit et de jurisprudence, 1951), p. 26.

5. This provision is a protection against the risk of proceedings being taken against a member for the purpose of preventing his presence and vote in Parliament. Under the Fourth Republic, 'immunity' also involved risks for the public. From 1946 to 1954, it covered the whole period of the member's mandate, including periods when Parliament was not sitting. This enabled members to publish, in the capacity of newspaper editors, articles that would

normally have been regarded as actionable. *The Times* (11 July 1949) published the following statement from a Communist paper published in Dakar: 'As frequent prosecutions for libel have been causing us serious expense, we have entrusted the management of our paper to a member of Parliament. It will no longer be possible to sue us for libel without first obtaining leave of the House.' In 1950, there were 256 requests for the suspension of members' immunity, of which 217 related to Communist Deputies (figures given in debate of 29 November 1950). From 1954, therefore, members who were editors were required to appoint co-editors who did not have the privilege of immunity. *v.* also, on some of the problems, the author's *French Politics: the first years of the Fourth Republic* (London, Royal Institute of International Affairs, 1953), pp. 293–4.

6. For details of the salaries of members of Parliament and Ministers, *v. Le Monde*, 6 May 1967.

7. Emile Blamont, in *Le Parlement dans la Constitution de 1958* (Paris, Jurisclasseur administratif, 1960, p. 11) notes that, after deductions, the Deputy or Senator receives a salary equivalent to that of a 'middle-rank civil servant'.

8. Senators are penalized only for failure to attend meetings of Committees. *v.* Règlement (*Assemblée Nationale*) for details of fines to which Deputies are liable. *v.* also Marcel Prélot, *Institutions politiques et droit constitutionnel* (Paris, Dalloz, 1969), p. 736.

9. Organic law of 7 November 1958 (*Journal Officiel*, 9 November 1958). This mentions the first five. The sixth was recognized by the amendment to article 27 of 1962. The amendment had originally included a seventh condition, that of obligations imposed by membership of local councils of the *département*, but the Constitutional Council (comprehensibly) rejected this. The *bureau* decides whether the excuse of *force majeure* is valid.

10. *v. Institutions politiques*, 1969, p. 737. *v.* also Pierre Viansson-Ponté in *Le Monde*, 8 November 1961:

> The sanctions that were to cure absenteeism, the rules regarding the imperative mandate, the elimination of proxy voting – in spite of the existence of the electronic system – have become a dead letter.

According to press reports, on the occasion of the censure debate of May 1967, 81 Deputies were absent on grounds of 'illness or family circumstances', and 63 on 9 June 1967. (*Le Monde*, 7 October and 15 June 1967.)

11. 'Les Banquettes vides', *Le Monde*, 27 November 1963. *v.* Pierre Viansson-Ponté in *Le Monde*, 8 July 1966: '... with ten members present, votes are recorded by 450'.

12. The *doyen d'âge* makes a speech prior to the election of the President of the Assembly, ostensibly to give his colleagues the benefit of his Parliamentary experience. In practice, this has sometimes been an opportunity to make a politically biased speech. The most striking example was that of the Communist Deputy, Marcel Cachin, in January 1948, which led to an amendment of the Standing Orders to prohibit any debate in future on the speech by the *doyen d'âge*.

13. An absolute majority is required for election at the first or second ballot, a simple majority only, at the third. In case of candidates receiving an equal number of votes at the third ballot, the eldest is elected. The President of the Senate is elected until the next partial renewal (three years). His functions are generally similar to those of the President of the Assembly, except that it is he, and not the President of the Assembly, who becomes interim President during a declared presidential vacancy (as in 1969, following General de Gaulle's resignation). The President of the Senate under the Fifth Republic is third in the order of precedence. The change in the rules regarding the interim presidency of the Republic may have been due to the fact that the Senate is never dissolved.

14. M. Jeanneney voted in 1939 and M. Herriot voted in 1949.

15. This was the position of the Radical Deputies in the Assembly elected in 1968, when they were affiliated to the Socialist party. Affiliates count as members of the group for purposes of representation in the permanent committees.

16. This statement is drawn up when groups are formed at the beginning of a new Parliament, and is published in the *Journal Officiel*.

17. This process takes a long time and was frequently used under the Fourth Republic (particularly by the Communists) as a method of obstructing Parliamentary business, since it was obligatory if requested by a majority of the Assembly, or when the Government had made a matter one of confidence. The rule was therefore changed and its use was restricted to certain specified important occasions.

18. The word 'committee' is used here to refer only to the standing or permanent committees forming part of the legislative process. These committees originally had different memberships: 60 each for the two dealing with foreign affairs and with finance; 90 each

for the two dealing with defence and with constitutional laws, legislation and administration; and 120 for the other two. The two with 90 members each were reduced to 60 after the departure of the Algerian members of the Assembly, since there would otherwise have been more seats on committees than there were Deputies. The odd 'one' for each was added in 1969 because, from 1967 onwards, the Assembly numbered 487. Six Deputies who belonged to no organized group (*non-inscrits*) were therefore excluded from membership of committees, since the organized groups have priority over isolated members. The President of the Assembly is, of course, not a member of any committee. In the Senate, defence and foreign affairs are dealt with by a single committee, but culture and social questions have one each. The numbers are in the main smaller, owing to the smaller numbers of Senators, but not proportionally so. They range from 38 to 75.

Of other committees, Special Committees are *ad hoc* committees which can replace the appropriate permanent committee to deal with any Bill, at the request of the Government or of the Assembly. The reason why relatively little use has been made of these is probably because Governments have feared bias in their appointment, whereas they know where they stand with the existing committees. Committees of Enquiry are set up to investigate special subjects as are Select Committees of the House of Commons. They must complete their work within four months. Supervisory Committees are concerned with the working of organizations in the public sector.

19. André Laurens, 'Le Métier de Député', in *Le Monde*, 8 October 1967.

20. A Government Bill is *un projet de loi*, a private member's Bill, *une proposition de loi*.

21. The 'urgency' procedure is provided for in article 45 of the Constitution and article 102 of the Standing Orders. If the Government declares a matter 'urgent', then the time allowed for consideration of it is reduced.

22. The organic laws mentioned in articles 6, 13, 23, 25, 27, 34, 47, 57, 63, 64, 67, 71, 82, 83 and 84 of the Constitution were all enacted by Ordinance during the transitional period between June 1958 and February 1959, when the Government had full powers. They concern the following subjects:

   (i) 24 October 1958. Rules governing eligibility and incompatibility (article 25).

(ii) 7 November 1958. Conditions of election of the President of the Republic (article 6).

(iii) 7 November 1958. Composition of the Assembly and term for which Deputies are elected (article 25).

(iv) 7 November 1958. Rules governing proxy voting (article 27).

(v) 7 November 1958. Organization of the Constitutional Council (articles 57 and 63).

(vi) 15 November 1958. Composition of the Senate and term for which Senators are elected (article 25).

(vii) 17 November 1958. Replacement of Deputies when disqualified from sitting (article 23).

(viii) 28 November 1958. Nomination to civil and military posts (article 13).

(ix) 13 December 1958. Salaries of members of Parliament (article 25).

(x), (xi), (xii) and (xiii) 19 December 1958. Organs of the Community (articles 82, 83, 84). These four organic laws are no longer effectively in existence.

(xiv), (xv) 22 December 1958. Organization of the Judiciary (articles 65 and 66).

(xvi) 29 December 1958. Organization of the Economic and Social Council (article 71).

(xvii) 2 January 1959. Organization of the High Court of Justice (article 67).

(xviii) 2 January 1959. Rules governing finance laws (articles 34, 47).

(xix) 4 February 1959. Numbers of Deputies representing Overseas Territories (article 25).

23. On the tactics, *v.* Philip Williams, *Crisis and Compromise* (Harlow, Longmans, 1964), pp. 263–8.

24. Organic law of 2 January 1959, articles 39 to 44.

25. Speech by M. Pineau to the 43rd National Congress of the Socialist Party.

26. *v.* Jean Gicquel, *Essai sur la Pratique de la Ve République* (Paris, Librairie générale de Droit et de Jurisprudence, 1967), p. 315: 'In a sense the budget is not so much voted as prolonged. With a disciplined majority, it becomes all but a formality.'

27. On the reform of the article of the Constitution providing for the Assembly to override the Senate, see the author's brief account in *Parliamentary Affairs*, Spring 1955.

28. *v.* speech by M. Léo Hamon in the Senate on 25 January

1951: 'a law is not defined in relation to the matter with which it deals; the definition is, juridically speaking, purely in terms of its form: a law is an act emanating from Parliament'.

29. The *Conseil d'Etat* is judge primarily of the legality, not the constitutionality, of executive acts. Appeals to it against the contents of a decree are on the grounds that the act complained of was not in itself permitted by the law under which the decree was issued, or that, even if permitted, it constituted in the circumstances a misuse of the power (for instance, by being a use of it that the law did not intend). But it now takes constitutionality into account if, in its view, the decree or rule complained of does not fall within the rule-making power (article 37, paragraph 1). In addition, under article 37, paragraph 2, the *Conseil d'Etat* becomes a judge of constitutionality, in the sense that it can refuse to authorize a decree amending a pre-1958 law, on the ground that the 1958 Constitution requires a law. Some lawyers have argued that it would be possible for the Government to challenge this ruling, if it could introduce a Bill having the same effects as the decree and then, by appealing to the Constitutional Council under article 37, hope to obtain a ruling that the matter came within the rule-making power.

30. Decision of 6 November 1962 (*v. Année politique*, 1962, pp. 687–8).

31. Prélot, *Institutions politiques*, 1969, p. 776. On how unevenly the scales are weighted, *v.* Maurice Duverger's examples (*Institutions politiques et Droit constitutionnel*, Paris, Presses universitaires de France, 1970, p. 820).

32. For instance, in 1964, the Constitutional Council declared that five out of seven proposed decrees relating to the organization of the radio and television services were matters for law and not for decrees. In July 1971, the Government was embarrassed by the Council's rejection of parts of a Government Bill to prevent banned 'leftist' groups from re-forming for illicit purposes. Article 3 of the Bill, which sought to revise the law of 1901 on the principles of freedom of association, was declared to be unconstitutional, on the ground that it infringed 'fundamental principles recognized by the laws of the Republic and solemnly reaffirmed in the preamble to the Constitution'. The right to freedom of association, said the decision, could not be curtailed by an administrative or even by a judicial authority, on the ground that the *object* of the association was illegal. (Decision of July 1971. *v.* text in *Le Monde*, 18–19 July 1971.)

33. *v.* for instance, M. Mollet's remark to General de Gaulle: 'He [i.e. the President of the National Assembly] affirms that there is a connection between the dissolution and motions of censure. But there is nothing in the Constitution to that effect.' (Interview at the Elysée of a Socialist delegation, reported in *France-Soir*, 27 September 1961.)

34. Decision of 19 March 1964 that the fundamental rules of the ORTF belonged to the domain of law, because it was a public corporation guaranteeing fundamental liberties by virtue of its mission of information and education. The functioning of the ORTF was governed by the law of 27 June 1964.

35. Academic jurists were almost unanimous that a law was required. The National Assembly received the views of eight eminent lawyers who all agreed that this was so. (*v.* view expressed by Professor Jean Rivero in *Le Monde*, 28–9 January 1968.)

36. The Deputy introducing the Bill was not seeking to extend Parliament's functions. If, however, his Bill had become law, Parliament's rôle in this field could not have been challenged in future.

37. The Government had four courses of action open to it at this stage:

(i) it could have introduced the measure by law;

(ii) it could have interpreted the Constitutional Council's decision as authorizing action by decree and risked appeals to the Council of State;

(iii) it could have consulted the Constitutional Council on the applicability of the *amendement Diligent* and risked another ambiguous reply; and

(iv) it could itself have introduced an organic law to complete article 34, which would automatically have been submitted for the approval of the Constitutional Council. In fact, it did none of these things.

38. At first, both the Assembly and the Senate included in their Standing Orders provisions for votes on resolutions as well as on Oral Questions with debate. The Assembly, however, withdrew the latter after a prolonged argument with the Government, but the Senate retained both, and resolutions were, in fact, voted in both Houses until the Constitutional Council ruled these articles of the provisional Standing Orders out of order. (Decision of 30 June 1959.)

39. Written Questions already existed under the previous régime

and some thousands are answered every year. Both questions and answers are printed in the *Journal Officiel*. Almost all are of only local or constituency interest. Oral Questions without debate are called by the President and the questioner is allowed to speak for five minutes following the Minister's reply. Oral Questions with debate are put by the questioner in a speech which can last from fifteen minutes to half an hour. The Minister then replies. Speakers in the debate are allowed up to fifteen minutes each, after which the Minister may make a final reply.

About four to five thousand Written Questions are put down per year. The following figures noted in the press give some idea of the numbers dealt with in the National Assembly: October to December 1963 (1180), April to June 1967 (2415), October to December 1969 (1162), April to June 1970 (1796).

The following figures show the numbers of Oral Questions put down and answered in the National Assembly: 1959, 392 (192 answered); 1960, 274 (100 answered); 1961, 269 (108 answered) (Pierre Avril, *Le Régime politique de la Ve République*, Paris, Librairie générale de Droit et de Jurisprudence, 1967, p. 109). These figures include questions with and without debate. Most of them M. Avril describes as 'trivial'. In 1967, of 308 Oral Questions with debate put down, 72 were answered, and of 208 without debate, 39 (Maurice Duverger, *Institutions politiques*, p. 806). In 1969, of 243 Oral Questions with debate put down, 27 were answered, 9 with a delay of one month, 8 with a delay of two months, 2 with a delay of three months, 8 with a delay of more than three months (*Assemblée nationale, Statistiques*, 1969, p. 31).

The following figures noted in the press give some indication of poor attendances at question time. On 22 November 1963, M. Malraux spoke to an audience of 8, dwindling to 5. In 1963 M. Pleven succeeded in getting a question on the agenda after a year of effort. The Minister's reply was made to an audience of 26 dwindling to 8 (*Le Monde*, 11–12 August 1963). Other audiences noted were: 29 May 1964 (12), 15 April 1966 (30), 22 April 1966 (42), 29 April 1966 (50), 2 June 1967 (10).

For an analysis of the subjects dealt with, *v.* Michel Ameller, *Les Questions, instrument de contrôle parlementaire* (Paris, Librairie générale de Droit et de Jurisprudence, 1964). He states that of 140 Oral Questions dealt with between 5 May 1959 and 16 December 1960, 75 were on social matters and the rest mainly of local interest. Only 4 were on foreign affairs and only 4 on defence. *v.* also Philip

Williams, *The French Parliament* (London, Allen and Unwin, 1968),
pp. 46–51.

40. The chairman of a special committee set up to consider ways
of improving Parliamentary efficiency (M. Habib Deloncle, UDR)
hoped that 8–10 *Questions d'actualité* a week could be treated rapidly
(*Le Monde*, 24 October 1969).

Questions d'actualité are read aloud by the President of the Assembly. The Minister then replies briefly and the questioner is
allowed two minutes to comment. In the first session (April to
June 1970) 109 questions were dealt with, the majority of them on
minor issues.

41. *v. Le Monde*, 10 July and 27 November 1970.

42. Figures quoted in *Le Monde*, 28–9 May and 16 June 1967,
15–16 December 1968. *v.* also articles by Pierre Viansson-Ponté in
Le Monde, 9 April 1964, 15–16 May and 8 July 1966. *v.* also reports
of absenteeism in the Finance Committee in *Le Monde*, 22 October
1964.

43. Quoted in *Le Monde*, 24 October 1969.

44. *v.* on this theme the speeches of the Presidents of both Houses
at the close of the April session 1970 (*Le Monde*, 2 July 1970).

45. On proposals for improvements, *v.* for instance, criticisms
and suggestions by Senator Armengaud (*Le Monde*, 9 April 1964),
which are in the main traditional in outlook; André Chandernagor
(Socialist Deputy) in *Un Parlement, pourquoi faire?* (Paris, Gallimard,
1967), p. 102, who wants more say by the opposition in the priorities accorded to questions in the Parliamentary timetable; Professor Georges Vedel (preface to *Report* of a Colloquium of the
Club Jean Moulin, 4–5 May 1968), who wants more time reserved
for private members' Bills; proposals by the President of the
Assembly (*Le Monde*, 27 November 1970); and proposals put forward by a committee of chairmen of Parliamentary groups (*Le
Monde*, 24 October 1969).

46. *Preuves*, November 1958, p. 13. He added: 'Yet the Assembly
could not find time for important debates on economic policy.'

47. A UDR Deputy, Pierre Bas, estimated that, in all, 10,595
private members' Bills were introduced during the Fourth Republic
(4281 in the first Parliament, 3588 in the second, and 2726 in the
short third Parliament), and that, of these, only 727 were voted
(*Le Monde*, 7 October 1967). In the first Parliament of the Fifth
Republic (1959–62) 513 Bills were voted, of which 46 were private
members' Bills (*Le Monde*, 25 November 1965). In the second

Parliament (1963–7) 436 Bills were voted, of which 53 were private members' Bills (François Goguel, 'Bilan du travail législatif' in *Projet*, March 1967), and in the short third Parliament (1967–8) 87 bills were voted, of which 18 were private members' Bills (Roger-Gérard Schwarzenberg, 'Les impasses de la Vᵉ bis', in *Projet*, September–October 1970, p. 95). Different sources quote somewhat different figures (but the discrepancies are slight). The majority of Fourth Republic private members' Bills were on trivial and minor matters, a number going through without debate. A considerable proportion of the Fifth Republic's much smaller number were introduced by Gaullist members. The whole trend of Gaullist legislation was towards a reduction in the number of Bills and a greater use of programme-laws or guide-line laws covering wide areas, the application of which was spread over several years. Purely statistical comparisons are, therefore, liable to be somewhat misleading as indications of the real significance of the dramatic fall in the number of both Government and private members' Bills under the Fifth Republic. (*v.* Alain Duhamel, *Le Monde*, 19 November 1970.)

CHAPTER IV

1. Statement made in the course of an interview to *Le Parisien libéré* (28 February 1946), in which M. Mollet spoke of the functions of the legislature as being to legislate – and so was opposed to government by 'decree-laws'. He added, concerning Parliament's function of supervision, that

> *Ce contrôle ne peut mettre en question l'autorité du Cabinet (je dis cabinet en préférence à gouvernement, car le gouvernement c'est à la fois l'Assemblée et le cabinet).*

2. *La France déchirée*, (Paris, Fayard, 1957), p. 9.

3. Darsie Gillie in the *Manchester Guardian Weekly*, 14 July 1949.

4. Article 13 of the 1946 Constitution. The law of 17 August 1948 saved appearances by distinguishing between matters traditionally and constitutionally recognized as being legislative, and subordinate matters that were not, or were not necessarily, legislative. In legislative matters the law must, as a minimum, lay down the 'essential rules', but the details could be filled in by executive measures. This was, in effect, an authorization of 'programme-laws'. In fact, however, Governments went considerably farther than this, and some subsequent measures were difficult to distinguish from the exercise by the executive of delegated legislative power. On this, *v.* Georges Galichon, 'Aspects de la procédure législative

en France', in *Le Travail parlementaire en France et à l'Etranger* (Paris, Presses universitaires de France, 1955).

5. Michel Crozier, *Le Phénomène bureaucratique* (Paris, Editions du Seuil, 1963), p. 296.

6. Francis Leenhardt, in the debate of 15 December 1961 (*Journal Officiel, Débats, Assemblée nationale*, 16 December 1961).

7. There was not an overall Gaullist majority in the National Assembly until after the 1968 general election, but the support in 1962 of some thirty members of the *Républicains indépendants*, who were very much the junior partner, and of about double that number in 1967, gave the Gaullists an effective *de facto* majority.

8. Peter Campbell, 'Cabinet and Constitution in France, 1951–6,' in *Parliamentary Affairs*, Summer 1956.

9. *v.* statement by Michel Debré to the *Conseil d'Etat* on 27 August 1958:

> The draft Constitution . . . includes certain precise procedural mechanisms, which would be out of place in a document of this kind, were it not for our realization that they are necessary in order to change our habits. To break bad habits, strict rules are required.
>
> (*Revue française de Science politique*, March 1959, p. 14.)

10. Though these reasons were often given, it is generally believed that General de Gaulle was responsible for the inclusion of article 23. In his statement of 8 August 1958 to the Consultative Constitutional Committee, he justified the need for Ministers to be independent of party and electors on the ground that they should be free to concentrate on national rather than on sectional interests.

11. Etienne Dailly, 'Les Suppléants, pourquoi faire?', *Le Monde*, 14 November 1969. In 1967, M. Couve de Murville told his electors that, if he were elected and remained a Minister, he would continue to defend the interests of the constituency (Pierre Avril, *Le Régime politique de la V*e *République*, Paris, Librairie générale de Droit et de Jurisprudence, 1967, p. 199).

12. Maurice Duverger, *Institutions politiques*, 1970, p. 695.

13. J.-M. Jeanneney, in *Le Monde*, 25 August 1970.

The incompatibility rule was not always easy to interpret and three difficulties are worth mentioning. The first (and least important) was related to the Bordeaux by-election. The organic law of 7 November 1958 refers only to 'acceptance' of office as disqualifying a Deputy (article 5). The Prime Minister had, of course, already accepted office and showed no sign of intending to relinquish it. Certainly, nobody expected him to resign (thus involving the resignation of the Government) in order to 're-accept' office after election. There were two earlier precedents of Ministers having won elections while in office and these were followed. M. Chaban Delmas resigned his seat within the month.

(On the legal implications of the Bordeaux election, *v.* Georges Vedel, 'Le Droit et l'élection de Bordeaux', *Le Monde*, 4 September 1970.)

Something of a problem had been created in 1962 by the rule that, during the month within which Ministers elected to the legislature must choose which office they wish to resign, they may sit in the National Assembly (or the Senate) but must not vote. The Gaullist majority in the December 1962 Assembly was fragile. In order to ensure a handsome majority for the President of the Assembly, who is elected at the beginning of a new Parliament, the Prime Minister delayed the announcement of the members of his Government (whose resignation following the defeat of the Government had taken effect only after the election). Deputies expecting to be appointed or re-appointed were, therefore, able to vote for the President of the Assembly. The following day, seventeen of them became Ministers and did not vote subsequently. They were replaced by their substitutes on 7 January, exactly one month after the opening of the session.

Another difficulty was created by article 6 of the Ordinance of 24 October 1958 (*Code électoral*, article L.O. 134) which states that 'A Deputy or a Senator, or a substitute replacing a member of a Parliamentary Assembly, cannot stand as a substitute in an election for the National Assembly or the Senate.' The reason for the provision is obvious. By doing so, some Deputies and Senators could have doubled their chances of election. But interpreted literally, this provision would have prevented all members, including those replacing Ministers, from presenting themselves as substitutes at an election held at the end of the five-year term. For Parliament is not then dissolved, and so members hold office until the opening of the session *following* the election. The Constitutional Council got round the difficulty by ruling that the 'incompatibility' became effective only when the 'substitute' entered the newly elected Assembly, which he did not do, of course, until he had replaced a Deputy who had resigned. What in effect the Council had done was to define 'substitutes' in such a way as to permit members to contest an election as *contingent* substitutes. With the opening of the new session, the fact that they have ceased to be members makes them eligible to become *effective* substitutes. The point was of some importance in 1967, since *all* the Ministers contesting the election had chosen as their substitute the sitting Deputy who had been their substitute in the previous election, and who, without the Constitutional Council's ingenious (if not very convincing) ruling, would have been disqualified from standing. (Decision of the Constitutional Council of 11 May 1967. *Journal Officiel*, 21 May 1967, p. 5004.)

14. Press Conference of 10 July 1969.

15. Quoted in *Le Monde*, 6 July 1966. Cf. statement on television of 28 September 1966, in which he defended ministerial candidatures on the ground that it was necessary for Ministers to show that they had the confidence of the electors.

16. Only two *Conseils de Cabinet* were held during the presidency of General de Gaulle (both during the premiership of M. Michel Debré). The *Conseil* did meet, however, during the interim presidency of M. Alain Poher, who was an anti-Gaullist presidential candidate. It should be noted that the word '*cabinet*' in French is generally used merely as a synonym for Government. The British distinction between Cabinet and non-Cabinet Ministers, which establishes a hierarchy determined mainly by the importance of the office, and sometimes also by the political standing of the Minister in the Prime Minister's view, has no equivalent in France.

17. General de Gaulle said at the end of his first septennate that he had presided over 420 meetings of *Conseils inter-ministériels* and 302 *Conseils des Ministres*. (Press conference of 9 September 1965.)

18. Under the Third Republic, junior Ministers were called *Sous-Secrétaires d'Etat*, and M. Guy Mollet included four *Sous-Secrétaires* in his 1956 Government. The largest Government of the Fifth Republic, up to 1971, that of 1969, included also the largest number of Secretaries of State (twenty). The smallest, that of December 1962, included four Ministers of State, seventeen Ministers and four Secretaries of State. M. Mollet's Government had included three Ministers of State, eight Ministers, one *Ministre-délégué*, twenty-one Secretaries of State and four Under-Secretaries of State. Secretaries of State did not attend meetings of the Council of Ministers under the Fourth Republic, unless the agenda included matters concerning their department.

19. Paul Morand, quoted by Marcel Prélot, *Institutions politiques et Droit constitutionnel* (Paris, Dalloz, 1969), p. 702.

20. 'Lettres à un ami anglais. I: Sur les cabinets ministériels', in *Revue administrative*, March 1971, p. 155.

Members of *cabinets* must not exceed ten for 'Ministers' and seven for Secretaries of State. This rule is to some extent evaded by the appointment of a certain number of 'unofficial' secretaries or *'chargés de mission'*.

21. *Sur quelques Maladies de l'Etat* (Paris, Plon, 1958), p. 36.

The author, René Massigli, himself by training a high official, was speaking of the period just after the second world war, when Governments often included a number of inexperienced Ministers.

22. Jacques Soustelle, *L'Espérance trahie* (Paris, Editions de l'Alma, 1962), p. 94.

23. Jean Gicquel, *Essai sur la Pratique de la Ve République* (Paris, Librairie générale de Droit et de Jurisprudence, 1967), p. 207.

24. The 'majority of the National Assembly' may ask for a special session; 'members of Parliament' have the right to propose amendments to the Constitution and to table Bills (*v*. articles 29, 89 and 39).

25. Prime Ministers of the Third Republic presented themselves, with their Governments, for the approval of the Chamber of Deputies. Prime Ministers of the Fourth Republic, up to 1954, presented themselves to the National Assembly alone, and were not officially appointed Prime Ministers (*investis*), but merely provisionally nominated (*désignés*) by the President of the Republic until a majority of the membership of the Assembly had accorded them a vote of confidence. From 1954 onwards, they presented themselves with their Governments and required only a simple majority to be *investis*. Prime Ministers of the Fifth Republic are appointed by the President and exercise the full powers of their office from the moment of appointment.

26. When M. Pompidou made his general declaration of 13 April 1966, he specifically announced that this procedure would be adopted in future.

Both the letter and the spirit of the 1958 Constitution [he said] leave the Government entirely free to decide whether or not to ask for a vote of confidence. . . . I believe that it is important, at the outset of the second septennate of the Fifth Republic, to create precedents. (*Journal Officiel, Débats, Assemblée nationale*, sitting of 13 April 1966, p. 620.)

M. Couve de Murville made his declaration on 17 July 1968. His statement was followed by a debate. M. Chaban Delmas made a declaration of general policy on 26 June 1969. It was followed by one speaker from each of five groups.

In addition to the declarations of general policy provided for under article 49 of the Constitution, Governments can make statements of information, or declarations, under article 132 of the Standing Orders. These can be with or without debate. If there is a debate, it is 'organized', and the Prime Minister winds up with a reply to speakers. If not, then the President of the National Assembly allows one speaker to reply to the Government. In neither case can declarations made under this article be followed by a vote. M. Chaban Delmas did, however, make a declaration of policy, followed by a vote of confidence, on 15 October 1970.

27. There were, however, objections to this procedure. On 13 June 1962, 280 Deputies walked out of the Assembly and signed a manifesto protesting against the Government's refusal to allow a vote following a foreign-affairs debate.

28. The proportion of one-tenth was generally thought to have been chosen in order to prevent the continuation of the Communist habit under the Fourth Republic of tabling purely obstructive censure motions. At the time that the Constitution was drawn up the Communist party was expected to have about fifty seats in the following Assembly. In fact it had only ten in the first and forty-one in the second.

29. *v. Règlement (Assemblée nationale)*, articles 149–53, on the procedure for the application of article 49 of the Constitution.

30. Socialists, Communists and the *Rassemblement démocratique*, which included the Radicals, together numbered 147 in the 1963 Assembly (Socialists 68 and Communists 40). In the 1967 Assembly, the Federation of the Democratic and Socialist Left numbered 121 and the Communists 73 (including affiliates). In the 1959 Assembly, the Socialists had numbered only 47, the Communists 10, and the Radicals 15. The total membership was then 576, but this included 66 members representing Algeria and the Saharan *départements* and 24 Overseas Deputies from States of the Community about to become independent. By 1960, the numbers had fallen to 552.

31. A bewildering number of statistics are produced to demonstrate the fall in the number of private members' Bills, and the numbers ruled out of order under articles 34 and 40. The figures for the numbers of Bills voted have been given in note 47 of

Chapter III. The figures given below of the numbers of private members' Bills tabled each year do not, of course, reveal how much of the reduction is accounted for by the limitations imposed by articles 34 and 40. Nor is it easy to estimate how many of those introduced were then ruled out of order under these two articles. Estimates given by Pierre Avril (op. cit., p. 43) and Philip Williams (*The French Parliament*, London, Allen and Unwin, 1968, p. 57n) both rely on the same article in the *Revue du Droit public* (May–June 1960), in which the authors first say that the grounds for ruling Bills out of order are often not known, and then make an estimate based on the year 1959 only. Moreover, the real impact of these two articles on the initiative of private members is assessable only if the number of *amendments* ruled out on the same grounds are known. Since the great majority of private members' Bills are really no more than amendments, the distinction between Bills and amendments is not necessarily meaningful.

PRIVATE MEMBERS' BILLS TABLED

	Total numbers	National Assembly
1957	852	804
1959	222	206
1960	196	158
1961	204	157
1962	109	75

(Figures quoted by Avril, op. cit., p. 43. Figures quoted by Jean Gicquel, op. cit., pp. 214 and 215, differ from the above and do not seem to make sense.)

32. *Journal Officiel, Débats, Assemblée nationale*, sitting on 6 May 1967. For further examples of this kind of lack of 'fair play' on the part of either the Government or the Conference of Presidents, *v.* Gicquel, op. cit., pp. 341–3.

33. Article 42 of the organic law of 2 January 1959 relating to the application of the finance law.

34. The word 'effectively' in article 42 of the organic law was intended to rule out the compensatory device that had allowed the provisions to be widely evaded under the Fourth Republic. Even in 1959, M. Paul Reynaud, a former Prime Minister and Finance Minister, was advocating the retention of the device. (Finance Committee of July 1959.) On this, *v.* Avril, op. cit., p. 57.

35. Statement made by M. Pierre Janot, a Gaullist Deputy, to the Consultative Constitutional Committee on 8 August 1958. (*Avis et débats*, 1960, p. 116.)

36. *v.* for instance, statement by M. Pierre Dumas in *Le Monde*, 15 February 1967:

> This guillotine-article, which is too often used, has been sharply criticized by the opposition, although its main objective is to maintain discipline in the ranks of the majority.

37. Avril, op. cit., p. 394.

38. Gicquel, op. cit., p. 314. Avril, op. cit., p. 382 gives the figure of 23 in the first Parliament and 58 in the second, but the second figure refers to the period up to June 1966 only. Gicquel gives the figure for the first Parliament as 19. For a detailed study of its use *v.* Pierre Avril, in *Revue du Droit public*, 1965, pp. 444–52.

The controversy over the meaning of the phrase in article 44(3): 'If the Government so requests, the assembly concerned accepts or rejects by a single vote the whole or part of the Bill . . . (*tout ou partie*)', was finally settled by a decision of the Constitutional Council of 15 January 1960 (*Journal Officiel*, *Débats*, *Assemblée nationale*, sitting of 2 February 1960). This recognized

> the right of the Government to request, at *any* point of the debate, a single vote, either on any part of the text of a Bill, with or without any amendments proposed or accepted by the Government, or on the whole Bill. The vote on the whole Bill is *necessarily and simultaneously* on all articles, or sections of articles, including amended articles . . . and is irrespective of whether they have been already voted on, or have been reserved when the Bill was submitted to the House.

It is pointed out by Jean Gicquel that this means that the Minister can, if he wishes, avoid all discussion on the separate articles of the Bill, by cutting short the debate when this stage has been reached. This, he concluded, quite accurately, is tantamount to reducing the vote to a referendum-type package deal (op. cit., p. 220).

It should, perhaps, be added that the old-style confidence vote also enabled the Government to impose acceptance or rejection, either of separate articles or of the whole bill, but not of undiscussed articles. Another difference was that Ministers and Governments were less able to count on emerging victorious from contests with the Assembly.

The *vote bloqué* was, of course, a much less effective instrument when used in the Senate, which sometimes welcomed the opportunity to defeat the Government and so try to use the *navette* in order to re-open discussion. But this could be no more than a delaying tactic, as the Assembly could always eventually override the Senate.

39. *v. Journal Officiel, Lois et Décrets*, 3 July 1959.

40. The procedure was introduced after the 1914–18 war and was used under the Third Republic in 1926, 1934 and 1935. In the last-mentioned case, decree-laws were described as having become the normal method of government. In 1937, the Senate refused to grant special powers to the Popular Front Government of Léon Blum, but granted them to his two successors. In all, between 1937 and 1939, 13 out of 26 months were periods of government by special powers. Under the Fourth Republic, the use of the power of delegated legislation under the law of 17 August 1948 was approved by the Council of State on certain conditions. These excluded use of the powers to change the constitutional rights in the Preamble of the 1946 Constitution. The powers were used in 1953, 1954 and 1956.

41. In addition to these powers granted under article 38, the exercise of special powers by the President of the Republic was authorized by referendum (April 1962) in order to enable the application of the Evian agreement following the end of the Algerian war.

42. In a television interview of 9 September 1967. (*Le Monde*, 11 September 1962.)

43. *Le Monde*, 4 May 1967.

44. *v. Documents français*, No. 2530 (11 April 1959), p. 19.

45. *v.* also Duverger, *Institutions politiques*, 1970, p. 721. The link between the programme and resort to article 38 is explicitly made in the first draft of the Constitution (article 34). *v.* Prélot, *Pour comprendre la nouvelle Constitution* (Paris, Editions le Centurion, 1958), p. 109.

46. The constitutionality was dubious owing to the President's political irresponsibility. Article 38's link of the powers with the Government's programme should, in constitutional theory, exclude the President, who has no programme. There was no doubt, however, that the unprecedented specification that the powers should be exercised by the President was a consequence of the known disagreement of the Prime Minister, M. Debré, with any policy of self-determination for Algeria. *v.* for instance, the Socialist statement

addressed to the Prime Minister in the debate: 'We would rather give our confidence to General de Gaulle than to you.'

47. *v.* a striking example of Government delaying tactics in Philip Williams, *The French Parliament*, pp. 85–9, which brings out very clearly the fact that the Government had not always some 'sinister' interest in delay!

48. M. André Chandernagor (Socialist) wanted to make Ordinances invalid if a Bill to ratify them was not voted within six months of being tabled. (*Journal Officiel, Débats, Assemblée nationale*, 13 September 1961, p. 2284.) The Bill was tabled on 13 December 1961.

49. For examples of this, *v.* in particular, Gicquel, op. cit., pp. 311–13. *v.* also the view expressed by Philip Williams (*The French Parliament*, p. 89) regarding 'the government's totally unscrupulous use of the facilities the constitution gave it'.

50. Avril, op. cit., p. 395. On this, *v.* statements made in the Assembly at the time, for instance, M. Legaret (*Indépendant*): 'To permit resolutions to be followed by a vote is to create an opportunity for an exchange of opinion. A refusal to allow them means that Parliament will be forced to reject the budget, or else, as it did in 1924, all Government proposals. It means substituting bad temper for frank explanations.' (Debate of 26 May 1959.)

M. Brocas (Radical): 'It is essential that Parliament should be able to express its political opinions by a vote other than a vote of censure.'

Speeches on these lines, and there were many of them, were less convincing regarding the merits of the vote than they were regarding the importance that Deputies attached to it.

51. Between 1959 and 1965, seven of these were held. (Gicquel, op. cit., p. 311n.)

52. For more detailed accounts of the relations between the Government and the majority group in the National Assembly, *v.* Jean Charlot, *Le Phénomène gaulliste* (Paris, Fayard, 1970), pp. 123–30, and Gicquel, op. cit., pp. 309–19, which is much more critical.

This co-operation, it must be stressed, was with the Gaullist group and not with the majority as such (including *Républicains indépendants*). It was not until the opening of the session of October 1969 that the Prime Minister met a 'permanent delegation of the majority groups'. This body, officially called the *Comité de liaison des Groupes de la Majorité*, formed in October 1969, included nine members of the UDR, six *Républicains indépendants* and three members of the PDM. Its official function was to maintain contacts between the Government and the Parliamentary majority, and also within the majority.

53. 'Le jour le plus long', *Le Monde*, 31 December–1 January 1962.

CHAPTER V

1. The previous exceptions to the 'mediocrity' rule were Poincaré in 1913 and Millerand in 1920, both of whom had been Prime Ministers, the latter, however, only for a period of a few months. Two (Doumergue and Poincaré) became Prime Ministers after their presidency. The other two Presidents who were elected for a second term were Grévy in 1886 and Lebrun in 1939. The first held office for eight years and eleven months; the latter for nine years and two months. General de Gaulle held office for ten years and four months.

Previous Presidents who resigned voluntarily were Grévy (1887), Casimir Périer (1895), and Deschanel (1920). Eight Presidents in all resigned, but the other four did so involuntarily, two (Lebrun and Coty) on the fall of the régime; two (MacMahon and Millerand) owing to conflicts with Parliament. Two were assassinated (Carnot in 1894 and Doumer in 1932). One died in office (Félix Faure in 1899). Only five completed their terms of office (Loubet in 1906, Fallières in 1913, Poincaré in 1920, Doumergue in 1931 and Auriol in 1953).

2. Cf. article 3 of the Constitutional Law of 25 February and article 7 of the law of 16 July 1875; articles 30, 32, 33 and 36 of the Constitution of 1946; and articles 9, 10, 13, 14, and 15 of the Constitution of 1958.

3. For rules governing the constitution of this court, *v.* organic law of 2 January 1959.

The provisions of article 68 of the 1958 Constitution and of article 42 of the 1946 Constitution are similar. Under the Third Republic, however, the Senate constituted the court to try both the President, if charged by the Chamber of Deputies with high treason, and Ministers, if charged with offences committed in the exercise of their functions. (*v.* article 12 of law of 16 July 1875.)

The method by which a President is charged with treason requires a special procedure. It is an 'open ballot' in Parliament, on a motion couched in identical terms in both Houses (article 68). Under the Fourth Republic, the vote was secret (*v.* article 57). Members of

Parliament elected at the beginning of a Parliament to serve as judges do not take part in the vote. (*v.* article 19 of the organic law of 2 January 1959 and articles 57 and 58 of the Constitution of 1946).

4. General de Gaulle used this right on formal occasions – on 15 January 1959, on the opening of the first Parliament of the régime; on 25 April 1961, announcing the application of article 16; on 20 March 1962, announcing the decision to hold a referendum (proposed by the Government) authorizing the application of the Evian agreements on Algerian independence; on 2 October 1962, announcing the decision to hold a referendum; and on 11 December 1962, on the occasion of the opening of the new session in the National Assembly, following the 1962 elections. This last message was much longer and its political content resembled that of a presidential broadcast.

President Pompidou addressed a message to Parliament on 25 June 1969, on the occasion of the opening of Parliament at the beginning of his presidential term of office. This, too, included a brief policy statement.

5. The difficulty of a counter-signature in the case of the appointment of a new Prime Minister, which was required under the Fourth Republic, was resolved by the provision that, after the President's nominee had obtained the confidence of the National Assembly, the decree appointing him was counter-signed by the outgoing Prime Minister. (*v.* Roger Pinto, *Eléments de Droit constitutionnel*, Lille, Morel et Corduant, 1952, p. 494.)

6. On 16 May 1877, after prolonged disagreement between the Monarchist President and the Republican-dominated Chamber of Deputies, the President virtually compelled the Prime Minister to resign, and, after the defeat of the following Government, dissolved the Chamber. The elections, in which the President intervened on behalf of Monarchists, returned another Republican majority. After a period of resistance, and when the Senate also obtained a Republican majority, the President took the advice offered to him by Gambetta during the election campaign – to 'give in or get out' (*se soumettre ou se démettre*) – and resigned in January 1879.

In 1887, Grévy resigned after a succession of refusals by politicians to accept his invitation to form a Government, though, in his case, this was merely the culmination of a series of efforts to get him to resign.

In 1924, after a period of much criticized presidential intervention in the Government's foreign policy, President Millerand found himself even more at odds with the *cartel des gauches* after its success in the election. His active rôle in the election campaign had proved to be the last straw, and successive nominees for the premiership refused to take office under his presidency, thus obliging him to resign on 13 June. In a message to Parliament on 8 June, he had warned Deputies that if they refused to listen to him and forced him to resign for political reasons, 'the President would be no more than the plaything of parties'. At that stage, politicians were prepared to welcome such a situation.

7. For instance, Presidents MacMahon and Grévy were actually responsible for the choice of Ministers of Foreign Affairs and War, and took an active part in the formation of Governments.

When Combes was *Président du Conseil* he deliberately left foreign affairs in the hands of the President and the Foreign Minister.

8. *v.* Marcel Prélot, *Institutions politiques et droit constitutionnel* (Paris, Dalloz, 1969) p. 680.

9. *v.* Pinto, op. cit., p. 469: '. . . *il faut regretter, à ce point de vue, la pratique inconstitutionnelle adoptée récemment en matière de décrets de grâce*'. He added (p. 502) that, in practice, the President could look into only the most serious cases, and that most of the thousands considered every year were, therefore, decided in reality by the Higher Council of the Judiciary. The President himself, however, claimed that he considered personally a great number of cases.

10. *v.* organic law of 22 December 1958, articles 16–18.

11. This is also the view of Duverger (*Institutions politiques*, 1970, p. 701) and implicitly that of Prélot (op. cit) though he does not say so in so many words.

12. In 1958, the presidential college included 81,764 electors, of whom 76,359 represented metropolitan France. Of these, 51% represented *communes* of under 9000 inhabitants, as against 53% in the senatorial college. With three exceptions, the presidential college in 1958 was the same as the senatorial college. In the presidential college, (i) representatives of Community assemblies voted; (ii) in villages with populations under 9000, Mayors and Councillors, not specially elected delegates, voted; and (iii) the over-weighting of small villages was slightly less marked.

13. *v.* for instance, message to Parliament of 2 October 1962 (*Année politique*, 1962, p. 677) and broadcasts of 4 October 1962 (Ibid., p. 678), 18 October 1962 (Ibid., p. 684), 26 October 1962 (Ibid., p. 685), 7 November 1962 (Ibid., p. 686).

14. *v.* speech to the *Conseil d'Etat* (*Revue française de Science politique*, March 1959), pp. 9–10:

> *Le régime présidentiel est la forme de régime démocratique qui est à l'opposé du régime d'assemblée. Sa marque est faite de l'importance du pouvoir donné en droit et en fait à un chef d'Etat élu au suffrage universel. ...*
>
> *Ni le Parlement dans sa volonté de réforme manifestée par la loi du 3 juin, ni le gouvernement lorsqu'il a présenté, puis appliqué, cette loi, n'ont succombé à cette tentation, et c'est, je crois, sagesse ... nous devons constater que cette conception ne coincide pas avec l'image traditionnelle, et, à bien des égards, légitime, de la République.*

15. Broadcasts from radio stations outside France's frontiers could not, however, be controlled, and some of these have a large French audience. Nor has it proved easy to find satisfactory formulae distinguishing news items (inevitably giving publicity to Governmental activities) from propaganda items. (*v.* decree of 14 March 1964 and *Journal Officiel*, 29 October 1965.)

16. As originally voted in 1958, the Constitution prohibited the use by the interim President of the powers given to the President (in articles 11 and 12) to accede to or refuse a request for a referendum, or to dissolve the National Assembly. The 1962 revision also prohibited the use of articles 49 and 50 (confidence and censure), and article 89 (Constitutional revision) during a presidential interim.

17. The President authorized the Prime Minister to deputize for him in the Council of Ministers on two occasions – 22 April 1964, when he was in hospital, and 30 September when he was in South America. He later cancelled the first meeting and also a further meeting due to be held on 14 October 1964. (*v.* Jean Gicquel, *Essai sur la Pratique de la Ve République*, Paris, Librairie générale de Droit et de Jurisprudence, 1967, p. 279, and *Année politique*, 1964, p. 74.)

18. Debate of 4 October 1962.

19. For text of this broadcast, *v. Année politique*, 1962, pp. 674-5.

20. Quoted in Léon Duguit, *Traité de Droit constitutionnel* (Paris, Boccard, 1924) p. 809.

21. Message to Parliament of 21 January 1947 and speech of 15 November 1951 to the foreign press.

22. Pinto, op. cit., pp. 470–1.

23. Statement by the President of the National Assembly on 19 September 1961, à propos of the question of the constitutionality

of a motion of censure during a period of national emergency as
defined by article 16.

24. Jacques Chapsal, *La Vie politique en France depuis 1940* (Paris,
Presses universitaires de France, 1966), p. 391.

25. 'Réponses à 12 Questions', *La Nef*, October 1965, p. 190.

26. *Le Monde*, 7 May 1960. *v.* also *Année politique*, 1960, p. 47.

27. *v.* text in *Année politique*, 1958, p. 551. The context is the
following:

The Constitution has been drawn up for this nation, this century
and this world in which we find ourselves. May it enable the country
to be efficiently governed by those whom it has mandated and to
whom it has accorded the confidence that constitutes its legitimacy.
May it make possible the existence, above the political battle, of a
national arbiter, elected by those citizens who themselves hold
public office, entrusted with the responsibility of ensuring the
regular functioning of institutions, with the right to appeal to the
sovereign people, and, in circumstances of great danger, responsible
for the independence, honour and integrity of France and the safety
of the Republic.

28. Prélot, *Institutions politiques*, 1969, p. 657.

29. *Commentaires sur la Constitution du 4 octobre 1958* (La Documentation française, Notes et Etudes documentaires, No. 2530,
11 April 1959, p. 7). *v.* also the President's own statement of his
'positive' rôle as an arbiter in *Avis et Débats du Comité Consultatif
constitutionnel* (Paris, Documentation française, 1960), p. 54.

30. Ibid., p. 8. cf. Michel Debré, *Revue française de Science politique*,
March 1959, p. 22. 'The President of the Republic, as is proper, has
no power except that of appealing to another power, Parliament.'

31. On General de Gaulle's references to his function of guide, *v.*,
for instance, speech of 28 December 1958: '*Guide de la France et chef
de l'Etat républicain . . . ;*' speech of 29 January 1960: '*J'ai pris, au nom
de la France, la décision que voici . . . l' autodétermination est la seule politique
qui soit digne de la France . . . C'est celle-qui est définie par le Président
de la République, décidée par le Gouvernement, approuvée par le Parlement;
adoptée par la nation française.*'

32. Press conference of 31 January 1964. (*Année politique*, 1964,
p. 421.)

33. The questions raised by this problem (which has not yet
presented itself) are: (i) would retirement of the President bring into
application paragraphs 4–6 of article 7, that is, the appointment of
an interim President? (ii) If so, would the first ballot be annulled, or,

since the aim of these provisions is to shorten the period of presidential vacancy, would the second ballot take place (that is, assuming that the President himself had not been a candidate)? (iii) If the President died, would the candidate who had been third on the list at the first ballot be allowed to compete, or would the single remaining candidate be considered as having been elected? For a discussion of the pros and cons of these possible solutions, *v.* André Passeron, *Le Monde,* 21–2 November 1965, and Maurice Duverger, ibid., 3 December 1965. On the analogies with provisions to cover cases where a single candidate for election to the National Assembly is left to contest the second ballot under the law of 29 December 1966, *v.* Gicquel, op. cit., p. 265. M. Gicquel suggests that the simplest solution would be the creation of an office of Vice-President.

34. Prélot, *Institutions politiques,* 1970, p. 687, where M. Prélot also states that the formal resignation of the Government on the election of a President, which was under the previous régime merely a polite gesture, is, under the present régime, a necessary resignation, 'following from the principle that the Government emanates from the President of the Republic'. This is an over-statement. Under article 8 (1), the President appoints directly only the Prime Minister.

35. Statement of 24 April 1964

36. On the President's dismissal of Ministers, *v.* Pierre Avril, *Le régime politique de la Vᵉ République* (Paris, Librairie générale de Droit et de Jurisprudence, 1967), pp. 238–9. For M. Debré's statement, *v. Le Monde,* 31 November–1 December 1965. In his book, *Ces Princes qui nous gouvernent* (Paris, Plon, 1957, p. 174), M. Debré had stated categorically that the Government ought to be responsible to the Head of State.

37. *v. Avis et Débats du Comité consultatif constitutionnel,* p. 118. Also quoted by M. Paul Reynaud, President of the Consultative Constitutional Committee, in a letter to *Le Monde* of 4 November 1965.

It has also been suggested that M. Pompidou's resignation in 1968 was, in reality, a dismissal, since he had intended to offer only the formal resignation of his Government, which was a traditional gesture following a general election. *v.* P. Rouanet, *G. Pompidou* (Paris, Grasset, 1969), p. 300.

38. Only a general outline of the President's broadcast of 16 September 1959, promising self-determination to Algeria, had been previously communicated to the Council of Ministers. The text of his broadcast of 4 November 1960 was not seen by the Government

until a recording of it had been dispatched for simultaneous broadcast in Algeria. The essentials of his speech of 28 June 1961, though revealed at a garden party the previous day, had, according to press accounts, not been communicated to the Government, or even to the Prime Minister. The imposition of an embargo on all arms for Israel, announced on 8 January 1969, certainly followed a meeting of the Council of Ministers, but Israel had been informed earlier. According to press accounts, the subject of the embargo was not on the agenda and Ministers learned of it from press telegrams from Israel. (*v. Le Monde*, 10 January 1969.)

39. *v. Le Monde*, 20–1 March 1960. The wording of the articles on special sessions is, however, somewhat different. The 1875 Constitution (article 2 of law of 16 July 1875) states that the President '*must*' (*devra*) call a special session, if the condition requiring an absolute majority of the members of both Houses is met. The 1946 Constitution (article 12) states also that the President of the National Assembly '*must*' (*doit*) call Parliament if the constitutional conditions are complied with. The 1958 Constitution merely states that 'Parliament meets in special session on the request of the Prime Minister or the majority of the members of the National Assembly' (article 29) and that 'special sessions are opened and closed by decree of the President of the Republic' (article 30). Article 13, which deals with the signature by the President of Ordinances and decrees, merely states that 'The President of the Republic signs such Ordinances and decrees as have been considered by the Council of Ministers.' This *could* (if the traditional practice is left out of account) be interpreted as meaning merely that no decree considered by the Council of Ministers is valid without the presidential signature. It need not necessarily mean that he is obliged to sign all that are presented to him.

40. *Revue française de Science politique*, March 1959, p. 11.

41. Letter of 18 March 1960 (*Année politique*, 1960, p. 640).

42. *Le Monde*, 24 March 1960. The author of the letter went on to quote Littré's *Dictionnaire général* in support of this interpretation!

43. On the other hand, the constitutionality of the referendum held in Algeria on 1 July 1962, in which the electorate voted in favour of independence, was criticized on the ground that the Constitution does not provide for a referendum in only a part of French territory. This objection was, in the circumstances, purely academic, since Algeria was by then politically recognized as

independent. The referendum merely brought out-of-date theory into line with political fact.

44. The President used this power in the constitutional revision of December 1963.

45. For text of the Bills submitted to these two referenda, *v. Année politique*, 1960, pp. 663–4 and 1962, p. 650.

46. The President of the Senate, M. Gaston Monnerville, described the referendum as a deliberate and outrageous violation of the Constitution. At a Radical party Congress (on 30 September) he used the term '*forfaiture*' (a dereliction of duty that, under the penal code, can be a serious criminal offence approaching treason. For once, the Radical party had been, if only temporarily, united! M. Monnerville was re-elected President of the Senate (following the three-yearly renewal), and made a powerful attack on the referendum from the Chair. (*v. Année politique*, 1962, pp. 680–4).

47. The Constitutional Council could not be consulted officially because consultation on the constitutionality of a referendum is not included among its functions. The President of the Senate tried to consult the Council, which ruled that it was incompetent. (*v.* decision of 6 November 1962, in *Année politique*, 1962, p. 687.) The Council of State had to be consulted, but its advice on legislation need not be taken and is never published. *Avis* of the Council of State and unofficial opinions of the Constitutional Council are generally known, however, and sometimes reported in the press. *Année politique* (1962, p. 107) simply states as a fact that both these organs were opposed to the referendum.

48. *v.* for instance, the following opinion expressed by M. Edgar Faure (who admitted to having voted No in the 1962 referendum, because he believed the procedure to be unconstitutional): 'This irregularity has now been regularized twice, first by the referendum and then by the general election.' (*Face à Face*, 31 May 1966, reported in *Le Monde*, 2 June 1966.)

49. Published in *Revue française de Science politique*, March 1959, p. 191.

50. *v. Année politique*, 1969, p. 20.

51. Speech in debate of 4 October 1962 on the Censure motion.

52. *v.* television interview with Michel Droit of 10 April 1969. (*Année politique*, 1969, p. 396.)

53. According to a report in *Le Monde*, 25 February 1966, there had been six cases under the Third Republic and three under the Fourth.

54. *Arrêt* of the Court of Cassation of 31 May 1965. An earlier *arrêt* had expressed a similar view.

55. It could be argued that, though the constitutional public authorities could function, they could not be guaranteed to function 'regularly' and without interruption, since part of the army was in a state of rebellion.

It could also be argued that the constitutional authorities could not function in Algeria, which was still part of France, or, alternatively, that the French constitutional authorities were not functioning normally owing to the arrest in Algiers (for four days) of a Cabinet Minister. None of these reasons seems satisfactory, nor did the Constitutional Council put any of them forward in its opinion. It appears clear from the text that the President decides and is not required to give his reasons.

For a fuller treatment of the problems raised by the application of article 16, *v.* W. Pickles, 'Special powers in France: Article 16 in practice', *Public Law*, Spring 1963.

56. *v.* organic law of 7 November 1958, Titre II, Chapitre VIII, articles 52–4.

57. The President broadcast a message to the nation on 23 April. The first '*décision*' announcing the application of article 16 was taken the same day. It stated that the Constitutional Council, the Prime Minister and the Presidents of the two Parliamentary assemblies had duly been consulted. The President sent a message to Parliament on 25 April, when it met for the normal session. This was regarded as being also a session held 'as of right' under article 16. The Prime Minister gave the news of the insurrection in a broadcast on 22 April, and made an appeal to the nation on the following day. He made a declaration to Parliament on 25 April.

(For texts of all these statements, *v. Année politique*, 1961, pp. 651–4.)

58. For a contrary view, *v.* Léo Hamon, 'A propos de l'article 16: quelques questions juridiques', in *L'Actualité juridique*, 20 December 1961, p. 664. M. Hamon appears to regard the detailed enumeration of the circumstances as amounting to fulfilment of the requirement of the organic law that the *Avis* must be '*motivé*'.

59. The organic law does provide an answer to one question, namely, what would be the constitutional position if some of the members of the Constitutional Council could not meet. Although the normal quorum is seven of the nine Councillors, in case of *force majeure* no quorum is required. (*v.* organic law of 7 November 1958, article 14.)

60. The only example of the President's having used his powers to override a constitutional provision during the emergency was the *décision* of 17 June 1961, which enabled him to remove judges in Algeria from their posts. Article 64 states that judges are irremoveable.

61. For text of this message, *v. Année politique*, 1961, p. 652.

62. The commentary on the Constitution published by La Documentation française, *Notes et Etudes documentaires*, 11 April 1959, p. 9, refers specifically to Parliament's right to bring the President before the High Court of Justice, but does not refer to the Constitutional Council's *Avis* in this connection. One possible reason for the apparently ineffectual rôle of the Constitutional Council is that General de Gaulle did not intend it to play any rôle. The draft text of the Constitution had merely provided for consultation of the Constitutional Council. The Consultative Constitutional Committee added a phrase requiring the Constitutional Council's agreement on the existence of conditions justifying the application of article 16. The final text specified that it must be consulted on the measures, but left out the requirement of agreement on the conditions of applying article 16. The organic law included the compromise of the '*avis motivé*'. *v.* Prélot, *Pour comprendre la nouvelle Constitution* (Paris, Editions le Centurion, 1958), pp. 84–7.

63. *v. Arrêt* 104 ('Arrêt Rubin de Servens') in *Les grands Arrêts de la Jurisprudence administrative* (Paris, Sirey, 1969) for the Council's statement of presidential powers under article 16, à propos of its rejection of the appeal against the setting up by the *décision* of 3 May 1961 of a special military court. An earlier appeal to the Court of Cassation had encountered a similar refusal by the judicial court to challenge the legality of a presidential decision.

The Council's justification of the right of appeal to an administrative court where measures belonging to the rule-making field were prolonged beyond the period of the emergency was that, since, under articles 34 and 37, these cannot be amended by law, they would otherwise escape the normal supervision of executive acts. (*v*. p. 501.)

As far as the initial decision of 23 April 1961 was concerned, the Council did appear to claim the right to judge what is called '*la légalité externe*', that is, its conformity with the constitutional prerequisites, namely, the consultation of the Prime Minister, the Presidents of the two Parliamentary assemblies and the Constitutional Council. (*v*. p. 497.)

64. André Guérin, in *Revue politique et parlementaire*, October 1961.

65. Broadcast of 2 October 1961 (*Année politique*, 1961, pp. 674–5). He seemed to be hinting, however, that in case of a future recourse to special powers he might make a less restrained use of them.

66. The Deputies in question announced their intention of bringing in a Bill to abrogate all decisions taken between 23 April and 29 September, on the ground that the last two, taken on 29 September, were contradictory. They were all right-wing opponents of the President. A Bill to amend the Constitution was tabled by the MRP Deputy, M. Paul Coste-Floret, and some of his colleagues on 24 October 1961, with the aim of clearing up some of the constitutional uncertainties revealed during the five months emergency period. It maintained the article, but added three additional provisions:

(i) If Parliament is able to meet (as it was in 1961), the special powers last for a maximum of 90 days;

(ii) The President of the Republic shall not have power to suspend or revise the Constitution;

(iii) The provisions of article 49 can be used during the emergency – that is, Government defeats and motions of censure are both permissible.

The authors of the Bill in their *exposé des motifs* expressly repudiated any linking of the procedures of confidence and censure with the right of dissolution.

Though the Bill was never voted, it expressed the views of many opposition Deputies, as a result of the controversy regarding the special session.

In *De Gaulle dans la République* (Paris, Plon, 1958, p. 146), M. Léo Hamon admits the theoretical right of the President to dismiss the Prime Minister under the powers given by article 16, but adds that, in unforeseeable circumstances, no Constitution can provide complete solutions for any eventuality. M. Coste–Floret's Bill would seem precisely to be trying to provide known rules to fit unknown circumstances.

67. Maurice Duverger, 'L'Article 16 et ses limites', *Le Monde*, 5 May 1961.

68. Léo Hamon, 'A propos de l'article 16 . . .,' op. cit., p. 668.

69. Letter of 31 August 1961, addressed to the Prime Minister (*Année politique*, 1961, p. 664).

In his message to Parliament of 25 April, the President had

clearly assumed that Parliament was meeting in normal session. Members of Parliament, however, regarded the April session as being both a normal session and one held 'as of right'. Their efforts to discuss the emergency then were, however, unsuccessful.

In fact, nothing in the Constitution justified the President's theory that Parliament's powers to legislate are limited to any one kind of session. All the same, he could, if he had wanted to do so, quite constitutionally have used his powers under article 16 to impose his own interpretation for the duration of the emergency. He did not do so, doubtless because this would have been politically unpopular and thus have led to the withdrawal of the support that Parliament gave to him during most of this period.

70. *v. décision* of 8 September 1961 (*Année politique*, 1961, p. 670).

71. *Décision* announced by the President of the National Assembly on 19 September 1961. The text, together with that of the President's letter to the Prime Minister, is published in *Revue du Droit public*, September–October 1961, pp. 1037–9.

72. Ibid.

73. *v.* for instance, the suggestion by André Guérin (*Revue politique et parlementaire*, October 1961, p. 46) that it was precisely because nothing in the Constitution prevented Deputies from 'turning out as many Governments as they pleased, without the possibility of the sanction of the dissolution being used against them' that the President finally ended the period of special powers.

74. *v.* statement in the debate of 16 December 1961 (*Journal Officiel, Débats*, p. 5676) by the Socialist Deputy, Francis Leenhardt, that the President had stated at a meeting with a delegation of the Socialist Parliamentary group:

Je n'ai jamais dit qu'il y avait lien entre dissolution et motion de censure.

In reality, nothing in either the Constitution or the Assembly's Standing Orders entitles the President of the Assembly to rule a censure motion out of order. His function is to inform the Government and the Assembly of its existence and have the text with signatures displayed. The Conference of Presidents then fixes the date of the debate. (*v. Règlement*, articles 150 and 151.)

75. On 5 September, the President of the Senate ruled one Bill out of order under article 40. The second, on an appeal by the Prime Minister to the Constitutional Council, was ruled out of order under article 41. In the National Assembly, the proposed legislation was also ruled out of order.

76. *v.* statement of 8 August 1958 to the Consultative Constitutional Committee (*Travaux préparatoires*, 1960, pp. 118–19). *v.* also *Mémoires d'Espoir*, I (Paris, Plon, 1970), p. 36.

77. Address to the *Conseil d'Etat* of 27 August 1958 (*Revue française de Science politique*, March 1959, p. 23). *v.* also statement to the *Cercle républicain* on 3 September 1958 (quoted in *Le Monde*, 5 September 1958).

78. Press conference of 31 January 1964. M. Pompidou's speech in the National Assembly, 24 April 1964.

79. Press conference of 2 July 1970. *v.* in particular, statement of January 1970 to the *Cercle de l'Opinion*:

> The President of the Republic is elected for seven years, but the life of a Prime Minister is probably shorter. . . . In the mind of a Prime Minister there is no place for the slightest feeling of envy or rivalry. On the other hand, the relationship is not one of strict subordination . . . it being understood that in the final resort direction comes from the Head of State and that, once it has been given, it is the Prime Minister's duty to take the appropriate action.
>
> (Quoted in *Projet*, September–October 1970.)

80. Pierre Viansson-Ponté in *Risques et Chances de la Ve République* (Paris, Plon, 1959), pp. 1 and 8.

81. Press conference of 27 November 1967 (*Année politique*, 1967, p. 399). Cf. statement of 31 January 1964 (*Année politique*, 1964, p. 421).

82. *L'Express*, 12 May 1960 (quoted in *Le Président de la Ve République*, Dossiers U², Paris, Armand Colin, 1970, p. 75).

83. *Mémoires d'Espoir*, I, p. 284. Earlier in the same volume, he merely specifies that the Prime Minister shall 'take action on important matters' only on the President's directions (p. 35).

84. Ibid., p 291.

85. Ibid., p. 301.

86. Ibid., p. 312. In volume II, *L'Effort*, he describes the Council of State's decision on the illegality of the *Cour militaire de Justice*, in 1962, as 'scandalous' and refers to the Council itself as a body acting 'in defiance of all obligations and traditions'. (pp. 47 and 78.)

87. This was clearly the fear of some politicians of the Fourth Republic at the time of General de Gaulle's brief contact with Parliament in June 1958. M. Georges Bidault's comment was:

'*Aujourd'hui musique de chambre, demain musique militaire*' (quoted in Jean–Raymond Tournoux, *Secrets d'Etat*, Paris, Plon, 1962, p. 339). The Communist Deputy, M. Kriegel–Valrimont said: '*après l'opération sédition, l'opération séduction*', and M. Mendès France: '*Il a appris un nouveau jeu. Quand on gagne on s'amuse toujours.*' (Quoted in Jean Ferniot, *Les Ides de mai*, Paris, Plon, 1958, p. 185.)

88. René Capitant in *Notre République*, 10 May 1963.

89. *Mémoires d'Espoir*, I, p. 291.

90. Ibid., p. 37.

91. Speech to the *Conseil d'Etat* in 1960 (quoted in *Le Monde*, 30 January 1960).

92. *Mémoires d'Espoir*, I, p. 291.

93. *Mémoires d'Espoir*, I, p. 34. *v.* also *Mémoires*, III (*Départ*), where he claims that during his period in the political wilderness from 1946–58, '*cette légitimité restait latente*'. *v.* also broadcast of 29 January during the revolt of 'the barricades' (*Année politique*, 1960, p. 639). In *Mémoires d'Espoir*, I (pp. 7–8) he defines 'legitimacy' as arising from the sentiment inspired and possessed by a Government (*un pouvoir*) that it incorporates national unity and continuity when the country is in danger.

94. *v,* for instance, press conference of 11 April 1961 (*Année politique*, 1961, p. 649).

95. *Preuves*, November 1958, p. 10.

96. *Secrets d'Etat*, p. 353.

97. *La Politique en France* (Collection U., Paris, Armand Colin, 1964), p. 243.

98. *Mémoires d'Espoir*, I, p. 285. The Prime Minister's contribution is compared to the second in command on board ship, who 'has his part to play alongside the Captain. Thus in our new Republic, the executive comprises a President charged with the responsibility for what is essential and permanent together with a Prime Minister who seconds him by dealing with day-to-day problems (*aux prises avec les contingences*).'

99. *v.* for instance, in *L'Espérance trahie* (pp. 94, 97 and 98) the description of meetings of the Council of Ministers given by M. Jacques Soustelle, who contradicts the President's affirmation that 'Everyone can ask to speak and permission is always given' (*Mémoires d'Espoir*, I, p. 286), saying that Ministers were, in reality, expected to concern themselves with their own departments, that there was little discussion, and often not even information regarding matters belonging to the 'presidential sector'. *v.* also Pierre Viansson Ponté

(*Le Monde*, 24 June 1969) who reports a new Minister as saying that, in meetings of the Council of Ministers presided over by General de Gaulle, the rule was that 'nobody spoke unless asked to, and nobody expressed an opinion opposed to that of the President'.

100. In general, the term *Conseil* is used for a committee presided over by the President and *Comité* for one presided over by the Prime Minister, but this rule is not by any means consistently adhered to. For instance, the *Comités de l'Elysée* – such as those set up early in the régime for Foreign Affairs, Algerian and African (including Madagascan) Affairs – are entirely presidentially appointed and the President presides. *Conseils restreints* are mainly inter-ministerial meetings, presided over by the President, but they may include high officials, or indeed anybody else whom the President chooses to appoint. These do not have any 'official' existence and, apart from brief reports of their meetings in the press, their activities remain largely unknown. Up to 1964, both the main defence committees (called *Comités*) were presided over by the President. Under the decree of 14 January 1964, reorganizing certain parts of the administration of the defence system, the *Comité de Défense* became the *Conseil de Défense*, apparently to the confusion of a number of Deputies.

101. 13 December 1961.

102. Avril, op. cit., p. 398.

103. *v.* article in *La Nef*, July 1959: 'M. Debré, existe-t-il?'. *v.* also Pierre Viansson–Ponté (*Le Monde*, 7 November 1961):

> In practice, anything and everything – the price of milk, the market for sugar, the Algerian negotiations or European policy – can be added one day to the reserved domain and removed from it the following day.

M. Viansson-Ponté goes on to quote the presidential decision to free Gaston Dominici (convicted of the apparently pointless murder of an English family) which, he says, was taken as the result of the President's seeing a programme about him on television.

For other examples of presidential personal interventions, *v.* Avril, op. cit., p. 225.

104. A Socialist Deputy (M. André Chandernagor) also accused the Prime Minister of unconstitutionality in counter-signing a measure that was itself unconstitutional.

105. *Journal Officiel* (*Débats, Assemblée nationale*), 25 April 1964.

106. 'La Lettre et l'Espoir', *Le Monde*, 26–7 April 1964.

107. *v.* for instance, articles in *Le Monde*, 6 October 1966, by Alfred Grosser, 8 October 1966 by Pierre Viansson-Ponté, and 17 November 1966 by Alexandre Sanguinetti; and M. Pompidou's statement in his press conference of 2 July 1970, in which he says that, faced with the dilemma of politically contradictory majorities in presidential and general elections, he would dissolve the Assembly. This does not, of course, settle the problem of what a President would do if the resulting election confronted him with exactly the same problem.

108. *v.* M. Poher's 12-point 'programme' published in *Le Monde*, 28 May 1969, which would not even have obtained anything like coherent support even among non-Gaullists. *v.* also questions raised by M. Giscard d'Estaing (*Le Monde*, 17 May 1969) on the significance of his previously published 'options' in the light of the actual majority in the Assembly, and M. Poher's unconvincing reply (*Le Monde*, 18 May 1969). As the election campaign proceeded, there was a tendency for journalists to treat these 'options' as a kind of programme put forward by a party leader hoping for a majority. As M. Pompidou pointed out (at Nice on 27 May 1969), if M. Poher were to obtain a majority it would be heterogeneous. Even M. Duverger, a supporter of the present quasi-presidential system, could only *note* M. Poher's 'dilemma', if he won, and found himself trying to apply his 'options' in an Assembly including some 350 Gaullists (*Le Monde*, 21 May 1969). On the problem of *les grandes options*, *v.* also Chapter I, pp. 22–3.

109. Speech at the *Cercle de l'Opinion* on 29 January 1970 (*Le Monde*, 31 January 1970).

110. *Institutions politiques*, 1970, p. 735.

M. Duverger's opinion that the existence of this new presidential status implies that a law voted by referendum could be repealed only by agreement between the President and the National Assembly has no foundation whatsoever in constitutional law, practice or common sense.

111. Alfred Fabre–Luce in *L'Or et la Bombe* (Paris, Calmann–Lévy, 1968), Chapter IV. '*Le chef de l'Etat a pris l'habitude de faire scandale deux fois par an dans une conférence de presse.*'

112. Pierre Viansson–Ponté, 'L'Année zéro de l'après-gaullisme', *Le Monde*, 4 October 1969.

113. *v.* in particular, statements of M. Chaban Delmas to the *Dîner-Débat des Echos* (10 December 1969), to the *Cercle d'Opinion*

(29 January 1970), and that of M. Pompidou in his press conference of 2 July 1970, all quoted in 'Les Impasses de la Ve bis,' by Roger Gérard Schwarzenberg (*Projet*, September–October 1970, pp. 926–7).

114. 'Libres Opinions. "Choix" ', *Le Monde*, 10 September 1966.

115. 'La Constitution, Demain,' *Le Monde*, 6 October 1966.

116. According to an opinion poll at the end of 1969 in the South-West, four-fifths of those questioned were in favour of the election of the President of the Republic by universal suffrage (*Le Monde*, 26 November 1969).

117. *Le Monde*, 12 November 1969. Cf. an opinion poll in 1967 which showed that, while 62% of those who replied thought that General de Gaulle had acted as the head of a majority party, only 21% thought that he ought to do this and 62% thought that he ought to remain outside parties. (Quoted in Philip Williams and Martin Harrison, *Politics and Society in de Gaulle's Republic*, Harlow, Longmans, 1970, p. 180 fn.)

PART II

CHAPTER VI

1. These figures do not take into account the period of provisional government from 1944 to the end of 1946, some extensive Government reshuffles and also those Prime Ministers who failed to form a Government, and so did not effectively hold office.

2. Some 'tendencies' represented in the National Assembly are not large enough to qualify as Parliamentary groups under article 19 of the rules of procedure. This figure, therefore, really under-represents the diversity of parties under the Fifth Republic. The Centre is heterogeneous, and the *Rassemblement démocratique*, which existed in the 1962 Assembly, was also heterogeneous. The Federation of the Democratic and Socialist Left formed one group in the 1967 Assembly, including Radicals, Socialists and representatives of the *Convention des Institutions républicaines*, which itself consisted of several political Clubs.

3. Jacques Fauvet, *La France déchirée* (Paris, Fayard, 1957), p. 26.

4. 'De la Montagne à M. Mitterrand', *Le Monde*, 4 January 1966.

5. *La Politique des Partis sous la IIIe République, 1933–1939* (Paris, Editions du Seuil, 1946), Vol. I, p. 20.

6. *Preuves*, February 1959.

7. *Le Monde*, 24 February 1970.

8. Robert de Jouvenel in *La République des Camarades* (Paris, Grasset, 1914), p. 89.

9. Ibid., p. 89.

10. *Les Idées politiques de la France* (Paris, Stock, 1932).

11. Jacques Fauvet, op. cit., p. 43.

12. *Le Populaire*, 9 March 1946.

13. *Le Monde*, 27 May 1955.

14. *v.* article in *Le Monde*, 25 February 1970, on the postponement of the revision of the Debré law of 30 December 1959. A Bill had been prepared, but the Government decided at the end of 1969 to prolong the Debré law for a year rather than risk reviving anti-clerical quarrels.

15. *La France déchirée*, p. 24.

16. *Le Régime politique français* (Paris, Editions du Seuil, 1955), p. 82.

17. *v.* motion voted on 13 July 1969 by the Socialist Congress. The section '*Orientation*' includes the statement that the party does not consider '*l'accession aux responsabilités gouvernementales.... comme le préalable absolu à la réalisation de ses objectifs*'. The party also rejected '*toute alliance avec les forces politiques représentatives du capitalisme, y compris la recherche de combinaisons centristes*'.

This decision came a month or so after the Socialist party *had* supported the Centrist presidential candidate, Alain Poher. The motion went on somewhat guardedly to say that there was no reason to '*s'isoler des forces démocratiques qui, sans se reconnaître explicitement dans sa doctrine, en viennent à dénoncer certains effets du régime capitaliste*'. It could reasonably be assumed that a number of 'Centrists' did belong to this category!

18. Address to Socialist students of the *Ecole normale supérieure* on 30 May 1947. *L'Œuvre de Léon Blum, 1945–7* (Paris, Editions Albin Michel, 1958), p. 431.

In fairness to Léon Blum, it should be added that he was distinguishing between the *exercise* of power in coalition with non-Socialist parties and the *conquest* of power for Socialism, and that the above-quoted remark referred specifically to the first of these alternatives. In the context of Socialist attitudes over the years, the statement can nevertheless be regarded as characteristic of much Socialist opinion at one time or another.

19. In reality, the Communists were the strongest party in terms

of voters throughout the post-war period (with the exception only
of the elections of June 1946, when they came second to the MRP)
up to 1966, when the Gaullists polled nearly two million more votes
at the first ballot. In subsequent elections in 1967 and 1968, the
Communists also came second to the Gaullists.

20. *Les Partis politiques* (Paris, Armand Colin, 1951), p. ix.

21. Ibid., pp. ix–x.

22. Quoted by Thibaudet, op. cit., p. 169.

23. Quoted by Jacques Fauvet in *Les Forces politiques en France*
(Paris, Editions *Le Monde*, 1951), p. 112.

24. *Les Partis politiques*, pp. ix–x.

25. Jean Guéhenno, quoted in Thibaudet, op. cit., p. 172.

26. Peter Campbell, in *Political Science* (New Zealand), September
1954.

27. *v.* the following description by the correspondent of the
Manchester Guardian (1 May 1956):

> Traditionally the new man arrives – probably from some forsaken
> region of South-Western France – with two thoughts in his
> mind: a sincere, inflammatory but vague distrust of the political
> system that rules in Paris: and a desire to obtain in Paris as many
> tobacconist's licences and other favours as possible for his friends
> at home. . . . The question always is how soon the second thought
> will prevail over the first and the deputy be safely absorbed into
> the Parisian system.

As evidence that this is also how the system works today, the
campaign of M. Pierre Messmer in Lorient in 1967 might be quoted.
On the phrase in one of his speeches, '*Je peux vous être utile*', a
commentator remarked:

> *Le ton est resté neutre de bout en bout. L'assistance n'a posé aucune
> question, maise elle a compris les sous-entendus des derniers mots: per-
> sonne ne peut mieux que moi assurer à Paris la défense de cette région.*
> > (*Le Monde*, 1 February 1967.)

The campaign of M. Jean-Jacques Servan-Schreiber in Nancy in
the by-election of June 1970 is no less illuminating on this point. He
was a new-comer to the region. The seat was held by a Gaullist.
His campaign was concentrated on the interests of Nancy.

28. General de Gaulle gave as one reason for refusing the special
session of the National Assembly requested under the provisions of
article 30 of the Constitution that Deputies were acting as a

pressure group for farming interests and that this was contrary to the requirements of article 27, which prohibits '*le mandat impératif*', that is, any specific instructions to a member of Parliament from an outside body.

Only one Parliamentary group has of recent years described itself as representative of a single interest, the '*groupe paysan*' in the last legislature of the Fourth Republic. It was a small group, mainly of right-wing Paris lawyers, whose 'peasant' affinities were not easily discoverable.

29. The Poujadist group represents an extreme case, in that its fifty or so Deputies (whose numbers were considerably reduced by the unseating of some) not merely represented almost exclusively the interests of small tradesmen, but were, in many cases, small tradesmen themselves. They behaved as a pressure group rather than a political party, though they did have views on other subjects, in particular, Algeria. They represented only a brief interlude in French political life, coming into Parliament in 1956 with some two and a half million votes and disappearing in 1958. But the organization representing their interests, the *Union de Défense des Commerçants et Artisans* (UDCA), continued to exist after their departure from Parliament.

30. Pierre Aubin in *Le Figaro*, 22 January 1967.

31. Given at a meeting in support of left-wing unity (*Le Monde*, 23 January 1970).

32. *La République des Professeurs* (Paris, Grasset, 1927), p. 171.

33. Pierre de Boisdeffre, *Lettre ouverte aux Hommes de Gauche* (Paris, Albin Michel, 1969), p. 22.

34. Quoted by Maurice Duverger in *Constitutions et documents politiques* (Paris, Presses universitaires de France, 1957), p. 208, with an inaccurate source reference. M. Duverger also gives other useful definitions of Right and Left.

35. André Siegfried, in *Le Figaro*, 13 November 1945.

36. *La Ve République* (Paris, Presses universitaires de France, 1959), p. 274.

37. *v*, in particular, Introduction and Conclusion of *La Politique des Partis sous la IIIe République, 1933–1939* (Paris, Editions du Seuil, 1946).

38. Herbert Lüthy, *The State of France* (London, Secker and Warburg, 1954), p. 30.

39. *Les Forces politiques en France*, p. 279.

40. Ibid.

41. *Les Français et la République* (Paris, Armand Colin, 1956), p. 20.

42. A minority decided to retain the adjective *'chrétien'* and so remained a separate movement.

43. *Tableau des Partis en France* (Paris, Grasset, 1930), p. 62.

44. *Le Figaro*, 13 November 1945.

45. *La France déchirée*, op. cit., p. 81.

CHAPTER VII

1. *Les Idées politiques de la France* (Paris, Stock, 1932), p. 242. Thibaudet defines liberalism as 'a system of coexistence in space', while traditionalism is for him 'a system of continuity over time'. In other words, the first is conditioned by reason and tolerance, the second by habit. Industrialism was 'the system (in the ideological sense) of industrial production'. In his view, each of these three belonged to a greater or lesser extent to the Right.

2. *Les Forces politiques en France* (Paris, Editions *Le Monde*, 1951).

3. *v.* article by Alfred Grosser in *Le Monde*, 24 September 1966.

4. Ibid.

5. This is not to under-estimate the value of the many excellent French studies of political behaviour in relation to economic, geographical, and historical factors, which make maps of French party strengths a fascinating and illuminating contribution to the understanding of why parties adopt the attitudes they do. The reader is advised to consult the detailed reports published in *Le Monde* during and after the elections, and the studies of parties and elections published in the *Cahiers* of the *Fondation nationale des Sciences politiques* (Paris, Armand Colin), in particular, François Goguel, *Géographie des élections françaises de 1870 à 1951* (No. 27), and *Nouvelles études de sociologie électorale*, 1954 (No. 60). The pioneer work is André Siegfried's *Tableau politique de la France de l'Ouest sous la troisième République* (Paris, Armand Colin, 1913, second edition, 1964). An interesting study is François Goguel's *Modernisation économique et Comportement politique* (Paris, Armand Colin, 1969).

6. 1951 hardly constitutes an exception, since the Communist party polled 4,934,000 votes. In 1958, the Communists polled only 3,882,204 votes at the first ballot, but this was still some 200,000 more than those received by the Gaullists. Since the size of the electorate increased over these years, and the percentage of those voting varied from one election to another, Communist strength is

more accurately indicated as a percentage of the votes cast. In 1946, at its peak in November, the party polled 28%; in 1958, its lowest point, 19% at the first ballot; in 1967, its highest point during the Fifth Republic, 22·5%; and in 1968, 21%.

7. The figures given by party spokesmen are:

1954,	506,250
1956,	429,000
1959,	425,000
1962,	405,482
1966,	425,000

No figures were given at the Congress in 1967, but at the meeting held to celebrate the 50th anniversary of the Communist party, Georges Marchais, the acting secretary-general, gave the figure of 400,000 (*Le Monde*, 29 December 1970). On 31 October the figure of 459,600 had been announced (*Le Monde*, 27 November 1970).

It is extremely difficult to discover the real membership of any French political party, but particularly difficult in the case of the Communist party, since published figures do not necessarily take adequate account of lapsed and non-paid-up membership. There is known to be a very rapid turnover in the Communist party. An enquiry in 1966 by the party showed that 44% of the members had joined the party since 1959 (*v. Le Monde*, 18 August 1966). In addition there have been from time to time specific allegations by Communists themselves of inaccuracies and even of the deliberate falsification of membership figures. For example, Charles Tillon (admittedly only following his expulsion from his 'cell') stated in a radio interview on 22 July 1970, that the party had then only 200,000 regularly paid-up members, and that meetings of cells were attended by only about 25% of the members (*v. Le Monde*, 24 July 1970). In his book, *Le Partisan* (Paris, Flammarion, 1963), Auguste Lecoeur accused Thorez of deliberately falsifying the post-war membership figures, when he gave them as a million (p. 280).

8. The outstanding exceptions to this rule were the votes of confidence on the formation of the Mendès France Government in 1954 and the Mollet Government of 1956. Both Prime Ministers explicitly stated that they were discounting Communist votes in their assessment of the degree of confidence expressed by the vote.

Of the 18 motions of censure from 1959 to 1971, the Communists voted for all but two, that of June 1962 (the seventh) which expressed right-wing opposition to the Evian agreements, and that of April 1966 (the eleventh), which criticized France's withdrawal from NATO the previous month. The Communists stated that this was 'the only positive aspect of Gaullist policy'. (*Le Monde*, 17 March 1966.)

9. The CGT paper, *Le Peuple*, opened a *tribune de discussion* on 1 April 1955 and the discussion continued up to June. The Communist demonstration that the improvement of the workers' condition was illusory was based on calculations of the percentage of the national income accounted for by wages, on the relation between incomes and hours of work and on somewhat doubtful estimates of profits. The difficulty of Communists was to avoid creating the impression that, if the workers' position under capitalism was *bound* to have this effect, then the value of the battle for improved conditions was questionable. This difficulty was surmounted by the argument of one of the two secretaries-general of the CGT, Pierre Le Brun, who agreed that the law of 'absolute impoverishment' was true as a general tendency, but maintained that its working could be checked by working-class action. (*v. Le Monde*, 11 June 1955.) As *Le Monde's* commentator remarked: 'if the standard of living falls, M. Frachon is right, because his theory is validated; if it rises he is right, because the working class has succeeded in preventing the capitalist machine from working'.

The interesting point about this argument is that it was revived nine years later in 1964 (*v. Cahiers du Communisme*, January 1964), when the Communist party was also finding it difficult to make headway in a situation of rising prosperity.

10. *v.*, for instance, the following description of the long-term effect of the Hungarian repression in *Le Monde*, 23 May 1959:

. . . The day that Russia fired on the workers a myth was destroyed.

The USSR has lost a kind of proletarian sanctity. It no longer has its halo.

11. In 1959 (2 June), Thorez was still affirming that the links between Algeria and France should be maintained, and this was the official party attitude even after President de Gaulle's declaration of self-determination on 16 September. Although, later, the party maintained that its views had never changed, and that it had always advocated peace by negotiation (*v.*, for instance, the speech by Thorez on 26 February 1962), in fact Communist views had fluctuated a good deal. When the rebellion broke out, *l'Humanité* (9 November 1954) had disapproved of it as being likely to play into the hands of colonialists. In March 1956, the Communists voted

for the Government's special powers on Algeria. On 20 May 1958, they voted for a motion expressing the nation's gratitude to the army. In 1959, the party approved of negotiations, but only if conducted from 'a position of strength' (*France nouvelle*, 12 February 1959). The first reaction of the Communists to General de Gaulle's approval of self-determination in 1959 was that it was 'a purely demagogic manœuvre' (*Cahiers du Communisme*, October 1959).

12. Among prominent Communists expelled during this period were André Marty (1952), Auguste Lecoeur (1955), Pierre Hervé (1956). Charles Tillon was expelled from the Central Committee, though not from the party. It is interesting to note that André Marty's post was filled by Roger Garaudy (himself expelled in 1970) and that Charles Tillon was again in trouble in 1970. Marty, Lecoeur and Hervé all published damaging attacks on the party leadership. Marty's *L'Affaire André Marty* (extracts from Marty's defence to the *bureau politique* published by a group of Communist sympathizers, Toulouse, 1952) was a long and documented account of his quarrel with the party. Lecoeur's *L'Autocritique attendue* (Paris, Editions Girault-St Cloud, 1955) was also a long statement of his case. Pierre Hervé's *La Révolution et les fétiches* (Paris, Table Ronde, 1956) was a highly sophisticated doctrinal dispute with the party.

13. A Communist Deputy, Marcel Servin, estimated that a million and a half Communists had voted for the Constitution in the referendum of 26 September 1958. The total 'No' vote was 4,625,000, whereas the Communists alone had obtained 5,600,000 votes in the 1956 elections. (*v.* statement to the *Comité central* at Ivry on 3–4 October 1958.) The November elections of 1958 also involved an estimated loss of a million and a half Communist votes, since 1956.

14. The reduction of Communist representation in the National Assembly to ten was financially as well as politically disastrous, since Communist Deputies contribute a large proportion of their salaries to party funds.

15. Since no left-wing victory was conceivable except with support from both the Communist party and parties to the right of the Socialists, Gaston Defferre's position was comprehensible. Communist support for him as a presidential candidate was valuable only if it involved him in no concessions to Communist demands that might alienate support from parties farther to the right. Communist insistence on French disengagement from military *blocs* was likely to be harmful to him, as was the Communist party's

militant anti-clericalism and collectivism. It was on the last two issues that the experiment of the *grande fédération* finally foundered.

16. Statement made at the Central Committee meeting at Ivry, 8–10 May 1963.

17. Statement made at Mulhouse in December 1964.

18. *v.* statement made at the Central Committee meeting on 4 January 1966. (*Le Monde*, 6 January 1966.) *v.* also interview by Waldeck Rochet reported in *Le Monde*, 30–31 July 1967.

19. Statement by Waldeck Rochet at the end of the *Semaine de la pensée marxiste*, 15 March 1966. (*Le Monde*, 17 March 1966.)

20. Ibid.

21. *v.* press conference by Waldeck Rochet of 6 September 1967.

22. *v.* statement by Waldeck Rochet to the Central Committee at Plessis–Robinson on 17 January 1968: '*La réalisation de l'unité de la gauche est une œuvre de longue haleine. . . .*'

23. The number of dissident student movements was still quite insignificant, however, and the orthodox point of view still triumphed at the student Congress in March 1965, but the debate had already begun. *v.* the special number of *France nouvelle* of February 1965 and the reply in the following number of the student paper, *Clarté*. About a hundred Communist university teachers sent a letter to Waldeck Rochet in February 1965 on the need for free discussion within the party. This was the first time for years that Communists had made a collective move of this kind. The official reply to them published in *l'Humanité* condemned them as guilty of '*activité fractionnelle*'.

24. *l'Humanité*, 16 February 1966.

Louis Aragon was a member of the Central Committee of the party. This was the first time a Moscow decision had been directly and frankly criticized by an important member of the party. *v.* also account in *Le Monde*, 17 February 1966.

Between 1960 and 1964 *l'Humanité* and five provincial papers had lost half their circulation, according to a report by Etienne Fajon to the *bureau politique* in Feburary 1965.

In 1964, the party produced what purported to be a facsimile of the underground edition of *l'Humanité* of 10 July 1940, with the aim of demonstrating the purity of the Communist resistance record. The authenticity of the appeal to resistance contained in it was immediately challenged. (*v. Le Monde*, 19 and 20 June 1964.) In his book, *Le Partisan* (Paris, Flammarion, 1963), Auguste Lecoeur returned to this theme and produced some impressive evidence in support of his claim that the document was a fabrication and that the Communist resistance record (which the Communists had exploited to great effect in the immediate post-war years) dated not from July 1940, but only from June 1941, when the Soviet Union was attacked by Germany (*v.* pp. 153–4).

The importance of this incident, as also of the revival of the theme of 'absolute impoverishment' (*v.* note 9 above), is that they both indicate the Communists' realization of the weakness of their position.

25. Statement by Georges Marchais on 3 May, when he attacked Daniel Cohn-Bendit. The Communist party was particularly annoyed by the latter's reference on 13 May at a PSU meeting to orthodox Communists as '*les crapules stalinennes*'. Before the end of May, Georges Séguy, the secretary-general of the CGT, was accusing students of holding 'irresponsible demonstrations' (*v. Le Monde*, 24 May 1968). On 26 May, the Communists published an appeal to intellectuals and students, stressing the evils of utopianism, anarchism and pseudo-revolutionary verbiage (*v. Le Monde*, 28 May 1968).

26. *v.* the Communist party's challenge to the Government on 21 May (*Le Monde*, 25 May 1968).

27. *v.* account of the CGT procession from the Place de la Bastille to the Carrefour Havre–Caumartin on 24 May. (*v.* also *Le Monde*, 26–7 and 28 June 1968.)

28. *v. Le Monde*, 2–3 June 1968. *v.* also Waldeck Rochet's statement on television on 12 June that 'the Communist party stands as a party of order and political wisdom, appealing to working-class discipline, voluntarily accepted' (*Le Monde*, 14 June 1968).

29. Television broadcast, reported in *Le Monde*, 16–17 June 1968.

30. Where the votes went was a question exhaustively studied in subsequent opinion polls. The general conclusion was that the Communists had lost some votes to both the PSU and the UDR, but that many Communists had abstained.

31. Statement by Waldeck Rochet on 21 August, 1968. (*v. l'Humanité*, 22 August 1968.) This was later watered down somewhat, but he never entirely withdrew it. The acting secretary-general, Georges Marchais, was accused of being a tool of Moscow (*v.* attack by Charles Tillon in *Le Monde*, 22 July 1970), but the editor of *l'Humanité*, René Andrieu, wrote on 27 July 1970:

S'agissant de la situation actuelle en Tchécoslovaquie, il est à peine besoin de dire qu'elle ne comble pas nos vœux, que nous ne sommes pas d'accord avec certaines mesures prises et qu'en ce qui nous concerne, nous aurions agi autrement. Mais cela dit, nous n'avons pas la vocation de donner quotidiennement des conseils aux autres.

32. Jeanette Vermeersch resigned from the political bureau on 22 October 1968 because the party was not sufficiently pro-Soviet on Czechoslovakia. Roger Garaudy continued to criticize the party's attitude regarding the Czech affair in the prolonged public discussion with the leadership that ended with his expulsion from all party offices.

33. *v.* Speech by Georges Marchais at Arcueil on 6 December 1969. (*Le Monde*, 15 December 1969.)

34. *Le Phénomène gaulliste* (Paris, Fayard, 1970), p.27.

35. The party had already accepted a manifesto '*Pour une démocratie avancée, pour une France socialiste*', as far back as December 1966, including a number of important doctrinal concessions to non-revolutionary viewpoints, such as the recognition that, at least for a start, only large concerns should be nationalized, that small firms as well as small and medium farms could be permitted, and that inheritance of 'the fruits of labour' was also permissible. Acceptance of the notion of passage to Socialism by legal means was also part of the 1966 manifesto.

36. *v. Tableau des Partis en France* (Paris, Grasset, 1930), pp. 163–5. He was talking about Socialists but, as he predicted (p. 165), what he said was to become applicable to Communists.

37. *Caliban parle* (Paris, Grasset, 1928), pp. 26–7.

38. On the later evolution of this party, *v.* Chapter 9.

39. In 1946, at its peak, the Socialist party had 145 Deputies and 350,000 members. It polled 21% of the vote. In 1962, its share of the vote at the first ballot was 12·65%. By 1965, it had lost one half of the votes and three-quarters of the members of the immediate post-war years, according to figures quoted at the 55th Congress, held in 1965. Its Parliamentary representatives in 1965 numbered 66, and 43 after the 1968 elections. In 1971, its membership was estimated to be at most 80,000.

40. Talks on the possibility of a common electoral front had been held at the beginning of 1962 (the *dîner d'Alma*), but the so-called '*Cartel des Non*', which was as near to an electoral alliance as the parties of the Left could get, provided only for *ad hoc* agreements, varying from constituency to constituency, on the best way to defeat the Gaullist candidate. Even so, the agreements were only partially adhered to.

41. Some Socialists found him too 'presidentialist' – too Gaullist – to be a satisfactory anti-Gaullist candidate. M. Defferre also involved himself in some complicated hypothetical arguments within the party (*v.* for example, the account in *Le Monde* of the Clichy conference at the beginning of February 1964), before going on to arouse doubts in the minds of his hoped-for supporters in other parties. In particular, there was some disagreement on what ought to be the relations between President and Prime Minister, on the precise functions of the President, and on how to avoid the danger of a dispute between the President and the majority in the National Assembly. (*v. infra* on the Federation of the Democratic and Socialist Left for a brief discussion of Socialist disagreements with their prospective partners.)

42. For a discussion of the differing viewpoints, *v.* article in *Le Monde* of 23 December 1964 and report of the discussion at the Socialist Information Conference of 4–5 April 1965 in *Le Monde*, 6 April 1965.

The Socialist Congress of June 1965 revealed the depth of feeling in the party about the future of State undenominational education if the Defferre Federation were to be created. M. Mollet clearly feared, too, that it would mean the erosion of some of the 'revolutionary' content of Socialism.

43. Six of the Defferrists resigned from the party *bureau* at the end of 1965.

44. This entailed dropping the description SFIO (*Section française de l'Internationale ouvrière*), which had been part of the party's official title since the unification of 1905.

45. There were at least four major problems, on each of which the party was divided, but the dividing lines differed in each case. They were:

(i) the problem of '*collégialité*'. Some supported the total elimination of hierarchy (Claude Fuzier); others (Pierre Mauroy) wanted a wide distribution of responsibilities, but accepted the need for a 'first secretary'. The second view prevailed.

(ii) *The question of admission to the party*. Some (e.g. Alain Savary) believed that the party should be open to all sections of the 'Socialist family'; others that certain Clubs should be only 'associated' with the Socialist party. The main point of dissension was the question of the admission of the CIR (*Convention des Institutions républicaines*), led by M. François Mitterrand. The UCRG (M. Savary's *Union des Clubs pour le Renouveau de la*

Gauche) joined the party. The UGCS split, the tendency led by Jean Poperen joining the party, that including MM. Desson and Hauriou remaining aloof. The CIR remained outside, but some of its members joined the party. The Club *Citoyens 60* remained outside.

(iii) *The problem of 'tendances'*. The old problem of the recognition of organized minorities within the party was finally settled, as it had been earlier by Guy Mollet, by the refusal to return to this tradition, though some (e.g. Arthur Notebard) wanted such minorities to be represented on the level of the 'bureau', but not of the Secretariat.

(iv) *The conditions on which a Socialist–Communist 'dialogue' should be resumed*. On this there were four major divergences. Some were opposed to the talks (André Chandernagor, Arthur Notebard, Gaston Defferre). Some were in favour of talks, but anxious to give first priority to maintaining the cohesion of the party (Pierre Mauroy). Guy Mollet and Alain Savary believed that the first priority was the struggle against capitalism and that the party should undertake not to accept Government office unless assured of the support of a majority of the working class. This section opposed all proposals for an understanding with Centre parties. Some of those on the Left of the party (Jean Poperen) wanted talks not merely with the Communist party, but also with the PSU and the CIR. On this issue, the final resolution of the constitutive conference represented a compromise in which talks were accepted in principle, but certain conditions laid down, though in general terms.

A fifth division came from the clash of personalities and their supporters. Gaston Defferre and Guy Mollet were personally as well as politically out of sympathy with each other. François Mitterrand and Guy Mollet agreed about talks with the Communists, but not on the question of the admission of the CIR to the party. Pierre Mauroy, Arthur Notebard, André Chandernagor were all really opposed to talks with the Communists, but disagreed with each other on other points.

46. The exact phrase was '*Le choix des partenaires doit cependant éviter toute exclusive qui résulterait de divisions politiques anciennes ou d'étiquettes héritées du passé.*' This could have been taken to justify a political understanding with the Centre, and the following paragraph, emphasizing the party's intention not to isolate itself from 'democratic forces that, without explicitly denouncing certain

consequences of the capitalist system, were in effect doing so in practice', reinforced that impression. Yet the specific repudiation of association with Centrism made it clear that these phrases were not intended to have that interpretation. Clarity was not, however, a characteristic of the declaration. *v.* also Chapter VI, note 17.

47. Alain Savary had left the Socialist party in 1958 to join the PSA, left the PSU in 1965 to form the UCRG, and had only finally rejoined the Socialist party after its reorganization, in 1969.

48. *v.* for instance, the joint declaration of the Federation of the Democratic and Socialist Left and the Communist party, published on 24 February 1968, which was as much a statement of the points on which they disagreed as of those on which they agreed. This was a point on which the Communist party specifically indicated its disagreement with the Federation (*v.* Section B. *Problèmes économiques et sociaux*).

49. *v.* for instance, François Mitterrand's statement of the position of the Federation on this point on 7 November 1968, at the Congress of the CIR:

Il n'est pas question de céder à la Grande-Bretagne ni de la dispenser de souscrire aux obligations du traité de Rome, mais il faut accepter de discuter.

50. *v.* for instance, the statement by Waldeck Rochet on 10 January 1968 (*Le Monde*, 12 January 1968):

Une négociation éventuelle de l'entrée de la Grande-Bretagne dans le Marché commun ne peut avoir lieu que si, au préalable, la Grande-Bretagne renonce à son alliance privilégiée avec les Etats-Unis et s'engage à pratiquer une politique indépendante et de coopération avec tous les pays d'Europe, c'est-à-dire, une politique impliquant la dissolution des blocs militaires, ce qui devrait conduire au non-renouvellement du pacte atlantique à l'échéance de 1969.

51. The specific articles of the Constitution that the Declaration suggested ought to be amended were: 11, 16, 19, 30, 34, 40–8, 49, 56–63, 65 and 89. There were slight differences between the Federation and the Communists with regard to article 19.

52. Georges Guille (Socialist Deputy), quoted in *Le Monde*, 27 February 1968.

53. *v. Le Monde*, 23 June 1970.

54. The new *Comité directeur* of 61 included 33 old faces and 28 new, of whom four represented the Clubs, two were former Radicals

and one a former member of the CIR. It was estimated, however, that 51 of the 61 seats were held by members of the former Socialist party.

55. Raymond Barrillon, in *Le Monde*, 15 October 1969.

56. The first secretary regarded the formation of André Chandernagor's movement as being contrary to party decisions of July 1969. The majority had then turned down the proposal for the recognition of organized minorities (*tendances*) inside the party. It had also condemned any *rapprochement* with Centrists. (*v. Le Monde*, 3 March 1970.)

57. This party, formed by the *maire* of Mulhouse, Emile Muller, was joined by another small dissident Socialist party, *Socialisme et Liberté*, run by the former Communist, Auguste Lecoeur, and a certain number of other Mayors tried to form similar movements.

58. Guy Mollet announced on 8 December 1968 that he would not be a candidate for the post of Secretary in the new party. In May 1969, he became the director of a party research organization, the *Office universitaire de Recherche socialiste* (OURS). There were those who believed, however, that he remained in effective control. As one member of the *Convention* put it: '*Le véritable patron demeure par personne interposée Guy Mollet*' (quoted in *Le Monde*, 19 July 1969). There was no clear evidence of the truth of this view during the first eighteen months of the existence of the new party, but M. Mollet certainly had a number of supporters and was in a position to exercise considerable influence, though he was himself no longer a member of the *Comité directeur*.

59. For texts of the two main motions voted on at the reunification Congress at Epinay-sur-Seine, *v. Le Monde*, 15 June 1971, p. 9. The new *Comité directeur* of 81 members included 28 representatives of the Mollet–Savary position, 23 of the Mauroy–Defferre positions, 13 supporters of M. Mitterrand, 10 of M. Poperen and 7 of the CERES. This composition represents a significant move to the Left, though not of a kind to be welcome to the Communist party, which described the conference as 'an obscure battle of the clans for the conquest of power'. (*l'Humanité*, 14 June 1971.)

60. The UDSR was originally a '*rassemblement*' of resistance movements that became a political party in 1946. It was Socialistic, though not Marxist, and included a number of Gaullist sympathizers. Its president was René Pleven, and, from 1951 onwards, M. François Mitterrand. Throughout the Fourth Republic, it formed, with a small group of overseas representatives, a Parliamentary

group of some 20 members. In the Senate, it formed part of the Radical *Gauche démocratique* group. Along with a number of small Radical parties, it formed part of the *Rassemblement des Gauches républicaines*, and became less Socialistic and more Radical in its politics. In 1958, it split into a small pro-Gaullist section, led by René Pleven and including Claudius-Petit, and a more left-wing section, led by François Mitterrand, which was opposed to the new régime. The former became in 1959 the *Union démocratique* and eventually merged with the Centre. The latter was virtually wiped out in the 1958 elections. M. Mitterrand himself was defeated, but two UDSR Deputies joined the predominantly Radical Parliamentary group, the *Rassemblement démocratique*.

61. The tendency of French Parliaments to accept Radical Prime Ministers or Presidents of Parliamentary assemblies was responsible for the description of the Radical party as *le parti des Présidents*, for, up to and including the Fourth Republic, Prime Ministers were called *Présidents du Conseil*.

62. The vote of Radical and allied groups increased by over a million and amounted to 13·4% of the vote, but this was due in large part to electoral alliances with the Socialists or the UDSR. It is never easy to give accurate figures either of Radical Parliamentary representatives or of Radical votes, owing both to frequent splits in the party and to electoral alliances on a constituency basis that can vary very much. Official election results usually quote figures only for 'Radical and allied groups'.

63. This did not mean that no Radical held office. A Radical Senator, Jean Berthoin, was a Minister for a short time. Edgar Faure became a Minister in 1966, but he had by then been moving steadily closer to Gaullism for some time. Former Radicals who became Gaullists included Jacques Chaban Delmas and Edgard Pisani.

64. The Radicals were divided among other things on Algeria, on European policy, on relations with the Socialists and on the Constitution.

65. In the first Parliament of the Fifth Republic, Radical Deputies had formed, together with left–centre Deputies belonging to a movement called *Libertés démocratiques*, a single Parliamentary group, the *Entente démocratique*. The two sections were usually referred to in the voting lists published in the press as *Section Radical-socialiste* and *Libertés démocratiques*. The group disappeared in the following Parliament, seven of its members joining the *Centre démocrate*, which was predominantly MRP. 26 Radicals joined the *Rassemblement*

démocratique, whose 39 members included in 1963 two members of the UDSR, three former right-wing Radical members of the *Entente démocratique* and eight isolated or affiliated members.

66. *Le Monde*, 26 January 1968.

67. Auguste Pinton, Senator for the Rhône, at Nantes, on 17 October 1968.

68. *v.* article by Gilbert Mathieu, 'Révolution ou vœu pieux', in *Le Monde*, 7 February 1970.

69. *v. La Nation*, 30 January 1970: '*On se demande quelles sont les véritables intentions de l'auteur: rénover le parti radical ou préparer la révolution de l'an 2000.*'

70. *v.* article by Maurice Duverger, in *Le Monde*, 7 February 1970.

71. *v.* Gilbert Mathieu, *Le Monde*, 7 February 1970.

72. Raymond Barrillon, *Le Monde*, 30 January 1970.

73. The acceptance on 15 February 1970 was accompanied by the requirement of modifications to meet certain objections. These included amendments to safeguard small estates and the retention of some form of national service.

74. There were ten candidates in all, including a Trotskyist, a right-wing extremist, a Centrist, a Socialist, a Communist, a representative of the PSU and two candidates of no political significance.

75. Pierre Viansson-Ponté in *Le Monde*, 1 September 1970.

76. Jean-Jacques Servan-Schreiber was a supporter of Pierre Mendès France from 1953 and while the latter remained a Radical. He continued to direct the weekly paper *l'Express*, until he became secretary-general of the Radical party, wrote a book opposing the Algerian war (*Lieutenant en Algérie*) and another on the danger of American economic penetration in Europe (*Le Défi américain*). He was the inventor of Monsieur X, a mysterious potential presidential candidate in 1965, who turned out to be Gaston Defferre.

77. A Socialist-Communist dialogue conducted by the Socialist side in the pages of the *Populaire* in the early months of 1964, and a number of round-table meetings of representatives of what was described as 'the Socialist family' (which included Socialist, PSU, CGT, CFTC representatives, together with members of the *Club Jean Moulin*), had led merely to familiar disagreements on doctrinal questions, such as the nature of revolutionary change, the rôle of the dictatorship of the proletariat, democratic centralism, and so on. In 1964, Guy Mollet put forward five conditions of co-operation with other parties. They were: 'to be a democrat, revolutionary, anti-

clerical, a patriot and an internationalist' (*Le Monde*, 20 October 1964). The second and third were, of course, unacceptable to the MRP and the fifth (in the sense understood by most Communists) was unacceptable to the Radicals.

78. The structure of the Federation was amended in 1967 following the elections, but the weighting was retained.

79. The Federation obtained four and a half million votes and 116 seats. The Socialists held 76 of these, the Radicals 24 and the *Convention* 16. In the previous Parliament, the Socialists had numbered 66 and the Radicals (included in the *Rassemblement démocratique*) 25. But the Communists also increased their representation from 41 to 73 and the PSU from one to four. The weakness of the Federation is indicated by the extent of their Deputies' dependence on Communist votes for election. It was estimated in 1966 that 45 of the 87 Deputies at that time included in the Federation could not hope to be re-elected without the support of Communist votes. Of 62 Socialist Deputies, 51, and of 25 Radical Deputies, 17 owed their election to the withdrawal of the Communist candidate at the second ballot. (*v. Le Monde*, 28 October 1966.)

80. The main affirmations in the Charter were:

(i) The need for certain guaranteed liberties, including the independence of justice, unbiased information, trade-union rights. . . .

(ii) The need to work for peace, through the return of France to the Geneva disarmament conference, the conversion of the French nuclear deterrent to peaceful uses, agreement on non-proliferation, a 'confederal' solution of the German problem. . . .

(iii) The need to construct 'Europe', through elected Assemblies, a common executive for the Communities, and the development of common EEC policies. . . .

(iv) The need to 'democratize' the National Plan, through extension of the public sector, tax reforms. . . .

(v) The need for social justice.

There were in all some 120 proposals for reform phrased in very general terms. A political declaration of 3 April 1967 reaffirmed the principles of the Charter.

81. The 1968 document, described as a joint declaration by the Federation and the Communist party, would be more accurately described as a summary of their disagreements. The agreements were on questions of principle, unrelated to time or to precise

proposals. The disagreements were precise and comprehensive. Those concerned with foreign policy have already been summarized in the section on Socialism, *v.* p. 191 and notes 48, 49 and 50. Those concerned with internal policy included:

(i) Nationalization, on which the Federation mentioned only two precise proposals, the Communists ten to twelve.

(ii) The electoral system, on which the Federation made no statement. The Communists were in favour of proportional representation.

(iii) The powers of President and of Parliament, on which there were significant differences. The Communists specifically expressed their opposition to the 'presidential system'.

82. The Federation was reduced from 116 to 57 Deputies. Communist strength fell from 73 to 34. Of the 57 representatives of the Federation, 13 were Radicals. The *Convention* lost 15 of its 16 members, only their President, François Mitterrand, surviving.

83. *v.* for instance, the statement by Michel Soulié: '*La tradition radicale s'oppose à toute espèce de contrôle rigide de la part des états-majors nationaux sur ce qui se passe dans les départements.*' (*Le Monde*, 22 November 1966.)

84. The '*contre-gouvernement*' was appointed on 5 May 1966, when seven members were announced together with the respective subjects on which they were to be spokesmen. The actual Gaullist phrase in *La Nation* (quoted in *Le Monde*, 7 May 1966) was '*une bonne idée publicitaire*'.

85. 'Le Choix de la Fédération', *Le Monde*, 10 May 1966.

86. The issue of 'fusion' provided a striking example of the process. Within the Federation, MM. Mitterrand and Defferre constituted the spearhead of the movement in favour of fusion, instead of the essentially 'confederal' organization of the Federation. The majority of the Socialist party, led at that time by Guy Mollet, were much less enthusiastic. Some Socialists were prepared for 'partial fusion', though only as a gradual process. Others, together with the Radicals, wanted no fusion at all. The result was that the Federation was condemned to statements of general principle committing no party to any action, since this was all they could agree on.

v. for instance, the debate on fusion reported in *Le Monde*, 23 January 1968, and the following statement by Gaston Defferre in reply to a question put by *Le nouvel Observateur*, reported in *Le Monde*, 25 January 1968:

If fusion between Radicals, members of the *Convention* and Socialists were possible now, I should be in favour of it. I am convinced that it is not possible. But let us make it quite clear that some Socialists do not want fusion at all, not even partial fusion ... To be against partial fusion is to be against fusion altogether.

CHAPTER VIII

1. *Le Phénomène gaulliste* (Paris, Fayard, 1970), p. 54.
2. *Institutions politiques* (Paris, Presses universitaires de France, 1970), p. 656.
3. M. Lecanuet in *Le Monde*, 27 January 1970.
4. *v.* for instance, one definition of Centrists as being:

middle class ... men and women who, in their professional life, have a sense of responsibility and do not see politics as belonging to the artificial world that classes men on the Right and on the Left, and whose criteria are represented by the question: 'Would you have voted for the execution of Louis XVI?'
(Alain Chevalier, 'Libres Opinions, rapprocher les Forces réformatrices', in *Le Monde*, 10 April 1970.)

5. Excluding, of course, the interim Blum Government of December 1946, which lasted only a month.
6. The figures refer to metropolitan France. During the Fourth Republic, MRP strength in the National Assembly was increased by the affiliation of a varying number of Overseas Deputies belonging to the group *Indépendants d'Outre-Mer* (IOM).
7. The worker-priest experiment in the 1950s represented one of the attempts made by Catholics to bridge the class as well as the religious gulf between themselves and the Marxist Left.
8. The MRP did not want to withdraw into opposition in 1959 because it hoped that General de Gaulle would be able to deal with the Algerian problem. The party was, however, itself divided on this, and a right-wing section, led by M. Georges Bidault, formed the movement *Démocratie chrétienne* in 1959, representing those MRP members whose policy was to keep Algeria French. The MRP was also much less critical than the Left opposition parties of the 'presidential' aspects of Gaullism. Nearly a quarter of the regional delegates to the National Committee were opposed to voting 'No' in the 1962 referendum, which proposed to amend the Constitution in order to provide for the election of the President by universal

suffrage. Prominent members of the MRP, in particular Paul Coste Floret, were in favour of a presidential system. At this stage, the Socialists were not yet reconciled to accepting the 1958 Constitution as permanent.

9. In the 1963 Parliament, seven MRP Deputies had been supported by UNR votes and a number of the 34 MRP Deputies had made commitments to the Gaullists. They formed, together with some 20 independent or Centre-Left Deputies, including René Pleven, former President of the UDSR, a Parliamentary group of 55 or so called the *Centre démocrate*, whose avowed aim was to avoid unconditional support for either Government or opposition.

10. This was the point of view of Pierre Pflimlin, who was anxious to preserve the Centrist character of the MRP.

11. *v.* for instance, his statement in a television interview in the programme *Face à Face*, on 12 September 1966: '*Nous ne formulons d'exclusive à l'egard de personne, à l'exception des communistes qui en ont d'ailleurs formulé à notre égard.*'

12. M. Lecanuet also stated that the MRP would not form part of a Government that included Communists. It was precisely on the issue of European unification that the five MRP Ministers had resigned from the Government in May 1962.

v. his reply on television to M. Pompidou, quoted in *Le Monde*, 29 September 1966, and his statement quoted in *Le Monde*, 4–5 December 1966.

13. In 1956, 12 out of 15 seats had gone to the MRP.

14. *Le Monde*, 3 May 1967.

15. What remained of the MRP from 1967 onwards formed part of the movement *Objectif 1972*, led by M. Robert Buron. It was estimated in 1967 that one-fifth of its members were former members of the MRP. (*v. Le Monde*, 12 December 1967.) Some joined the Socialist party at the 1971 reunification Congress.

16. Statement of 12 February 1968 (quoted in *Le Monde*, 14 February 1968).

17. The plan of February 1968 was mainly concerned with economic and social policy and recommended, along with aid for the economy, increasing provision of schools, universities and houses, increased family allowances, support for farm prices and the reform of the private sector. *v. Le Monde*, 30 January and 13 February 1968.

18. Statement of the *Centre démocrate* National Convention at Nantes, quoted in *Le Monde*, 26 October 1971.

19. Alain Duhamel, 'Les Centristes ont le cœur à gauche mais ils votent à droite', *Le Monde*, 27 March 1971.

20. According to opinion polls, up to September 1962 only one Frenchman in five thought that the party's 1958 success would be lasting. In September 1962, 33% were uncertain of the future of the party. (*v. Le Phénomène gaulliste* by Jean Charlot, Paris, Fayard, 1970, p. 19.)

21. *v.* for instance the speech made by General de Gaulle at Rennes in July 1947, in which he referred to Communists as having 'made a vow of obedience to the orders of a foreign organization aiming at domination led by the masters of a Slav great power'. (Quoted by Henry Coston, in *Partis, Journaux et Hommes politiques d'hier et d'aujourd'hui*, Paris, Lectures françaises, 1960, p. 291.)

22. The Gaullists voted for the Barangé law in 1951, thus classing themselves on the Right in the eyes of all left-wing parties except the MRP, which also voted for the law and so went through a period of some five years of estrangement from the other left-wing parties.

23. The text of the Bayeux speech is reproduced in the *Annexe* of the *Année politique* for 1946 (p. 543), and an extract from it is given in English in the Appendix of David Thomson's *Democracy in France since 1870* (London, OUP, 1964), p. 324.

24. The Gaullists voted against the treaty setting up the European Coal and Steel Community as well as that providing for a European Defence Community.

25. There was some excuse for this attitude in the 1950s. The RPF programme in 1950 included – along with the plan for '*l'association capital–travail*', constitutional reform and the rejection of a coalition with any other party in the 1951 elections – the following specific proposals regarded by all politicians of the Left as expressing right-wing views:

(i) the right of the President to dissolve the National Assembly and to hold a referendum;
(ii) the replacement of the Senate by a functional second Chamber;
(iii) State aid to Catholic schools.

26. There were Social-Republican Ministers in the Mendès France Government of 1954 and the Faure Government of 1955. The Mollet Government of 1956 and the Gaillard Government of 1957 each had one Social-Republican Minister – M. Chaban Delmas.

27. The first split in the RPF had occurred in 1952, when 27 right-wing Deputies formed a small dissident group, *Action*

républicaine et sociale (ARS) and later joined their spiritual home, the *Centre national des Indépendants*. General de Gaulle's announcement of the severance of his relations with the Parliamentary group followed Gaullist defeats in the municipal elections of 1953. The rump of Gaullist Deputies sustained heavy losses in the 1956 general election and by 1958 numbered only 21, disunited on almost everything except their opposition to European integration. In the four years from 1954 to 1958, Gaullism undoubtedly increased the weakness of the '*système*' by helping to defeat six Governments. In the late 1960s there was still a Gaullist movement outside Parliament described as the *Rassemblement du Peuple français*, but it was admittedly inactive. (*v*. Charlot, op. cit., p. 188.)

28. As created in 1958, the UNR included four distinct and incompatible elements:

(i) the rump of the Social Republicans;

(ii) the movement formed by Jacques Soustelle, himself a Social-Republican Deputy, *L'Union pour le Renouveau français*, which represented the point of view held by French settlers in Algeria;

(iii) the *Convention républicaine* led by Léon Delbecque; and

(iv) the *Comités ouvriers pour le Soutien du Général de Gaulle*.

The last two were formed expressly for the election campaign of 1958. Most of the supporters of *Algérie française* left the movement, and Soustelle was expelled after the insurrection in Algeria in January 1960.

29. Speech to a *journée d'études parlementaires de l'UNR-UDT*, 22–5 October 1960. Quoted in Charlot, op. cit., p. 93.

30. The actual fusion took place after the election, but there was an electoral alliance between the UNR and UDT.

31. Roger Frey, in an interview in *La Nouvelle République* (15 January 1963). Cf. the statement by the former party Secretary, Jacques Baumel, that Gaullism ought to be 'the real Centre party'. (*Le Monde*, 2 March 1965.)

32. The statement was made at a UNR Congress at Bordeaux on 15 November 1959. What he actually said was:

Le secteur présidentiel comprend l'Algérie, sans oublier le Sahara, la Communauté franco-africaine, les affaires étrangères, la défense. Le secteur ouvert se rapporte au reste. . . .

The importance of the statement in this context is not its constitutional validity or otherwise, which is discussed elsewhere, but the fact that this was accepted as a political fact by the Gaullist party.

M. Chaban Delmas defended it later precisely on the ground that he was speaking at a party congress, and as a member of the party, and intended his remarks to apply only to the party. (26 April 1962.)

33. 15 November 1962.

34. Charlot, op. cit., p. 127.

35. *L'UNR – Etude du pouvoir au sein d'un Parti politique* (Paris, Armand Colin, 1967), p. 23.

36. Pierre Viansson-Ponté in *Le Monde*, 24 December 1963. It should, perhaps, in fairness, be added that he went on to say that the Gaullist party had 'nevertheless falsified enough predictions, defied enough laws and dissipated enough illusions to make its opponents give up treating it with irony and scorn'.

37. In 1964, of some 470,000 municipal Councillors, only 22,500 were Gaullists (*v. Le Monde*, 7 July 1964). In 1965, of the twenty largest provincial towns, only Bordeaux had a Gaullist Mayor, M. Chaban Delmas, who had been Mayor since 1947. *v.* also the article by Alain Duhamel commenting in 1967 on the Gaullist failure to establish local roots, as well as on the failure of their directing organs to evolve a policy of their own (*Le Monde*, 5 April 1967). The 1971 municipal elections produced little change.

38. Regional representation in the *bureau politique* of the Parliamentary party was provided for under article 24 of the UDR *Statuts* of 9 July 1968.

Regional *journées d'études* were held between October 1968 and February 1969 at Marseilles, Charleville, Bordeaux and Tours.

39. This was provided for by the presence of two non-Gaullist party members as 'associate' members of the *bureau exécutif* of the movement. One, Phillipe Dechartre, was, in fact, the leader of the *Convention de la Gauche Ve République*, but the other, Marie-Madeleine Dienesch, was a former member of the MRP. Under article 4 of the *Statuts*, 'double membership', that is, the right to belong, in effect, to two different parties, was officially recognized. As Jean Charlot points out (op. cit., 1970, p. 133) this was a tradition dating from the party's '*Rassemblement*' days. It had existed in the early years of the RPF, when it was sometimes described as '*la bigamie*'. In those days, the MRP objected to double membership, and Radicals and the near-Radical UDSR were the main members of the Gaullist 'intergroup' in the second Chamber, the Council of the Republic.

40. *v.* M. Pompidou's speech at Lille: 'Apart from the appeal to men from other political families, the meaning of these *Assises* for me is their opening up of our movement to the young.'

41. The French phrase was '*démocratie, renouveau, élargissement, relance, efficacité et implantation locale*'.

42. For a summary of the declaration, *v. Le Monde*, 5 April 1967. The party clearly continued to regard its electoral ace of trumps as the image of '*efficacité*'. See, for example, M. Pompidou's definition at Lille of the party's task as being to demonstrate that its members were 'men of progress with ideas for the future'. After Lille, youth and efficiency were linked. Jean Charlot (op. cit., 1970, p. 136) points out the use by Gaullist propaganda in 1968 of the 'youth' *motif*, in phrases on posters, for instance, calling on the public to 'build the France of tomorrow' with the UDVᵉR, associated with slogans on modernization.

43. Ibid.

44. The new party Constitution following the Lille conference was agreed on 9 July 1968.

45. During the election campaign, the Gaullists adopted the label: *Union pour la Défense de la République* (UDR). After the elections, they retained the initials, but the party called itself henceforth the *Union des Démocrates pour la République*.

46. In April 1968 a membership campaign was announced, but it was not until August, that is after the May events and the June election, that the increase in membership became so striking. By then, the secretary-general was claiming 500 new members per day (*Le Monde*, 6 September 1968). In March 1969, however, the official membership, based on the number of cards sent to the local party federations, was 180,000. Jean Charlot (op. cit., 1970, p. 135) considers this (along with all other party membership figures based on this procedure) to be a considerable over-estimate of the true figure, which was probably in the region of 160,000 paid-up members. This, however, is a relatively high figure for individual membership of a French political party, and only the Communist party would normally expect to claim more members. The Socialist party never reached 100,000 members after its brief post-war peak in the 1940s.

47. *v.* for instance the statement by René Capitant on Europe I (*Le Monde*, 11 June 1968), expressing hopes for something like 'workers' co-operatives' within firms.

48. *v.* decision of 19 September 1969 to reconstitute the UDT (*Le Monde*, 23 September 1969).

49. *v.* for instance, M. Léo Hamon's objections to the reconstitution of the UDT on the ground that the group might become 'the PSU of Gaullism'. (*Le Monde*, 1 October 1969.)

50. Pierre Viansson-Ponté in *Le Monde*, 10 September 1969.

51. On this *v.* Charlot, op. cit., p. 189 and also Manifesto of the *Union gaulliste populaire* (*Le Monde*, 28 April 1970), together with policies announced at the second National Council (*Le Monde*, 11 August 1970).

52. *Le Monde*, 4–5 February 1968.

53. *Le Monde*, 28 November 1967.

54. Maurice Duverger, *Institutions politiques et Droit constitutionnel* (Paris, Presses universitaires de France, 1970), p. 654.

55. *Le Monde*, 28 February 1971.

56. *Le Monde*, 2–3 May 1971.

57. In July 1966, M. Giscard d'Estaing sent a personal letter to about 38,000 *maires*, appealing for the support of all those who were not committed to the UNR–UDT. (*v. Le Monde*, 14 July 1966.)

58. Figures quoted in *Le Monde*, 20 December 1969.

59. *v.* statement quoted in *Le Monde*, 26 March 1966. A number of *Républicains indépendants* were opposed to the 1962 Constitutional reform introducing presidential election by universal suffrage. Though M. Giscard d'Estaing was himself in favour of the reform, he believed that the régime should remain Parliamentary.

60. In a television interview (*Face à Face*, 15 February 1966), M. Giscard d'Estaing emphasized the need for the majority to represent

the so-called European tendency, expressed at the first ballot [i.e. of the presidential election the previous December], the 'liberal' tendency, in the political sense of that term – I do not mean economic liberalism, but one that implies a certain desire for dialogue and discussion.

61. It is difficult to generalize on this point, because M. Giscard d'Estaing himself held more moderate views than some members of his party.

62. In 1965, a *Républicain indépendant* stood at the first ballot of the presidential election. It must be remembered, however, that nominations are individual and this did not commit the party to support him.

The 'Yes – but' policy, announced on 10 January 1967, was also described by M. Giscard d'Estaing as '*un Gaullisme réfléchi*', an attitude unacceptable to authentic Gaullists. The Prime Minister, M. Pompidou, condemned this qualified Gaullism: 'You cannot govern with *buts*' (television broadcast of 20 January 1967). The

Party programme of 13 September 1966 emphasized that it was *'centriste, libéral et européen'*, which could perhaps be taken as a summary of the significance of the 'but'. M. Giscard d'Estaing himself voted *'Non'* in the 1969 referendum. (*Le Monde*, 16 April 1969.)

63. *v.* statement to the press on 17 August following the 1967 election in which he summarized the party's criticisms of Gaullist policies.

CHAPTER IX

1. One contributor to the monthly *Défense de l'Occident* did describe himself as a Fascist (*Le Monde*, 1–2 March 1970), and the right-wing paper *Rivarol* (12 June 1969) described the paper *l'Elite européenne* as Fascist. The movement *l'Ordre nouveau* vigorously defended itself against accusations that it had Fascist tendencies. There was no clearly discernible Fascist influence among right-wing movements between 1968 and 1970.

2. The movement at first called itself *Mouvement national de Progrès*. The names of both M. Tixier-Vignancour's and M. Le Pen's movements are typical of right-wing tendencies.

3. The three Sidos brothers all played an active part in right-wing activism at the time of the Algerian war. Pierre Sidos was a founder of the movement *Occident*, in 1964. (*v. Le Monde*, 28 February–1 March 1965.)

4. M. Tixier-Vignancour himself was a supporter of the removal of Marshal Pétain's ashes to the military cemetery at Douaumont, and he acted as defence Counsel for two of the most prominent of the activists in the Algerian war – Jean-Marie Bastien Thiry, shot in 1963 for his part in the attempted assassination of General de Gaulle at le Petit Clamart the previous year, and General Salan, who was sentenced to life imprisonment in 1963 for leadership of the 1961 'revolt of the Generals'.

5. *Le Monde*, 7 February 1966. On the programme, *v. Le Monde*, 10 May 1966. M. Tixier-Vignancour was elected to the National Assembly in 1956 when he was the leader of the *Rassemblement national*. At that time, he was opposed to the régime, describing it as powerless to arrest national decadence.

On the *Rassemblement national* in the 1950s, *v. Partis, Journaux et Hommes politiques* by Henry Coston (Paris, Lectures françaises, 1960), p. 201.

6. Among those amnestied in June 1968 were MM. Georges

Bidault and Jacques Soustelle, General Salan, and Colonels Broizat, Lacheroy and Argoud, together with eight other members of the OAS. (*Année politique*, 1968, p. 47.)

7. *Le Monde*, 28 February 1970.

8. Ibid., 3 March 1956.

9. The movement's candidate is not however the Comte de Paris. It disapproved of his support for General de Gaulle's Algerian policy – though it was really no more than passive acquiescence. (*v. Le Monde*, 3 March 1965.) A breakaway nationalist movement formed in 1954 by Pierre Boutang, *La Nation française*, was much closer to the Pretender.

10. *Le Monde*, 28 February 1970. The following pages owe a great deal to this article and to those published on 1–2 March and 3 April 1970 on the situation of the extreme Right and the extreme Left.

11. *Le Monde*, 28 February 1970.

12. The movement *Action nationaliste* also claimed to be 'intransigently nationalist'. It accused the Right in general of being 'activist' rather than 'militant' and added: 'We are nationalist militants and not anti-Marxist activists.' (*Le Monde*, 28 February 1970.) It is, however, a sectional rather than a national movement, representing mainly students in one institution.

13. Declaration to the press on 31 March 1970 (*Le Monde*, 1 April).

14. One of the founders of the pre-war movement *l'Ordre nouveau*, Robert Aron, in a protest against any association of the two (*v. Le Monde*, 25 March 1970) emphasized the earlier movement's defence of democratic ideas and explained its original encouragement of Franco-German *rapprochement* as being intended to prevent Nazism. With the development of Nazism, he said, relations between the pro-German and the other members of *l'Ordre nouveau*, such as himself, had steadily worsened.

It is certainly true that the pre-war movement was a movement of the Left, and in spirit representative of the Syndicalist and federal thinking of Proudhon. But it did have what were generally regarded at the time as corporatist undertones that aroused suspicions in some quarters as to the authenticity of its 'leftism'. On this, *v.* the author's 'Intellectual ferment in France', in *Politica*, March 1936.

15. *Le Monde*, 1 April 1970. Declaration to the press by leaders of some right-wing movements.

16. *v. Le Monde*, 2 November 1968.

17. For a summary of left-wing organizations in 1970, *v.* 'Panorame de l'extrême Gauche révolutionnaire', in *Le Monde*, 3 April 1970.

18. A number of small, anarchist movements emphasizing special doctrines have had an intermittent existence – '*Conseillistes*', for instance, who existed at the time of the *Commune*, and had a brief revival in 1956, believed in the creation of a Communist society through the development of soviets; '*abondantistes*' advocated workers' management.

19. The *Lambertistes* wanted a world revolution against capitalist society and were opposed to Kremlin bureaucracy. They also wanted action through democratically run councils of elected delegates, subject to recall by their electors at any time, set up in factories, *départements*, and on the local level. They believed in '*l'Etat-commune sans bureaucratie permanente, sans armée ni police permanente*', which would seem to bring them almost into the anarchist camp.

20. The AJS did not agree with other '*gauchistes*' in attacking the Communist party, but held that all working-class parties ought to be associated in the common struggle. (*v. Le Monde*, 26 March 1970, and account of the debate at the UNEF Congress in *Le Monde*, 5–6 April, 1970.) Its members emphasized the need for the workers to defend what working-class action has won (*la défense des acquis*).

21. The Pablist tendency formed the '*tendance marxiste révolutionnaire*' of the Fourth International.

22. Coston, op. cit., p. 492.

23. The pre- and post-war youth sections of the French Socialist party were both openly Trotskyist.

24. In August 1968 this paper, together with *Servir le Peuple*, disappeared and it was said that both would be replaced by a new pro-Chinese paper, *Le Drapeau rouge*.

25. Twelve movements were dissolved on 12 June 1968, of which the best-known were:

Daniel Cohn-Bendit's *Mouvement du 22 mars*	(Anarchist)
Jeunesse communiste révolutionnaire	(Trotskyist)
Fédération des Etudiants révolutionnaires	" "
Parti communiste internationaliste	" "
Organisation communiste internationaliste	" "
Voix ouvrière	(Maoist)
Union des Jeunesses communistes marxistes-léninistes	" "
Parti communiste marxiste–léniniste de France	" "

26. Alain Geismar also wrote in the Maoist paper *l'Idiot international*, which announced the appearance of yet another periodical in July 1970, to be called *Journal du Mouvement du 27 mai, un Eté chaud*. (*v. Le Monde*, 2 July 1970.) The same paper (19 June 1970) announced

the formation of an organization called *Secours rouge*, by seven left-wing movements, of which at least four were Maoist. Its aim was to protect militants and immigrants from 'police, judicial and employers' repression'.

27. This charge led to renewed protests on the Left, which regarded his arrest as constituting evidence of 'a general policy of repression' (*v. Le Monde*, 4 April 1970). M. Jean-Paul Sartre took over the editorship of the paper, which was perpetually being seized by the police (M. Sartre claimed in *l'Idiot international* in May that there had been four seizures). His evident intention was to challenge the authorities to arrest him. (*v.* his article in *Le Monde*, 27 May 1970.) He also acted as a 'patron' of two other Maoist papers published in 1971 – *J'accuse* and *Tout*. In June 1971, M. Sartre was charged with libelling the police in articles published in *l'Idiot international*.

The Maoist arguments were condemned by two Trotskyist weeklies (*Lutte ouvrière* and *Rouge*) as '*putschisme*'.

It is not the workers [wrote Henri Weber in *Rouge*] who are resorting to revolutionary violence in order to resolve their problems; it is the militants of *La Gauche prolétarienne* who are carrying out acts of revolutionary violence in the name of the workers. In Marxist theory, this policy is called *putschisme*. Its effect is to isolate revolutionary groups and mark them out for repression.

(Quoted in *Le Monde*, 28 March 1970.)

Georges Kaldy, in *Lutte ouvrière*, criticized the policy of *La Gauche prolétarienne* on the ground that

If the extreme Left cannot convert the proletariat to its ideas and join in the battles waged by the proletariat, then all that violent action and verbal radicalism will do is to put the workers at the mercy of orthodox or Stalinist reformism.

(Ibid.)

By mid 1971, the Maoist movement seemed to be in difficulties and several of its papers were no longer appearing.

28. Quoted in *Le Monde*, 24 March 1970.

29. Interview with Jean-Paul Sartre, published in *Le nouvel Observateur*, quoted in *Le Monde*, 22 May 1968. Daniel Cohn-Bendit specifically emphasized the importance of spontaneity (*la spontanéité*

incontrôlable), and the undesirability of any efforts 'to canalize or utilize to advantage the action that it has unleashed'.

30. *Le Monde*, 28 April 1970.

31. When five members of a Maoist commando appeared before a court charged with using violence against a citizen in the public service, together with acts of violence involving some 44,600 francs worth of damage, one of them – a university teacher of thirty-three – explained that the action was necessary 'in order to extend the right of youth to revolutionary initiative'. (*v. Le Monde*, 2 and 8 May 1970.) This action had taken place on 23 January. There were a number of similar commando actions in April and May, on printing works, for instance, and the offices of certain papers described as 'bourgeois'. In one week in May alone, there were eight such attacks in Grenoble and two in Paris, in which plastic bombs were used.

It was estimated that in the incidents of March 1970, in the university of Nanterre alone, 400,000 francs worth of damage was done. The university had already suffered considerable damage in previous incidents and was frequently the scene of fights between Leftists and Communists. (*v. Le Monde*, 18 March 1970.)

32. *v. Le Monde, Libres Opinions*, 'Toute la Vérité', 27 May 1970.

33. The Central Committee of the Communist party declared in July 1968 that Leftism was the most pressing danger. This was still one of the party's main preoccupations in 1972.

34. Two PSU Deputies were elected in the 1962 election; four in the 1967 election (including Pierre Mendès France); none was elected in 1968, but Michel Rocard was elected in a by-election in October 1969, in which he defeated M. Couve de Murville. In the National Assembly, the PSU Deputies were affiliated for administrative purposes with the Socialist party, or the Federation of the Democratic and Socialist Left during the few years that this existed. M. Rocard was *non inscrit*, that is, attached to no group.

35. The PSU put forward four points as a basis for discussions with the Communist and Socialist parties at the end of 1964. These were either so vague as to be meaningless or obviously unacceptable to Socialists. (*v. Le Monde*, 27 November 1964.)

36. There were ups and downs. In 1964, membership fell to below 10,000. It had recovered by 1967 and reached a peak of 15,000 at the time of the May revolution. (Figures given at the 1969 Congress at the beginning of March 1969.)

37. These figures relate to votes cast at the first ballot, as given by

the Ministry of the Interior. PSU votes are given in 1958 under the heading of *Divers gauche*, and therefore do not relate solely to the PSU, but it is probable that they relate mainly to that party. In terms of votes cast, the strength of the dissident Left was given as 347,298 in 1958, the PSU vote in 1968 as 874,212, with a separate figure for other dissident Left of 163,679.

38. The Paris Federation of the PSU called it a 'neo-Centrist' organization, accepting by implication the integration of part of the working-class movement in neo-capitalism (*v.* vote at the Congress of 6–7 June 1965, expressing hostility to the inclusion of the MRP in a Federation of the non-Communist Left).

39. *Le Monde*, 13 May 1966.

40. Ibid, 21 January 1967.

41. The UCRG later joined the FGDS (see below).

42. Quoted in *Le Monde*, 25–6 June 1967.

43. *v.* statement by Michel Rocard (*Le Monde*, 21 May 1968): 'The PSU believes that all those who no longer agree to passive acceptance of the structures of a reactionary State should take affairs into their own hands.'

v. also the following extract from a PSU resolution of 28–9 June 1969:

> The main task of Socialist forces is not to prepare electoral alliances, but to work for the development of industrial battles for higher wages within a framework involving the disequilibrium of the system and the overthrow of the régime through the transfer of power to the workers (*le renversement du régime par l'instauration du pouvoir des travailleurs*).

v. also statement on Europe I on 30 October 1969 (*Le Monde*, 1 November 1969).

v. also the following statement by M. Marc Heurgon, then assistant secretary-general of the PSU: 'We are not interested in installing M. Mitterrand or M. Waldeck Rochet in the Elysée. It is inside factories, in the universities and in local areas that Socialism will be built up.' He went on to say that ... '*un affrontement violent avec le régime reste prévisible.* (PSU meeting at Lille on 1 November 1968.)

44. A resolution passed at a meeting held at the end of June 1970 provides a perfect illustration of the PSU's situation. By 255 out of 470 card votes the delegates voted to maintain the *status quo*. The minority consisted of 30 votes cast for a Trotskyist point of view;

73 pro-Maoist votes; and 90 cast by the Federation of the Paris region (traditionally a maverick in dissident left-wing politics) which in effect accepted the majority view, but wanted to suspend talks with the Communist party. (*v.* figures in *Le Monde*, 28–9 June 1970.)

The *reductio ad absurdum* was the decision of Alain Badiou to form a Maoist group of his own, since he was dissatisfied with the Maoist section of the PSU of which he was the leader, and none of the other Maoist organizations was exactly what he was seeking! (Quoted in *Le Monde*, 27 March 1970.)

45. *v.* summary of the new movement's manifesto in *Le Monde*, 22–3 February 1970.

46. For an account of the trade-union side of this dispute, *v.* Chapter X.

47. Communist tactics were well described as being to: '*garder le ton révolutionnaire sans faire la révolution*'.

48. All the evidence indicated that many workers voted for the Radical candidate in the by-election held at Nancy in June 1970, in spite of the fact that the Communists opposed him and the PSU described him as a neo-capitalist, whose ideas constituted a new and dangerous brand of technocratic reformism. One of his opinions was that the traditional form of the 'class struggle' was hopelessly out-dated.

49. Quoted in *Le Monde*, 27 June 1970.

50. *Humanité rouge*, commenting on the PSU programme as expounded at the Congress of March 1969. (Quoted in *Le Monde*, 5 August 1970.)

51. In *Le Monde*, 12 May 1970.

52. An opinion poll on Clubs at the beginning of 1965 estimated their social composition as follows: middle class 32%; liberal professions and top management 27%; students 22%; manual and white-collar workers 14%; craftsmen 4%; farmers 1%. Figures published in the official Bulletin of the *Club des Jacobins*. (*v. Le Monde*, 21–2 February 1965.)

53. The *Club des Jacobins*, which existed during the Fourth Republic, was originally independent Radical, then *Mendèsist*. The *Club Jean Moulin* inherited a spirit of wartime resistance and was very European. The Club *Citoyens 60* was Socialist, *Objectif 72* (from 1972, *Objectif Socialiste*) both Socialistic and European.

54. Jean Cluzel of the Club *Positions*, in the inaugural address at the *Assises de la démocratie*, held at Vichy 25–7 April 1964, and attended by some 11 Clubs, including the *Club Jean Moulin* (Paris),

the *Cercle Tocqueville* (Lyons) and *Démocratie nouvelle* (Marseilles), *Citoyens 60* (Paris), the *Club des Jacobins*. These and some 35 other Clubs, more politically committed, met on 6 June on the initiative of MM. Mitterrand and Hernu, to form the *Convention des Institutions républicaines*, which was duly formed in October of that year as a federation of a number of Clubs.

55. The Club *Démocratie nouvelle*, in a letter to M. Defferre. Quoted in *Le Monde*, 6 December 1966.

56. Jacques Piette, quoted in *Le Monde*, 1 November 1966.

57. The *Convention des Institutions républicaines* claimed to represent 50–60 Clubs by 1965, of which the most important were the *Club des Jacobins*, *Citoyens 60*, *Jeune République*, *France Forum*, and the *Ligue des Droits de L'Homme*. It is not possible to give any accurate description of organizations and members, because for one thing conferences were attended by a number of representatives who did not belong to the *Convention*. These either came as observers, or were members of political parties, attending and speaking in their individual capacities.

58. *v. Le Monde*, 31 March 1966.

59. *v.* Letter to *Le Monde*, 2 April 1966.

60. For instance, M. Giscard d'Estaing's Club *Perspectives et Réalités*, dated from the beginning of 1966 (*v.* above, Chapter VIII, Conservatism). Some of the Gaullist organizations were, in effect, Clubs, and in September 1970, Edgar Faure announced the formation of a *Club pour un nouveau Contrat social*, including a number of Deputies, whose aim was to discuss political problems. In 1967, the Radical Congress noted that Radical Clubs were becoming more and more numerous. In the same year the PDM announced the formation of a Club called *Centre d'études Progrès et Démocratie moderne*. The Socialists had their *Club Jean Jaurès*, and their organizations for study and research, CERES and (from 1969) OURS. In 1968, the CFDT trade-union Confederation announced its interest in the formation of '*groupes de liaison*' aiming at 'discussions of long-term political problems, in a context divorced from partisan obligations and from conditions imposed by electoral considerations', which was exactly the aim of many of the Clubs. (*v.* article in *Le Monde*, 18 January 1968, by André Jeanson, president of the CFDT.)

61. *Citoyens 60* and the *Vie nouvelle* groups also remained outside the Socialist party, and announced their intention to concentrate on discussions of problems affecting the family, education etc.

62. Quoted in *Le Monde*, 24 July 1970.

63. In July 1970 the CIR set up a university organization, *Club Démocratie et Université*, aimed at making a special appeal to intellectuals in favour of left-wing unity. The UGCS section led by M. Poperen formed in September 1970 a Club called *Etudes, recherches et information socialiste*, publishing a Bulletin, *Synthèse-Flash*. In the summer of 1970, the *Club des Jacobins* was protesting against the attitude of 'certain of their friends' (i.e. in the CIR) towards the Communist party – an attitude that the president described as '*le suivisme à l'égard du PCF*' (*v. Le Monde*, 24 July 1970). The CIR was opposed to the support given by the president of the *Club des Jacobins* to M. Servan-Schreiber's candidature in the by-election at Bordeaux. Unity on the Left was, in fact, as divisive an issue in the Clubs as in the Socialist party!

CHAPTER X

1. *Les Groupes de pression en France* (Paris, Armand Colin, 1957).
2. The *Charte d'Amiens* was the resolution voted at the end of the CGT Congress of 1906. The relevant passages are:

> The CGT unites, regardless of political beliefs, all workers who are conscious of the struggle that will be necessary in order to get rid of the wage system and the employing class.

> ... since economic action must be directed against the employers, if the trade-union movement is to achieve maximum results, the unions as such should not concern themselves with parties and sects, which can work independently from, and parallel with, the unions for the transformation of society.

3. *v.* for instance, the speech by Georges Séguy, quoted p. 275.
4. In the 1970 municipal elections, 36 out of the 41 members of the Government contested the election; of these, 28 were elected, 7 defeated and one retired.
5. M. Pierre Mendès France is reported to have said that when he was Prime Minister in 1964 he received some forty to fifty callers a day, ranging from individuals to official delegations, together with an enormous mail, and that in addition he was subjected to a great deal of personal lobbying by Deputies. (*v.* Meynaud, op. cit., p. 138.)
6. For a more complete study of the rôle of pressure groups, *v.* Meynaud, op. cit., and Henry W. Ehrmann, *Organized Business in France* (Princeton, N.J., Princeton University Press, 1957) on

employers' organizations. There is little up-to-date material, but aspects of the subject have been discussed in articles in the *Revue française de Science politique* (*v.* in particular September 1962, where Jean Meynaud discusses the real extent of the changes brought about by the demotion of Parliament). *v.* also Philip Williams and Martin Harrison, *Politics and Society in de Gaulle's Republic* (Harlow, Longmans, 1961), Chapter 9.

7. *v. Le Monde*, 2 April 1971, and *l'Humanité*, 1 April 1971. It is interesting to note that the CFDT, no longer associated with Catholicism since 1964, includes teachers' unions that adopt the traditional left-wing anti-clerical position.

8. *v. Avis aux Ouvriers*, adopted by the Paris Municipal Council on 26 April 1791, which reproves workers for meeting as a body to discuss and issue decisions fixing arbitrarily the price of their labour, when they ought to be working. Workers are reminded that a coalition to fix wage levels would evidently be contrary to their own real interests, as well as being illegal, and a threat to public order and the interests of the community (quoted in J.-D. Reynaud, *Les Syndicats en France*, Paris, Armand Colin, 1963, p. 28).

9. Small, organized groups of Catholic workers had existed in France since the late 1880s, but they did not become a strong force until after the formation of the CFTC, which united a number of Catholic unions.

10. The most influential of the independent trade-union movements is the *Fédération de l'Enseignement national* (FEN), with some 280,000 members in the 1960s (*v.* Reynaud, op. cit., p. 127). Among other independent movements is a small anarcho-syndicalist *Confédération nationale du Travail*, formed in 1946, and a *Confédération française du Travail*, formed in 1967 by the union of three smaller organizations, preaching absolute independence of trade-unionism and politics. In 1970, this movement was claiming 300,000 members and demanding an equal right to present candidates in the elections to the *Comités d'Entreprise* (*v. Le Monde*, 13 August 1970).

11. The CGC, generally estimated to have about 150,000 to 200,000 members, is usually non-militant and is non-Marxist. It dates from 1944.

12. Reynaud (op. cit., p. 127) quotes an outside source as giving a membership figure of 450,000 for the CFTC and 380,000 for FO in 1960. Later, the split in the CFTC reduced the membership of the CFDT in 1964, but the May events considerably increased it after 1968, though possibly only temporarily. It could perhaps have

amounted to 700,000 in 1970, but the figures for FO certainly fell considerably between 1960 and 1970. In 1967, the CGT gave its own membership figures as 1,942,523, a slight increase on the figures given two years earlier. In 1969, it claimed 2,400,000 (*v. Le Monde*, 31 January 1970). FO and the CFDT do not normally publish figures. Though CGT membership no doubt increased after the May events, the figure quoted is almost certainly an over-estimate.

The difficulties of estimating trade-union membership are increased by the fact that even when figures are given, they are usually some eighteen months in arrears, as calculations have to be made of the numbers of the cards distributed to branches that are, in fact, taken up by members. The figures given include many who, in Britain or the United States, would be recorded as not fully paid-up.

13. National bargaining is conducted in accordance with the principle of 'representativeness', that is, by the most representative of the workers' and employers' associations, which means in practice the organizations affiliated to the main employers' organization, the CNPF, and the three workers' confederations (together with the CGC, where its interests are concerned), or with the main farming associations or tradesmen's organizations, where these categories alone are involved. The tests that the Government is required to apply in deciding 'representativeness' are membership, independence, income, experience and seniority. Both sides are, in practice, dependent on the State to an extent which gives the Government a vital rôle. The 1968 Grenelle negotiations, for instance, were conducted by the Prime Minister in person, in meetings with representatives of both sides of industry.

(On the development of the system, *v.* Val Lorwin, *The French Labour Movement*, Cambridge, Mass., Harvard University Press, 1954, Chapter XI.)

14. Factory branches (*Sections d'entreprise*) have become more important in large firms, but for bargaining purposes these are still unofficial subdivisions of the local *syndicat*. It is the *syndicat* which bargains with the employer.

15. Reynaud, op cit., p. 119.

16. Reynaud (op. cit., p. 123) estimates that, in 1963, the funds of the strongest CGT unions did not exceed some tens of thousands of francs. In other words, no union in France has anything like the reserves possessed by the large British and American unions.

17. Meynaud, op. cit., p. 72.

18. The miners constitute a partial exception to this rule. The only serious strike of any duration during the first eleven years of the Fifth Republic was the miners' strike of 1963, which lasted a month. The most serious of the Fourth Republic strikes involving mainly a single industry was the miners' strike of 1948. Reynaud (op. cit., p. 125) notes the existence of a small strike fund in the CFTC miners' unions from 1950. The miners' example was followed by railway workers, engineers and postmen in the CFTC unions, but with an immediate fall in membership.

19. In 1970, FO claimed that over 50% of its members were in the private sector, as against 40% in 1968. *Le Monde*, 19 August 1971.

20. On the attempts of the CGT to explain away this awkward conclusion, *v.* Chapter VII, note 9, p. 376.

21. Conference of 16–17 April 1966. This position was reaffirmed by the 1969 Conference of 18 March, which rejected all contacts with the CGT while it remained under the control of the Communist party, but expressed willingness for talks with the CFDT and the independent teachers' organization, the FEN.

22. In France, these services are financed by contributions from workers and employers (mainly the latter) and administered by elected representatives of trade unions and employers. The Ministry exercises general supervision. The reorganization of the services in 1967 provided for State responsibility for unemployment insurance.

23. At a press conference, the CFDT president, André Jeanson, referred to the students and workers as fighting the same battle. The CGT was never under that illusion! (*v. Le Monde*, 22 May 1968.)

24. At the 1970 CFDT Congress, some 70% of the delegates were under 40, and the average age of the 1,000 or so delegates was said to be 35. A quarter were under 30. (*v. Le Monde*, 10–11 May 1970.)

25. The normal CFDT phrase, '*l'antagonisme des classes*', was used by the president. One spokesman described the CFDT as '*une organisation marxiste libertaire*', a description not likely to endear it to the CGT at the time (*Le Monde*, 6 May 1970).

26. CGT Congress of 16 November 1969.

27. Georges Séguy to the Railway Workers' Union (quoted in *Le Monde*, 22–3 November 1969). He went on to declare that 'the CGT will never become the arena for political activities of the kind that have destroyed the UNEF'.

28. *v.* exchange of letters between Georges Séguy and Michel Rocard (*Année politique*, 1969, p. 203).

29. In 1936, the original name was changed to the *Confédération*

générale du Patronat français. Along with the trade-union organizations, this was dissolved by the Vichy Government of 1940–4.

30. Quoted in Ehrmann, op. cit., p. 103. The CNPF is reported to have advised its members to vote against de Gaulle in 1965.

31. The *Chambres des Métiers* have also existed since 1925, representing small craftsmen (*artisans*). They have a similar clientèle to that of the UDCA and play a similar rôle to that of *Chambres de Commerce*, namely, as local organizations expressing opinions on economic policies.

32. On this *v*. Ehrmann, op. cit., p. 144.

33. Meynaud, op. cit., p. 163.

34. On this *v*. for instance the statement of representatives of trade-union movements on 'participation' in *Le Monde*, 9 July 1968, apropos of the Capitant plan.

35. Williams and Harrison, op. cit , p. 147.

36. *v. Année politique*, 1965, p. 164. It should be added, however, that this faint praise was accompanied by criticisms that the statement left too much power in the hands of employers.

37. Ibid.

38. *v. Le Monde*, 20 October 1970.

39. On the relations between farmers' organizations under the Fourth Republic, *v*. Gordon Wright, *Rural Revolution in France* (Stanford, Calif., and London, Stanford and Oxford University Press, 1964).

40. Ibid., p. 130.

41. *v*. the view expressed by Gordon Wright (op. cit., p. 150) that the generation of leaders of the JAC in the 1950s made it into 'the most dynamic force for change in rural France'.

42. Michel Cointat (UDR Deputy for Ille-et-Vilaine and later Minister of Agriculture) in *Le Monde*, 26 November 1969. *v*. also the evidence of Henri Mendras, member of the Vedel Commission, that 'the rapid industrialization of agriculture, though theoretically desirable, is open to criticism on economic grounds and is socially impossible'. (*Le Monde*, 8 October 1969.) He could have added that it was also unthinkable for political reasons.

43. Other organizations included the *Fédération des Unions commerciales, artisanales et des petites Entreprises* (FUCAP), consisting mainly of moderates in the *départements* of Drôme, Ardèche, Gard and Vaucluse, which was responsible for a number of demonstrations in 1970, mainly in the South; the *Fédération des Industriels, Commerçants et Artisans de la Sarthe* (FICA), which was opposed to

demonstrations; the *Fédération des Unions commerciales et artisanales de la Sarthe* (FUCAS), which favoured them. The Communist attitude was to support 'legitimate claims', but to oppose what the party called '*des actions aventuristes et illégales*'. (*l'Humanité*, 27 March 1970.) The *Mouvement de Défense de l'Exploitation familiale* (MODEF), formed in the early 1960s, was a more left-wing movement, opposed to the FNSEA, and was mainly active in the South-West.

44. *v.* p. 291 seq.

45. Quoted in *Le Monde*, 5 July 1963.

46. Between 1962 and 1967, the number of students increased by 14% per annum. (*Le Monde*, 22 November 1967.)

47. Relations between universities and the police date from a regulation of the First Empire, allowing police to enter university buildings only in three circumstances: 1) fire; 2) in pursuit of offenders caught in the act; and 3) only then, when called in by the Dean of the Faculty, or whoever is responsible for the building. A distinction is made between university premises to which the public are not admitted (*domaines fermées*), and which still enjoy this *franchise universitaire* (that is, the right of the university to exclude the police) and university premises that are crossed by traffic routes, where there is police surveillance, as for instance in Paris. The situation at the university of Nanterre is a special one, in that when it was built in 1964 it was a 'campus' with no public roads running through it, and responsibility for maintaining order, therefore, remained in the hands of the Dean of the Faculty of Arts, to whom power had been delegated by the Rector. Now motor roads cross the campus, but the situation with regard to the police has been modified only to the extent that police surveillance is allowed by night. By day, a request from the Dean is still required. The university authorities want this surveillance extended to daytime. The inability of successive Deans to maintain order led to intervention by the Minister, and police difficulties have been increased by the unwillingness of Deans to admit police to university buildings (as opposed to the grounds). Feelings on the question of *la franchise universitaire* were so strong that the authorities feared that to risk a head-on clash between police and students would make the situation worse. In practice, of course, the ability of rioting students to take refuge in the building made the task of the police impossible. The case for the authorities was that, in the event of a clash with the police, student solidarity would probably lead to moderates going over *en masse* to the side of the extremists.

48. 'Open university' summer schools were, in fact, run in 1968 by students in several universities. That in Grenoble attracted some 200, mostly young people, and debates were mainly political and concerned with the May events. That in Montpellier was rather more successful in obtaining working-class participation, but even then it was not estimated to account for more than 10% of those present. (*v. Le Monde*, 20 August 1968.)

49. *v.* statements by Jacques Sauvageot in *Le Monde*, 7 June and 6 July 1968.

50. Though revolutionary, Trotskyists in this organization were in favour of retaining what advantages had been obtained under a capitalist régime.

51. *v.* account of the Congress in *Le Monde*, 3–4 April 1970. The 59th Congress, at the end of February 1971, was organized in total confusion, the two remaining political organizations within the UNEF, *UNEF–Renouveau* and the AJS, being at loggerheads as to whether there was or was not anybody qualified to take a valid decision on behalf of the movement.

52. Two other organizations shared the more moderate views of the FNEF. They were the *Mouvement universitaire pour la Réforme* (MUR), formed in May–June 1968, and the *Comité de Liaison étudiant pour la Rénovation universitaire* (CLERU) formed as the result of a pre-1968 split in UNEF. CLERU regarded the solution of university problems as essentially a long-term affair, and wanted a complete rethinking of the idea of 'pluridisciplinarity', teaching methods, and attitudes to culture, the individual and democratization.

53. Alain Geismar, a young university teacher of 29 at the time of the May revolution, resigned from his post as secretary-general of SNE-sup during the events, because he could not combine it with the active political rôle he wanted to play. He joined the Maoist organization, *La Gauche prolétarienne*, and wrote for its monthly, *l'Idiot international*, which preached revolutionary activism. This movement was banned in May 1970 along with two other organizations, which were, in reality, part of the same movement, on the ground of their incitements to violence. Alain Geismar was arrested in June 1970 for direct provocation to violence against the police, to which a later charge of reconstituting a banned organization was added, and on 22 October 1970, was sentenced to 18 months' imprisonment. He was the author of several often quoted revolutionary statements, including that affirming that '*les seuls bons flics sont ceux qui sont à l'hôpital*'. (*v. Le Monde*, 11 March 1970.)

54. The SNI is affiliated to the independent *Fédération de l'Education nationale*, which includes a number of unions and has a membership of some 200,000 to 250,000. It by no means includes all teachers' unions in the State system. Secondary and university teachers' unions are in the main outside it.

55. *v. Le Monde*, 17 January 1969.

56. Ibid., 3 December 1970.

57. Frédéric Gaussen in ibid., 25 February 1970.

58. Alfred Grosser in ibid., 28 February 1970.

59. Ibid., 18 February 1970.

CHAPTER XI

1. *v.* for instance, the following statement by Léo Hamon, the Government spokesman in M. Chaban Delmas' Government of 1969:

The real inspiration of Gaullism is the combination and alliance of the principles of order and movement, which have been for too long opposed to each other.

2. M. Roger Frey at the *Assises* of the UNR–UDT at Nice in November 1963. (Quoted by Jean Charlot in 'Le Parti dominant', *Projet*, September–October 1970, p. 951.)

3. 'La logique de la Situation', *Le Monde*, 14–15 February 1971.

4. Pierre Viansson-Ponté in 'Les grandes Vacances de l'Opposition', *Le Monde*, 8 October 1969.

Bibliography

Only the most important of the sources published in book form are quoted. In addition, the *Année politique*, the *Revue française de Science politique* and the *Revue du Droit public* contain much useful material. Some references to these are given in the Notes, but they are far from complete. The works by Pierre Avril and J. Gicquel cited below both include a comprehensive bibliography, giving a number of references to periodicals.

(i) IN FRENCH

GENERAL BACKGROUND

FAUVET, J., *Les Forces politiques en France*, Paris, Editions *Le Monde*, 1951.
— *La France déchirée*, Paris, Fayard, 1957.
— *La Quatrieme République*, Paris, Fayard, 1959.
SIEGFRIED, ANDRÉ, *Tableau des Partis en France*, Paris, Grasset, 1930.
— *De la IVe a la Ve République*, Paris, Grasset, 1958.
THIBAUDET, ALBERT, *Les Idées politiques de la France*, Paris, Stock, 1932.
RÉMOND, RENÉ, *La Droite en France de 1815 à nos Jours*, Paris, Aubier, 1954.

THE CONSTITUTION

AVRIL, PIERRE, *Un President pourquoi faire?*, Collection Jean Moulin, Editions du Seuil, 1966.
— *Le Régime politique de la Ve République*, Paris, Librairie générale de Droit et de Jurisprudence, 1967.
BAGUENARD, J., MAOUT, J-CH. and MUZELLEC, R., *Le Président de la Ve République*, Dossiers U², Paris, Armand Colin, 1970.
BELORGEY, GERARD, *Le Gouvernement et l'Administration de la France*, Collection U, Paris, Armand Colin, 1967.

BURON, ROBERT, *Le plus beau des Métiers*, Paris, Plon, 1963.

CHANDERNAGOR, ANDRÉ, *Un Parlement pourquoi faire?*, Paris, Gallimard, 1967.

CHENOT, BERNARD, *Etre Ministre*, Paris, Plon, 1967.

Documentation française, la, *Notes et Etudes documentaires*

— No. 2530 (11 April 1959) *Commentaires sur la Constitution.*

— No. 2755 (25 February 1961) *Le Conseil constitutionnel.*

— No. 2959 (31 January 1963) *Les Domaines respectifs de la Loi et du Règlement d'après la Constitution de 1958.*

— No. 3072 (12 March 1964) *Documents relatifs aux Rapports du Gouvernement et du Parlement sous la première législature de la cinquième République.*

DUVAL, H., MINDU, P. and LEBLANC-DECHOISAY, P. Y., *Référendum et Plébiscite*, Dossiers U², Paris, Armand Colin, 1970.

DUVERGER, MAURICE, Thémis, *Constitutions et Documents politiques, Textes et Documents*, Paris, Presses universitaires de France, 1957.

— *La Vᵉ République*, Paris, Presses universitaires de France, 1959.

— *La VIᵉ République et le Régime présidentiel*, Paris, Fayard, 1961.

— *Institutions politiques et Droit constitutionnel*, Paris, Presses universitaires de France, 1970.

DUPUIS, G., GEORGEL, J. and MOREAU, J., *Le Conseil constitutionnel*, Dossiers U², Paris, Armand Colin, 1970.

GAULLE, CHARLES DE, *Mémoires d'Espoir*, I and II, Paris, Plon, 1970 and 1971.

GICQUEL, J., *Essai sur la Pratique de la Vᵉ République*, Paris, Librairie générale de Droit et de Jurisprudence, 1967.

GOGUEL, FRANÇOIS and GROSSER, ALFRED, *La Politique en France*, Collection U, Paris, Armand Colin, 1964.

LONG, H., WEIL, P. and BRAIBANT, G., *Les grands Arrêts de la Jurisprudence administrative*, Paris, Sirey, 1969.

MASSIGLI, RENÉ, *Sur quelques Maladies de l'Etat*, Paris, Plon, 1958.

MITTERRAND, F., *Le Coup d'Etat permanent*, Paris, Plon, 1961.

PRÉLOT, MARCEL, *Pour comprendre la nouvelle Constitution*, Paris, Editions le Centurion, 1958.

— *Institutions politiques et Droit constitutionnel*, Paris, Dalloz, 1957 and 1969.

Règlement de l'Assemblée nationale, Paris, Imprimerie de l'Assemblée nationale.

Travaux préparatoires de la Constitution, Paris, Documentation française, 1960.

PARTIES AND INTEREST GROUPS

BOISDEFFRE, PIERRE DE, *Lettre ouverte aux Hommes de Gauche*, Paris, Albin Michel, 1969.

BRUCLAIN, CLAUDE, *Le Socialisme et l'Europe*, Paris, Collection Jean Moulin, Editions du Seuil, 1968.

CHARLOT, JEAN, *Le Phénomène gaulliste*, Paris, Fayard, 1970.

COSTON, HENRY, *Partis, Journaux et Hommes politiques d'hier et d'aujourd'hui*, Paris, Lectures françaises, 1960.

DEBRÉ, MICHEL, *Mort de l'Etat républicain*, Paris, Gallimard, 1947.

— *Ces Princes qui nous gouvernent*, Paris, Plon, 1957.

— *Au Service de la Nation*, Paris, Stock, 1963.

DUVERGER, MAURICE, *Les Partis politiques*, Paris, Armand Colin, 1951.

FABRE-LUCE, ALFRED, *Le plus illustre des Français*, Paris, Julliard, 1962.

FAUVET, JACQUES, *Histoire du Parti communiste français*, Paris, Fayard, 1965.

FAUVET, JACQUES and MENDRAS, HENRI, *Les Paysans et la politique*, Paris, Armand Colin, 1958.

GARAUDY, ROGER, *Pour un modèle français du Socialisme*, Paris, Gallimard, Collection Idées, 1968.

HAMON, LÉO, *De Gaulle dans la République*, Paris, Plon, 1958.

LIGOU, DANIEL, *Histoire du Socialisme en France, 1871–1961*, Paris, Presses universitaires de France, 1962.

MARTINET, GILLES, *La Conquête des Pouvoirs*, Paris, Collection Histoire immédiate, Editions du Seuil, 1968.

MENDÈS FRANCE, PIERRE, *La République moderne*, Paris, Gallimard, 1962.

MEYNAUD, JEAN, *Les Groupes de pression en France*, Paris, Armand Colin, 1957.

MOLLET, GUY, *13 mai 1958, 13 mai 1962*, Paris, Plon, 1962.

— *Les Chances du Socialisme*, Paris, Réponses à la Société industrielle, Fayard, 1968.

NICOLET, CLAUDE, *Le Radicalisme*, Paris, Presses universitaires de France, 1957.

PHILIP, ANDRÉ, *La Gauche: Mythes et Réalités*, Paris, Aubier, 1964.

REYNAUD, J–D., *Les Syndicats en France*, Paris, Collection U, Armand Colin, 1963.

SERVAN-SCHREIBER, JEAN-JACQUES, *Ciel et Terre, Le Manifeste radical*, Paris, Editions Denoël, 1970.

SCHUMANN, MAURICE, *Le vrai Malaise des Intellectuels de Gauche*, Paris, Plon, 1957.

VIANSSON-PONTÉ, PIERRE, *Les Gaullistes*, Paris, Editions du Seuil, 1963.

(ii) IN ENGLISH

BROWN, L. NEVILLE and GARNER, F. L., *French Administrative Law*, London, Butterworth, 1967.

CAMPBELL, PETER, *French Electoral Systems and Elections since 1789*, London, Faber & Faber, 1965, 2nd edn.

CAUTE, DAVID, *Communism and the French Intellectuals, 1914–1960*, London, André Deutsch, 1964.

CHARLOT, JEAN, *The Gaullist Phenomenon*, London, Allen & Unwin, 1971.

DUVERGER, MAURICE, *The French Political System*, Chicago, Ill., Chicago University Press, 1958.

EHRMANN, HENRY, *Organized Business in France*, Princeton, N.J., Princeton University Press, 1957.

GAULLE, CHARLES DE, *Memoirs of Hope*, London, Weidenfeld & Nicolson, 1971.

GOGUEL, FRANÇOIS, *France under the Fourth Republic*, Ithaca, N.Y., Cornell University Press, 1952.

MACAUD, CHARLES A., *Communism and the French Left*, London, Weidenfeld & Nicolson, 1963.

PICKLES, DOROTHY, *France, the Fourth Republic*, London, Methuen, 1958.

PICKLES, W., *The French Constitution of October 4th 1958* (introduction and annotated text), London, Stevens, 1960.

RENDEL, MARGHERITA, *The Administrative Functions of the French Conseil d'Etat*, London, LSE Research Monographs, 6, 1970.

RIDLEY, F. and BLONDEL, J., *Public Administration in France*, London, Routledge & Kegan Paul, 1964.

WILLIAMS, PHILIP M., *The French Parliament*, London, Allen & Unwin, 1968.

— *French Politicians and Elections, 1951–1969*, London, Cambridge University Press, 1970.

WILLIAMS, PHILIP M., and HARRISON, MARTIN, *Politics and Society in de Gaulle's Republic*, Harlow, Longmans, 1971.

WRIGHT, GORDON, *Rural Revolution in France*, Stanford, Calif. and London, University Presses, 1964.

Index